Claiming Rights and Righting Wrongs in Texas

Number Fifteen:

Rio Grande/Río Bravo
Borderlands Culture and Traditions

Norma E. Cantú, General Editor

Claiming Rights and Righting Wrongs in Texas

Mexican Workers and Job Politics during World War II

Emilio Zamora

Foreword by Juan Gómez-Quiñones

Texas A&M University Press
College Station

First edition

This paper meets the requirements of ANSI/NISO Z39.48-1992 (Permanence of Paper).
Binding materials have been chosen for durability.

An earlier version of chapter 3 appeared as "Mexico's Wartime Intervention on Behalf of Mexicans in the United States," in *Mexican Americans and World War II,* edited by Maggie Rivas-Rodríguez (Austin: University of Texas Press, 2005), and is reprinted here with the permission of the University of Texas Press.

An earlier version of chapter 6 appeared as "The Failed Promise of Wartime Opportunity for Mexicans in the Texas Oil Industry," in the *Southwestern Historical Quarterly* 95 (January 1992): 323–50, and is reprinted here with the permission of the Texas State Historical Association.

Library of Congress Cataloging-in-Publication Data

Zamora, Emilio.
Claiming rights and righting wrongs in Texas : Mexican workers and job politics during World War II / Emilio Zamora ; foreword by Juan Gómez-Quiñones.—1st ed.
p. cm. — (Rio Grande/Río Bravo ; no. 15)
Includes bibliographical references and index.
ISBN-13: 978-1-60344-066-0 (cloth : alk. paper)
ISBN-10: 1-60344-066-6 (cloth : alk. paper)
ISBN-13: 978-1-60344-097-4 (pbk. : alk. paper)
ISBN-10: 1-60344-097-6 (pbk. : alk. paper)
1. Alien labor, Mexican—Texas—History—20th century. 2. World War, 1939–1945—Mexican Americans. 3. Mexican Americans—Employment—Texas—History— 20th century. 4. Mexican Americans—Texas—Civil rights—History—20th century. 5. Mexican Americans—Texas—Social conditions—20th century. 6. Discrimination in employment—Texas—History—20th century. 7. United States—Foreign relations—Mexico—20th century. 8. Mexico—Foreign relations—United States—20th century. 9. United States. Committee on Fair Employment Practice—History—20th century. 10. League of United Latin American Citizens—History—20th century. I. Title. II. Series.
HD8081.M6Z36 2009
331.6'272076409044—dc22

2008024039

This book is for Angela, Clara, and Luz.

May it always remind them of our wonderful life together.

Contents

Foreword

Multiple forms of agency by diverse persons, along with intended, unintended, and contradictory consequences in a complex sociopolitical environment, is the broad topic of this work by historian Emilio Zamora. The research that he generates is informational, interpretive, and innovative. There is fine detailing here, to be sure, including all the nuances involving human beings who either do or do not resolve challenges of employment under racialized circumstances. The author adds colors and shadings in exhaustive detail through informed descriptions, rich analyses, and critical commentary. Like most thoughtful social historians in this country, Zamora addresses one of its major themes, namely, the persistence of racial and ethnic inequalities, even as positive measures to mitigate them are promoted and, to some extent, effectuated by public officials and government agencies.

The work also takes up other major points of debate in U.S. historiography, among them the efficacy of gradualism in promoting change. Gradualism is the option preferred by functionaries and many activists. Historians often follow by studying the slow and uneven quality of gradualist change and implicitly endorse it, preferring this option to stagnation or radicalism. Zamora parts with them. He questions why the proverbial "American" optimism limits the possibilities of choices beyond moderate gradualism. His work illuminates how the preference for slow change by public agencies and institutions grant a low priority to the interests and desires of the Mexican community.

As Zamora points out, the conventional black-white paradigm is not about numbers, whether blacks outnumber Latinos nationally or locally. This paradigm is a distorting optic for examining both ethnic and class specifics in the United States; it denies and limits the presence and progress of a Latino population, including the Mexican. It is also a manipulative tool for both liberals and conservatives to foment invidious distinctions and thwart substantive social change. Zamora also brings to mind the many historians of U.S. development who assign a positive role to U.S. business unionism with its emphasis on wages and benefits. Historians often view trade unions as proponents and facilitators of progressive change. In contrast, Zamora finds them to be equivocal or negative to Mexican progress. He accomplishes this with a vast number of bibliographic sources, including rich government and personal archives that allow him to widen his lens to consider the actual experience and role of Mexicans on the job. In the end, the study raises important questions concerning the real versus fictionalized history of the United States.

Zamora delineates how racist restrictions circumscribed life for many persons of Mexican descent in the Southwest, particularly in the state of Texas. These restrictions were consistently challenged by Mexican individuals and organizations from the mid-nineteenth century through the years of World War II. Mexicans were disadvantaged in all spheres of life—socially, politically, and economically—precisely because they were Mexicans. Mexican pro–civil rights activists concluded that the 1940s were a propitious time for change. The climate and conditions of World War II encouraged the pursuit of job equality. The chance for success felt viable. Mexican activists believed that job equality would contribute significantly to enhancing the quality of their lives in the years to follow.

Zamora relates a thoughtful unfolding operational strategy and accompanying tactics to secure job equalities for Mexicans in a wartime economy. The Texas economy was, of course, intimately linked to the United States' emerging role in the global economy, and Texas shared important ties with Mexico and its wartime bid to gain U.S. support for the modernization of its economy during the postwar period. As Mexico and the United States initiated their new cooperative relations, Mexican officials sought an independent negotiating course that came to include interventions on behalf of Mexican civil rights and job equities. Zamora documents the actions of the civil rights activists, federal functionaries, state officials, and representatives of Mexico who were deployed under the important and unequal dispensation of the United States federal executive. He also explains how and when Mexicans and their allies made use of international norms, Mexico's advocacy policy, and the United States' Good Neighbor Policy to fight for civil and labor rights, sometimes in conjunction with African Americans and their organizations.

This seminal study is a continuation of Zamora's already outstanding work, evident in *The World of the Mexican Worker in Texas.* In the pages that follow, he extends his interpretations into the social and political history of the mid-twentieth century, explaining the consequences of public policies. The New Deal state, together with the boom created by a wartime economy hold proverbial status in the imagination of scholars, pundits, and laypersons alike who prefer to see significant social and economic betterment beginning at midcentury without taking sufficient notice of the persistence of inequality and the important role that the Mexican struggle has played in that story. Here too Zamora adds to what we know about the unequal development of social relations in U.S. history.

With his characteristic method of meticulous research and cogent thinking, Zamora offers balanced views on a number of persistent issues like the role of the state in mediating social relations, the impact of a booming economy in promoting and arresting change, the inconsistencies and opportunities in interracial and working-class unity, the contradiction between declared egalitarian values and the reality of racialized inequality, the internationalization of racial discrimination and its potentially transformative effects on domestic issues, and the possibility of a revitalized Mexican diplomatic posture before the U.S. government.

Juan Gómez-Quiñones, Professor
Department of History
University of California at Los Angeles

Acknowledgments

This history, like many other histories of Mexicans in the United States, is more than the worthwhile scholarly enterprise of recovering a still neglected past and explaining how one situates their experiences within the larger world of peoples, processes, and institutions in the United States and Mexico. It is also an account that has been influenced by my ongoing experiences in the Mexican community of the United States, particularly in its social movement for dignity and equal rights. This does not mean that presentist notions have diminished my ability to render credible and reliable interpretations of the past, but rather that the Mexican social movement has always motivated me to write on its history and the changes that it has sought.

Whether motivated by the belief in the perfectibility of human nature, a dedication to democratic principles, allegiance to international norms, the hope in reconciliation, a confidence in legal remedies, or simply a righteous desire to set things right, present-day activists in the Mexican community have helped me better understand and appreciate our predecessors. The participation of tens of thousands of immigrants without legal status in the recent proimmigrant demonstrations, for instance, harken back to the fight for workers' rights in the 1940s and the risks that leaders and members of the rank and file often faced; in 2006 it meant and continues to mean their possible deportation and the further deterioration of their already tenuous social situation. The national Defend the Honor protest against the conscious exclusion of Mexicans in a 2007 documentary on World War II, on the other hand, reminds me that researchers continue to edit Mexicans out of U.S. history and that my work joins in the larger effort to counter this trend.

The movement is extensive and instructive for anyone formulating and answering history research questions. It includes studies, conferences, and publications on the crisis in the schools, the legal challenges on behalf of the unjustly incarcerated, the leadership training programs among the youth, protests against the contamination of our environment, the cultural and community-building activities of university and nonuniversity organizations, the organizing work among immigrant workers, lobbying for equal rights before governmental bodies, and the spiritual sustenance and guidance provided in our homes and places of worship. Angela Valenzuela and I have been associated with these and other activities through LULAC, the Intercultural Development and Research Association, the Texas Center for Education Policy, the Mexican American Legal Defense and Educational Fund, the Texas Criminal Justice Coalition, the American G.I. Forum, the Mexican American Legislative Caucus, Austin Voices for Education and Youth, the Mission Texas Coalition, the National Hispanic Institute, Teatro Vivo, the University of Texas Center for Mexican American Studies, the Division of Diversity and Community Engagement, the University Leadership Initiative, the Hispanic History of Texas Project, the "Comadres" Network, Las Latinitas, El Buen Pastor Presbyterian Church, and the University of Texas Latino Faculty and Staff Association. This is my brief tribute to them and their work.

I also want to acknowledge the undergraduate students in my classes on Mexican American history—especially Clint La Fuente—who read portions of my manuscripts as required reading and helped me see my work from many, sometimes unexpected, vantage points. Graduate students at the University of Texas with whom I have nurtured professional, as well as personal relationships have been especially helpful with their observations, suggestions and encouraging words. They include Manuel Callahan, María Sofía Corona, Claudia Cuevas, Alan Goméz, María Gonzalez, Beatriz Gutiérrez, Toni Herrera, Linda Jackson, Miguel Levario, Verónica Matsuda Martinez, Dennis Medina, Hortensia Palomares, Kristen Petros, Linda Prieto, Virginia Raymond, Lilia Rosas, Cristina Salinas, and Brenda Sendejo. My manuscript was also a source of conversation with José G. Pastrano, Lisa Yvonne Ramos, and David Urbano, graduate students from other universities.

Our University of Texas community also includes staff and faculty who have given me encouragement and support. I am especially grateful for my longstanding professional and personal relationship with José Limón, professor in English and director of the Center for Mexican American Studies, as well as for my close associations with Professors Robert Abzug, Ricardo Ainslie, Richard Flores, Doug Foley, John Gonzalez, Gloria Gonzalez-Lopez, David Gracy, David Leal, Ann Martínez, John McKiernon Gonzalez, Martha Menchaca, Maggie Rivas-Rodríguez, Lorene Roy, Andrés Tijerina, Alan Tully, and Richard Valencia. Mary Helen Davila, Luis Guevara, Dolores García, and Elvira Prieto also helped and encouraged me. Archivists Margo Gutiérrez, Christian Kelleher, and Donald Gibbs have always been courteous and helpful at the Mexican American Library Collection.

Colleagues across the country have also played a part in the preparation of this manuscript by commenting on my writings and formal presentations. Juan Gómez-Quiñones, a longtime friend and fellow traveler in the

Mexican cause, has been one of my most trusted advisors. I also received help from scholars like Carlos Blanton, Roberto Calderón, Ignacio García, Ines Hernández-Avila, Nick Kanellos, Mario Montaño, David Montejano, Victor Nelson Cisneros, Irene Owens, Antonio Ríos Bustamante, Rodolfo Rosales, Guadalupe San Miguel, Dennis Valdés, Zaragosa Vargas, and Devra Weber. Other friends and colleagues from far and near who have shared much with me and my family during the preparation of my book are Sam Barrocas and Teresa Carrillo, Georgina "Coca" Bravo, Dolores Carrillo, Lisa Catanzarite, Tom Cohen and Lisa Fuentes, Nora Comstock, Ana Correa-Yañez, Juan and Martha Cotera, Randy Hanson and Catherine Milun, Sandra Hernandez, Linda McNeil, Tatcho and Cindy Mindiola, Terry McKenna, Roel and Irene Montalvo, Carlos and Rosanna Moreno, Ernesto Nieto and Gloria de Leon, Catherine Mooney, Terrie Rabago, Joann and Rupert Reyes, and Olga Vazquez.

I wish to acknowledge the generous research support from the University of Houston and the University of Texas that made it possible for me to visit important archival institutions in Mexico and the United States. Although the Fulbright-García Robles Foundation provided me research support for another research venture, I used some of the time to complete the manuscript for publication in 2007. I am also grateful for the help that I received from the archival staff at the University of Texas, the University of Houston, the Houston Metropolitan Library, the University of Texas at Pan American, Texas A&M University at Corpus Christi, the National Archives and Research Administration, the University of Michigan, the Archivo de Relaciones Exteriores, and el Archivo de la Nación. My acknowledgments would not be complete if I did not also express my appreciation to Diana L. Vance, Jennifer Ann Hobson, and Mary Lenn Dixon for their very friendly and professional assistance at Texas A&M University Press. I am especially grateful to Philip Bansal and his fine editing skills.

My relations once again served as my most important source of love and support that made it possible for me to remain focused on my work. In my extended family, I will always be grateful for the way everyone so effortlessly resumes conversations after what always seem to be long separations. My parents, Emilio Hinojosa Zamora and Eudelia Solis de Zamora, have been pillars in our family and in their community of La Feria, Texas. My brothers and sisters—Noelia, Elia, Rolando, Cecilia, Leticia, Norma Alicia, Ricardo, and Aida—have always been devoted to them even as they raise their own families. I also appreciate Carlos and Helen Valenzuela as well as Alex Valenzuela and Valerie Robles and their families for the care and love that they have given Angela, Clara, Luz, and me. The memory of Olguita, Joey, and Helen lives in us.

I am especially grateful to Angela, Clara, and Luz. Our love and respect for each other has sustained our emotional and intellectual growth as individuals and as a family. I will always associate this book with our good times together and especially the joy that Angela and I felt as we helped Clara and Luz blossom into the smart, beautiful, and caring young women that they have become. I will also remember that I completed the book surrounded by a host of new friends in *la noble ciudad de* Guanajuato, México, and that I wrote it with dear Angela by my side: my confidence builder, my wordsmith, my advisor, my defender, my loyal companion, my personal model of care, beauty, and love.

Claiming Rights and Righting Wrongs in Texas

Chapter 1: Introduction

This study examines employment discrimination, social inequality, the Mexican cause for equal rights in the United States, and the role that the government played in reinforcing and ameliorating the socially marginalized position that Mexicans filled in the urban and rural settings of Texas.[1] One of my central arguments is that Mexicans made significant occupational gains during the Second World War but Anglos and African Americans benefited more from wartime opportunities and thereby recovered faster from the hard times of the Depression. The different rates of occupational mobility that also occurred in the Mexican community led to greater internal class differentiation, a trend that continued beyond the war years. The racial and class inequalities were striking because they emerged at a time of unprecedented opportunity made possible by wartime production and an expanded governmental apparatus that promoted the full, efficient, and nondiscriminatory use of the available labor supply. Wartime recovery was both obvious and unequal for many, including Mexicans.[2]

The promise and the disappointment of the New Deal were most evident in the ubiquitous wartime language of justice and democracy that public officials, journalists, and other war enthusiasts used to elevate the conflict in Europe to a moral battle between a just cause and a fascist agenda.[3] The high-sounding declarations made by the United States against injustice and oppression affirmed egalitarian values, validated social causes at home, and

"Americans All, Let's Fight for Victory—Americanos Todos Luchamos por la Victoria," 1943. (Artist: Leon Helguera. Rare Books and Texana Collection, World War II Posters, University of North Texas, Denton, Texas.)

encouraged marginalized groups to hope for change. The disillusionment came when public officials and segregationists outside of government questioned the idea of a more just and democratic society in the United States or proposed a gradualist approach to change, which often amounted to public appeals for understanding instead of official prohibitions against racial discrimination.

This study contributes to the history of home front causes by focusing on the response to discrimination, segregation, and inequality in Texas by the League of United Latin American Citizens (LULAC), the leading Mexican civil rights organization in the country at the time. Although LULAC was not the only Mexican organization to note the moral inconsistency of opposing or delaying change while fighting for justice and democracy abroad, it was one of the most visible and consistent in its actions.[4] In addition to protesting discrimination and inequality in Mexican daily life, LULAC councils collaborated with other groups throughout the state, including the Mexican consulate and government agencies such as the Fair Employment Practice Committee (FEPC), the office that was responsible for implementing President Franklin Roosevelt's Executive Orders 8802 and 9346, which prohibited discrimination in war industries, government employment, and unions. They also spoke on behalf of all Mexicans, regardless of nativity, and made rhetorical calls for the application at home of the Good Neighbor Policy, the U.S. initiative that promoted unity and understanding in the Americas.

Persistent inequality at a time of great material and ideological promise achieved even greater importance when officials from the United States and Mexico gave discrimination a central place in their relations, elevated it to a level of hemispheric importance, and made Texas the testing ground for the application of the Good Neighbor Policy. The international emphasis on race and civil rights extends the reach of this study and distinguishes the Mexican wartime experience from those of other ethnic and working-class groups in the United States.[5] This study shows how Mexico gained a negotiating advantage on behalf of Mexicans in the United States and strengthened the cause against racial discrimination, a worldwide issue that achieved greater importance in the Americas as the war progressed. Mexico's intervention involved a consular campaign against discrimination in the United States and collaborative ties with LULAC's own crusade for equal rights in Texas. The United States responded by extending its Good Neighbor Policy from the field of hemispheric relations to the domestic arena of racialized social relations. Mexico's determined critique of racial discrimination coincided with the wartime understanding of nonintervention and mutual consultation in the Good Neighbor Policy and with the State Department's concern that Latin America and Mexicans in the United States were fertile ground for Axis influence.

To understand how the high-sounding wartime principles of justice and democracy applied to race relations in the United States, one must examine the collaborative work between LULAC and the Mexican consulates, on the one hand, and, on the other hand, the interagency response within the U.S. government to this collaboration, especially in the context of the government's security concerns over the border region and the Southwest. To this end, the study focuses on the joint advocacy campaign and the U.S government's labor initiatives, which were especially evident in the work of two agencies, the United States Employment Service (USES), an arm of the War Manpower Commission involved in regulating the farm labor supply, and the FEPC, the agency involved in managing labor relations in the more critical war industries.[6]

My intent is to demonstrate that the state both reinforced and ameliorated inequality at the same time that its agencies sought the full and efficient use of all available labor. Open declarations against racial discrimination notwithstanding, federal and state officials were primarily committed to meeting the wartime demands on the economy and they promoted racial understanding and goodwill as long as such initiatives did not interfere with the high production levels that the war effort required.[7] Mexican consulate staff and LULAC members, on the other hand, made use of the Good Neighbor Policy to promote their cause against discrimination in the United States, despite the apparent limits that the U.S. state and its wartime agenda placed on their work.

The important vantage point that the Mexican experience provides for the history of the U.S. home front bears restating. Their socially marginalized position allows us to posit that discrimination figured prominently in maintaining inequality despite the opportunities for significant recovery that the wartime economy and an activist state provided. Also, the political response by LULAC underscores the importance that Mexicans gave discrimination and inequality as wartime issues in American life and in intergovernmental relations. These interpretations acquire added significance when one considers that other Mexicans and African Americans also met the same fate and responded in like manner at a time of unprecedented possibilities for change. Moreover, the intervention of the Mexican government on behalf of Mexicans and the decision by the State Department to demonstrate its good will with Good Neighbor Policy initiatives in Texas internationalize the story and bring the themes of intergovernmental relations, racial discrimination, civil rights, and an activist state into sharper focus. To restate matters further, the Texas home front story has deeper implications than one would ordinarily suppose.

This study fills gaps in the historical literature and combines the findings and interpretations of various relevant works to construct a new history of the U.S. home front.[8] Histories of Mexico and Texas in the 1940s that treat history in broad synthetic terms offer an opportunity to supplement and complement the scholarly record. Juan Gómez Quiñones's two-volume history of Mexican politics, for instance, addresses some of the major trends that run their course through the 1940s, including discrimination, inequality, labor and civil rights activity, and an activist state, but his primary interest was in providing a broadly conceived work that covered over three hundred years. David Montejano, on the other hand, provided an analysis of racialized social relationships in Texas and credited the period of the Second World War for major social and political changes that brought noticeable benefit to the Mexican community, but his treatment of a 150-year period left little room for an in-depth examination of the home front experience. George N. Green also took pause at the Texas home front, but made his most important contribution to the 1940s with his overarching history of conservatism and its challengers between 1938 and 1957. More recent examples of broadly conceived histories include works by scholars like Ben Proctor and Randolph B. Campbell. They examined the Texas home front experience with useful comprehensive essays on the twentieth century. Ernest Obadele-Starks, on the other hand, made some note of Mexican workers in the Texas Gulf Coast in his well-received study on black unionism in the South.[9]

Other general studies have given greater attention to the Mexican at the home front. Guadalupe San Miguel's work on educational segregation and Mexican self-help and protest activity in Texas follows a long chronological path while paying close attention to LULAC and the effects of the Good Neighbor Policy on race relations during the 1940s. Mario García also took time in his study on leadership and identity to address the history of LULAC in Texas and some of its civil rights work during the Second World War. Scholars like George J. Sanchez, Matt García, Carlos K. Blanton, and Arnoldo de León have likewise incorporated the 1940s more fully into the social and political history of Mexican communities in California and Texas. Vicki Ruiz, on the other hand, has made significant contributions to Mexican history with studies on women that have addressed the Second World War experience.[10]

Scholars from Mexico and the United States who have internationalized their respective national histories with studies on themes such as intergovernmental relations, interchanges between Mexican communities on both sides of the border, and immigration also provide important information and frameworks for understanding Mexicans in Texas during the 1940s. Luis G. Zorrilla and Blanca Torres have written two of the most important works on the history of relations between Mexico and the United States that focus on the period of the Second World War. The authors are balanced in their approach and analysis and provide an assessment of the important political and material contributions made by Mexico to the war effort as the principal U.S. ally in the Americas.[11] Gómez-Quiñones and David R. Maciel, on the other hand, have contributed to the growing body of literature that addresses the history of nongovernmental relations between Mexicans on both sides of the international border, a field that informs most of the study. They have done this with their individual scholarship as well as with programmatic initiatives involving anthologies with authors from both countries, binational scholarly conferences, and other cooperative activities.[12]

The work by the labor economist Walter Fogel figures prominently in this study, especially in the area of employment discrimination. He provided some of the earliest evidence of a seemingly permanent condition of racialized occupational inequality in the five major southwestern states between the 1930s and the 1960s. Fogel concluded that although Mexicans made important occupational gains, especially during the war years, discrimination restricted them to a lower mobility rate and contributed to a disparity that continued largely unabated into the 1960s. Mario Barrera seconded Fogel's findings by noting the unparalleled occupational gains that Mexicans made between 1930 and 1970 in California, Arizona, New Mexico, and Texas. He also called attention to discrimination as an explanation for the continuing concentration of Mexicans in the lower occupational ranks, as well as in the bottom segments of the higher-skilled occupations. The quantitative studies by Fogel and Barrera contributed much to our understanding of employment discrimination and inequalities that defined relations within the Mexican community and between Mexicans and members of the larger society. Their work, however, lacked context and the kind of explanation that a social history typically provides.[13]

Useful focused studies on Mexicans at the home front or related topics have not been completely absent. Mario García, for instance, addressed the emergence of a Mexican social movement in Los Angeles that expressed an ethnic identity borne out of the patriotic days of the Second World

War. Richard Santillán's article on "Rosita the Riveter," on the other hand, supplemented women's history with contributions by Mexican women war workers in the Midwest. Gerald D. Nash contributed a notable essay to the general experiences of Mexicans during the war years in his well-cited book on the American West while George N. Green contributed one of the earliest articles on Mexicans and the Good Neighbor Commission, the agency that purported to investigate and settle complaints of discrimination in Texas during the Second World War. Articles by Emilio Zamora on Mexican oil workers in the Texas Gulf Coast and the FEPC and intergovernmental relations in the Americas during the war also contribute to our understanding of employment discrimination, inequality, and the intervention of the Mexican government on behalf of Mexicans in the United States.[14]

The historical literature on the FEPC includes an important study by Clete Daniel that examined the agency's first, short-lived visit with Mexican workers in the Southwest in 1942. He pointed out that discrimination in the nonferrous industry of West Texas, New Mexico, and Arizona was widespread and that it created a serious obstacle to upward occupational mobility. Daniel also reported on the dedicated work of a field examiner named Ernest Trimble and the courageous efforts by Mexican miners and smelters to bring their grievances before the FEPC. Daniel did not, however, examine the work of the FEPC in other parts of the Southwest, nor did he analyze Mexico's important interventionist role. Finally, he failed to attend to the civil rights movements in the Mexican and African American communities and the advocacy campaign for equal rights by the Mexican consuls. Daniel's study nevertheless serves as an important point of departure for an understanding of the FEPC in the Mexican community.[15]

Early texts on Mexican history also guided this study, including Raul Morín's *Among the Valiant,* Carey McWilliams's *North From Mexico,* Pauline Kibbe's *Latin Americans in Texas,* and Alonso Perales's *Are We Good Neighbors?*[16] The authors examined the hard times of the Depression, New Deal legislation, and the momentous organizing struggles of the period, as well as the harsh social conditions facing the largely working-class Mexican population during the 1930s and their efforts at surviving, protesting, and changing these conditions. They also addressed the Mexican battlefield contributions, their experiences recovering from the Depression, and the continuing marginalization during the war years.[17]

Together, these firsthand works offer a foundational treatment of the Mexican experience at the home front. Morín documented the battlefield sacrifices that Mexican newspapers and activists noted during and after the war in their public calls for equal treatment at home. McWilliams provided personal and historical accounts of the Mexican community as an ethnic group and bottom segment of the working class. He was especially critical of discrimination as a major obstacle to the improved employment opportunities offered by an expanding wartime economy. Their unequal treatment, he argued, prevented Mexicans from recovering from the hard times of the Depression to the same extent as other workers. To illustrate the problem, McWilliams examined the difficulties they faced in agriculture. Although their wages improved during the war, the slow movement of workers out of agriculture plus the expansion of the immigrant population in rural areas and the growth of the migratory workforce seemed to lock them in place as laborers. Kibbe also acknowledged the dire conditions under which Mexicans lived and worked in urban and rural Texas settings. She pointed to the battlefield contributions of Mexicans and made use of the Good Neighbor Policy to call for a better understanding of Mexicans in the United States and improved relations with Latin America, especially Mexico. Perales, on the other hand, documented conditions of discrimination and inequality in Texas using accounts contributed by leading Mexican activists and numerous affidavits by aggrieved Mexicans whom he interviewed.

Perales's book has special appeal as the single most important compilation of primary records that addressed the Mexican experience at midcentury. The book's descriptions and interpretations of discriminatory practices are especially valuable sources of information for understanding the Mexican home front as well as the broader southwestern context. Edited by one of the most prominent Mexican civil rights leaders between the 1920s and the 1940s, *Are We Good Neighbors?* brings together a collection of essays, speeches, newspaper articles, and affidavits that are unmatched in originality, understanding, and boldness. The quality of the essays owes much to the fact that their authors were public figures with established reputations for speaking and acting on discrimination and segregation.[18] They used moral, Christian, and constitutional arguments and the ever-present egalitarian language of the war years to critique discrimination and to justify their calls for equal rights. The authors also analogized the fight on the battlefield with the cause for equal rights at home. The fight at both places was the same: it sought peace, understanding, and equality among nations as well as between groups and individuals at home. Perales drove this point home with his double-meaning book title, *Are We Good Neighbors?*

The antisegregationist voices in Perales's book also mounted the overarching argument that no appreciable dent was made on social inequality during the 1940s, even with the help of an expanded wartime economy and an activist state. Morin, McWilliams, and Kibbe acknowledged that recovery opportunities had brought some relief, but that Mexicans had recovered at a slower rate than other groups and the problem of unequal relations remained virtually untouched. They added that discrimination and segregation were extending inequality into the postwar period. The challenge for the state, according to Perales and his writers, was to treat discrimination forthrightly and to incorporate Mexicans more effectively and equally into mainstream society.

Perales's book includes three works that were especially influential to this study. Carlos Castañeda, the highly regarded borderlands historian from the University of Texas at Austin and an intellectual standout in LULAC, wrote them: "The Second Rate Citizen and Democracy," "Testimony at Fair Employment Practices Act Hearings, March 12, 13, 14, 1945," and "Statement on Discrimination Against Mexican-Americans in Employment." Castañeda declared that "economic" discrimination made Mexicans second-class citizens in the same way that it marginalized African Americans in the South. Race prejudice, he added, led to employment discrimination, the root of racial inequality, and to the "undemocratic, un-American, and un-Christian" practice of treating Mexicans as social inferiors. This denied them equal rights and ultimately led to the "destruction of the basic principles of democracy" that the United States was proclaiming throughout the world. Although his writings were poignant and convincing, his importance to this study lies elsewhere.[19]

Castañeda contributed more than well-written statements against discrimination and the second-class status of Mexicans. His prior work as an official of the FEPC also added authoritative weight to Perales's book.[20] As the field examiner of the Dallas FEPC office in 1943, the director of the San Antonio office and special assistant to the chairman on Latin American workers in the Southwest in 1944 and 1945, and as an active member of the 1945 campaign to make the FEPC a permanent agency after the war, Castañeda had been well-positioned to observe employment discrimination against Mexicans and blacks throughout the Southwest. His writings provided credible evidence that employment discrimination reinforced inequality in the Southwest as well as in the Midwest and the Far West. Castañeda's active association with LULAC, beginning soon after the organization's founding in 1929 and continuing during the war years, gave added credibility to his observations.

I became interested in Castañeda's important role as an intermediary between LULAC and the FEPC and as a vantage point from which to begin constructing a home front history of Mexicans in Texas. His biography and the historical literature on the civil rights organization, however, provided little help. Félix D. Almaraz and Mario García focus most of their attention on his personal life and his work as a historian. García also addresses Castañeda's participation in LULAC, but neither he nor Almaraz provide a full account of his association with the FEPC and LULAC during the Second World War.[21]

Most of the histories of LULAC, like the general historical studies of the Mexican community, also gloss over the Second World War. Typically, historians point out that wartime opportunities helped Mexicans recover from the Depression, and they note, to a lesser extent, that they did not recuperate as well as Anglos. LULAC, meanwhile, was weakened by the loss of membership to the draft and was only able to maintain a minimum of protest activity against discrimination and segregation in the schools and in public establishments. The general impression then is that Mexicans recovered somewhat from the hard times of the 1930s and that LULAC had to wait until the postwar period to resume an expanded civil rights activity with legal action and electoral politics that had a decidedly conservative agenda: it shunned Mexican immigrants, embraced an exaggerated form of patriotism, and adopted whiteness as its principal political strategy for access into American society.[22]

Although the recent focus on whiteness largely looks at the period after the Second World War, it has generated a central critique against LULAC involving the "other-White" strategy that was also present in the 1940s. Whiteness studies remind us that race permeates society and that Mexicans are not immune to its influences, particularly the alleged propensity for some of them to claim racial privilege by virtue of their official designation as whites and their socially constructed position in the "middle" of the racial structure that grants them political maneuverability. This interest, however, has not always resulted in well-grounded conclusions, including the claim that organizations like LULAC made use of the official designation of Mexicans as "White" to break with the black cause and, in some important cases, deliberately and even spitefully maintain the edifice of race. The historian Mario García offered a relevant critique to a similar generalization in the 1980s that suggested the organization had reinforced internal divisions by using citizenship to claim constitutional rights.[23]

García's call for a fuller account of LULAC's political work apparently has been lost on some "Whiteness" scholars like Ian F. Haney Lopez, who has focused on the other white strategy that many Mexicans used between the

1930s and the 1960s. Haney Lopez has assumed that the official designation of Mexicans as whites favored them in a significant way and suggested that when Mexican leaders claimed equal rights on the basis of their identification as Whites, they were exercising this "privilege" and essentially abandoning the fight against pernicious distinctions based on race. Some Mexicans may have had the opportunity to make political use of their whiteness and dissociate themselves from the African American social movement. The whitening process, including the social conditions and political exigencies under which Mexicans of different class backgrounds, nativity, and racial makeup could make use of the "privilege," however, is still underexamined. Scholars, for instance, have preferred to explain why Mexicans would make use of this "privilege" without telling us how and why segregationists would also use the whiteness designation as a tool to deny Mexicans the right to claim equal rights. More importance should also be given to the Mexican leadership who recognized the strategic opportunity and responded in the most reasonable and appropriate manner as the other white group and with the same sense of righteous indignation that one finds in other fights for civil and labor rights. This minimally calls for tentative observations, rather than the following kind of misleading generalization by scholars like Haney Lopez: "Mexican American civil rights organizations, including the League of United Latin American Citizens and the GI Forum" attacked segregation "not on the ground that this racial practice was morally wrong, but because Mexicans were ostensibly white."[24]

The historian Neil Foley has made a stronger case for a self-serving and divisive form of racial privilege as a primary explanation for the use of the other white strategy among Mexicans. That this view is far from achieving a consensus is demonstrated by Carlos K. Blanton's recent critique. He examined the correspondence between George I. Sanchez, a LULAC leader and University of Texas professor who is credited with preparing important legal cases that used whiteness on behalf of Mexican plaintiffs, and two prominent members of the African American community, Thurgood Marshall, the famed attorney who represented the National Association for the Advancement of Colored People (NAACP) before the U.S. Supreme Court in *Brown v. Board of Education* and Charles Johnson, the eminent black sociologist and president of Fisk University. For the first time on record, Blanton's study makes a substantial case for viewing whiteness in broad terms, as part of a general Mexican strategy against racial inequality that at times operated in unison with African American civil rights leaders.[25]

The debate over Mexicans and whiteness raises important questions that this study seeks to clarify. To what extent, for instance, was the other white strategy a restricted plan of action that excluded blacks and undermined the cause for equal rights? One could also ask to what extent a Mexican political identity, in conjunction with other strategies like the use of a manpower policy, the Good Neighbor Policy, or the campaign in favor of civil rights legislation, reinforced or undermined the racial structure. The point here is to broaden the field of evidence and thereby the analysis beyond general and often insufficiently grounded impressions. With a broader lens that investigates inequality, governmental action, and community responses to social disparities, this study aims to examine varied instances in which Mexicans used their whiteness, singly and in cooperation with black civil and labor rights leaders, to promote the cause against discrimination and segregation, particularly in the workplace.[26]

While the whiteness literature raises important questions regarding race as a broad unit of historical analysis, interethnic relations, and the significance of the Mexican cause, historical works on the FEPC offered little help in understanding Castañeda, the Mexican community, and the fight against discrimination and segregation in a broad internationalist setting. With the exception of the previously noted works by Daniel and a dissertation by Lou Ella Jenkins, the pertinent histories on the FEPC, race, and the state fail to acknowledge Castañeda and the FEPC's work in the Mexican community. The glaring gap no doubt reflects the overriding governmental concern with blacks during the war as well as with the conventional practice among historians to treat race, labor, and the cause for equal rights primarily in black and white terms and to deny the participation of Mexicans as subjects and agents in U.S. history. This is evident in at least four important works. The respected historian Merl E. Reed purports to study the FEPC and other federal agencies in the South but restricts his attention to blacks. Daniel Kryder also excludes Mexicans from his examination of race conflict and the role that the state played in managing it in the workplace and in the army. Roger W. Lotchin applauds the growing work on the home front in the West and calls for its further expansion with only a couple of references to Mexicans and without mentioning relevant works on their history in the Southwest. A recent essay by William J. Collins on wartime production, race, and the FEPC does not mention Mexicans at all.[27]

These gaps notwithstanding, scholars have provided a thorough examination of the FEPC with notable studies on its history among various groups throughout the country. They have acknowledged that the agency contributed an important chapter in the history of labor, race, civil rights, and the activist state of the New Deal era. Although the agency was largely ineffective because of an insufficient budget and the opposition of segregationists in local areas and the southern congressional bloc in Washington, it exposed discrimination as a serious issue in home front production and encouraged the cause of labor and civil rights among African Americans. Historians have also documented the black political offensive, the work of an activist state, and the dramatic expansion of a wartime economy.[28]

Some findings in the historiography of the FEPC assumed special relevance during the early stages of this study, especially when read next to observations that Castañeda and other writers offer in Perales's book. For instance, African Americans also shared in the recovery experience of the Second World War and trailed behind whites. The shared experience of Mexicans and blacks gives greater weight to the significance of discrimination and inequality in U.S. history. It also calls for a broader consideration of discrimination and the role of the state in combating it. Discrimination, in other words, was a more widespread experience if we include Mexicans in the equation, especially in Texas where they outnumbered blacks in the 1940s. One could add that the combined experience suggests an even more ineffective and complicit state.[29]

While the secondary literature does not provide much on Castañeda and his work in the area of employment discrimination, the rich archival records of the FEPC opened up new research possibilities for this study. The collection included complaints from Mexican and black workers, correspondence among agency officials, workers, and industry representatives, accounts of investigations by FEPC examiners, reports on working conditions and organizing efforts, official findings that mostly favored complainants, and FEPC directives that ordered settlements of the complaints and adoption of the country's nondiscrimination policy. The records also contained the views of aggrieved workers on issues like wage and upgrading discrimination, political analysis by civil rights leaders, debates among FEPC officials over investigative strategies, relations with local activists, and arguments by company and union officials who opposed the agency's findings and directives.

FEPC materials also revealed the central role that Castañeda played in the agency's work, especially in Texas. He opened the first FEPC office in the Southwest after the El Paso office had closed. As the agency's first Mexican field examiner, his primary responsibility was to solicit complaints from mostly Mexican and black workers in the Texas-Louisiana region, investigate them, and negotiate settlements with management and the unions who were implicated in the cases of discrimination. As the special assistant to the chairman on Latin American workers in the Southwest, Castañeda assumed the added responsibility of working with Mexican complainants in the entire Southwest and parts of the West. He also received special instructions to maintain good relations with government officials, community leaders, and minority organizations. Castañeda continued his work in the San Antonio office and worked closely with LULAC and members of the Mexican Consulate, primarily in Texas.

The voluminous records associated with Castañeda's early investigation of the oil industry on the Texas Gulf Coast served as the basis for my first attempt to study the FEPC and Mexican workers in wartime industries.[30] The oil cases were "thick" with information on working conditions, workers' complaints, the practice of discrimination, the FEPC's implementation of the president's executive orders, and Castañeda's collaboration with Mexican groups in the Southwest. The study confirmed the observations that Castañeda made in Perales's book regarding widespread discrimination in wartime industries. The most obvious corroboration involved weekly reports written by Castañeda and other FEPC officials that told of hiring, wage, and job classification discrimination and the difficulties they faced in enforcing the nation's nondiscrimination policy in employment. The claims by the workers, often substantiated by FEPC investigations and findings, as well as admissions of guilt by employer and union representatives, were also important. The oil study, a revised version of which appears as chapter 6 in this book, raised three research questions that guided my subsequent research.

The first question had two parts: to what extent did discrimination limit recovery for Mexicans in the oil industry during and after the war, and what difference did the FEPC make? Castañeda acknowledged in his reports as well as in correspondence with his superiors that Mexicans managed to secure employment in the oil industry, but that discrimination limited their entry and concentrated them in low-wage, low-skill occupations like janitors, members of cleaning crews, and assistants to skilled workers. He also claimed that Mexicans and blacks faced discrimination in other critical wartime industries as well as in less critical, or essential industries, like agriculture and construction. The implication was that the unequal access to higher-paying and higher-skilled jobs was extensive, and that this experience explained inequality between Mexicans and Anglos and among Mexicans that, according to authors like Montejano and Gómez-Quiñones, extended into the 1980s. Castañeda also expressed concerns over the FEPC's lack of enforcement powers and the reluctance among other agencies to promote the nation's nondiscrimination policy. The USES, according to Castañeda and other FEPC officers was the major culprit in agriculture and urban-based war industries. On the other hand, he openly acknowledged that the federal government responded to claims of discrimination and that the FEPC encouraged workers to hope for industrial democracy with findings and directives that favored them.

The second research question emerged mostly from Castañeda's correspondence with leaders representing LULAC councils, unions, NAACP locals, and Mexican consulate offices: how can the collaborative relationship between FEPC officials and activists help us better understand the implementation of government policies that addressed discrimination and inequality? The record pointed to a community of liberal as well as conservative activists who built relationships with the FEPC and other agencies. Tensions arose and agency officials tried to maneuver between the different expectations generated by the president's executive orders. Ethnic leaders expected the state, through agencies such as the FEPC, to make good on the promise of wartime recovery. Segregationists, on the other hand, either opposed the application of the nondiscrimination policy or insisted on a gradualist approach. Castañeda, like his counterparts in the agency, mediated these countervailing influences.

The cooperative relationship between the FEPC, LULAC activists, and Mexican consulate officials raised a third important question: given the degree and persistence of occupational discrimination against Mexican workers during the war, why did the government wait so long before waging a sustained effort in the Southwest? Although the agency briefly opened up an office in El Paso in 1942, it did not initiate a concerted effort until the summer of 1943, almost two years after the announcement of Executive Order 8804. FEPC officials had occasionally suggested that the agency was not more active among Mexican workers because they did not usually submit the complaints needed to start an investigation. The large number of complaints received at the El Paso office contradicted this view. Also, more complaints could have been generated in 1941 and 1942 if the FEPC had opened additional offices in the Southwest and if officials had given greater publicity to their work. There are other, more likely explanations for the government's delay. In the minds of Washington officials, Mexicans largely represented a regional immigrant or ethnic community and as such did not occupy a central position in the national policy arena of race and race relations. Moreover, Congress did not provide the FEPC with the necessary appropriations to expand into the Southwest until 1943, when Roosevelt issued his second executive order.

An enabling budget no doubt contributed to the expanded purview of the FEPC. This factor alone, however, does not explain the government's newfound interest in workers in the Southwest. An answer lay in the correspondence between officials in the State Department; the Office of the Coordinator for Inter-American Affairs (OCIAA), the office responsible for implementing the Good Neighbor Policy; and the Secretaría de Relaciones Exteriores (Mexico's Foreign Affairs Office). These records strongly suggest that U.S. government officials decided to give more policy attention to Mexicans in response to pressure from Mexico and their own concern with security issues in the Southwest. More specifically, they feared that claims by Mexican officials and Mexican organizations in the United States would encourage protests by Mexicans and that this could trigger conflict with segregationists and worsen a perceived security problem in the Southwest. They were also concerned that if discrimination could not be abated, or if its critics drew greater public attention to it, the Good Neighbor Policy and the inter-American system of cooperation under construction in the Americas would be jeopardized. A fuller explanation of the FEPC's policy change and the way it reflected a new, broader government view of Mexicans appears in chapter 3.

The correspondence between Castañeda and Adolfo G. Domínguez, the Mexican consul in Houston, and Carlos Calderón, the general Mexican consul in San Antonio, also revealed that the Mexican government had decided to vigorously assist its nationals in the exterior. The Mexican government had consistently promoted this policy, but it now appeared to pursue it with a greater sense of urgency.[31] The war had encouraged Mexico to take a more active role, largely in response to critics of the Mexico-U.S. wartime alliance, but also as a way to test the sincerity of the United States in building understanding through its Good Neighbor Policy. The State Department and the governments of the states located along the Mexico-U.S. border now had to contend with a more daring Mexican state. Mexican officials, apparently emboldened by the new inter-American spirit of cooperation, demanded that the State Department direct federal agencies to address the problem of discrimination. Promoting the ideal policy of improved understanding across the racial divide meant that agencies such as the FEPC would now seek to integrate Mexicans into their work.[32]

Texas emerged as the key site in the story of an expanded Good Neighbor

Policy. This too resulted largely from pressure originating in Mexico especially during the 1942 negotiations over the Bracero Program, the labor importation program that Mexico and the United States negotiated as a wartime measure of cooperation.[33] Mexico's negotiators were concerned over the large number of complaints of discrimination filed throughout the early 1900s against Texas employers, especially farmers. They negotiated an agreement with basic protections for Mexican contract workers and refused to send them to Texas as a way to publicly pressure the United States into advocating for the rights of Mexican nationals and U.S.-born Mexicans. Texas officials, under pressure from farmers who also wanted Braceros, took a cue from the State Department and adopted their own version of a good neighbor policy in 1943. Washington had extended Texas officials the necessary financial support to establish the Good Neighbor Commission. Mexico, nevertheless, kept the ban in place insisting that the good neighbor initiatives were not improving race relations in Texas. They continued to make this point for the duration of the war. Texas had clearly become a test case for the Good Neighbor Policy and no amount of official neighborly behavior could deter Mexico from using Texas to make a case for effective official interventions against discrimination.

The intergovernmental focus on Texas underscored the importance of the unprecedented alliance that LULAC and the Mexican consular corps forged on behalf of Mexican nationals and U.S.-born Mexicans. LULAC's collaboration with Mexico's advocacy campaign as well as its work on behalf of Mexican workers through its association with Mexican consuls and the FEPC challenges some basic assumptions in the history of Mexicans in the United States. LULAC primarily acted as a civil rights organization but one cannot deny that its mostly upwardly mobile U.S.-born middle-class leaders also made cause with the largely working-class Mexican population. They professed an ethnic or "Mexican Americanist" orientation, but they did not deny the opportunity to also make common cause with Mexican nationals as well as blacks during the war years.[34]

LULAC's record during the 1940s stands out because its leaders were clearly intent on making use of new opportunities that included Mexico's advocacy campaign in the United States and the implementation by the FEPC of the nation's nondiscrimination policy in employment. Although LULAC's pan-Mexican stance in the area of labor rights seems exceptional next to its conventional view as a moderate or conservative civil rights organization, it minimally calls for a reassessment of its politics during the national emergency. This does not necessarily mean, however, that LULAC stands completely apart from its history before and after the war. LULAC continued other long-term campaigns, including actions against segregation in the schools; fights against discrimination in public establishments like restaurants, swimming pools, theaters and grocery stores; and support for civil rights legislation that could benefit Mexicans as well as African Americans. LULAC also made full use of the egalitarian language associated with the war effort, which invigorated its discourse with continuing allusions to moral, divine, and constitutional rights. Additionally, its members and leaders often combined their official designation as whites, interventions from Mexico, and what Montejano calls the Anglo's racial ambivalence towards Mexicans to fashion a wedge strategy for civil rights legislation and workers' rights. Although the civil rights organization stands out during the 1940s for its collaborative strategy and far-reaching hemispheric orientation, LULAC councils occasionally diverged from their favored course of action. The evidence also suggests continuities that extended into the postwar period.[35]

The general inclination of numerous organizations to use the language of justice and democracy, on the other hand, suggests that the wartime spirit of egalitarianism also influenced the Mexican community into adopting a broad, inclusive approach to civil rights. My own work shows that José de la Luz Saenz, a LULAC founder, a prominent leader during World War II and a contributor to Perales's book, was especially important in preparing the rhetorical ground for a "Double V" campaign. His World War I diary and the numerous newspaper articles he wrote between the wars were constant reminders to the Mexican leadership, if not the general Mexican public, that the declared democratic principles associated with the war effort justified their call for equal rights. Not unlike the connections African American leaders were making between the home and war fronts, Saenz made special note of military service and battlefield sacrifice by Mexicans to emphasize their right to equal treatment in the United States. In this way, Saenz and others, like Perales and Castañeda, appropriated the wartime language of democracy and justice to recast the Mexican cause for equal rights in hemispheric terms. They did this by representing their movement as an integral part of the larger effort to democratize relations in the Americas and to build a united front against autocratic powers around the world. Mexican civil rights leaders, in short, were broadening their claims for equal rights at home by becoming Americans abroad.[36]

LULAC and the Mexican consulate, of course, were not the only ones that spoke out against discrimination and inequality. The archives of the FEPC, the USES, the WMC, and the Mexican Foreign Affairs Office contain numerous records indicating that other organizations and individuals participated in the cause, often in collaboration with each other. The workers who submitted complaints of discrimination to the FEPC and requested the assistance of LULAC and consular representatives in this effort must also be acknowledged as important participants. The members of the Laredo union of miners and smelters, on the other hand, did not limit their political work to requests for FEPC investigations; they also pursued bread-and-butter issues as well as the unity of Mexicans across the international border. Still others submitted complaints to the FEPC as disgruntled members of unions associated with the American Federation of Labor (AFL) or with the Congress of Industrial Organizations (CIO) or as workers that the unions had excluded and disregarded, at times in collaboration with their employers. Journalists like Ignacio Lozano, the editor of *La Prensa*, the popular daily from San Antonio, also championed the rights of workers and gave consistent support to organizations and individuals that espoused change. The numerous mutual aid societies, Masonic orders, and consulate-affiliated Comisiones Honoríficas operating throughout the state also supported workers' rights, often as a result of the involvement of some of their members in unions and the grievance process that the FEPC afforded them. Other organizations did the same, including the famed pecan shellers' union from San Antonio and members of confederations like the Congreso de Habla Española, the Confederación de Trabajadores Latino-Americanos, the Confederación de Organizaciones Mexicanas y Latinoamericanas emerging out of Galveston and Houston, and the Mexico-based Confederación de Trabajadores Mexicanos en Norteamérica. LULAC councils, however, worked most closely with the FEPC and the Mexican consulate.[37]

The next chapter examines the experience Mexicans had in the labor market and the contradictory role that the state played in managing their relations with employers. I measure their occupational mobility in light of unprecedented wartime opportunities and explain their lower rate of mobility by pointing to discrimination in workplaces and governmental policies that both ameliorated and reinforced inequality. More specifically, I examine the wartime experiences of Mexican workers as they moved from rural to urban areas to replace their agricultural positions with better-paying jobs in rapidly expanding industries such as oil, garment, meatpacking, construction, and transportation. The USES was in large part responsible for the slow movement of Mexicans out of agriculture. I contend that discrimination also limited their movement into nonagricultural pursuits. This explains why observers such as Castañeda could claim that Mexicans had recovered from the Depression, while simultaneously lamenting the persistence of inequality.

Chapter 3 studies the intervention by Mexico, the response by the State Department, and the emergence of Texas as a key site for negotiating the application of the Good Neighbor Policy. Mexican officials were successful in urging the State Department to address the issue of discrimination as an obstacle to the inter-American alliance. The subsequent interagency campaign to "incorporate" Mexicans into the war effort involved the decision to broaden the Good Neighbor Policy into the domestic arena. A principal concern in this chapter is to demonstrate how the shift in the Good Neighbor Policy led to the more determined work by the FEPC in the Southwest and other areas where Mexicans predominated. It also underscores the importance of Texas in Mexico's intervention on behalf of U.S.-born and Mexico-born Mexicans, often in collaboration with the FEPC and LULAC.

Chapter 4 introduces LULAC's civil and labor rights program of action and more fully addresses its political relationship with the consular corps of Mexico. LULAC leaders also organized their own challenges against racial discrimination and inequality in business establishments, schools, and workplaces. The organization's association with Mexican consuls gave added legitimacy and political strength to their cause at the same time that their collaboration with the FEPC allowed them to negotiate Mexican workers' rights as issues of domestic and hemispheric importance. This activism was especially evident in Texas, where state officials instituted their own Good Neighbor Policy to convince Mexico to lift the Bracero ban, and LULAC, in association with Mexican consuls, called for a law prohibiting racial discrimination. Although LULAC and Mexican consuls typically called for a protected legal status for Mexicans, their leaders at times promoted a broader view of civil rights legislation that could have included African Americans. The Mexican cause in Texas also joined the larger effort to improve understanding among the American nations by introducing the issue of discrimination during discussions on human rights at international meetings held in Mexico City and San Francisco.

Chapter 5 looks more closely at efforts by the FEPC on behalf of Mexican workers and at the political debates that the FEPC stimulated on states' rights, on the enforcement abilities and responsibilities of federal agencies like the FEPC, and on the Good Neighbor Policy as an overarching project seeking racial understanding in Texas. The work of the FEPC demonstrated some sincerity in the application of the Good Neighbor Policy at home.

Mexican officials also contributed to the effectiveness of the agency when its personnel pointed to the alliance in the Americas to pressure employers to accept the agency's directives and adopt the nation's nondiscrimination policy.

The last two substantive chapters focus on the working conditions that Mexicans faced in wartime industries and the role that the FEPC played in implementing a nondiscrimination policy. The cases investigated by the FEPC pitted Mexican workers against obstinate manufacturing firms and unions, whose representatives promoted policies and practices intended to discriminate against Mexican and black workers. The chapters underscore the importance of discrimination in keeping Mexicans as well as blacks from making full use of employment opportunities in the high-skilled and high-wage firms in wartime industries. They also demonstrate how Castañeda and other FEPC officials collaborated with LULAC and Mexican consulate representatives. Lastly, they show that the support of LULAC and Mexican consuls, as well as international pressure, brought greater attention to discrimination against Mexican workers and that the workers were emboldened as a result.

Chapter 6 examines the conditions under which Mexicans and blacks worked in three refineries in the Texas Gulf Coast oil industry and the use of a union contract and understandings between union and company representatives to segregate workers according to race. The FEPC failed to resolve workers' grievances at the Shell, Sinclair, and Humble refineries located in the Houston area in large part because Anglo unionists refused to accept the agency's findings and directives and management claimed that it feared a work stoppage and conflict if they disagreed with the segregationists. The CIO unions at Shell and Sinclair and the independent workers' organizations at Humble had similar contractual understandings that limited the number of minority workers who could be hired, assigned them to the unskilled jobs, and denied them upgrading opportunities. In all three instances, workers' representatives joined with company officials in admitting that these arrangements constituted discrimination and violated the nation's nondiscrimination policy. The workers and their representatives claimed that Anglos refused to work next to Mexicans, suggesting racial animus among their members. The issue of job control explains these racial predilections as Anglo workers used their collective power to defend what they believed were hard-won gains now being threatened by minority workers and an intrusive federal government. The measure of their feelings against the FEPC and minority workers became evident in 1945 when Anglo workers from Shell staged a race strike to express their opposition against the agency's finding of discrimination and the company's acceptance of a directive to upgrade some minority workers.

Chapter 7 offers additional findings of discrimination and a refusal by company and union representatives to abide by directives that favored the workers. The Mexican workers, some of whom belonged to the unions in the plants, and local LULAC councils followed the regular grievance procedures, but they met resistance and, ultimately, defeat. Although the chapter begins with an examination of two manufacturing firms in Corpus Christi, it focuses on the one that witnessed a protracted fight. The company, Southern Alkali, and its CIO union jointly maintained and justified a segregated order, much like in the Houston refineries. A striking difference was the near absence of African American workers in the Corpus Christi plants despite their noticeable presence in the community. There were other differences, especially in the way that the company was able to undermine the work of the FEPC. In one instance, company representatives capitalized on some negotiating errors that Castañeda committed. On another occasion, they instituted an English-language aptitude examination for new hires and continuing workers as a subterfuge to circumvent FEPC directives and rid the company of Mexicans. All along, company officials argued that they had to reject the FEPC directives because of opposition by the Anglo workers, a claim that was corroborated by the union officers.

The book's final chapter summarizes the study's findings and assesses the significance of the work of the FEPC, as well as LULAC and consular officials, in assisting Mexican workers to recover from the Depression with the help of a mostly failed state-sanctioned process of conciliation. The chapter also concludes with a discussion of the major political actors and their goals in the home front story of Mexican workers in Texas. I underscore change in employment, social relations, and relations between LULAC and the Mexican government, but give special attention to continuities such as inequality, the Mexican claim for equal rights, and an activist state. I also discuss the World War II experience for Mexicans in Texas in light of general trends among the general population in Texas and Mexicans in other parts of the United States, especially in the Southwest.

Taken together, these chapters offer a home front study of Texas that is at once broad and focused. The book treats larger questions related to an activist state, civil rights, wartime recovery, and hemispheric relations at the same time that it directs our attention to Mexican workers and the persistence of discrimination and inequality into the postwar period. My study has benefited from the work undertaken by numerous authors. I build on their individual findings and conclusions on unprecedented employment opportunities, continuing discrimination, inequality and hardship, women's rights and gender inequality, political struggle, the rise of the liberal-urban coalition, the conservative tradition in Texas, and the slow eradication of Jim Crow. One of my purposes is to fill an obvious gap in the historical literature with new findings and interpretations based on previously unexamined records. I also offer an original and synthetic work on Mexican workers in Texas during the Second World War.

Chapter 2: Wartime Recovery and Denied Opportunities

"If there's anything I hate worse than a Nigger, it's a damn Mexican," proclaimed a World War II veteran from South Texas.[1] Daniel Schorr opened his 1945 article in *The New Republic* with the veteran's quote to explain how a resurgence of racial thinking in the postwar period threatened the "modest" occupational gains and new "yearnings" for a better life that Mexicans realized during the war. According to Schorr, "Texan bigotry and economic discrimination" had maintained a "holding action" during the war and now sought to continue business as usual. He may have exaggerated his accompanying claim of a "conspiracy" by Anglo government officials, business owners, and journalists. Schorr did not, however, overstate his critique of discrimination as a major obstacle to employment opportunities for Mexicans during the war and as an impediment to a brighter future during the postwar period.[2]

For Schorr, discrimination explained the racial division of labor and the inequalities that affected Mexicans in the 1940s. With this explanation, he did more than legitimate the voice of the protesting civil rights movement in the Mexican community. He also joined in the effort to bring national attention to Mexicans and to broaden the discourse over discrimination and minority rights beyond the prevailing focus on African Americans. Schorr also noted one of the central arguments that the Mexican civil rights leadership made during the 1940s: discrimination denied Mexicans employment opportunities and the chance to share equally in wartime recovery.

"Luchamos por La Libertad de Todos," 1939–1945, Coordinador the Asuntos Interamericanos, Washington, D.C. (Artist: E. McKnight Kauffer. Franklin D. Roosevelt Presidential Library and Museum, Hyde Park, New York.)

The problem of unequal recovery was especially evident in agriculture where government agencies like the USES collaborated with farmers to contain Mexican workers in the fields and packing sheds. The policy of containing farm labor, a more institutionalized rendering of pre-war policies and practices of labor repression, slowed farm workers' movement into urban areas and impeded their entry into the better-paying industries. Castañeda and other FEPC officials also noted discrimination in the higher-paying wartime industries that the government designated as critical or essential to wartime production. The critical industries included munitions, aircraft construction and repair, chemicals, synthetic rubber, iron and steel, shipbuilding, petroleum refining, and nonferrous metals. Mexican workers were concentrated as laborers in these industries as well as in a second tier of urban-based industries that the government classified as essential to the war effort, including agriculture, construction, garment and textile, and meatpacking. The story of unequal recovery and the unfulfilled hope of wartime opportunity can be best appreciated by first reviewing the significant industrial and economic changes that the war brought to Texas.[3]

Wartime Growth and Expansion

Although there were doubts that production could meet the wartime demand, the nation's industrial machine exceeded even the more generous expectations. War production, for instance, quadrupled in 1942 and surpassed the combined manufacturing output of the Axis powers. A significant share of production occurred in Texas where manufacturing recorded major growth with its added value increasing from $453,105,423 in 1939 to $1.9 billion in 1944. Increased production allowed Texas to pass its pre-war position as an industrially underdeveloped state and join the rest of the nation with its modernizing regional economy. The California economy showed the most impressive signs of recovery in the Southwest, growing at a fast rate, adding 1.3 million jobs during the 1940s and increasing employment by nearly 60 percent, a rate that was twice as high as in Texas. The Texas economy, however, remained a major production site in the Southwest, especially in oil, agriculture, aircraft construction and repair, shipping, munitions, and military installations.[4]

Increased industrial activity did more than improve job opportunities for Texans. It also contributed to significant population growth and urbanization

Table 2.1. Total population and percent population change in Texas, 1920–1950

Year	*Population*	*Decade*	*Numeric change*	*Percentage change*
1920	4,663,228	1910–1920	766,686	19.7
1930	5,824,715	1920–1930	1,161,487	24.9
1940	6,414,824	1930–1940	590,109	10.1
1950	7,711,194	1940–1950	1,296,370	20.2

Source: Texas State Data Center, Department of Rural Sociology, Texas A&M University, College Station, Texas.

during the first half of the twentieth century (see table 2.1). The state registered its first impressive growth spurt between 1920 and 1930, but from 1930 to 1940 Texas recorded its lowest increase since the 1860s. The war years, however, witnessed a significant demographic recovery. The number of residents almost reached the eight million mark as early as 1945, registering a 24 percent rate of growth since 1940. The general trend of demographic growth during the 1920s, followed by decline in the 1930s, and then recovery in the 1940s paralleled similar trends among Mexicans and blacks. Mexicans, however, suffered a more significant decline in the 1930s and a more impressive demographic recovery in the 1940s. The more dramatic population growth in the general population of the 1940s occurred in urban centers like Houston, Dallas, and San Antonio (see appendix 1).

The number of employed workers also increased significantly during the war years. Their numbers increased from 86.6 percent to 92 percent between 1940 and 1945. Much of the increase occurred in the critical war industries that employed around five hundred thousand workers during the middle of the war, although essential industries like agriculture and construction also registered significant increases. As urban-based industries lured increasing numbers of workers into urban areas, the civilian labor force became less dependent on farm employment. As a result, nonagricultural employment in towns and cities rose from 33.4 percent to 37 percent during the war years. Rural Texas contributed as many as five hundred thousand workers to the cities during this period. Despite the efforts by farmers to dissuade agricultural workers from leaving, a steady stream of them headed to urban areas where wartime recovery was most promising. Workers who entered Texas from other states also contributed to the growth of the workforce. Mexican immigrants, on the other hand, played an especially important role in replacing the departing agricultural workers. They also joined the rural-to-urban migration to fill unskilled and semiskilled positions in urban areas, although to a lesser extent than U.S.-born Mexicans.[5]

The Texas economy began its recovery around 1936. The nation's preparedness program and the wartime economy that followed it, on the other hand, spurred the state to unprecedented levels of production. The wartime need for military training facilities, for instance, stimulated early growth throughout the state. Constructing the new roads, runways, firing ranges, military buildings, and homes for the congregating workers contributed to booms in the construction and lumber industry as early as 1939. The pace of construction quickened as workers built or expanded the fifteen army posts and forty air bases in the state that accommodated more than a million military trainees during the war. Military establishments also became important sources of government contracts and offered employment in the building of living quarters for military families.[6]

The wartime demand on the state's economy triggered growth and expansion elsewhere. Agriculture, for instance, began producing cotton, cattle, and vegetables at previously unimaginable rates. Aside from contributing to improved earnings for farm laborers and packing shed workers, war production intensified the processing of agricultural products in nearby towns as well as in cities such as Dallas, Fort Worth, Houston, San Antonio, and Laredo. Although oil did not have to recuperate from the effects of the Depression to the same extent as other industries, it too witnessed significant growth as the war boosted crude oil production and hastened the development of related industries, especially the petrochemical industry in the Gulf Coast region. Shipyards along the Gulf Coast and in the Orange-Beaumont-Port Arthur region and aircraft factories in the Dallas-Fort Worth area likewise responded to the demands of the war with new and expanded operations. Adding to the recovery experience were the large vegetable and citrus processing plants in the Rio Grande Valley, the munitions factories located throughout the state, the smelters at places such as El Paso and Laredo, and the sulphur operations on the Gulf Coast.

The recovery process in Nueces County, on the lower Gulf Coast, reflected the statewide changes that were evident in the late 1930s. Cotton production was a mainstay for the port city until the Depression set in. Farming, however, began to recover by 1933. The large number of cotton pickers who returned to the area and the growing number of ships carrying cotton from the Corpus Christi docks signaled this change. Other industrial developments quickened economic activity. In 1933, the Pittsburgh Plate Glass

Young cotton picker near Corpus Christi, 1942. (Photographer: Howard R. Hollem. Farm Security Administration, Office of War Information Photograph Collection, Library of Congress.)

Company and the American Cyanamid Company initiated the construction of a chemical plant valued at the formidable sum of $7 million. The county also modernized its port between 1934 and 1935 and significantly improved its shipping capacity. The port's tonnage passed the million-ton mark for the first time in 1935 and reached almost three tons the following year. Oil production in the county also increased as a record number of nearby oil wells supplied "black gold" to the five local refineries and the petrochemical plant, all built between 1938 and 1942. The economy grew even more during the years that followed.[7]

Cotton picker near Corpus Christi, 1942. (Photographer: Howard R. Hollem. Farm Security Administration, Office of War Information Photograph Collection, Library of Congress.)

Port officials launched other improvements to accommodate the increased production in oil, alkali, synthetic chemicals, and cotton. The result was another dramatic increase in shipping tonnage during the war. The construction industry also grew significantly as it built new industrial plants and homes for the workers and their families migrating into the area. Merchants shared in the growing prosperity by increasing their stock and expanding their operations. Signs of robust entrepreneurship included an imposing hotel, a large office building, and a one hundred thousand-dollar stadium that seated more than twelve thousand spectators. A crowning achievement was the construction of a large military training facility. Congress authorized the building of the naval air station in Corpus Christi in 1940. Its civilian and military personnel rose to well over ten thousand within a few years.[8]

The signs of "progress" were not lost on South Texas historians J. Lee Stambaugh and Lillian J. Stambaugh when they credited the one thousand-mile Intercoastal Canal for advancing the commercial fortunes of ports along the Texas Gulf Coast and connecting them with Mexico and places as far away as

Mississippi. The inland waterway, extending over eighteen counties between the Sabine and the Rio Grande rivers, provided a safe alternative to shipping in the open waters of the Atlantic Coast and the Gulf of Mexico where freighters and tankers were thought to be at the mercy of enemy submarines. Coastal shipping carried almost sixteen tons of sulphur, petroleum, and other vital war supplies by the end of the war, an increase of over 100 percent since 1940. Increased wartime shipping resulted in dramatic industrial and demographic growth all along the coast. This meant increased agricultural production in deep South Texas where large numbers of packing sheds mushroomed alongside the highly productive cotton, vegetable, and citrus fields of the Rio Grande Valley. Places like Corpus Christi and the upper Gulf Coast, on the other hand, were able to extend their pipelines, increase their refining capacity of oil, and expand related industries like gas, sulphur, and drilling technology.[9]

The expansion of the military establishment also boosted wartime recovery. The U.S. government placed a record number of military training bases in the state, influenced by the Texas congressional delegation and by the fair weather in the state. The new and expanded military posts like the Laredo Army Field, the Tri-City Air Base in the McAllen area, Camp Swift in Austin, Fort Crockett in Galveston, and Hensley Field near Dallas provided more jobs and attracted additional workers into the state. The training facilities were nowhere more significant than in San Antonio. The military complex had already been a mainstay in the pre-war economy. Before the war, for instance, the buildings and land occupied by Fort Sam Houston, the headquarters of the Army's Eighth Service Command, were worth $19 million. The military installation included Camp Travis, Dodd Field, and a site at Leon Springs, northwest of San Antonio. Next to Fort Sam Houston, Kelly Field had operated as a training site for airmen since World War I. Other important military camps added to the pre-war mix. Built in 1917, Camp Normoyle, a technical supply depot, was near the downtown area, while Brooks Field, a few miles to the south, supported a flying school. Randolph Field, fifteen miles northwest of the city, functioned as the army's main training center for airmen. According to a local journalist, the pre-war army contributed $19 million to the local economy in official purchases, construction contracts, and numerous other consumer activities.[10]

San Antonio's military training complex grew significantly during the war. Brooke General Hospital, located in Fort Sam, expanded as the army's main physical rehabilitation center. Kelly Field merged with Duncan Field in 1942 and became the army's major aircraft repair site in the country. The sprawling enterprise of five square miles included hangars, machine shops, assembly plants, laboratories, air strips, offices, and barracks. Kelly, San Antonio's largest wartime industrial establishment, employed thousands of civilian workers until the government shut it down in the 1990s. Camp Normoyle also increased its demand for labor beginning with the construction of a vast site for housing formidable arsenal and training quarters. The air force, on the other hand, took over the local municipal air base and established Stinson Field in 1942. Brooks Field also expanded and increased its annual operating budget to about $2 million. The government invested well over $11 million in Randolph Field, allowing it to assume a greater role in training air cadets. San Antonio's military presence eventually covered fifty square miles. The civilian workforce in the city's twelve military installations reached 38,297 by the early part of 1943.[11]

Pay improved as more jobs became available. By 1943, wages had doubled in South Texas in large part because agriculture expanded so rapidly. Earnings from picking cotton increased from $1.25 to $2.25 per hundred pounds between 1941 and 1943. Workers who joined the rural-to-urban migration and secured jobs in urban industries registered even more significant improvements. In some instances, they increased their income to six or seven dollars a day. Skilled workers in the oil refineries at Beaumont, Houston, and Corpus Christi even boasted previously unimagined benefits like overtime pay and vacation leave. The unprecedented levels of production and the significant advantages that they brought ended or ameliorated the hard times of the Depression. Mexican workers, however, did not share equally in wartime recovery.[12]

An Uneven Road to Recovery in Agriculture

On the eve of the entry by the United States into the Second World War, Mexicans were heavily concentrated in agriculture. Approximately five hundred and fifty thousand farm workers and the great majority of approximately five hundred thousand migratory workers were Mexicans. Around fifty thousand Mexicans, some of whom doubled as migratory workers, labored in the packing sheds of South Texas, mostly in processing, packing, and shipping. Although exact figures are not available, observers agreed that Mexicans maintained their concentration in agriculture throughout the 1930s and 1940s and that renewed immigration beginning during the late 1930s increased the size of their rural and urban workforces to unprecedented levels.

Migratory labor camp, Sinton, 1940. (Photographer: Russell Lee, Farm Security Administration, Office of War Information Photograph Collection, Library of Congress.)

Their concentration in agriculture did not mean that they did not benefit from job opportunities during the war. Some of them moved out of the farms and secured better employment in urban areas. Also, those that remained in agriculture enjoyed significant improvements over their prior conditions. These gains, however, were not sufficient to overcome inequalities.[13]

The social disparities associated with farm work had their antecedents in the 1910s and 1920s, during a period of significant growth in the agricultural industry. Successful recruitment campaigns along both sides of the border and in the interior of Mexico, along with the relaxed enforcement of immigration laws, flooded the farms, tipped the negotiating balance in favor of the farmers, and aggravated the problems of long hours and low pay for working families. Another result was the growth of migratory farm labor, a predominantly Mexican workforce from South Texas and northern Mexico that periodically took to the road in search of higher wages in other parts of Texas and outside the state. Although the migratory strategy allowed working families to maximize their earnings with better wages and family labor, the experience was not always good. The occasional misfortune on the road or the unrealized promises of full and fair employment at their points of destination, as well as the low wages and temporary employment that awaited them upon their return often undermined their overall income. This explains why Mexican farm workers from South Texas remained the poorest and most exploited group in the state throughout the first half of the twentieth century.[14]

The seasonal nature of farm production, that is, the overlapping production cycles of citrus, vegetable, and cotton encouraged Mexican farm workers to join the migratory trail in search of newly maturing crops, better pickings, and higher earnings. When a season ended, migratory workers moved to other promising places and eventually back to their home areas to take temporary jobs as laborers in local industrial sites like the packing sheds of the Rio Grande Valley, construction projects in Corpus Christi, or the pecan shelling plants of San Antonio. In some cases, working families remained in towns or cities along the migratory trail or they completed the cycle by returning to communities immediately across the Texas-Mexico border where they also eked out a living as temporary laborers. They remained in their rural communities, towns, and cities until they once again decided to follow the crops. The demographic spill into the towns and cities helped to double and sometimes triple the Mexican population in interior cities such as Corpus Christi, San Antonio, Austin, and Houston, as well as in places immediately across the border like Matamoros, Reynosa, and Nuevo Laredo.

The Depression set in with declining consumption patterns that undermined production and caused unemployment and underemployment figures to rise dramatically. The government-initiated programs of relief and recovery offered some respite from the hard times of the Depression, but conditions seemed to worsen, at least until Franklin Roosevelt's rejuvenated New Deal program and the war preparedness program brought new hope for recovery in the late 1930s. For the lowly farm worker, the future remained precarious. Even recovery measures like the government's crop reduction program compounded their misfortune. It drove record numbers of farm workers out of their jobs, while farmers mostly denied them a share of the program's benefits. Mexican immigrant workers were among the most affected by the hard times. They were disproportionately represented among the farm workers as well as in the urban-based unskilled and semiskilled work force that functioned as a reserve labor pool for area farmers. In many instances, they were the first to be assigned reduced hours of work or to be released altogether. With few alternatives before them, some resorted to the familiar memories of the homeland as refuge, and emigrated. Others rejected the imagined security of Mexico and decided to escape their misfortune by moving their families into nearby towns and cities.[15]

The growing urban population, however, could not escape poverty and even impoverishment.[16] More importantly, they came face to face with a menacing nativist movement that sparked an anti-Mexican crusade. The movement began with public calls to limit government relief to the U.S.-born on the grounds that resources were too scarce to share with immigrants. Anti-immigrant sentiments grew, especially after local officials and journalists joined in blaming immigrants for the hard times and calling for their expulsion as a way out of the crisis. The gathering conflict was especially evident in the urban areas of the Southwest, although it also extended into places in the West, Midwest, and the Deep South. The political crisis, however, was not confined to the immigrants largely because nativists were not always able to make nativity distinctions among the Mexicans. As a result, large numbers of U.S.-born persons, typically the children and grandchildren of Mexico-born parents, joined an unprecedented movement of immigrants back to Mexico during the early 1930s.[17]

Historians estimate that at least five hundred thousand Mexicans returned to Mexico. In some cases, state and federal agencies conducted searches in Mexican communities and work sites, rounded up persons who appeared to be foreign-born and arranged for their deportation to the closest Mexican border town. In other situations, Mexicans decided that they could no longer endure the scapegoating or survive the hard times in the United States. They made their own preparations to repatriate, at times with the ready encouragement of U.S. government officials and the help of local Mexican consulates and Mexican community organizations. Mexican government officials, feeling the pressure from critics at home for not intervening effectively on behalf of its nationals in foreign soil, added to the exodus by establishing colonization projects to accommodate the émigrés with farming land along the Mexican border. According to Mercedes Carreras de Velasco, the projects failed primarily because the government did not keep its promise of financial and technical support. The failed colonization effort underscored the overall experience of hundreds of thousands of persons who returned—or were made to return—to an even more destitute Mexico.[18]

The war brought change and much welcomed relief. It reversed the dismal production trends of the Depression and triggered another massive movement of workers from Mexico, many of whom joined the resident farm labor force while others entered urban labor markets. According to government sources, farm labor in the state quadrupled in size to at least seven hundred and fifty thousand workers in 1943, with Mexicans assuming the majority among them, especially in the packing sheds and the migratory work force. Their earnings in the citrus, vegetable, and cotton fields doubled over 1941 rates. By 1942, cotton farmers in East Texas had increased daily

Five young field workers wearing football padding, ca. 1945. (José De Los Santos Collection, U.S. Latino & Latina WWII Oral History Project, University of Texas at Austin.)

wages to as much as $1.50. In the San Antonio area, farm workers earned between $1.25 and $2.50, substantially higher amounts than the $0.75 and $1.50 rates of the previous year. Although wages varied widely, depending on the area and the time of the season, a growing number of farmers paid daily wages of $2.50 and above by 1944. Cotton-picking rates also increased to as much as $1.25 per hundred pounds. This meant that an experienced picker could earn between $3.00 and $3.50 a day, depending on the time of the season and the quality of the cotton.[19]

Wartime improvements did not necessarily rid the country of the familiar structures of inequality that were evident in Texas. The lack of comparable wage data makes it difficult to gauge the lower standing of Mexicans relative to their Anglo counterparts on the farms. Some scholars, however, provide sufficient information to comment on the different rates of movement out of agriculture. Walter Fogel notes that Mexicans moved out of Texas farms at an impressive rate, yet they could never overtake their Anglo counterparts during the 1940s and 1950s. The percentage of Mexicans in Texas agriculture, according to Fogel, dropped from 51 to 32 percent of all employed Mexicans between 1930 and 1950. This meant that 19 percent moved out of farm employment. Anglos, on the other hand, escaped the farms at a faster pace. Their numbers dropped from 47 to 17 percent during the same period. According to Fogel, 30 percent of Anglos made the move, most probably into wartime industries. He concluded that "Mexican Americans were not able to improve their relative occupational position because the position of others rose so sharply."[20] Agnes E. Meyer, a journalist reporting on farm labor in the Rio Grande Valley, explained the different rates in 1946 by noting that Mexicans seemed destined to be migratory workers, while the proportionally smaller number of Anglos were exceptions to their group's more favorable experience: "With the Mexican, migration is a professional way of life. With the Anglo it is usually proof that everything else has failed."[21]

Despite the wage increases in farming, government studies found continuing impoverishment among the Mexican farm workers living in rural and urban areas during the early 1940s. They attributed much of their condition to racial prejudice, more specifically, to the practice of paying Mexicans as little as possible on the grounds that they were accustomed to living on less than Anglos or that they were destined to receive less pay than Anglos. One researcher underscored the consequence of racial thinking by noting that none of the Mexican families in the Rio Grande Valley met the government's minimum earning standard, even when they supplemented their income with migratory and child labor.[22]

Freezing Farm Labor

A study of inequality in the Texas rural labor market would be incomplete without explaining how farmers and the state immobilized agricultural workers during the war years. According to an official directive from the WMC, the agency that was responsible for regulating the nation's labor supply, the partnership with the farmers pursued a policy of containing labor to ensure that agriculture had the necessary workers to meet the growing production demands.[23] Government officials continually justified their work among farm workers in Texas with references to this "freezing" policy. Although officials often claimed to be assuring employment and reliable earnings to the farm worker, the labor distribution program favored the farmer by maintaining a large and mostly immobilized workforce of poor and powerless farm workers.[24]

Regulating the Mexican farm labor supply began before the Second World War. Farmers had encouraged the flow across the international border and directed it throughout the state since the late nineteenth century to ensure a sufficient number of workers during harvest time and to guarantee that they stayed long enough to complete the work. Some of the most popular methods of controlling the labor supply included cooperative recruitment campaigns and wage-fixing arrangements. Never able to completely immobilize a labor force that was inclined to take to the road in search of better opportunities, farmers turned to more formal methods including vagrancy laws. They convinced county governments to establish the legal means whereby law enforcement officials could round up workers accused of leaving the farms before the harvest was completed and return them to the complaining farmers.[25]

Searching for even more effective methods of control, farmers convinced the state government to establish the Texas Farm Placement Service in the 1910s. Government officials, under pressure from labor organizations that feared competition from the growing Mexican worker population, also wanted to contain them in the farms as much as possible. The program that emerged was an officially sanctioned effort headed by the state's labor commissioner and assisted by the Texas Employment Service (TES) and the Department of Agriculture. Program officials fulfilled their regulatory function by assigning agricultural agents to survey labor needs prior to the harvests and to route the workers from farm to farm until they returned to their home areas. The effort continued with federal assistance until the mid-1930s, at which point the TES assumed responsibility for the program.

The Depression brought important changes. It reduced agricultural production and shifted some of the government's attention from the farmers' alleged needs to urban-based nativist campaigns. When agriculture began its recovery, however, farmers regained their influence and resumed their calls for the effective regulation of the workforce. The government responded with even greater resolve once it became clear that the war required greater efficiency in agricultural production. By 1941, the government's new Farm Labor Program had incorporated the labor repressive practices of the past into a more extensive and effective apparatus. The Farm Security Administration (FSA) and its successor, the Office of Labor, in the Department of Agriculture, had supervisory responsibilities over the program. In 1942, the WMC added another administrative layer when it assigned direct regulating responsibilities over farm labor to one of its major agencies, the USES. This decision was part of a larger plan to give the USES control over state employment agencies and to centralize the WMC's regulatory function over the nation's workforce.[26]

When the USES took over the TES, it inherited the agency's vast experience in regulating farm labor. The USES also made use of one of the longest-running farm development initiatives in Texas when it contracted with the Agricultural Extension Service (AES) from Texas A&M University to assume the responsibility for administering the Farm Labor Program beginning in 1943. The AES was primarily responsible for coordinating farm extension services sponsored by the Department of Agriculture and state agricultural colleges. County agricultural and home demonstration agents typically assisted Anglo farmers and their families with technical support and assistance in farm and home management activities. The AES had functioned as part of the Extension Service in the Department of Agriculture since 1915. It worked with the FSA and the Texas Farm Placement Service and collaborated with the USES beginning in 1941. More importantly, the AES and the TES brought into the new federal-state partnership a working relationship with local chambers of commerce and the Texas Farm Bureau, the Texas Cotton Ginners' Association, the Texas Citrus Exchange, and the Texas Fruit and Vegetable Growers and Shippers.[27]

Although the Farm Labor Program only included a state supervisor, five assistants, two field assistants, and five migratory state labor assistants, it operated within a vast network of county organizations that often shared memberships with the relatively more independent farm groups like the Farm Bureau. The three major county organizations involved in administering the Farm Labor Program were the Farm Labor Advisory Committees, the Land-Use Planning Committees, and the Farm Labor Councils. The Farm Labor Advisory Committees included at least five farmer representatives who made recommendations or suggestions to local agricultural agents and other Farm Labor Program employees on the general operation of the program. The Land-Use Planning Committees mostly included farmers. They also operated at the county level and advised the farmers and the Farm Labor Program on important planning matters such as planting schedules and labor needs.[28]

The Labor Councils were composed of the members of the Labor Advisory Committees, representatives of farm organizations, ministers, local, county, and federal officials, and other residents who, according to an AES official, "were interested in seeing that the maximum amount of labor would be made available." The Labor Councils maintained public support for the Farm Labor Program with publicity campaigns and communications with influential persons in local communities, often in cooperation with other community organizations and County Agricultural Victory Councils (county-based organizations with large numbers of farmers and their spouses), including approximately 10,037 "community Victory leaders" and 42,008 "neighborhood

Victory leaders" throughout the state. The county associations functioned within their respective statewide networks, and their parent organizations also cooperated fully with the Farm Labor Program, the USES, and other agencies.[29]

The vast collaborative structure assisted farmers in recruiting workers from Mexico. International laws that prohibited the recruitment of workers in foreign soil and Mexican government policies that discouraged immigration may have impaired the effort somewhat, but did not prevent it. Farmers and their organizations simply drafted the workers as they crossed into the United States, and they secured the help of the USES to assist in the process. Typically, the USES certified local labor needs with U.S. immigration authorities along the border, who relaxed their enforcement practices and allowed the immigrants to cross. Once the workers arrived on Texas soil, the farmers recruited them and USES agents assisted the farmers in transporting the workers by truck or rail to their destinations.[30]

The introduction of new workers was part of a larger scheme to regulate the farm labor supply. Recruiting workers along the border met an alleged labor need that was made all the more convincing by the growing number of workers who joined the migratory labor force, entered the military, or traveled to urban areas in search of better-paying jobs. Encouraging the labor flow across the international line, in other words, accompanied the efforts to control its movement within the state's borders. Regulating the growing migratory workforce became one of the most significant challenges to the Farm Labor Program largely because out-of-state recruiters, as before, encouraged the movement of workers into the beet fields of the West and Midwest. Sugar beet companies, according to numerous USES labor market reports, siphoned off between twenty and thirty thousand workers during the 1941 and 1942 cotton seasons despite the strict state laws that required the recruiters to pay high registration and recruitment fees.[31]

Government officials and farmers responded to migratory labor with some tried methods like joint recruitment efforts, wage-fixing understandings, and compatible planting schedules to minimize competition for the available workers. The Farm Labor Program, however, placed much of its faith on the long-standing and now-expanded procedure of stationing agricultural agents along the migratory routes to direct the migratory flow and to ensure that workers did not take to the road prematurely. The agents typically conducted pre-harvest surveys among the farmers to estimate needs and then stationed themselves along the two major migratory routes out of South Texas. Agents located on the major roads leading out of the Lower Rio

Grande Valley interviewed the migrants to determine the size and destination of the flow. They recorded each crew leader's name, the number in the crew, the type and license number of their conveyance, their planned destination, and whether their employment was assured or not. The officials then routed the crews without prearranged employment to Texas farmers who had previously indicated a need. In some instance, the agents even redirected workers with assured employment to other places that reported more critical needs. The crews left the check points at Riviera and Encino with "letters of introduction" intended to direct the flow, as the workers were expected to present them to farmers, FSA officials, and USES staff along the migratory route. The agents, in turn, supplied the workers with information on available jobs on the trail and promised to urge the farmers to pay them well.[32]

Although these interventions may have reduced the workers' idle time, guaranteed good pickings, and increased their earnings, the agents were primarily interested in maintaining adequate supplies of workers. This does not mean that government officials had no concern over working and living conditions or did not occasionally express empathy towards the workers and their families. At times, they reported on the destitute conditions of the migrants, especially when midwestern labor recruiters reneged on their promises and left families stranded in places far away from their homes. These favorable changes in the official outlook, whether sincere or not, were encouraged primarily by the war emergency. They also justified greater oversight on the movement of migratory workers. This became especially evident when USES officials enlisted the help of Mexican consuls and community leaders to more effectively regulate their movement.

According to Pauline Kibbe, the executive secretary of the Good Neighbor Commission, Mexican leaders were incorporated into the labor program when the Farm Labor Office of the Texas A&M University Extension Service inherited from the USES the responsibility for routing and placing farm labor throughout the state.[33] A case in point was the State Farm Labor Advisory Committee which met on November 28, 1944, at College Station. It included nine "Latin Americans," representing LULAC, the Mexican Chambers of Commerce in Texas, Rafael Linares, Vice-Consul of Mexico at Galveston, and Manuel C. Gonzales, the LULAC Governor of Texas and attorney for the Mexican Consulate General in San Antonio. Although the Mexican participants sought to protect the migratory workers from unscrupulous midwestern recruiters with greater publicity in Spanish on the routing services of the USES, they did this while promoting the efficient regulation of the farm labor supply.

The overriding interest in immobilizing workers may have trumped good intentions. Mexican leaders, not unlike other supporters of the Farm Labor Program, however, believed that it benefited farm workers. Government officials, after all, often stated that the program sought the full employment of farm workers and promised to protect them from dishonest farmers. Gonzales expressed this view soon after the College Station meeting. He notified LULAC councils throughout the state that "I have agreed to lend the fullest cooperation to the work of the Federal Government and the A&M College" and urged the local organizations to form committees "which will serve as the link between the cotton pickers, the farmers, and the College representatives in the adjustment of any difficulties that might arise, such as housing, sanitation, school, food supply, and wages." Farm Labor Program officials, according to Gonzales, were interested in "bettering their [farm workers'] living conditions, improving transportation facilities, and at the same time putting them to work in places where they are most needed." Gonzales added LULAC's advocacy and patriotic signature to his recommendation; LULAC members had a responsibility to help "our people in your locality" at the same time that they assisted "the Federal Government to produce the most for the boys at the front who are making it possible for us to enjoy the blessings of a free country."[34]

Well-meaning statements notwithstanding, farmers and government officials also conceived new techniques such as lobbying draft boards to exempt farm youth during harvest times. The extent of their influence is difficult to determine; however, farmers clearly benefited from preferential treatment.[35] Communications between Congressman Richard Kleberg from South Texas and Paul McNutt, the head of the WMC, in the summer of 1942 indicate as much. Farmers had been urging Kleberg to negotiate a labor importation program with Mexico to offset an alleged labor shortage. Although Mexico would eventually agree to such a program, as will be demonstrated in a later chapter, its officials refused to send contract workers, or Braceros, to Texas. Kleberg nevertheless saw that a labor importation program would grant the USES greater control over the immigrant flow and make the agency more effective in "the freezing of certain men at their labor posts."[36] McNutt, not convinced that Mexican workers were circumventing the USES's freezing policy or that a critical shortage existed, reminded Kleberg that draft boards were already checking the alleged labor hemorrhage. The boards, noted McNutt, used deferments throughout the state as a form of "limited 'freezing'" because the exemptions "are subject to termination" if workers left their employment in the farms.[37]

Another novel regulatory technique involved the application of a clearance procedure that the WMC and the USES used in urban-based industry. Clearance slips allowed released workers to demonstrate that they had completed their work and secured the necessary authorization to seek employment elsewhere. When workers tried to circumvent this procedure by visiting USES offices in response to announced job or training opportunities in nonagricultural sites, officials typically instructed them to return to their original employers in the farms or in the packing sheds. The USES's practice of rejecting transfer requests out of agriculture accompanied other methods of control.[38] They also denied or delayed gas and rubber allotments to individual families or truck drivers contemplating travel to other parts of the state or the country.[39]

Officials associated with the Farm Labor Program also waged campaigns to convince women and youth to join the workforce, especially in agriculture. At other times, they persuaded local authorities to shorten school terms and free the students for work in the farms. They also convinced agencies such as the National Youth Administration (NYA) and the Works Progress Administration (WPA) to temporarily release trainees and workers from their contractual obligations during harvest times. As with the recruitment of workers along the border, farmers and labor agents justified the conscription of persons in the NYA and the WPA by stating that the labor supply could not meet the wartime demand. The introduction of new workers, however, often exceeded the demand; when it did, the farmers tipped the negotiating weight to their side.[40]

Regulatory measures did not go unchallenged. Workers at times evaded the controls and left the state or traveled to urban areas like San Antonio, Houston, or Dallas. Others volunteered for military service. The activated workforce of women and youth also posed special problems. Inexperience, military conscription, and the attractive jobs in urban areas meant that farmers could not always depend on them. The recruitment of Mexican nationals was not without its difficulties either. Mexican authorities, upset over reports of discrimination, discouraged some workers from leaving and, as noted previously, even refused to send contract workers, or Braceros, to Texas. Texas farmers, of course, often circumvented Mexico's immigration policy and the Texas ban and continued to recruit large numbers of workers along the Texas-Mexico border. A defiant Mexico nevertheless hampered their efforts during the war.

The failure to fully regulate the farm labor force often reflected the farmers' inability to maintain wage understandings or to adjust wage agreements to match earning possibilities elsewhere. They broke ranks in response to the recruitment efforts by sugar beet companies, the constant draw of urban-based industries, and the difficulties involved in recruiting workers along the border. These problems at times resulted in tensions between the farmers and the collaborating agencies. USES officials, for instance, often complained to their superiors in Austin and Washington that farmers disregarded their advice to maintain minimum wages. They also accused farmers of fabricating claims of labor shortages. Eugene Butler, the editor of *The Progressive Farmer,* responded for the farmer by noting disdainfully that "farm experts," that is, government officials, often questioned the legitimate claims of labor shortages.[41]

Despite important challenges, the Farm Labor Program largely succeeded in regulating the farm labor supply. The records of the USES demonstrate that farmers maintained high productivity levels in large part because the state assisted them in maintaining the necessary labor supply and minimizing disruptions that the workers could have caused by taking to the road or initiating other labor actions. This occurred throughout the state as the Farm Labor Program also incorporated Anglo and black workers into their regulatory scheme. Mexican workers, however, remained a central concern as evidenced by the program's practice of concentrating Mexican migratory workers in labor camps to further regulate their movement in the production of cotton.

Labor Camps as Sites of Control and Contestation

One of the most far-reaching efforts to regulate the movement of farm labor involved labor camps and the construction of camping grounds, or reception centers, on the migratory trail. The official explanation for the Farm Labor Supply Center Program, popularly known as the Migratory Labor Camp Program, was that federal and state officials were providing clean and adequate housing for the large numbers of migratory workers that often arrived to a locale suddenly, and quickly overwhelmed the capacity of local farmers to provide for them. Although USES and Farm Labor Program officials emphasized the goodwill of the state, other reasons occasionally emerged.[42] One of them involved the unwelcome reception that workers often received from townspeople and their subsequent decision to refuse work in areas where they were not wanted. The camps thus helped to prevent conflicts at the same time that they provided farmers and government officials a new and outwardly obliging means of directing the movement of workers across the state. The Labor Camp Program also provided "home economics" instruction in hygiene, nutrition, and maternal care, a measure intended to assist the needy Mexican families and the anxious Anglos, who were concerned about maintaining cultural homogeneity and control over their local social environment.[43]

Although the FSA and the Labor Office in the Department of Agriculture began constructing the campsites in the late 1930s, Congress authorized the former agency in 1943 to build and operate the facilities. The Labor Camp Program established nine camps and over twenty reception centers throughout South, East, and West Texas. The centers in places like Harlingen, Corpus Christi, and El Campo provided toilets, running water, and a place to park and rest. The camps at McAllen, Weslaco, Harlingen, Raymondville, Robstown, Sinton, Crystal City, Princeton, and Lamesa offered more permanent quarters. A 1944 report by Kibbe offered a description of a typical South Texas site, the Robstown camp.[44]

The camp had two types of living quarters to accommodate as many as twelve hundred persons at one time. Apartments rented for $1.25 a week and housed up to five persons. At their disposal were community showers and toilet facilities and a laundry room, complete with electric irons and sewing machines. Larger families lived in the twenty-six four-room houses with private baths that rented for $2.25 a week. Upon registering in the camp offices, administrators directed the workers and their families to the clinic where two nurses gave them free physical examinations and medical and dental treatment if necessary. An adjoining "hospital" provided childbirth care. Camp administrators ensured the general upkeep of the camp and a community center provided a nursery for children below six years of age. The community center also offered the residents recreation and religious services and meeting space for Camp Council, the governing body with worker representatives drawn from four sections in the camp. The camp also functioned as a labor recruitment and distribution center. Camp administrators and agricultural agents usually assessed labor needs in the area and directing the camp residents to the different farms.[45]

Reflecting the liberal New Deal view of social rehabilitation, Kibbe described the camps as necessary sites for the socialization of needy families in the modern methods of hygiene, child rearing, childbirth, and self-government. She also expressed the prevailing wartime imperative of making full use of the available labor supply by acknowledging that the facilities represented a boon for local farmers. The camps saved them the trouble of providing housing for the workers. Moreover, the camps maintained a stable number of workers who would travel to and from local farms. Kibbe's emphasis on the generosity of the state and her otherwise condescending description of Mexicans were clearly intended to draw support for the camps among concerned Mexicans and anxious Anglos. The more independent observer, Agnes E. Meyer, offered a different account in the progressive *Texas Spectator.*[46]

Meyer was more concerned with the practical intentions of the camps than with the goodwill of the state or Kibbe's perceived need to allay cultural concerns regarding Mexican child rearing customs and home-tending practices. Basing her observations on conversations or interviews, possibly with Caesar Hohn, an official with the AES and the director of the Farm Labor Program, and H. H. Williamson, the vice director of the AES, Meyer noted that the Labor Camp Program primarily intended to keep racial tensions from destabilizing the labor market. Although prejudice and discrimination precipitated the tensions, worker dissatisfaction triggered official concern, according to Meyer. Agricultural agents who had been told to acquaint themselves with the migratory workers, "seeing how they lived, studying their problems, finding out what they wanted done, and getting a line on their faults," reported at least four concerns among the workers.[47]

The workers resented the discrimination that they faced in stores, restaurants, theaters, and other business establishments, especially the "No Mexicans Allowed" signs that appeared as soon as they started arriving in a given area. They also complained that farmers did not provide them sanitary working and living facilities and, as a consequence, they remained unclean for weeks and even months at a time. Anglos, they added, justified discrimination with the view that all migratory workers were dirty and posed health risks to their communities. Workers also reportedly stated that they could not trust farmers who promised better pickings and earnings because they lied so much. Lastly, the workers resented that employers treated them "like cattle" and they sometimes found "a distinct pleasure to run off and leave him with his cotton unpicked."[48]

Agricultural agents, according to Meyer, confirmed the workers' claims of prejudice and discrimination against Anglo farmers and business owners. Farmers were accustomed to describing Mexicans as dirty and undependable and believed that they should encourage the workers to leave immediately after their work was completed. Anglo business owners and other residents in towns that received large numbers of migratory workers agreed with the perception of Mexicans as "dirty people" and thought they should remain in the farms as much as possible. Montejano has reminded us that some Anglos, especially farmers and business owners who depended on Mexicans as workers and customers, did not always express these views. The general reaction to Mexican migrants and discontent among the workers, however, was sufficient to alarm farmers and government officials that anti-Mexican feelings and attitudes could disrupt agricultural production.

Meyer and her informants concluded that the Labor Camp Program intended to stabilize labor relations primarily by allaying the political and economic concerns among Anglos. The camps, on the one hand, provided migratory families from South Texas and Mexico important social and health services as well as a regularized process for securing steady employment at a dependable rate of pay. These services also encouraged the workers to stay away from town. This pleased farmers who were assured a ready supply of workers in a single location and Anglo town residents who had become wary of the social and health consequences of the seemingly foreign cultural practices among the congregating workers. The labor camps brought immediate social and economic benefits to some workers, but they also helped farmers better manage the labor supply and minimize the conflict with anxious urban residents and business owners. The magnitude of the initiative as well as its justification as an emergency war measure also reinforced the public view of the state as a responsible arbitrator of social and labor relations.

Temporary Job Transfers

To further understand the concentration of Mexicans in Texas agriculture, it is necessary to examine yet another important wartime method that farmers and the state used to "freeze" Mexican labor. The practice involved the temporary transfer of Mexican farm workers into local construction sites in need of unskilled and semiskilled labor. Once the construction work was completed, USES officials typically returned the workers back to the farms or other construction sites. They also shifted the mostly Anglo construction workers from one skilled job to another, usually across the state. The USES normally arranged for transporting the skilled and often unionized workers over long distances while they made use of the idle agricultural workers living close to the construction site. This arrangement approximated a closed shop that employers ordinarily rejected as a compulsory hiring hall imposed by unions. In this case, however, employers offered the mostly Anglo union members a hiring preference. Moving workers to fill labor needs in other industries and places ordinarily could be seen as a rational and effective

Applying for work at USES office, Corpus Christi, 1940. (Photographer: Russell Lee, Farm Security Administration, Office of War Information Photograph Collection, Library of Congress.)

method of labor distribution. Selective job transfers that temporarily assigned Mexicans to the lesser-skilled jobs and Anglos to the higher-skilled occupations in construction, however, reinforced a racial division of labor. Although the USES played the major role in arranging the temporary transfers, other agencies such as the WMC and the AES also took part.[49]

Construction, like agriculture, was an essential industry in Texas particularly because of the large number of building projects involving military training bases, airports, and public housing for new workers migrating into the urban areas. Construction also registered one of the fastest growth rates during the early part of the war years. By 1942, it already claimed a work force of approximately three hundred thousand. Like farmers, construction companies and their contractors faced formidable challenges in managing the available labor supply. The problems included unpredictable weather, intense labor competition, the scarcity of skilled and experienced workers, the military draft, and the high cost of transporting workers between construction sites. This was partly resolved by using local agricultural labor

Migratory workers in front of an employment agency, Corpus Christi, 1949. (Photographer: Russell Lee, Russell Lee Photographic Collection, Center for American History, University of Texas at Austin.)

for the lower-skilled jobs and the largely itinerant Anglo workers for the higher-skilled positions. The policy was applied throughout the state, with the cooperation of farmers and construction companies, their contractors, and the unions of predominantly Anglo construction workers.[50]

For USES officials, accommodating the wishes of the contractors and farmers no doubt seemed a reasonable application of their wartime charge to facilitate the full and effective use of the available labor supply. The Mexican agricultural workers who remained in South Texas after the completion of their "Big Swing" across the state and the Midwest congregated during the winter and most of the spring in places like the Rio Grande Valley and the Winter Garden Area, and in cities such as San Antonio and Corpus Christi. The growing number of underemployed and unemployed workers was as predictable as the seasonal return of the migrants.[51]

Mexican farm workers in the Rio Grande Valley and in San Antonio, like their African American counterparts to the northeast, discovered that they could often depend on the USES to help them find temporary and better-paying work in construction. However, they rarely had the opportunity to upgrade their position into the skilled ranks. Also, the USES rarely offered them a chance to join their training programs. Lastly, neither the agency nor the unions assisted them in securing jobs elsewhere.[52]

Temporary employment for laborers at Camp Swift located outside Austin demonstrated how effective the USES, construction companies, and farmers could be. Once the cotton picking season of 1941 ended and the USES had routed some of the idle workers to other farms or nearby processing plants, officials directed the remaining workers to Camp Swift as a construction company stepped up its work there. The company usually began to release its laborers between May 10 and May 25, the days when cotton chopping and onion picking began. Their temporary employment and better pay in construction and military camps was a boon for the workers who usually remained unemployed between seasons. Work, however, was temporary and the USES did not always guarantee employment between seasons. The construction company typically released a large number of their laborers at harvest time. In March 1942, for instance, it announced that it would discharge five thousand workers within three months.[53]

In another case involving the Tri City Air Base in Edinburg, USES officials consulted with area farmers before they recruited a large number of Mexican farm workers to work at the construction site. The USES registered the workers and assigned them to the contractor as his requests came in. The officials also made arrangements with other USES offices, union representatives, and the local contractor to identify and transport a smaller number of Anglo workers from other areas in the state to fill the skilled positions. Once the skilled workers were identified, union representatives and the construction company negotiated the terms of their employment. When the work neared completion, USES officials informed union representatives of skilled jobs in other parts of the state and assigned the workers to vacant positions. The USES also directed the Mexican laborers to return to their old jobs. Some secured employment at other construction sites in the area as laborers. The majority returned to the fields and canneries, while others rejoined the migratory workforce.[54]

Contractors and union representatives often played a key role in locating and placing the Anglo skilled workers. On some occasions, the unions initiated contact with the USES with prior understandings or agreements that the skilled jobs were reserved for their members. A representative for the Noser Construction Company from the Rio Grande Valley, for example, secured carpenters, painters, and plumbers through a local AFL union. The contract was consummated when the company and the union supplied the local USES office with a list of the skilled jobs that were to be made available and the corresponding names of the union members who met the stated needs. Meanwhile, the construction company selected laborers from a list of available farm workers prepared by the local USES office.[55] At Corpus Christi, the contractors and union representatives also worked closely with the USES to fill the skilled and semiskilled jobs at the Naval Air Station with Anglo workers from other parts of the state. The USES officials certified their list of skilled workers and agreed to recruit the laborers among the local farm workers.[56]

Job control for the predominantly Anglo unions involved other benefits. If their membership was not large enough to meet the USES requests, the unions recruited mostly Anglo workers from sister organizations or among nonunion members in the area. In some cases, the unions recruited Anglo farm workers living in the local labor camps. In this way, the unions extended their influence and control over skilled jobs in construction. Union officers also increased their membership by demonstrating their ability to secure good-paying jobs for Anglos in construction. The overall consequence was to reinforce racial thinking, promote the idea that unions functioned primarily as racial cartels rather than workers' organizations, and maintain a racial division of labor.[57]

The USES's cooperation with segregationists appeared unwarranted in many cases, especially since transporting skilled workers, often over long distances, may have cost more than training local workers with experience in construction work. Moreover, government policy dictated that agencies such as the USES encourage the nondiscriminatory transition from laboring positions to semiskilled jobs, and from semiskilled to skilled employment to meet the growing need for specialized workers in industries like construction. The influential farmers and their organizations, however, supported the unequal labor transfers because the temporary work arrangements provided needed employment to idle workers and maintained a labor force in reserve that could be released once the harvests began. Independent contractors, company representatives, and union officials, on the other hand, insisted on Anglo referrals for the skilled jobs primarily on the grounds that unionized and nonunionized Anglo workers did not want to work next to Mexicans.

The inter-industrial arrangement, however, was not without problems. As noted earlier, some workers refused to stay in one location, preferring instead to join the migratory workforce and optimize their farm earnings with the use of the entire family. The farmers' frequent claims of labor shortages and their anxious and often racially laced demands for government assistance in securing Mexican labor often meant that noncompliant workers could undermine their controlling schemes. The workers also unsettled rural labor markets when they took advantage of new opportunities outside agriculture and construction. The movement to the urban areas thus represented a bargaining act that defied rural inequalities. Joining industrial labor in the towns and cities of Texas also meant that the arriving workers could share in a higher level of recovery, especially if they obtained jobs in the war industries. Unequal job opportunities, however, also awaited them in the urban areas.

Inequality and Urban Workers in Wartime Industries

Labor market reports by the USES provide a basis for gauging the movement of Mexicans into the wartime industries, the source of the more desirable jobs in urban areas. The reports analyzed quantitative, interview, and observational data collected at wartime industries in the seventeen major industrial areas of the state. These industrial areas had a workforce of approximately three hundred and sixty thousand workers, a significant portion of the total number of workers in the state's wartime industries, which reached between five hundred thousand and seven hundred and fifty thousand during the middle of the war. The agency was responsible for maintaining reliable information on the size, skills, and movement of the workforce, the breadth and rate of productive activity, the labor needs of industry, and the effectiveness of government regulation in industrial and labor relations. Data collection and analysis were also necessary to meet the agency's major day-to-day responsibility of matching workers with available jobs and to train workers whose skills did not match industrial needs. This involved record-keeping on labor pools and job requests, job referrals, and training programs.[58]

One of the earliest USES reports offered a rare encouraging view of minority employment in wartime industries: "Minority race groups, which include negroes and Mexicans, are gradually being given more consideration; and the scope of work opportunities for these workers is being broadened."[59] Most early accounts, however, acknowledged that segregation posed a formidable obstacle to the full and effective use of all available workers. One USES official, for instance, predicted during the middle of 1943 that "only when the normal supply has been entirely depleted" could minority workers expect equal employment opportunities. Subsequent reports concluded that

Workers at the Kimble Wool and Mohair Company warehouse, Junction, 1940. (Photographer: Russell Lee, Farm Security Administration, Office of War Information Photograph Collection, Library of Congress.)

wartime industries utilized Mexican, blacks, and women workers slowly, even as the draft and the growing labor demand severely reduced the "normal" supply of workers in the state.[60]

Although USES reports placed much of the source of the problem at the gates of the industrial plants, the agency was not without fault. USES offices, for instance, maintained separate files for Anglo, black, and Mexican job applicants, and its staff usually referred Anglos to the skilled jobs and the Mexicans and blacks to the lesser-skilled positions, often in accordance to the requests submitted by segregationist employers in urban and rural areas. USES officials could claim, as they often did, that they had to maintain segregated records in order to accommodate the mostly discriminatory job requests that they received. Segregationist employers, on the other hand, blamed Anglo workers who opposed the hiring of Mexicans and blacks. The logic that cemented the collective segregationist claim thus centered on the claim that Anglo workers would protest fair hiring practices, disrupt production, and undermine the war effort. Such a dire consequence might have been possible in the segregated environment of the Second World War, but

Members of Club Femenino Chapultepec selling War Bonds in downtown Houston, 1940s. (Melesio Gómez Family Collection, Houston Metropolitan Research Center, Houston Public Library, Houston.)

USES officials rarely, if ever, challenged the employers or tested their claim of potentially disruptive Anglo workers. Whether intentional or not, the USES thus enabled an unequal rate of entry into wartime industries and further reinforced the kind of racial division of labor that Daniel Schorr observed in 1945.[61]

Women broke into the war industries earlier and with greater ease. It was not uncommon, even as early as 1941, to see women replace men who had taken up jobs vacated by other men who had entered the military. An anonymous USES official described this queuing process: a man who was drafted while working at a foundry was replaced by someone in an auto supply store. The process continued when a taxi driver took the place of the supply store clerk and a woman became the driver. Although women typically replaced men in the least desirable jobs during the first year of the war, they filled better-skilled and better-paying jobs as production increased and men moved up or joined the military. Racial preference often complicated the story of gender discrimination as Anglo women fared better than their minority counterparts. Training programs administered by federal agencies

Celebrating Christmas at the Lone Star Bag and Bagging Company, Houston, 1939. (Joe Rodriguez Family Collection, Houston Metropolitan Research Center, Houston Public Library, Houston.)

and larger industrial plants such as North American Aviation from Dallas, for instance, favored Anglo women over Mexican and African American males and females.[62]

In October 1942, women represented 9.2 percent of the state's workforce in the war industries, a slight improvement over the previous year. They mostly worked as low-wage labor in the service and food industries. Women numbered approximately four hundred and fifty thousand during the early part of 1943, when they began to near the peak of their participation in the wartime industries that the USES surveyed. Aircraft construction and repair plants claimed a female workforce of 34 percent, the largest proportion in wartime industries. Foundries hired the second-largest group of women. As the war progressed and production picked up, however, employers hired more women and war industries increasingly assigned them semiskilled and skilled positions. By December 1943, they constituted 23.1 percent of the workforce in war industries. Another way to appreciate women's entry into wartime industries is to compare their rate of incorporation to males. In 1943, women were hired almost three times faster than men. The woman's share of wartime employment, however, dropped to 20 percent in 1944 and to 19 percent in 1945, largely because production slowed down and military veterans were replacing them.[63]

Blacks represented 5.8 percent of the workforce in wartime industries in July 1942. Their representation came close to approximating 11 percent, their proportion of the total state population, as it increased to 8.8 percent within a year and to 10.3 by July 1944, the last time that the USES recorded their labor participation figures. Blacks made their gains mainly in construction, garment work, and food processing; industries like chemicals, nonferrous metals, aircraft, shipbuilding, ordnance, and iron and steel registered a lower level of black participation. Although they almost doubled their labor participation rate between 1942 and 1944, blacks also remained concentrated in the lower-skilled and lower-paying jobs.[64]

The USES did not provide a labor participation rate for Mexicans, although Castañeda claimed in 1945 that they never exceeded a 5 percent share of the workforce in the state's war industries.[65] Even with Castañeda's imprecise reference to "war and essential industries," a 5 percent estimate is striking, especially since the Mexican portion of the state's population very possibly reached 15 percent by the mid-1940s. Castañeda's observation on the poor rate of entry into the wartime industries was not the end of the story.[66] He added that Mexicans faced formidable barriers after they secured jobs in the war industries: "Such industries as have given employment to Mexican labor have restricted them to common or unskilled labor jobs largely, regardless of their ability, training, or qualifications. In the oil, aircraft, and mining industries, in the numerous military installations, in the munitions factories and shipyards, and in the public utility corporations, such as gas, light, and transportation companies, their employment has been limited and their opportunities for advancement restricted."[67] As the war progressed and the labor supply became depleted, Castañeda observed that employers gave "the Mexican American a try, but not without the greatest reluctance and misgivings." USES reports confirmed this. Wartime industries largely denied employment to Mexicans during the first years of the war and employed them slowly by the latter part of 1944.[68]

WMC utilization reports also support Castañeda's contention that Mexicans gained greater entry towards the end of the war. Its September 1944 report, for instance, noted that wartime and essential industries were integrating Mexican, as well as black and female workers. Although the report credited the utilization "recommendations" of WMC and USES officials for

Josephine Ledesma, airplane mechanic instructor, Randolph Field, San Antonio, 1941. (Josephine Ledesma Papers, U.S. Latino & Latina WWII Oral History Project, University of Texas at Austin.)

the change, it also noted that the increasing vacancies left by departing male Anglo workers created pressures on employers to integrate the workforce. The report's reference to specific cases involving Mexican, black, and women workers who secured industrial employment may not reflect the reluctance that Castañeda noted, but the overall view did point to low rates of entry.[69]

In most cases involving white women, government officials reported their placement in jobs vacated by white men. Mexican and African American workers also benefited from increasing opportunities, although they typically filled positions when no other workers were available, either because the supply had been depleted or white women refused the jobs that were available. In Tyler, for instance, the USES helped two companies recruit local African American women when white women rejected the jobs. In one of the cases, white women declined night shift jobs and in another, they turned down low-wage jobs. In both instances, the employers placed the African American women in segregated work sections. In Big Spring, an employer was convinced to give up his request for white women and accept "Latin American"

Aircraft workers, Mauldin Aircraft Company, Mauldin airport, Brownsville, 1947. (Abraham Moreno Papers, U.S. Latino & Latina WWII Oral History Project, University of Texas at Austin.)

women, the only workers who were available in the area at the time. An "oil company" and union from Big Spring also agreed to forego their contractual understanding against the hiring of Mexican workers because no others were available to fill the available jobs.[70]

Castañeda offered additional information on the experiences of Mexicans within wartime industries. They were noticeable as laborers in munitions, aircraft construction and repair, oil refining, and smelters, especially in regions where they predominated. Oil refineries in the Houston area, Corpus Christi, and El Paso, as well as smelters in Laredo and El Paso hired them primarily as laborers, although sites like Braniff Airways and Pan American Airways in Brownsville and the Texas Mining and Smelting Company from Laredo assigned some of them semiskilled or skilled positions. Industrial establishments along the border where Mexicans were in the majority, as well as military installations, especially in the San Antonio area, generally had a better record of placing Mexicans in the higher-skilled and better-paying positions.[71]

USES employment registration data from 1942 on Anglo, Mexican, and black women workers over fourteen years of age in San Antonio and Dallas suggest that the agency's job and training referral service contributed to different labor participation rates (see table 2.2). Since no comparable data for men is available, the following analysis of women workers offers a reliable approximation for the labor market experiences of the different racial groups and the role that the USES played in determining their labor participation

Table 2.2. Female population and registrants at United States Employment Service Offices, San Antonio and Dallas, 1942, by race

City	*Population*	*% of city population*	*Registrants*	*% of registered workers*
San Antonio				
Anglos	163,316	55.8	923	64.4
Mexicans	98,901	33.8	254	17.7
Blacks	19,447	6.6	256	17.9
Dallas				
Anglos	262,829	80.7	4,487	85.7
Mexicans	7,699	2.4	46	0.9
Blacks	47,879	14.7	703	13.4
Totals				
Anglos	426,145	72.5	5,410	81.1
Mexicans	106,600	18.1	300	4.5
Blacks	67,326	11.5	959	14.4

Sources: USES Labor Market Reports for Texas, May 15–June 15, 1942, 62, and April 15–May 15, 1942, 111.

rates. The trustworthiness of the data is reinforced by the significant differences in the proportional representation of Anglo, Mexican, and black women among USES job registrants. Anglo women, for instance, outdistanced Mexican and black women as registered workers in USES files at San Antonio. They made up 64.4 percent of the total number of available women workers (1,433) that the USES registered in San Antonio, while Mexicans and blacks registered less than 18 percent each.[72]

The disparity was especially glaring when compared with the corresponding population figures for each group in San Antonio. The proportional registration figures for Anglo women exceeded their share of the female population in San Antonio (55.8 percent). Mexicans, on the other hand, claimed one-third of the city's female population, yet only accounted for less that 18 percent of the total number of workers that the USES registered as available workers for industrial employment. Blacks fared better with a low population figure (6.6 percent) and a higher registration rate (17.7 percent) that approximated the Mexican record. Anglos and blacks, in other words, registered a higher representation rate in the San Antonio office of the USES.

Comparable data from Dallas also suggest that Anglos benefited from job placement assistance to a greater extent. Anglo women represented a significantly larger number (262,829) and portion of the total female population (80.7 percent); and a considerably higher number (4,487) and share of the USES registrants (85.7) than in San Antonio. Neither Mexican nor black women registered better rates than in San Antonio, although a significantly larger number of the latter (703) appeared in the list of USES registrants. The low absolute and relative figures for Mexican women were striking. Overall, Anglo women from San Antonio and Dallas benefited from their larger population size and the USES's employment and job training referral services. Mexican women constituted the second largest group of working age women, but drew the notice of USES officials to a significantly lesser extent than Anglo and black women. This is especially obvious when one considers that Mexicans were the only ones who failed to make the registration list at a rate that equaled or exceeded their share of the total female population.

Despite the favored position of Anglo women in the Texas labor market and in the job placement record of the USES, Mexican and black women also benefited from the new employment opportunities. The USES reported that a large percentage of minority women also left their homes for industrial employment in urban areas, although agriculture continued to be their principal employer. African American women, however, seemed to have done better than Mexican women in securing industrial employment in the cities. They typically replaced upwardly mobile Anglo women. Mexican women joined in this replacement process to a lesser extent. The USES reports often failed to note them, suggesting that they did not work in wartime industries in appreciable numbers. On several occasions, agency personnel noticed that the numbers of Mexican women in wartime industries were smaller in both absolute and proportional terms.[73]

Mexican immigrant workers fared the worst in war industries. An indication of this was their near total absence from the USES labor market reports on the principal war industries in the state. The records of the WMC and the FEPC offer much qualitative information in reports and memoranda that point to discrimination as a major explanation for their bottom position in the urban labor market. Job training programs operated by the WMC and private employers like North American Aviation at Fort Worth, for instance, typically placed Mexican immigrants at the bottom of the queuing process. Also, FEPC officials often accused local USES offices of assigning Mexican immigrant workers to agricultural jobs and of claiming questionable security concerns as an explanation for their failure to assign them to wartime industries such as munitions and aircraft construction. Their defense was that employers and Anglo workers insisted that Mexican immigrants were security risks by virtue of their nativity. Restrictions on the hiring and training of foreign-born workers almost always affected Mexicans and not European-origin immigrants, according to the records of the FEPC and the USES. The discrimination was especially evident in security sensitive industries such as shipbuilding and aircraft construction.[74]

Security breaches and the possibility of Anglo reactions to the hiring of Mexican nationals no doubt represented pragmatic concerns at a time of war. Employers, however, were obligated to observe the nation's nondiscrimination policy established by Executive Orders 8802 and 9346 and agencies like the USES were responsible for insuring that the policy was implemented. In the case of Mexican immigrants, this minimally meant that employers could appeal security restrictions and the USES could justify such appeals on the grounds that the president's executive orders prohibited discrimination on the basis of national origin, that Mexico was a wartime ally, and that the demand for labor was critical. None of these imperatives seem to have mattered until immigrant workers from Texas began to complain to the FEPC and agency representatives as well as Mexican officials relayed their concern to the USES. This led to an administrative agreement in 1944—involving the military, the USES, and U.S. Civil Service Commission—that guaranteed foreign-born persons equal employment opportunities in wartime industries. Although the long clearance procedure continued to deny Mexican nationals equal opportunities to jobs or positions in training programs, the agreement reaffirmed a nondiscrimination policy and minimized a long-standing obstacle to wartime recovery for immigrant workers.[75]

The 1944 agreement and the belated yet welcomed attempt to accommodate immigrant workers indicate that discrimination and government agencies did not always keep Mexicans from enjoying the full benefits of equal employment opportunities. The FEPC and the intervention of the Mexican government, as we shall see in succeeding chapters, also helped working families realize the promise of recovery offered by an expanding wartime economy. The more mundane, everyday initiatives that workers took to protest conditions or expand opportunities in wartime industries require some attention to demonstrate that Mexican workers in nonagricultural industries also expressed concern over their working conditions.

Mexican workers in war industries, like their brethren in agriculture, often took to the road in search of better opportunities, at times in violation of job clearance requirements. USES officials on numerous occasions claimed that Mexican workers moved between essential industries like agriculture and construction and some war industries for the purpose of pressuring employers to adjust wages in an upward direction. According to a 1942 USES report, the movement of Mexican workers was extensive and driven by the possibility of better wages: "One of the major factors affecting the supply of farm families is the ease with which farm workers can secure jobs on war construction projects or in war industrial plants at higher wages than farmers are able or willing to pay."[76]

The strategy of withholding one's labor was understandable in agriculture and even construction where laborers earned some of the lowest wages in Texas. War industries, on the other hand, generally offered appreciably higher wages. Some war industries, however, offered laboring wages that were only slightly higher and even lower than in some farms and construction sites. This is the reason that the mercury and zinc mines at Shafter, Alpine, and Dumas, for instance, always had a difficult time securing enough workers. Mining companies in the Big Bend region insisted on paying the low rate of thirty cents an hour despite workers' protests and job desertions. The increased demand for mercury in 1942 eventually forced them to raise the pay. This allowed the mine operators to attract some of the disaffected miners back to work.[77]

In other instances, Mexicans quit their jobs in war industries during the cotton picking season to optimize their earnings with the use of the entire family. Employers like American Smelting from Corpus Christi periodically reported a turnover in their maintenance and leaching departments that corresponded with onion work in March, April, and May and cotton picking from July to October. Although there is no evidence that American Smelting responded by raising their wages, its representatives occasionally reported that they rehired some of the departing workers after the harvests.[78]

Pirating employers also helped. A case in point occurred at the El Paso Union Depot in the fall of 1942. Representatives of the Railroad Retirement Board had recruited forty of them in Santa Fe, New Mexico, for work on a railroad line in California. While awaiting transportation, a labor agent representing the Spreckels Sugar Company from California surreptitiously approached them and convinced thirty of them to leave with promises of better earnings. Although the labor agent may not have delivered on his promises, the workers demonstrated a willingness to seek better working conditions despite prior arrangements with other recruiters. A USES official from El Paso concluded that "such incident illustrated just how keen has become the competition for common laborers on the part of out-of-town employers."[79]

Sometimes workers simply refused to work. Spontaneous work stoppages were used to advance a negotiating point or simply to register a protest without any hope of winning concessions. One such group of Mexican workers left Fort Worth's McKinley Iron Works in 1944, after their employer changed the pay time, and possibly extended the work week, from Saturday noon to Saturday evening. That same year saw an undetermined number of Mexican workers quit the Texas Mining and Smelting Company from Laredo because they had tired of the low wages that they were receiving. Striking workers may have returned to their old jobs and the same wages, but not before they had demonstrated that wartime industries did not always provide workers the opportunities that they expected.[80]

Conclusion

The denial of equal opportunities in wartime industries was only one part of the story of unequal mobility among Mexicans and between Mexicans and the rest of the worker population. The consistently higher concentration of Mexicans as farm workers points to a slower movement out of agriculture. Mexicans' lower mobility rate is best understood by examining their containment in agriculture. Farmers, in collaboration with state and federal agencies, stepped up their efforts during the war to regulate the movement of farm workers. The workers, in turn, entered into an informally bargaining process by regularly taking to the road and evading labor repressive measures.

Regulating the Mexican farm supply added a new feature to the pre-war procedure of controlling their movement. The USES included farm workers in a larger regulatory scheme intended to fully and effectively utilize the available labor supply in Texas. Other researchers have focused on the various methods used by agriculturists to keep Mexican workers immobilized in the farms. They have given little attention, however, to the government's broad policy of "freezing" Mexican farm labor in place and the role that the USES played in implementing the official course of action during a period of unprecedented job growth.

The USES reports, Castañeda's observations, and anecdotal evidence reported in other government agency sources, reveal important trends. Increased production led to growing employment opportunities, which, in turn, led to an observable improvement in the lives of working families. Improvements were most striking when a worker left the farm and found employment in the higher-wage firms normally associated with the major industries that were doing business with the government. Anglo men, followed by Anglo women, recorded some of the most impressive rates of participation in war industries, especially in the fastest growing ones that were offering the most attractive working conditions and upgrading possibilities.

Mexican and black male workers were next in the queuing process. Minority women and Mexican immigrant workers followed. While minority workers generally benefited less than Anglos, Mexican and black males took advantage of wartime opportunities to a greater extent than their female counterparts. Mexicans as a whole, however, benefited less than other groups in wartime industries. Like their brethren in agriculture, they took to the road or protested their condition in other ways. The unequal experience that they faced in the highest reaches of the recovery experience underscores the pervasive nature of discrimination and its significance in maintaining the racial division of labor in wartime Texas. At the same time that discrimination, labor policies, and skill differences contributed to variations in the recovery experience, a rapidly growing wartime economy provided the basis for much of the occupational improvement that Mexicans experienced during the Second World War. This naturally directs our attention to the other major explanation for wartime recovery, an activist state with New Deal proclivities that also acted on behalf of workers.

Although the USES obstructed the movement of Mexicans out of agriculture and retarded their incorporation into war industries, the multifaceted state also intervened to bring benefits to Mexican workers. The president's executive orders prohibiting discrimination in public employment, unions, and wartime industries, along with the establishment of the FEPC to enforce the orders, contributed to their recovery. The question that we must ask is to what extent did such a policy help to offset the labor-repressive work of the USES? Also, how did discrimination undermine this possibility? Before we address these questions, however, it is necessary to determine why the state paid any attention to discrimination against Mexicans at all. This is a reasonable question since the government had not previously taken such notice and even waited until 1943 to launch an official campaign on behalf of aggrieved minority workers in the wartime industries in Texas. To answer these questions we now turn to Mexico's intervention on behalf of Mexican workers, its alliance with LULAC, and the decision to expand the Good Neighbor Policy into the domestic arena and direct the FEPC's attention to Texas and other parts of the Southwest.

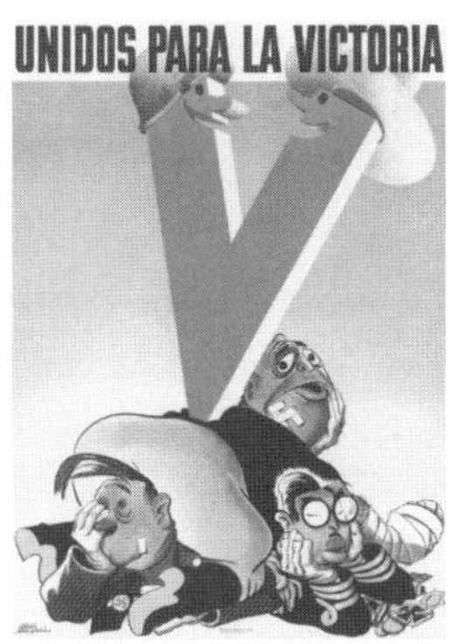

Chapter 3: Elevating the Mexican Cause to a Hemispheric Level

Mexico and the United States had never been on friendlier terms than in 1943 when President Manuel Avila Camacho hosted U.S. diplomats at his country's Independence Day celebration. The war, according to historian Lorenzo Meyer, had compelled the neighboring countries to end "the period of confrontations" in their relations. By 1943, the Good Neighbor Policy in the United States had produced a record number of treaties and official proclamations of cooperation, and Mexico had become the principal partner of the United States in crafting the inter-American alliance, the system of wartime cooperation and reciprocity in the Americas. Avila Camacho and members of his cabinet affirmed the wartime partnership when they appeared at the Independence Day celebration with three special guests of honor: George Messersmith, the U.S. Ambassador to Mexico, Nelson Rockefeller, an assistant secretary of state and the director of the OCIAA, and Coke Stevenson, the governor of Texas.

Messersmith and Rockefeller were logical choices for broadcasting good neighborliness. Messersmith was an active and popular ambassador and Rockefeller was the director of the OCIAA and the chief architect of the Good Neighbor Policy in Latin America. Texas's prominence in U.S. trade with Mexico also made the governor's appearance understandable; however,

Unidos Para La Victoria. Cartoon depiction of a giant "V" with G.I. helmet and a vaquero hat pinning Mussolini, Hirohito, and Hitler, n.d. (Artist: Antonio Arias Bernal. The Holland Collection of World War II Posters, Center for Southwestern Research, University of New Mexico, Albuquerque, New Mexico.)

he was there mostly to mend fences. In 1942, Mexico had signed a treaty to provide war workers, or Braceros, for farms and railroads in the United States, but refused to send them to Texas citing the state's inhospitable reputation toward Mexicans. Stevenson, under pressure from farmers to negotiate an end to the ban, and compelled by State Department officials to promote racial understanding, often found himself currying favor with Mexican officials. Mexico welcomed his expressions of goodwill, but refused to end the ban during the entire period of the war.

The give and take between Mexico and Texas reflected a larger process of negotiations over discrimination against Mexicans in the United States. Mexico, in other words, singled out Texas as it pressured the State Department to extend the Good Neighbor Policy from the hemispheric theater of diplomatic relations to the home front stage of ethnic affairs. The State Department responded to pressure from Mexico by initiating a domestic program in 1942 to "rehabilitate" the "Spanish-speaking," a term that included mainland Puerto Ricans but that focused on Mexicans. The OCIAA took command of the program which sought to improve Anglo-Mexican understanding by recognizing Mexican home front contributions and publicizing Mexico's favored nation status in the Americas. The State Department and the OCIAA emphasized the application of the Good Neighbor Policy in Texas and thus contributed to making the state a key public site in the negotiations over discrimination.

Although Mexico's influence explains much of the growing engagement, home-grown concerns within and outside U.S. government circles also contributed to bringing the policy home. State Department officials, for instance, welcomed improved relations to counter the suspected, and often exaggerated, influence of German operatives with their shortwave radio messages beaming into Mexican homes in the Southwest. The wartime language of democracy which called for the application of egalitarian principles at home also encouraged changes in hemispheric relations. Adding to these influences was the fear of social strife in some government circles. Much of this apprehension centered on the growing agitation around the issue of discrimination, especially the public protestations by Mexican government officials that were made primarily in conjunction with LULAC.

This chapter outlines how Mexico helped to make discrimination a central issue in wartime relations. It also examines how a diplomatic concern joined with domestic fears over security and social tensions in the decision by the OCIAA to apply the Good Neighbor Policy to race relations at home. Adding to the diplomatic and domestic mix were the efforts by Mexican civil rights leaders—especially in Texas—to insert their cause for civil rights into the arena of international relations. The chapter ends by explaining how the FEPC joined the OCIAA-headed program and broadened its work to include complaints by Mexican workers. The FEPC's expanded efforts, made possible by a second executive order in 1943, illustrates how the earlier policy shift in the OCIAA contributed to a sharper official focus on Mexican workers in wartime industries in Texas, a central concern in this book.

Building Hemispheric Unity

Latin American countries had sought unity and understanding since at least the time of their independence movements in the early 1800s. They renewed their unifying initiatives in the late 1800s when the United States presented interventionist threats in the region. Paradoxically, the United States led a renewed effort at pacific relations in the late 1930s with its Good Neighbor Policy, a plan of action that, according to Roosevelt and Rockefeller, sought inter-American unity and new, more cooperative and reciprocal relations befitting good neighbors. Roosevelt announced the policy during his first inauguration as a call for worldwide unity against the possibility of global strife. Soon thereafter, he gave it hemispheric focus and meaning as a rallying cry for inter-Americanism. Although historians disagree on the intent of the Good Neighbor Policy—some see it as a continuation of a politics of hegemony while others as a radical break with a past of military intervention, political interference, and distrust—they generally concur that Latin America saw it as an opportunity to redefine relations on more favorable terms.[1] Thus, it was not uncommon for Mexican officials like Dr. Francisco Castillo Nájera, Mexico's wartime ambassador to the United States, to describe the new relations with metaphoric allusions to "a united family of nations" in the Americas.[2]

Mexico welcomed the chance to become a major partner in building inter-Americanism. This became obvious as Mexico began signing a succession of cooperative agreements with the United States to build a united political, economic, and cultural front against the Axis threat. In an equally important act of cooperation, Mexican officials worked tirelessly to encourage other Latin American countries to embrace wartime unity. Although Mexico's leaders were sincere in promoting unity and understanding, they also sought to prepare the ground for more cooperative relations with the United States during the post-war period. They believed that the war offered a rare opportunity to improve future relations, open up new possibilities for trade and economic assistance, and place Latin America on a more equal footing with the United States.[3]

Avila Camacho revealed his wishes soon after his inauguration in December 1940 when he distanced himself from his predecessor's distrust of the United States. While President Lázaro Cárdenas had refused to take sides, Avila Camacho and his renowned foreign affairs secretary, Ezequiel Padilla, embraced the Allied cause and Roosevelt's wartime leadership in Latin America. Avila Camacho also settled the oil crisis, a source of serious international conflict that he inherited from the Cárdenas administration. He signed "El Acuerdo del Buen Vecino," whereby Mexico paid the claims of U.S. oil companies in favorable terms and the United States extended loan credits to stabilize the peso. The Mexican president expressed his clearest commitment to unity when he instructed Padilla to promote inter-Americanism with the United States at its helm. Days after Avila Camacho's inauguration, Padilla informed the U.S. embassy that Mexico was ready to establish a Joint Mexican-United States Defense Commission. He also assumed a leadership position in building Latin American unity with rousing speeches at the meetings of foreign ministers. In the early part of 1941, he began calling on Latin American countries to join with the United States in the fight against the Axis powers and their ideas of racial superiority, a matter of no small concern in Latin America. Padilla was less explicit, but no less serious, when he justified unification as a way to prepare the ground for the new relations that Mexico and other Latin American countries expected with the United States.[4]

Cooperative initiatives did not mean that Mexico's political leadership or its press wholeheartedly embraced the idea of new relations with the United States. Critics of Avila Camacho's hopeful embrace warned that the United States could not be trusted. The United States, after all, had grabbed more than half of Mexico's territory in 1848 and had returned hundreds of thousands of destitute Mexicans during the Depression without any regard to the social and political problems that Mexico was to face in receiving them. The steady stream of criticism that journalists and political leaders directed against the Avila Camacho administration accompanied equally effective reminders that Mexican diplomats should focus on discrimination in the United States as the central point of contention in diplomatic relations. The artists, labor leaders, journalists, and public officials who came together in 1943 as the highly influential Comité en Contra el Racismo added weight to this concern by continually equating racial prejudice in the United States with the claims of racial superiority in Germany.[5]

Apprehensions diminished when Japan attacked Pearl Harbor on December 7, 1941, and Mexico responded even more favorably to the United States' appeals for unity. Mexico broke relations with Japan on December 8 and, soon thereafter, with Germany and Italy as well. Mexico also stepped up its support for hemispheric unity alongside the United States. Padilla, for instance, on his way to the January 1942 Rio de Janeiro Conference of Foreign Ministers, endorsed the U.S. recommendation that Latin Americans sever relations with the Axis powers. He expressed the official commitment to hemispheric unity that diplomats from throughout the Americas had been expressing throughout the 1930s, albeit with even greater force: "An American nation had been brutally set upon. One of the twenty-one flags of the continent of brotherhood had been treacherously assailed."[6]

Despite Mexico's embrace of the inter-American cause, some officials approached the alliance with caution. This became evident during the brief military crisis that occurred on the border soon after Pearl Harbor. Fearing a Japanese invasion on the West Coast, Mexico and the United States took defensive measures that resulted in a military face-off at Tijuana–San Diego and Mexicali-Calexico, where Mexican troops prevented their U.S. counterparts from entering to fortify Baja California in defense of the Pacific coast. The popular former president Cárdenas, who was then acting as the military commander of Baja California, Sonora, and Sinaloa, rebuked the U.S. claim that Padilla had given permission for a military incursion into Mexico and ordered General Roberto Calvo Ramírez to stand up against the U.S. threat to Mexican sovereignty on the border. The confrontation was averted when the commander of the U.S. forces retreated and officials from both countries negotiated an agreement whereby Mexico guaranteed military surveillance on its Pacific coast and allowed the United States to set up radar installations in its territory. Cárdenas, obviously concerned about the limits of cooperation, visited Tijuana soon after the crisis had died down and reportedly conveyed to Calvo Ramírez the now famous view on the overbearing neighbor, "Not even as friends could we allow them to enter because how could we then remove them."[7]

The idea of continental defense acquired even more importance after Mexico announced that German submarines had sunk two of its oil tankers, the Potrero del Llano on May 13, 1942, and the Faja de Oro nine days later. By the end of the month, other tankers were sunk and Mexico had declared war on Germany. Other Latin American countries stepped up their efforts to build a wartime alliance with the accompanying agreements of cooperation. One important agreement allowed the United States and Mexico to draft each other's nationals living within their borders. Other understandings included a decision by Mexico to contribute critical military supplies, such as rubber, copper, and tungsten, to U.S. wartime industries. The best-known treaty, known as the Mexican Labor Agreement, created the Mexican Farm Labor Supply Program, or Bracero Program, in August 1942. The program supplied U.S. farmers and railroad companies with hundreds of thousands of Mexican Braceros during the war.[8]

Negotiating Discrimination

As the terms of wartime cooperation were being drawn, Mexican officials and journalists continued to sound a discordant note in the otherwise harmonious refrain of wartime cooperation. They continued to agree on the inter-American alliance, but warned that discrimination against Mexicans posed an obstacle to unity if U.S. officials did not openly address it—they wanted words matched in deeds.[9] Their concern was especially evident during the negotiations over the Bracero Program. At the same time, critics in major Mexico City newspapers began calling on the government to negotiate a treaty that guaranteed protections to Braceros, as well as noncontract workers who were independently migrating into the United States. Some of them, including members of the Chamber of Deputies, feared that discrimination against Mexicans would undermine popular support for wartime unity and, as a consequence, impair relations and undermine inter-Americanism. Mexican officials, already concerned over the possible depletion of the labor force through immigration and the moral implications of racial discrimination, also may have sought to demonstrate a measure of negotiating independence to quiet their detractors. Discrimination was a central issue in the discussions over the Bracero Program, beginning in February 1942, as well as during subsequent negotiations to extend the life of the international agreement.[10]

The Bracero Program meetings gave Mexican officials their first important opportunity to negotiate protections for aggrieved Mexicans, but it was the earlier attack on Pearl Harbor that encouraged the United States to link the idea of hemispheric unity to racial discrimination at home. By the middle of December 1941, OCIAA officials were offering three explanations for their newfound interest, including "repercussions in Latin America," meaning statements of protest by Latin American governments, especially Mexico, against the problem of discrimination facing the Spanish-speaking communities in the United States. OCIAA officials also reported tensions between

Discrimination sign, Dimmitt County, 1949. (Photographer: Russell Lee, Russell Lee Photographic Collection, Center for American History, University of Texas at Austin.)

the Spanish-speaking and the larger U.S. society, as well as a lack of recognition and even negative images of Latin American allies in the war effort. They added that a history of discrimination and segregation had marginalized the Spanish-speaking population and isolated them from the war effort. This was an obvious reference to an often-expressed fear within government circles that "fifth-columnists" and Axis shortwave broadcasts could encourage dissent among an aggrieved Mexican population in the home front. These problems, according to OCIAA officials, required bringing "the Good Neighbor Policy into effective operation within the United States."[11]

The U.S. embassy in Mexico also participated in the deliberations over broadening the scope of the Good Neighbor Policy. Soon after the meetings over the Bracero Program began, the U.S. embassy sent a report to the State

Department and the OCIAA's Coordination Committee in Mexico with a plan of action that had been in the works for some time. The report, entitled "Suggested Method of Improving the Situation," linked the negotiations over the Bracero Program with discrimination in the United States and called on the government to direct its agencies to treat discrimination as an impediment to cooperation with Mexico.[12]

The increased attention on Mexicans was also evident among government officials in the United States, according to Will Alexander, the head of the Minority Groups Branch of the Office of Production Management (OPM). He reported during the latter part of February 1942: "The matter of an overall program for the government in dealing with the problems of Spanish-Americans is under discussion here [Washington, D.C.] between the various agencies in the government that now have some responsibility in this general field."[13] The discussions reported by Alexander reached fruition when the OCIAA extended the purview of its Good Neighbor Policy into the domestic arena.[14]

Rockefeller expanded the work of the OCIAA by adding the Division of Inter-American Activities in the United States in March 1942. The purpose of the division was to encourage federal agencies to join in a program to improve the image of Latin America and to promote interethnic understanding in the United States. Within a month, the OCIAA gave focus to the Division of Inter-American Activities by establishing the Spanish and Portuguese Speaking Minorities Section. The Minorities Section was to oversee the agency's work on Mexican-Anglo relations and to challenge prejudice and discrimination with public programs that offered financial assistance, encouraged self-help actions, and propagandized wartime unity on the home front. The Minorities Section included three employees and a temporary budget. Within a year, it had grown to at least five employees in Washington and a larger number of field representatives with an improved appropriation for local and regional projects. The Inter-American Division and the Minorities Section also participated in the larger OCIAA effort to coordinate an interagency campaign against discrimination. The same government edicts that reformulated the OCIAA's program of activity also directed government agencies to expand their reach into Mexican communities to more effectively address discrimination and cooperative relations with Mexico.[15]

Although the Mexican government must be credited as a major influence in the decision by the State Department to expand the purview of the Good Neighbor Policy, nongovernmental actors from the United States were also instrumental in the OCIAA's more determined plan to address discrimination. Carey McWilliams, the commissioner of immigration and housing in California, noted this in his classic study, *North from Mexico.* He suggested that prominent southwestern leaders had convinced Rockefeller to establish the Minorities Section with a coordinated letter-writing campaign beginning in October 1941. Until then, the Inter-American Division, according to McWilliams, had been more concerned with organizing "trifling ballyhoo campaigns" that focused on improving relations with Latin American countries rather than on efforts to address discrimination and the need for improved relations between the Spanish-speaking and the rest of society. The establishment of the Minorities Section, McWilliams added, signaled a major programmatic change as well as a shift toward relations between Anglos and Mexicans. The public began to see that these relations were no longer only a matter of domestic concern, but "an integral part of the much larger question of finding the basis for a new accord between the Anglo part of the hemisphere and the Spanish part."[16]

McWilliams's proposition that the work of the Minorities Section influenced public thinking on race relations may have been overly optimistic, especially since other nonstate actors like U.S. farm and railroad interests had also increased their pressure with claims of labor shortages and demands that their government negotiate a labor importation program. The United States' commitment to promote good neighborliness at home, on the other hand, may have been enough to convince the Bracero Program negotiators to continue their work after a pause in the discussions. U.S. and Mexican officials had slowed the negotiations for fear that the predictable discrimination that Braceros would face could draw publicity, harm relations, and undermine the war effort. Immediately after the OCIAA had established the Minorities Section in April 1942 and Mexico had declared war on the Axis powers in May 1942, the negotiations were resumed.[17]

When negotiators from the Office of Foreign Affairs and the Department of Labor and Social Provisions came back to the bargaining table in June 1942 they again strengthened their hand by raising old grievances. Jaime Torres Bodet, Mexico's under secretary of foreign affairs, reported that Mexico was concerned that Mexicans had been returning penniless from the United States during the 1930s, making their situation "worse after they returned than before they went." He suggested that the problem of "social readjustment" was a serious concern in the Avila Camacho administration. His clear intent, however, was to underscore that Mexico was expending precious political capital by agreeing to establish the program and that the United States had to reciprocate with contractual guarantees that shielded the workers from discrimination. This was the same bartering technique that Torres Bodet and fellow Mexican officials used when they asked that the United States act on the problem of discrimination in the first place.[18]

The Mexican negotiators also claimed that the United States had not helped Mexico receive the tens of thousands of destitute repatriates left jobless by the Depression. Because of this, they proposed a program of labor guarantees that the Chamber of Deputies had drawn up years earlier in anticipation of a possible repeat of the abuses of the 1930s. The action by the Chamber of Deputies made it obvious that the United States had to offer contractual guarantees if farmers and railroad companies were to receive the workers that they claimed to need. The United States agreed to a number of the stipulations dictated by the Chamber of Deputies, including free return transportation, a minimum wage, individual contracts, and, most important, the continuing review and approval of the program by the Mexican government. The United States had never consented to such broad oversight even though Mexicans had complained of discrimination throughout the late 1800s and early 1900s, underscoring the fact that the war and the United States' desire to repair relations with Mexico had turned the tide.[19]

Intervening on behalf of the more than 320,000 Braceros who worked in U.S. farms and railroads had significance far beyond the program. Aside from allowing Mexican inspectors to visit Braceros in their camps and work sites, the treaty established the minimal conditions which Mexico would expect for Braceros in the United States, including a guarantee that Executive Order 8802 protected them from discrimination. This, as we shall see, strengthened Mexico's hand on many occasions when it spoke for Mexican nationals as well as U.S.-born Mexicans. Noncontract workers, moreover, were often encouraged to express their own concerns because the labor guarantees more often than not exceeded the conditions under which they labored. In other words, the negotiated contracts theoretically represented the minimal conditions that Mexico wanted for all Mexican workers.[20]

Soon after the Bracero Program was agreed to, Mexico and the United States announced a more general understanding regarding the rights of each government to intervene on behalf of its nationals. The Consular Agreement of 1942, the first of its kind between both countries, stipulated that consular agents could "protect" the rights of their citizens by representing them before federal, state, and local authorities in the host country. The "protective" policy declaration had special significance for the Foreign Affairs Office because it broadened Mexico's right to intervene on behalf of its nationals beyond the possibilities offered by the Bracero Program agreement.

Although the United States had the same theoretical right to speak for its citizens, the understanding represented an especially important opportunity that Mexico used to lobby for Mexican rights in the United States. It also demonstrated a major concession by U.S. officials who were making their own home front assessments to justify the unprecedented changes in intergovernmental relations.[21]

Preparing the Ground

While U.S. officials pondered the idea of extending the Good Neighbor Policy into the domestic arena, the Office of Facts and Figures, the agency responsible for disseminating information about defense efforts and policies, joined with the OCIAA and the FEPC in conducting field studies that informed and encouraged the decision.[22] In hindsight, the studies did not seem necessary since academic and government researchers had already generated much information on the social conditions of Mexicans for at least four decades. The researchers, however, did not only seek to confirm the prior findings of poverty, discrimination, and inequality affecting Mexicans in the United States. They also sought to measure the level of Mexican discontent and the degree to which Mexican and U.S. government action and the political influence of the left and the right on the Mexican community could trigger an Anglo reaction. In sum, the researchers wanted to determine the degree of social tension, a general wartime policy concern, and the possibility of eruptions with security implications on the border region.[23]

Paul Horgan, a western historian and librarian for the New Mexico Military Institute, prepared the first report for the Office of Facts and Figures. Harkening back to the still fresh memory of the 1917 Zimmerman note and claims of a German conspiracy in Mexico during World War I, he warned that the United States was vulnerable to German aggression and intrigue along the border primarily because of the presence of large numbers of Mexicans who were not fully aware of U.S. war aims. Horgan next made the unsubstantiated, yet provocative claim that German agents were promoting dissension by promising Mexicans the return of Texas, New Mexico, Arizona, and California "as the fruits of successful alliance against the United States." He added that Axis shortwave broadcasts were reaching Mexican homes in the Southwest and alleging widespread anti-Catholic and anti-Mexican sentiments in the United States. Hogan recommended a vigorous Americanization campaign, a project primarily intended to win the presumably reluctant

Mexicans over to the war effort by acknowledging their battlefield and home front contributions. His proposal was not limited to a Mexican audience. Hogan also suggested that the initiative should promote a more realistic and considerate public view of Mexicans. He also recommended that officials publicize the campaign, primarily through radio and public programs in the Southwest, and seek the assistance of outwardly patriotic Mexican civil rights leaders.

One month after the Horgan report, the OCIAA sent David J. Saposs to Texas, New Mexico, Arizona, California, Colorado, and Illinois. Saposs, a labor economist who was to become the director of the OCIAA's Minorities Section, submitted one of the most comprehensive reports. Like Horgan, he emphasized poverty and social inequality to support his view that continuing discrimination aggravated social tensions and posed security risks. Saposs noted that the Mexican community was "probably the most submerged and destitute minority group in the United Sates." He added that discrimination undermined relations with Mexico and jeopardized hemispheric unity.[24]

Discrimination, according to Saposs, offered the best single explanation for problems ranging from unemployment, low wages, migratory work, low school attendance, illiteracy, juvenile delinquency, chronic illnesses, and poor housing. The Mexican community, he added, experienced some of the most flagrant discrimination in public places such as restaurants and parks. Saposs also reported widespread prejudice—the Anglo community mostly regarded them "as inferiors." Inequality, discrimination, and long-standing prejudice, Saposs concluded, constituted the ideal mix for conflict that could disrupt production and undermine the war effort.[25]

With some exaggeration but obvious intent, Saposs warned that agitators, especially the ones that favored the Axis cause, made use of the misery among the Mexicans to provoke racial strife. Others, especially leftists, were exaggerating discrimination and inequality with the clear intent of causing conflict. Although Saposs's unflattering views of Mexican leaders amounted to a blanket denunciation, his concerns seemed to be limited to an individual from Phoenix whom he described in unbecoming terms. He was also especially troubled by the intense political environment of Los Angeles that he described as "bizarre." The place included everything "from shysters of various sorts, thru Latino Politicos, fascist and Communist fronters, each with its peculiar machinations and cliques."

While he clearly sought to discredit leaders from the right and the left, Saposs was mostly impressed with the politically conservative and moderate

Mexican leadership. He took special notice of LULAC, especially its self-help and community development work with other like-minded organizations in Colorado, New Mexico, Texas, and Illinois. For Saposs, LULAC could be trusted to embrace a governmental initiative to improve understanding and social conditions. Despite this encouraging note, Saposs cautioned Rockefeller that even the more agreeable civil rights leaders would manipulate the issue of discrimination for greater political effect.[26] He added that "the enemies of a better understanding and closer cooperation are capitalizing on the disadvantages and disabilities of the resident Latin Americans in order to block a satisfactory implementation of the good neighbor policy. It is the general opinion that our office must interest itself in this situation, and aid in any attempt to improve conditions so as to counteract enemy propaganda."[27] The best way to counteract such propaganda, according to Saposs, was to promote social improvements. Saposs also recommended that the United States recognize Mexican immigrants as war workers. This would acknowledge a popular and official view in Mexico and strengthen hemispheric unity.[28]

Vincenzo Petrullo, a creative southwestern writer and author of a report to the FEPC, corroborated many of the earlier findings, especially the ones related to security and international relations. Petrullo admitted that some Mexicans were frustrated with official neglect and recognized that unrest was also possible among them, although it "cannot yet be definitely labeled as the penetration of foreign political movements." The public expressions of concern over discrimination among Mexicans, nevertheless, presented a clear and present danger of Nazi manipulation, according to Petrullo.

Petrullo reiterated Horgan's observation that great cultural distance kept Mexicans beyond the reach of an Americanizing influence. Discrimination that in some instances "is greater than that practiced against the Negroes," encouraged bitterness and discontent in the Southwest and Mexico, a problem that for Petrullo "constitutes a serious handicap to the effectiveness of the Good Neighbor Policy." Petrullo spoke in greater detail about Mexican political groups such as the right-wing Acción Nacional and Sinarquista organizations that were allegedly fomenting dissension in the Southwest. Like Horgan and Saposs, he spoke about LULAC in favorable terms. The organization, Petrullo noted, included intellectuals, businessmen, and professionals who openly critiqued discrimination and government inaction but professed what he considered a genuine form of Americanism. This finding must have brought welcome relief to officials who were concerned that racial tensions might erupt into racial conflict. Four months after the field studies had been completed and the Minorities Section had been established, however, U.S. officials grew alarmed when tensions came close to a breaking point at Los Angeles.[29]

The Los Angeles Troubles

The troubles began in August 1942 when the Los Angeles Times began warning of delinquency among Mexican youth. The police had arrested hundreds of young Mexicans as suspects in a murder near a swimming place named Sleepy Lagoon. Twenty-two of them were tried and twelve were convicted of the crime. The courts exonerated the young men within two years but not before the media had exposed an undercurrent of racism with biased reporting and prejudiced depictions of Mexican youth as juvenile delinquents. The press coverage as well as the equally undeserved racial characterizations attributed to city officials troubled Mexico and the resident Mexican community. According to State Department and OCIAA officials, who were very concerned about security, the Mexican response and the possible Anglo reaction to their claims of discrimination provided added justification for good neighborly action. The Zoot-Suit or Pachuco "riot" that erupted later, in May–June, 1943, confirmed the fears of racial strife and led State Department and OCIAA officials to think that more could occur.[30]

Walter Laves, the director of the OCIAA's Inter-American Division, arrived in the city on October 1942. He came to moderate the gathering conflict, soon after the court convicted the Sleepy Lagoon defendants and the Los Angeles County grand jury held open hearings to investigate the outlandish claims that Mexican youth were naturally prone to violence. Laves met with numerous journalists and local officials as well as with persons who testified on behalf of the Mexican community before the grand jury. He and Alan Cranston, from the Minorities Section of the Office of War Information, urged journalists and local officials to exercise restraint because discrimination was causing resentment among the Mexican leadership in Los Angeles and officials in Mexico. Laves also used the opportunity to promise the Mexican community and its allies that the government would intervene with a program of "rehabilitation" for their "submerged" population. Rehabilitating Mexicans, an idea similar to the Americanizing one previously offered by Horgan, had two meanings in government circles—government agencies would seek to improve the Mexican social condition and promote a public awareness of their contributions to the war effort. When he returned to Washington, Laves used the Los Angeles case to secure permanent funding for the Minorities Section and continued vigilance on Mexican-Anglo relations as a potential source of conflict.[31]

Laves felt that the trouble at Los Angeles revealed widespread prejudice and underscored a moral dilemma for the United States, that is, it was leading a war against fascism while many of its citizens were seconding Nazi proclamations against an "inferior" race. Anglo prejudice, coupled with a growing number of Mexican complaints submitted to the OCIAA, also worried Laves. He was concerned that Anglos might react if they perceived that the OCIAA favored Mexican causes, especially if they believed that "fifth-columnists" were agitating Mexicans and disrupting the home front peace. This may explain why Laves opposed hiring someone with "Mexican or other Latin American blood" to head the Minorities Section.[32]

While Laves and Cranston concentrated their attention on Los Angeles, Mexican officials expressed concerns through private diplomatic channels.[33] This would change soon after critics in Mexico and the United States noted Mexico's reluctance to speak forthrightly about the troubles in Los Angeles. By the latter part of 1942, Mexico began to break with the conventional method of negotiating privately for Mexicans in the United States. Mexican officials were now just as apt to appeal to the court of public opinion as they were to communicate their concerns privately, through the Mexican embassy and the State Department. This emphasis on public discourse was clearly intended to answer critics at home and to assert Mexico's negotiating hand. The public criticism leveled against Mexico's preference for quiet diplomacy in the Sleepy Lagoon case, as well as during the subsequent Zoot-Suit "riot," also may have contributed to the decision to pursue the more public form of negotiation.

In directing Washington's attention to Los Angeles, Laves was seconding the finding in the field studies that discrimination was a major cause of Mexican poverty and inequality and that government inaction could impair relations with Mexico. He also expressed concern about triggering an Anglo reaction to government action. Laves concluded, however, that it was not enough to propagandize the contributions of Mexicans at the war and home fronts or, as McWilliams and his fellow protesters had indicated earlier, U.S. government officials could no longer expect that a public relations campaign would satisfy their critics. It was necessary to expand the Good Neighbor Policy and direct a government campaign against racial discrimination at home.

The decision to broaden the Good Neighbor Policy took on even greater significance when Mexico announced in June 1942 that they would not send Braceros to Texas until state officials acted decisively on discrimination. The ban, aside from proclaiming that prejudice was especially evident in Texas, allowed Mexican officials and Mexican civil rights leaders to sustain the public discourse over discrimination and to offer an increasingly popular home front solution, civil rights legislation. As in Los Angeles, the OCIAA intervened by urging local and state officials to address discrimination as an issue of wartime significance. This time, however, the public deliberations in Texas revealed a more energetic intervention by Mexico as well as an activist alliance with LULAC.[34]

The Texas Ban

Mexico's campaign against discrimination in Texas was more than a strategy to draw public attention to the problem or to test the sincerity of the United States in applying the Good Neighbor Policy at home. It also represented a break with a past of relatively quiet and guarded diplomatic negotiations over cases of discrimination brought before consulate offices. Mexican officials were no doubt encouraged to broadcast their concerns and petitions as popular support for the inter-American alliance increased and the clamorous left softened its demand that Mexican officials stand up to the United States. They were now tenacious and even uncompromising with frequent public statements that reaffirmed Mexico's principled opposition to racial prejudice and discrimination throughout the world and concern for the welfare of Mexicans in the United States.[35]

The public statements against discrimination in Texas by Padilla and consular officials like Carlos A. Calderón, the Mexican consul general at San Antonio with jurisdiction over the South Texas region, and the responses by Texas and U.S. officials amounted to a continuous process of public negotiation. Writers for Spanish- and English-language periodicals added to the public discourse by regularly reporting and commenting on the Texas ban while Mexican civil rights leaders and members of the Mexican consular corps in Texas became increasingly vocal in the press. They openly solicited complaints and submitted them to Mexican and U.S. authorities and called on the state to take effective actions. State Department and OCIAA officials, meanwhile, advised their counterparts in Texas on how to respond to Mexican demands, all along admitting publicly that the United States recognized that discrimination was a central issue in hemispheric relations.

State authorities usually minimized the extent of discrimination at the same time that they announced that the Good Neighbor Commission (GNC) was resolving individual complaints and leading an "educational" campaign to improve racial understanding among Anglos. They insisted that the GNC's "gradualist" approach avoided disruptions that Anglo segregationists would surely cause if pushed too hard. Mexican government officials and LULAC officers, on the other hand, preferred an immediate solution in the form of civil rights legislation. Moreover, they often accused state officials of indulging and even encouraging the opposition.

Although LULAC came highly recommended by the authors of the field reports and eventually assumed an intermediary position between Mexican and U.S. authorities on the issue of discrimination, the organization's association with the Mexican consuls, especially its participation in the public heated discourse over racial distinctions, raised some doubts in U.S. governmental circles. In the summer and fall of 1942, for instance, the San Antonio office of the Federal Bureau of Investigation (FBI) was conducting surveillance on the local LULAC council primarily because of the organization's critique of discrimination as an impediment to unity at the home front and in Latin America.

Although an early report concluded, "There was found practically no evidence of any pure Spanish [Falangist] activities in this division," the FBI continued investigating LULAC councils. The steady vigil that the agency maintained over LULAC councils reflected a larger concern over dissidence in the Mexican community. The FBI also posted agents in other Mexican organizations like Masonic orders, mutual aid societies, communist organizations, and sinarquista, or Falangist, groups in the Rio Grande Valley, San Antonio, Houston, and Dallas. The suspicions over LULAC, however, seem to have been lifted by the end of 1943 when the organization became the government's clear choice over the left-wing and right-wing organizations as well as the less Americanized groups like the more numerous Masonic orders and mutual aid organizations. The rancorous debate that the ban generated during the latter part of 1942 and early part of 1943 may have contributed to this temporary suspicion of LULAC. Their patriotic language and close association with the Mexican government, on the other hand, probably helped to transform their image in government circles.[36]

The announcement of the ban took effect soon after August 1942, when the Mexican and U.S. government signed the Bracero Program agreement. Although the State Department immediately registered its displeasure, South Texas farmers were unable to muster a concerted protest because they were already well into their 1942 harvest. By the early part of 1943, however, when farmers began preparations for the new cotton-picking season, they raised the issue with state officials and congressional representatives from South Texas. The Texas Farm Bureau followed with a well-organized campaign for an end to the ban that included urgent appeals to state and federal authorities. The letters and petitions that bureau officials attached to their communications claimed that the ban was aggravating an already serious situation—the military draft and the rural-to-urban migration had depleted the labor supply at the same time that the war placed higher production demands on agriculture. State Department officials, on the other hand, often questioned the labor shortage claim, largely because they believed that Texas farmers made full use of the existing farm labor supply, including women and youth who were entering the workforce in increasing numbers. The political support that farmers secured from Texas and USES officials, however, made their claims compelling enough for the State Department to call for an end to the ban. Mexico's firm position and the spotlight that it placed on discrimination, on the other hand, were sufficient to draw the State Department into the fight.[37]

By the summer of 1943, the Texas Farm Bureau had hired Cullen Briggs, a former judge from Corpus Christi, to represent the farmers in private consultations with state and federal officials. He contacted William P. Blocker, U.S. consul general in Ciudad Juárez, Chihuahua, and both men convinced Tom Sutherland, the field representative of the OCIAA in Texas, to secure the State Department's help. Meanwhile, Briggs consulted privately with Governor Stevenson, Congressmen Richard M. Kleberg, and U.S. embassy officials in Mexico City. During these private negotiations, Briggs and Ambassador Messersmith devised a proposal for a separate Good Neighbor Policy in Texas. The ambassador sent the plan to Stevenson and urged him "to curb discrimination where it exists and to wipe it out altogether." Although the details of the Briggs-Messersmith plan are not entirely known, there is little doubt that the Farm Bureau and the State Department played a role in private consultations with state and federal officials as well as in the decision by Stevenson to bring Texas in line with the Good Neighbor Policy.[38]

Prompted by the expressed concerns of Texas farmers and instructions from State Department officials, Stevenson called on members of the Texas legislature to prepare a bill that outlawed discrimination against Mexicans. In June 1943, the state's 48th legislature passed the Caucasian Race Resolution, a narrowly constructed statute that extended protections to Mexicans as another white group.[39] The decree, otherwise known as House Concurrent

Resolution 105, declared it unlawful to discriminate against Mexicans in "all public places of business or amusement." With this action, Texas legislators ostensibly extended civil rights protections to Mexicans, regardless of nativity. However, they limited the prohibition to discrimination against Mexican consumers at private businesses and they skirted the problem of discrimination against African Americans. Clearly, the framers of the resolution did not wish to address discrimination against Mexicans in workplaces or schools nor did they intend to lighten the segregationist burden that blacks endured. The legislators, however, affirmed the "other white" claim that Mexican civil rights activists were making at the time. The resolution, in other words, reinforced Mexico's contention that discrimination was an issue of hemispheric importance and validated whiteness as a civil rights claim. Stevenson's subsequent overtures bolstered the good neighborly cause.[40]

Soon after the Texas legislature acted, Stevenson proclaimed a Texas version of the Good Neighbor Policy. The measure called on Texans, especially public officials, to treat Mexicans with greater understanding and respect as an expression of wartime solidarity at home and abroad. Discrimination, he added, could hamper "the prompt and full utilization of all resources in this great emergency." Stevenson also announced that discrimination in business establishments against Mexicans constituted a violation of the state's policy as noted in the resolution: "and though not punishable by criminal prosecution may be subject to civil action in the courts." In August, Stevenson took yet another step to demonstrate that Texas had turned a new leaf in race relations. Based on advice from Sutherland and approximately $17,000 from the OCIAA, Stevenson established the GNC. The agency was to investigate and settle Mexican complaints of discrimination against business establishments and to promote a public program of good neighborliness throughout the state. Although the GNC had a limited purview, Stevenson placed the agency in the governor's office and appointed leading business and community leaders to its board.[41]

Apparently convinced that the governor's initiatives would satisfy Mexico, Stevenson and Messersmith made public a letter, written jointly by them, to Padilla in which the governor pronounced the state's commitment to good neighborliness and made another appeal for Braceros. Optimism faded quickly when Padilla openly applauded the effort but rejected the appeal. He promised to continue entertaining the request for Braceros as long as Texas could demonstrate significant improvements in race relations.[42] Padilla added that if Texas took resolute actions such as effective legal sanctions against discrimination in the form of substantial fines, Mexico "would gladly extend the cooperation of our workers in the fields of the State of Texas." Obviously, Padilla was not convinced that the legislature's action had met his demand for an effective antidiscrimination law.[43]

The decision by Stevenson to embrace the Good Neighbor Policy was significant because it involved a consensus among farmers, state officials, and federal authorities that Texas should bring its resources to bear on the problem of discrimination. Mexico's influence was equally important. Officials like Messersmith and Stevenson could insist privately that they were primarily seeking to end the ban and to secure the Braceros that Texas farmers needed, but Mexican authorities like Padilla could claim that they had forced Texas to act against discrimination.[44]

Additional events had placed the wartime relations between the two countries in sharp relief and brought added attention to Texas. This included a series of meetings between Avila Camacho and Roosevelt on April 20 and 21, 1943, in Monterrey, Nuevo León, and Corpus Christi, Texas. Mexican and U.S. presidents had not met since Porfirio Díaz and William H. Taft convened in Ciudad Juárez and El Paso on the eve of the Mexican Revolution. Moreover, no U.S. president had ever traveled into the interior of Mexico. The extended amount of time that the presidents spent on their trip from Monterrey to Corpus Christi as well as their friendly public appearances underscored the importance that they gave to wartime unity and cooperation. They also affirmed strong support for the inter-American alliance.[45]

During the historic meeting, the presidents proclaimed the agreement whereby each country could draft into military service the nationals of the other residing within their borders and declared that Mexico would send additional Braceros to the United States, except to Texas. Their discussions also led to the formation of the Mexican-American Commission for Economic Cooperation, the agency that formalized economic activity between the two countries. In his public statements, Roosevelt stressed interdependence, nonintervention, and the Good Neighbor Policy as guiding principles in the new relations between Mexico and the United States. He added that the system of cooperation, "whose strength is now evident even to the most skeptical, is based primarily upon a renunciation of the use of force and the enshrining of international justice and mutual respect as the governing rule of conduct by all nations."[46] Avila Camacho emphasized that Mexico and the United States had a special responsibility to demonstrate that the Good Neighbor Policy could work. The rest of Latin America, according to the Mexican president, looked upon them as "the natural bridge of conciliation between the Latin and the Anglo-Saxon cultures of the continent."[47] Avila Camacho added an oblique reference to racial thinking at the home front alongside a concern over foreign intervention when he noted, "We desire to live together free of the perpetual threats which derive from those who seek supremacy in foreign and domestic affairs."[48]

Avila Camacho's public statements were general and discreet, as one would expect in such high-level meetings between heads of state. His subordinates, however, were less restrained by diplomatic protocol. This was evident days after the Avila Camacho–Roosevelt meeting. Luis L. Duplán, the Mexican consul at Austin, issued a widely circulated report that publicized Mexico's official view that discrimination in Texas was a major impediment to wartime understanding and cooperation in the Americas. Duplán, acting under standing instructions for consuls to bring complaints of discrimination before authorities, sent his report to numerous officials, including George I. Sanchez, the state director of LULAC and the head of the Texas-based OCIAA-sponsored Committee of Inter-American Relations.[49]

Padilla and two consular officials in Texas, Calderón and Adolfo G. Domínguez, the Houston consul, amplified Mexico's view in June, soon after the outbreak of the so-called Pachuco riots in Los Angeles.[50] Padilla, no doubt smarting from accusations by Mexican civil rights leaders in Los Angeles that he had done little on behalf of the Mexican youth that were attacked by U.S. servicemen, publicly affirmed his commitment to the victims of the violence and announced a broad effort to expose discrimination as a major hindrance to effective unity in the United States and Latin America.[51] Discrimination was a problem of such international proportions, according to Padilla, that it required immediate and far-reaching action in the form of legislation that outlawed it. Calderón followed with a similar public appeal that he, Padilla, and others would continue to present as a precondition for the lifting of the Texas ban.[52]

After the Los Angeles riots and during the legislative hearings on the Caucasian Race Resolution, Padilla also gave an interview to the Houston Post in which he underscored the significance of discrimination by analogizing the work of segregationists with fifth columnists who were intent on undermining unity in the United States and among allied nations in the hemisphere. Domínguez also stated that anti-Mexican prejudice was so ingrained that private citizens and local officials were averse to the idea of a Good Neighbor Policy, even in the best of times in the history of relations between Mexico and the United States. This lag, Domínguez noted, gave Mexico sufficient reason to continue protesting "the deplorable and unjustified practice that we are witnessing." Domínguez also offered a delicately stated observation on the work of the Mexican consulate on behalf of U.S.-born Mexicans. He conceded that foreign governments could not openly advocate on behalf of U.S. citizens lest they be accused of violating sovereignty laws. Domínguez, however, added an important qualification. Discrimination and the "Nazi principles" that impelled it constituted a compelling infringement on human rights, a violation of the very democratic principles that elevated the Allied and inter-American cause to a higher moral ground. His suggestion was resolute and far-reaching. Mexican officials, like their U.S. counterparts, were obligated to end discrimination, regardless of the place where it occurred or who was involved.[53]

While Domínguez put forward Mexico's broadest interpretation of its advocacy policy in the United States, Padilla struck an unwavering negotiating posture in large part to support Mexican consuls and LULAC leaders who were jointly or separately promoting a campaign for equal rights in Texas. LULAC leaders like Alonso Perales, Manuel C. Gonzales, George I. Sanchez, and Carlos Castañeda, for instance, were busy lobbying and testifying in support of the Caucasian Race Resolution at the same time that Padilla and Mexican consuls were condemning the entire practice of discrimination and calling for legislative remedies. LULAC officers and consuls, on the other hand, helped Mexican officials maintain their critical stance by soliciting complaints of discrimination and submitted them along with reports that lamented the slow progress in Mexican-Anglo relations as well as in the more general area of race relations.

Although Mexican consuls and LULAC activists often spoke against race discrimination as a whole, they maintained a focus on Mexicans by targeting the GNC and the Caucasian Race Resolution to demonstrate the state's lackluster record. The state agency, the centerpiece of the Good Neighbor Policy, was supposed to hear complaints, render fair decisions on the merits of each case, and reach settlements with the parties involved. Mexican consuls and LULAC representatives from San Antonio, Austin, and Houston conducted their own sincerity tests by bringing hundreds of complaints before the GNC and monitoring its work. They also claimed that GNC officials limited their work to promoting public understanding, especially with Latin America, and failed to support additional antidiscrimination bills before the Texas Legislature. Consulate and LULAC representatives expressed the same disappointment in local newspapers and announced a coordinated campaign to put pressure on Texas officials.[54]

The next episode in the public negotiations over the ban occurred in September 1943 when Padilla invited Stevenson to Mexico's previously noted

Alonso Perales, ca. 1949. (Photographer: Russell Lee, Russell Lee Photographic Collection, Center for American History, University of Texas at Austin.)

Independence Day celebration. Stevenson, still perturbed by Padilla's rejection of his good neighborly initiatives during the summer, used the opportunity to conduct a well-publicized tour in Mexico to demonstrate that he was sincere about improving Mexican-Anglo relations in the state. The tour took him to the four Mexican states bordering Texas: Tamaulipas, Coahuila, Nuevo León, and Chihuahua. The official receptions and welcoming statements that state officials extended to the governor gave added legitimacy to his goodwill tour. At Chihuahua, for instance, the interim governor expressed confidence that Stevenson would successfully implement his state's Good Neighbor Policy.[55]

George I. Sanchez, ca. 1940. (Nettie Lee Benson Latin American Collection, University of Texas at Austin.)

The Mexican government clearly welcomed the opportunity for rapprochement with the governor. Avila Camacho and other Mexican officials, however, continued to insist on the ban. This two-track diplomacy was obvious when Avila Camacho and Padilla granted Stevenson a place of honor at the National Palace, while Alejandro Carrillo, a congressman aligned with the famed leftist labor federation La Confederación de Trabajadores Mexicanos, chairman of the Committee on Mexicans in the Exterior, a faculty member of the National Workers' University of Mexico, and former Mexican consul in San Antonio, announced Mexico's continuing support for the ban during the patriotic celebration in San Antonio.[56]

The San Antonio daily, *La Prensa,* announced that Carrillo delivered a message of concern from Avila Camacho. According to Carrillo, the president "follows with great interest the experiences of Mexicans who find themselves in Texas and in the other entities of the United States."[57] Not unlike Domínguez and other Mexican officials, Carrillo did not limit himself to the problem of discrimination against Mexicans, but leveled a major broadside against racial discrimination as a whole. He pointed out that the wartime relations between Mexico and the United States, "present the opportunity to consolidate the Mexico-American friendship, to avoid cases of racial discrimination that are absolutely contrary to the democratic spirit evident in all the American nations, where the worth of human beings is not measured by

Manuel C. Gonzales, 1930s. (Nettie Lee Benson Latin American Collection, University of Texas at Austin.)

the shape of the cranium, the color of their skin or their eyes; the acceptance of this false theory would be tantamount to declaring ourselves followers of Hitler."[58]

If Texas officials still had doubts regarding Mexico's opposition to discrimination and its commitment to the ban, these were dispelled after the Mexico City festivities, during a meeting between Padilla and members of the newly created Committee on Mexicans in the Exterior in the Chamber of Deputies. The committee proclaimed that its members would remain focused on "the numerous cases of racial discrimination affecting Mexicans." They also urged Padilla to advise Mexicans over the radio about taking their complaints of discrimination to their local consul. Stevenson's inopportune statements during a Mexico City press conference may have prompted this action. The governor, according to William P. Allen, the editor of the *Laredo Times,* told a group of Mexican journalists with personal knowledge of discrimination in Texas that the complaints were few and highly exaggerated. Allen reported to the ever-vigilant Sanchez that the governor "tried to minimize these facts to a half a dozen incidents."[59]

Stevenson was obviously sounding the limits of the Good Neighbor Policy; he did not publicly agree that discrimination was as serious as the Mexican consuls and civil rights leaders described it. Also, he may not have

Carlos E. Castañeda, ca. 1940. (Nettie Lee Benson Latin American Collection, University of Texas at Austin.)

seriously intended to significantly change relations between Mexicans and Anglos. He was mostly interested in conceding the necessary measure of good neighborliness to lift the ban. The narrow and generally ineffective influence of the state's Caucasian Race Resolution and the GNC suggests this. The state's reluctant view of discrimination became more evident when the state ended its Good Neighbor Policy at the same time that Mexico was forced by circumstances along the border to drop the ban.

Mexico ended the ban in 1947 primarily because farmers were able to circumvent it. Although Texas farmers were denied Braceros during the war and often found it difficult to evade the Mexican policy that discouraged Mexicans from migrating into Texas, they were always able to recruit workers along the border. When growing numbers of Mexicans migrated to the Mexican side of the border, between 1945 and 1947, it became easier for Texas farmers to recruit them. In 1947, U.S. border officials at El Paso underscored Mexico's futility in stemming the flow when they encouraged Mexicans to cross onto U.S. soil, legalized their status, and made them available to farmers and their recruiters. Historians attribute the end of the ban to this incident.[60]

Mexico's use of the ban to negotiate an end to discrimination in Texas, however, had allowed Mexico, often in collaboration with LULAC, to wage a civil rights campaign on behalf of U.S.- and Mexico-born Mexicans in the United States. The campaign also extended its rhetorical reach into the general area of human rights and the cause against discrimination as a whole. Mexico selected Texas as the major test site for the Good Neighbor Policy because it was a principal point of destination for Mexican immigrants, the state's agricultural industry was highly dependent on Mexican labor, and Texas had the largest concentration of Mexicans in the United States. Mexicans from Texas also registered the greatest number of complaints of discrimination with Mexican government offices. Although Texas officials dictated the terms of the negotiations with a narrow focus on discrimination in business establishments and a program of public education to encourage Anglo understanding, the vigorous negotiations with Mexico elevated discrimination to a higher level of domestic and hemispheric importance. Mexico's ban and the open debate over discrimination that it stimulated in Texas also reinforced the wartime language of justice and democracy and prepared the ground for bringing the Good Neighbor Policy home. The expanded project, coordinated by the OCIAA, called on government agencies to extend their reach into Mexican communities. The work of the FEPC in Texas illustrates a key part of this transition, the attempt to more fully incorporate Mexican workers into the war effort.

Coordinating the Effort

Soon after the establishment of the Bracero Program and while the State Department was addressing the Sleepy Lagoon case in Los Angeles and the political wrangling in Texas, the OCIAA acted on another front that brought attention to Mexican workers in the Southwest. It called on other federal agencies to join in a campaign to address problems affecting the Mexican community. By the end of 1942, the OCIAA was hosting interagency meetings that included the FEPC, indicating that government officials gave employment discrimination a great deal of importance. According to Laves, the OCIAA was to keep a "weather eye" open for trouble and act as if "riding herd on the rest of the federal bureaus." The FEPC, like other governmental agencies, thereafter acted more deliberately in providing Mexicans the wartime opportunities offered to other workers. The renewed interest in Mexicans led the FEPC to establish regional offices in the Southwest during the summer of 1943, and it led to a substantial increase in the number of Mexican complaints of discrimination against wartime industries and unions. The FEPC, as some historians have pointed out, may have failed to produce significant changes in the segregated workplaces of wartime industries. It also may have been slow in coming to the aid of Mexican workers, almost two years after its creation. The OCIAA campaign, however, made a difference in bringing the FEPC to places like Texas. The measure of its success would be determined by the federal government's unprecedented attention to Mexicans in the Southwest as well as by the FEPC's investigations, settlements, and the encouragement that it gave the Mexican cause for equal rights, a subject that will be examined later in the study.[61]

As previously noted, some government agencies had already noticed the Mexican community during the early 1940s. This interest, however, remained limited until the OCIAA established the Minorities Section and initiated its coordinated campaign. The WMC is a case in point. The agency established the Minority Groups Branch within its Office of Production Management, and it set up the regional FEPC office in El Paso during the summer of 1942. This was a departure from the apparent indifference that the FEPC had demonstrated in October 1941, when it convened its first Southwest hearing on employment discrimination in Los Angeles that focused on African American workers. A preponderant national concern for blacks and a lack of resources during its early history may explain the agency's focus, even when its attention was being drawn to the Southwest. This changed soon after the spring of 1942, around the time that Will Alexander was reporting a new Washington interest in Mexicans and the OCIAA was establishing its Inter-American Division and Minorities Section. It was at this time that the FEPC, under instructions from the WMC, set its mark on the Arizona–New Mexico–West Texas region.[62]

The FEPC office in El Paso was responding to complaints from public officials, like Senator Dennis Chavez, a central figure in a national network of Mexican leaders that included LULAC members. He claimed that discrimination was so widespread in the three-state region that it was impairing production in a critical industry, denying Mexicans equal employment opportunities, and undermining relations with Latin America, especially Mexico. Once the WMC decided to investigate the numerous complaints submitted by Mexican workers, its representatives began to voice similar concerns that linked employment discrimination with Mexican rights and inter-American relations. As public officials expressed their concerns, the FEPC staff in El Paso set out to implement the nation's nondiscrimination policy. Ernest G. Trimble, the principal field representative in El Paso, found that the mining companies practiced widespread discrimination and maintained racially segregated workplaces. His efforts to settle workers' complaints, however, failed because the companies resisted FEPC findings and directives and the agency did not have the necessary authority to enforce the nation's nondiscrimination policy.[63]

In addition to the problem of recalcitrant employer representatives, who either denied discrimination or stalled compliance with FEPC directives, disagreements among the agency's officials on whether to seek plant-by-plant or industry-wide settlements undermined Trimble's work. The final setback occurred when the State Department blocked the FEPC's decision to hold an industry-wide hearing in El Paso scheduled for September 1942. State Department officials feared that the public hearing would draw public attention to discrimination and impair relations with Mexico. They were also concerned that Mexico would capitalize on admissions of discrimination to challenge the United States' Good Neighbor Policy in the Americas. Some Mexico officials agreed to minimize public discussion over discrimination; they had not yet embraced the idea of fully publicizing their views. The FEPC closed its El Paso offices and practically ended its brief fight with the copper industry until the OCIAA prompted it to renew its efforts and the president's Executive Order 9346 of May 1943 made it possible for the FEPC to expand its operations into other parts of the Southwest.[64]

The FEPC's early efforts coincided with the initial flurry of government interest in the Mexican community that the OCIAA encouraged during the first half of 1942. The OCIAA had been calling on other agencies to promote good neighborliness and its representatives had successfully moderated the conflict at Los Angeles in the fall. The work of coordinating an interagency campaign began later, in November 1942. In the meantime and for the duration of the war, the OCIAA sponsored or encouraged educational and public information activities that promoted good neighborliness primarily in southwestern communities. This included the establishment of inter-American committees responsible for coordinating the "neighborly" activities of local organizations. The OCIAA encouraged these organizations and projects to assist Mexicans with their everyday material needs and to direct public educational campaigns in support of wartime unity and racial understanding.[65] The OCIAA also provided financial and technical support for self-help efforts at the Barelas Community Center, founded by LULAC in Albuquerque, and the Taos County Project. The OCIAA also helped to launch the GNC and a community project in Chicago.[66]

Laves called the first interagency meeting to order on November 13, 1942. The participants included the OCIAA, the State Department, the Bureau of the Budget, the War Production Board, the War Labor Board, the Board of Economic Warfare, and the Office of Price Administration. The purpose of the meeting was "to explore the possibilities of using the facilities of the various agencies in an effort to deal with the Spanish-speaking minority problem in general, and the Los Angeles situation in particular."[67] The collaborating agencies were encouraged to see their work as an important contribution to hemispheric unity. The OCIAA staff was especially interested in assisting the Department of Agriculture, the War Relocation Authority, and the Farm Security Administration to jointly address claims of discrimination against Braceros.[68]

By the time the OCIAA called the second interagency meeting on December 10, 1942, the Office of the Budget had approved its operating fund. This allowed the agency to fund more "inter-American" activities and to further advance its coordinating work. The meeting included twenty-four participants from fourteen government offices, a clear indication that the wartime program on the Spanish-speaking had acquired more importance. Laves chaired the meeting and the participants agreed on new areas of emphasis for the "comprehensive program." Representatives from the Office of War Information reported on their public relations work in Los Angeles, while others from the California Farm Security Administration and the State Department informed the meeting on diplomatic and logistical issues related to the Bracero Program. Laves also spoke about the OCIAA's renewed work, including a major emphasis on employment discrimination against Mexicans in wartime industries. This focus was also evident in the statements by Lawrence Cramer, the Executive Secretary of the FEPC, and Alexander, the OPM official who announced in February 1942 the beginnings of the OCIAA-led campaign.[69]

Cramer was especially active in the second meeting. He reported that the FEPC had been investigating "the alleged discrimination of Mexican workers by six or seven industries in the Southwest," and that three of them had agreed to comply with the president's executive order. His hope was that settlements in selected "major cases" would "bring the rest of the industries along." Alexander added that the "worst situation in the country" was in Texas and that "the worst offenders" were the oil companies of the Texas Gulf Coast. Alexander's comments foretold the agency's major offensive in Texas. By July the FEPC had established its regional office in Dallas and begun its investigation of the oil refineries of the Texas coast. By the summer of 1943, when the FEPC had established its Dallas office, the manpower agency was cooperating closely with the OCIAA, knowing that its work involved more than the full utilization of workers without regard to racial, national origin, or religious differences. It was also part of a broader national campaign to promote the Good Neighbor Policy and build hemispheric unity.[70]

Conclusion

The delayed attention that the FEPC gave Mexicans achieves special significance when cast within the diplomatic realm of the Second World War. This larger setting involved an uncommon combination of foreign pressures and domestic concerns over the incorporation of a socially "isolated" group with close ancestral ties to a co-belligerent and ally. The intervention of the Mexican government, moreover, served as the overriding factor in the decision by U.S. officials to give expression to what Rosario Green and Peter H. Smith have elsewhere described as intermestic concerns, a preoccupation with issues that are international and domestic "at the same time."[71] The policy decision to "rehabilitate" the Mexican community and to improve interethnic understanding required that federal agencies, including the FEPC, incorporate Mexicans more fully into their areas of responsibility. To state this differently, Mexicans from the United States partly entered the center stage in the political arena of minority and labor politics by way of an international, or more precisely hemispheric, body politic. Mexican government officials, facing criticism for their agreements of cooperation with the North Americans, wished to demonstrate a measure of independence by testing the United States' Good Neighbor Policy, especially its declared wartime aim of improving understanding and goodwill throughout the Americas. The give and take between Mexican and U.S. officials played out dramatically around the Texas ban. It involved the conventional private channels of communication; but it was the frequent public claims and promulgations that began in the last half of 1942 that gave the negotiations their unique character.

Broadcasting discrimination as an obstacle to inter-American unity and publicly negotiating individual settlements or Good Neighbor Policy decisions was significant in another way. Although Mexico's policy and advocacy on behalf of Mexicans in the United States theoretically contradicted the principal of nonintervention, the key building block in the edifice of continental unity, it functioned as a separate point of diplomatic understanding, one that stressed human rights in another domestic jurisdiction and that redefined and further broadened the area of cooperation between Mexico and the United States. The foreign ministers from Latin America had insisted on the principle of nonintervention during their meetings in the 1930s and early 1940s, hopeful that the need for continental unity would cause the United States to end its history of military and diplomatic interference in the internal affairs of its southern neighbors. The U.S. agreed to this form of nonintervention and demonstrated it during the Mexican oil crisis. When Cardenas expropriated the oil industry and the oil companies demanded that the United States intervene on their behalf, Roosevelt retreated from a confrontation with Mexico and reinforced international legal understandings on national sovereignty. This affirmation, however, did not question Mexico's legal right to protect its subjects in another country nor did it lead the United States to claim an overriding legal jurisdiction over foreign-born persons within its borders. Instead, Mexico was able to proceed, if only for the duration of the war, with its vigorous campaign for Mexican rights in the United States without upsetting other noninterventionist sensibilities in the Americas. Mexico also made use of international norms and its own official repudiation of racial discrimination around the globe to strengthen its advocacy work for Mexican rights as well as the larger issue of human rights in the United States.

The U.S. government's continuing entry into the world of labor and minority rights during the war had its advantages and disadvantages for the Mexican population in the United States. The promotion of the Good Neighbor Policy and the use of a language of justice, democracy, and reciprocity that was associated with it provided the justification for quick and, to some extent, effective attention to the problems of discrimination and inequality. Of special significance was the way that the war emergency created by Pearl Harbor prompted governmental agencies to consolidate and advance their previously unfocused and ineffective efforts. This attention, however, was mostly dependent on the broader campaign to build hemispheric unity, especially Mexico's bargaining ability to encourage the United States to act on behalf of Mexicans. For reasons that are still not known, Mexico discontinued its forthright policy of advocacy for Mexican rights after the war. The Mexican community in the United States was thus left to elaborate its cause for equality largely without the help of the Mexican government.

Mexico's intervention nevertheless produced observable results. Using its position as a key ally, Mexico influenced the United States to broaden the scope of its Good Neighbor Policy. This resulted in converting discrimination and the plight of Mexicans in the United States into issues of hemispheric importance. Although much of the focus of the United States' expanded Good Neighbor Policy continued to be Latin America, the attention that Mexicans received was unprecedented and may have encouraged them to expect the U.S. government to assume a more active role on their behalf. Moreover, it loosened the hold of segregation and anticipated a more active role that the state was to play in their lives and the lives of other minority groups during the postwar period. One can only conjecture on the extent to which more determined and effective state action and improved recovery experiences could have contributed to a more equitable experience for Mexicans on the home front.

State action, a primary subject in this chapter, offered a singular opportunity for correcting or ameliorating the problem of inequality in society. Whether prompted primarily by pressures from the Mexican government or initiated mostly as a concern within the United States' body politic, the activist state offered a limited and ineffective response to the prejudice and discrimination that contributed significantly to Mexican inequality. Historians agree that the lack of resources and conservative opposition in places like the South and the Southwest contributed to the lack of effectiveness of the OCIAA and the FEPC, the two agencies that played a central role in bringing the Good Neighbor Policy to the home front. The public negotiations over Braceros in Texas magnified other problems. Despite initially impressive initiatives and some public support for them, the State Department, the OCIAA, the Texas legislature, and the governor's office maintained a greater interest in securing an end to the ban than in effectuating substantial changes in social relations. This narrow approach, whether reflecting a moderate New Deal outlook or the path of least resistance in a conservative environment, limited the purview of the state to discrimination in business establishments and an emphasis on improving the public's view of the Mexican. Texas officials also may have decided to restrict the terms of the negotiations because they feared that the Mexican government, LULAC activists, and African American civil rights leaders would push for a more broadly constructed civil rights law.

LULAC played a central role in drawing attention to Mexicans in Texas. In the process, the organization did more than collaborate with the Mexican government and figure in the decision by the U.S. government to apply its Good Neighbor Policy at home. At the same time that LULAC helped to internationalize the Mexican cause in the United States, it became the leading civil rights organization in the Mexican community. LULAC's rise to prominence had two origins. The close relationships that individual leaders had with Mexican consulate offices explains to some extent their participation in joint campaigns on behalf of U.S.-born and Mexico-born Mexicans. Washington officials clearly viewed LULAC as a moderate and favored alternative to other Mexican organizations. The favored treatment that LULAC enjoyed added to its legitimacy as the primary Mexican civil rights organization during the war. LULAC leaders, as we shall see in later chapters, also contributed to the organization's rise to prominence with energetic and astute political campaigns on behalf of Mexicans in the United States.[72]

At other times, LULAC may have acted primarily as a moderate and middle class organization that argued for the rights of the U.S.-born Mexicans with a narrow claim of whiteness and U.S. citizenship. During the war, however, its leaders also used the discourse of good neighborliness and collaborated with the Mexican government in crafting a strategy that emphasized a common cause with Mexican nationals and a critique of racial discrimination as a whole. This is not to say that LULAC activists did not emphasize whiteness in challenging racial discrimination or that they did not use citizenship to make moral and constitutional arguments on their behalf. Their political ethos was broad. It included a Mexicanist, or internationalist, identity that stressed their bonds as Mexicans as well as a Mexican Americanist, or ethnic, orientation that focused on U.S.-born Mexicans. LULAC also critiqued racial discrimination and embraced a labor plank to accompany its well-known fight against discrimination in the schools and public establishments. The following chapter provides a closer examination of LULAC to explain how the fortuitous diplomatic circumstance created by the war encouraged the organization to make use of the FEPC to elaborate a campaign for labor rights.

Chapter 4: The Fight for Mexican Rights in Texas

In 1943, when the owner of the American Café in the Texas panhandle town of Levelland refused to serve a Mexican farm worker, Texans learned how quickly Mexican officials could turn a local case of discrimination into an issue of international importance. At another time, it would have been a routine, though serious, matter for the Mexican government to ask the State Department to investigate an act of discrimination. But by 1943, Mexican officials had become more assertive and at times uncompromising, especially when local Spanish-language newspapers, Mexican consuls, and Mexican civil rights leaders would join in openly condemning discrimination. Mexican officials, as well as LULAC leaders with whom they often allied themselves, were bold with their repeated use of the wartime language of democracy, generously punctuated with references to the United States' Good Neighbor Policy and Mexico's position as its principal ally in the Americas.

The United States government usually responded immediately to complaints that arrived in consular offices and the Mexican embassy. Time and again, the State Department agreed with Mexico's claims against discrimination by invoking the United States' commitment to improved relations in the Americas and by interceding in cases like the Levelland incident. The ensuing discourse, along with the efforts to settle local cases of discrimination, reproduced the larger process of inter-American cooperation. No longer was discrimination against Mexicans a domestic issue or kept out of diplomatic sight as back-channel communication. Stated differently, the war against

"El Grito de Guerra." (Artist: David Arreola, Secretaría de Gobernación, Mexico. Harry Ransom Humanities Research Center, University of Texas at Austin.)

fascism opened a Mexican fight on the home front against discrimination that matched the Double V campaign associated with the African American cause.

This chapter examines the LULAC's push for civil and labor rights and its relationship with two national initiatives: Mexico's advocacy policy and the United States' Good Neighbor Policy. LULAC's collaborative middle position was exemplified by Manuel C. Gonzales, who was the secretary general of the organization in Texas during the war and the legal counsel for the Mexican consulate at San Antonio between the early 1930s and late 1940s. George I. Sanchez and Carlos Castañeda also demonstrated their organization's mediating position by serving prominently in U.S. and state government positions. Their links to the corresponding national policies provided LULAC leaders an opportunity to advance their claims for equality with the language of justice and democracy as Americans, in the original sense of the word.

An international emphasis on the Mexican fight over civil and labor rights may seem to be directing our attention away from the domestic space that the FEPC and LULAC inhabited for most of their history. This discussion, however, would represent a digression if the FEPC had not been caught up in the politics of intergovernmental relations and LULAC had not joined with Mexican consulates in devising a broad political agenda during the Second World War. But they did. Moreover, FEPC officials understood that their work on behalf of Mexican workers had a bearing on relations with Mexico. LULAC leaders were also conscious of the international importance of their politics. They spoke openly, although not always in agreement, among themselves or others about the difficult conditions under which Mexicans worked, and they looked to Mexico, the FEPC, and the Good Neighbor Policy to help workers share in the recovery opportunities of the war. This can be best understood by first examining how LULAC made use of Mexican and U.S. policies to address discrimination in Texan schools and businesses.

The Educational Campaign

Despite LULAC's focus on discrimination in workplaces and business establishments, it is best known for its fight against discrimination and segregation in schools. Although other groups had a similar focus, LULAC was the first organization to lead a wide-ranging response to the problem of unequal educational opportunities. The organization began its work in 1930, less than a year after its founding, when it supported lawyers in the preparation of a legal challenge against school segregation at the Del Rio Independent School District in Southwest Texas. The Texas courts found it unconstitutional to segregate Mexican children on the basis of their national origins. The ruling declared, however, that the district had segregated Mexican children on acceptable pedagogical grounds, that is, the children received separate instruction because they lacked English language skills and attended irregularly or enrolled late because of their parents' migratory work. The decision may have undermined the racial justification for segregation, but it left intact the separate and unequal condition that Mexican plaintiffs were challenging. The disappointing court decision, along with the high legal costs, the dearth of attorneys willing to lead other legal fights, and the need to build a more effective base of support, may have discouraged LULAC members from continuing a legal strategy during the war. Instead, they adopted what educational historian Guadalupe San Miguel has called "a politics of persuasion," or a piecemeal approach to encourage greater civic participation among Mexican parents and to pressure school districts and public officials to improve local conditions.[1]

The politics of persuasion produced important results in the 1930s. In San Antonio, LULAC mobilized a successful school improvement campaign that placed pressure on local and state school officials to address problems such as underenrollment, overcrowded schools, and poor facilities. San Miguel also credits LULAC for playing a major role in establishing La Liga Pro-Defensa Escolar, a federation of over seventy-two community organizations committed to changing the predominantly Mexican schools in the West Side of San Antonio. He suggests that despite the successful organizing appeals of LULAC and others, public officials responded inconsistently and, as a result, San Antonio saw little change in their Mexican schools. The war, however, gave LULAC and their allies an added reason for continuing their politics of persuasion.[2]

When state education officials took the good neighborly cues from the State Department and the OCIAA and began to demonstrate greater interest in the Mexican community, the civil rights leadership opted for the less confrontational approach. The welcomed change involved the appointments of key individuals to important educational policy-making committees. Leading these appointments was Sanchez, the University of Texas professor who was the president of LULAC in 1941 and the director of the university-based Executive Committee on Inter-American Relations in the Southwest in 1943. That same year, he became the chair of the Statewide Committee on

Inter-American Education in the State Department of Education. Castañeda and Connie Garza Brockette, a longtime educator in Texas, also served on the committee. The following year Garza Brockette became the director of the Division of Education and Teacher Aids in the OCIAA in Washington. Sanchez, Castañeda, and Garza Brockette had known each other, primarily through LULAC, and they continued to collaborate with Anglo allies in the educational reform efforts of the war years. Other Mexicans were named to the Planning Committee and the Production Committee which were responsible for promoting inter-American understanding in the schools partly by developing teaching materials that incorporated the Spanish language and Latin American subjects into the curriculum.[3]

Adding to the change was the 1941 initiative by the state legislature that allowed school districts to include Spanish-language instruction in selected grades beyond the second year. The measure was inspired by the wartime spirit of inter-American cooperation and most probably suggested by Sanchez and other officials associated with the State Department and the OCIAA. The legislation expanded Spanish-language instruction and integrated Latin American cultural activities into the curriculum.[4] Teacher training programs at colleges and universities—Texas College of Arts and Industries in Kingsville, Southwest Texas State University at San Marcos, Our Lady of the Lake College in San Antonio, the University of Texas at Austin and Sul Ross University at Alpine—joined in the effort by incorporating the idea of inter-American understanding into their academic programs and teacher training workshops. The workshops and the curriculum that the teacher-participants developed often received funding from the OCIAA and coincided with LULAC efforts to establish parent-teacher organizations and to encourage the participation of Mexican parents in their schools. The promise of inter-American education, however, began to fade.[5]

Despite the important appointments, curricular changes, and teacher education programs, LULAC leaders became discouraged by the slow rate and narrow breadth of change. They were especially disenchanted with education officials who seemed more interested in improving relations with hemispheric allies than in ending segregation and even acknowledging the presence of Mexicans in Texas. The curricular changes, for instance, typically incorporated cultural representations from Latin America and dismissed local Mexican communities. Segregation in the form of separate facilities and classrooms also remained in place. Educational reform in Texas, in other words, revealed the limits of inter-Americanism. Despite the frequent allusions by federal and state officials to a broadly conceived program of action that included Mexican-Anglo relations in various areas of national life, the focus on international relations largely dictated educational change.[6]

Sanchez leveled one of the clearest critiques against the deceptive nature of inter-American education. He urged Anglo administrators and teachers to promote hemispheric unity by recognizing the educational needs of Mexican children at the home front. While speaking before the National Congress of Parents and Teachers in 1942, Sanchez added that the continuing problems of discrimination and segregation did "more harm to Pan-Americanism than a shipload of Nazi agents." Discrimination, he believed, tested the United States' ability to live up to its promise of good neighborliness to the 120 million Spanish-speaking people in the Latin American republics. Sanchez connected the problem of discrimination to the reluctance to fully acknowledge the Mexican in the classroom when he concluded that it was simply unjust and downright un-American to be "interested in the Mexican across the border but not in the one across the tracks."[7]

Against the Denial of Service

LULAC leaders also devoted much of their time to the denial of service in public establishments. Perales, for instance, collected hundreds of affidavits from aggrieved Mexicans claiming discrimination and submitted them to state and federal agencies, including the GNC. He also made the list and other related materials available to U.S. officials, including Senator Chavez. Perales and other civil rights leaders also addressed the problem extensively in the press, obviously believing that their claims would encourage additional complaints and strengthen the overall cause.[8] The denial of service was not necessarily more common or momentous than discrimination in the schools or at work. But it was more public and often more dramatic, especially when the press and civil rights leaders publicized the most flagrant cases involving Mexican servicemen, farm workers, and diplomats.

LULAC leaders gave wide publicity to cases involving Mexicans in the U.S. military partly to underscore the view that Mexicans deserved equal treatment by virtue of their battlefield contributions. Denying them service suggested contempt of the highest order because neither military service nor personal sacrifice seemed to exempt them from discrimination.[9] Their impressive military record and the sense of indignation that the offended servicemen and their families expressed also added drama to the problem. Mexicans were among the first Americans to see action in the Pacific theater.

One out of every four soldiers in the infamous Battan death march was of Mexican origin. Mexican families from Texas sent more soldiers per home to the front. Mexican military personnel were also well represented in the death and casualty lists of South Texas. Their record continued unfolding at war's end. More than two hundred and fifty thousand Mexicans, including approximately fifteen thousand Mexican nationals, served in the U.S. military. Although their record of bravery and gallantry would not be completely known until after the war—they received a higher proportion of Medals of Honor and Silver Stars than any other ethnic group in the country—newspapers provided a day-by-day account of their disproportionate contribution to the war in the form of casualty and death figures as well as an impressive number of commendations.[10]

Servicemen and their families may not have contributed the most complaints to the discourse over discrimination; however, they registered them in growing numbers, and their spirited complaints attracted much public attention. Salvador Guerrero, a young recruit from West Texas, expressed a familiar form of resentment after the war: "Though we Mexican Americans had contributed zealously to the crusade to save democracy from Hitler, the war had done little for the Mexican Americans of San Angelo. For one thing, we were still refused service at various public places, even when wearing our uniforms."[11] Their greater sensitivity to discrimination no doubt reflected a realization that even battlefield sacrifices could not guarantee them equal consideration at home. The large number of complaints registered by Mexican servicemen during the war also resulted from their greater movement on furlough or on the way to report for duty. While traveling beyond their familiar environments they often entered segregated businesses inadvertently. On the other hand, some of the soldiers may have anticipated an unfriendly reception and decided to assert their rights, bring attention to the need for wartime unity, and confront the discriminatory behavior. Pvt. George M. Villarreal suggested this much in a letter to Governor Stevenson when he related a case of discrimination against a fellow serviceman in his hometown of San Benito: "when we were in civilian life it was OK to be push[ed] around, but now in War time—well it's tough in this way."[12]

The most celebrated case involved Sgt. Macario García, a resident of Sugarland, native of Villa Costaño, Coahuila, México, and the third Mexican soldier to receive the Congressional Medal of Honor. The LULAC council from Houston had honored García as a war hero in September 1945. Shortly thereafter, a local civic club decided to also pay him tribute with a luncheon. On the way to the function, the uniformed García stopped at the Oasis Café

President Harry S. Truman pinning the Congressional Medal of Honor on Sergeant Macario García, 1945. (John J. Herrera Collection, Houston Metropolitan Research Center, Houston Public Library, Houston, Texas.)

in nearby Richmond for a cup of coffee. The waitress, according to García, announced that, "Mexicans were not served at that place." When he protested, a fight broke out with the owner and an Anglo customer armed with a baseball bat. Injuries prevented García from reaching the Houston luncheon. The well-publicized incident, according to Castañeda, "aroused much heated comment" among government officials and the press in Mexico as well as Mexican civil rights leaders in Texas. The commonly heard concern was that discriminatory practices in Texas contradicted the egalitarian principles that the United States was proclaiming.[13]

Denials of service involving Mexican government officials also triggered protests. Although these cases were less common than the ones involving servicemen, they too elevated discrimination to a level of international proportions because the practice disregarded diplomatic protocol and underscored that prejudice was widespread. Federal and state officials from the United States frequently admitted the affronts, issued statements disavowing discrimination, and communicated their displeasure with the offending parties. They just as often stated that their citizenry was generally lagging behind the official lead offered by the Good Neighbor Policy. It is impossible to know the extent to which stubborn segregationists impaired the wartime policy of racial understanding and how a cultural lag may have contributed to the problem. The consequence of discrimination against Mexican public officials was clearer. A report by Leonard Outhwaite, a Farm Security Administration official, underscored the official concern when he pointed out that discrimination against Mexican public officials as well as business persons was impairing relations with Mexico.[14]

Mexican diplomats and other well-placed individuals often traveled between Mexico and the United States on official business. Their movement exposed them to segregated businesses throughout the state. The staff and families of Mexican consuls were especially vulnerable. They often traveled to Mexican communities to participate in local festivities, investigate complaints of discrimination, and inspect the patriotic and philanthropic work of their affiliate organizations, the Comisión Honorífica and the Cruz Azul. Although the consulate staff may have often been uninformed about the segregationist businesses that they visited, their hosts were not. Some of the Mexican officials may have decided to challenge the owners of these establishments once local Mexicans apprised them of the practice. The relatively few complaints that they registered, however, suggest that they most often declined this opportunity and chose to make the fight on the basis of the complaints that they received from local residents. When such cases occurred, however, the position and status of Mexican officials usually drew a swift reaction and considerably more public notice than other confrontations with discrimination. A case in point is the highly publicized incident involving Eugenio Prado and a restaurant in Pecos, a town approximately 150 miles east of El Paso.

Prado was a senator from Mexico, a respected medical doctor, and president of the Chamber of Deputies, or the Mexican Congress. Prado was not alone when the owner of the Lone Star Cafe refused him service in March 1945. Accompanying him were two other members of the Mexican Chamber of Deputies, Arturo Chávez and Teófilo Borunda. All three represented the border state of Chihuahua. We do not know the total number in the group or why they were in Pecos. The editors of *La Prensa* made a reference to official wartime business when they reported that the group was on a "good neighbor tour." Although the newspaper reports from San Antonio and Mexico City noted that the affront was first and foremost a slight against Prado and Mexico, they also pointed out that discrimination was extensive in Texas and that it undermined democracy and the war effort.[15] The "Pecos Incident," in other words, reminded everyone that some Texans insisted on treating Mexicans differently regardless of how this contradicted the United States' alliance with Mexico and its declared wartime aim of promoting and protecting the democratic rights of Mexicans in the United States.[16]

The editors of *La Prensa*, well-versed in international norms, offered one of the more striking critiques by noting how the Prado case contradicted the high-sounding statements associated with efforts at building inter-American unity. According to the newspaper, the U.S. secretary of state, Edward R. Stettinius, only days before the incident had announced to the Mexican Congress that "the era of international inequality has disappeared," and that "all nations, big and small, powerful and weak, have the same rights before the law." The editors also noted that the delegates to the Chapultepec Conference—the Inter-American Conference on Problems of War and Peace—had recently proclaimed in Mexico City "the victory of brotherhood and the defeat of the doctrine of racial superiority." It had not been long, they added, since the United States began its preparations to attend the founding meeting of the United Nations "where a new world will be established on the basis of justice and democratic principles." At this time of great optimism, after a long process of building international safeguards against "the ominous dangers of the hour," "a sinister citizen from Texas" turned down Prado, Chavez, and Borunda because they were Mexicans.[17]

Writers for *La Prensa* were not alone in dramatizing the Prado case. Perales also referred to it in newspaper articles, public presentations, and testimony before a congressional committee that was conducting hearings on the bill introduced by Senator Chavez to extend the life of the FEPC beyond the war. In Mexico City, *Fraternidad,* the official organ of the highly regarded Comité en Contra el Racismo, also covered the incident alongside other stories that compared segregationists in Texas with Nazis in Europe. Enrique González Martínez, the president of the Comité, drove the point further with a statement of protest that Perales circulated widely in the United States. A group of Mexican residents from Pecos also joined in sensationalizing the case and in pointing out that discrimination victimized Mexicans regardless of nativity. In a letter to *La Prensa* and the governor's office, Alfonso A. Orozco noted, "There is hate, resentment, animosity and discrimination against Latin Americans in the city of Pecos. We are denied our right to enjoy our American rights." His emphasis was on a right derived from his American, or hemispheric, citizenship and discrimination as an everyday experience, a point that migratory farm workers also understood.[18]

Migratory workers faced more rejections in businesses than servicemen or highly regarded visitors from Mexico. The growth of the migratory workforce contributed to the higher incidence of discrimination. The number of migratory farm workers in a particular locale varied depending on the seasonal nature of agricultural production, that is, the workers congregated in different places as the cotton plants maturated in a northern and northeastern direction. Also, growers in the southeastern, central, and western parts of the state allotted more land to cotton production during the war and consequently drew more workers when their crops matured. The sudden appearance of large numbers of migratory workers increased the anxiety level among Anglo residents who were already bothered by the presence of local Mexicans. The USES offered one of the more reliable estimates of the migratory workforce. In 1923, its staff contacted as many as three hundred and twenty-five thousand migratory workers heading to Texas farms and out-of-state destinations, mostly in the Midwest. By 1939, the figure had increased to five hundred and fifty thousand. More than 80 percent of them were Mexican.[19]

As previously noted, most of the farm workers began their trek in northern Mexico and the Rio Grande Valley. The migratory pattern converged at border points such as Brownsville, McAllen, Laredo, and El Paso and grew exponentially as it moved in a northern and northeastern direction. They first harvested cotton in the Rio Grande Valley and traveled up the Gulf Coast towards Corpus Christi and the Central and North Texas regions. The workforce moved into West Texas around October, November, and December and then traveled back for the onion harvest in the Laredo area and the fruit, vegetable, and bean harvest in the Rio Grande Valley and the surrounding region. Families spent most of the winter doing off-season work in the fields as well as other laboring jobs in the South Texas towns. The cycle began again in the early part of the summer.[20]

West Texas towns located on the migratory route became especially known for the unfriendly reception that they extended to Mexican farm workers. Although farmers in the area welcomed and even recruited them, numerous residents in the towns reacted against the large numbers of Mexicans seeking provisions, a haircut, or a movie on Saturdays. Adding to the tension and conflict were self-respecting and daring farm workers who would not stomach the rejection. On some occasions they, like some servicemen and the occasional Mexican official, accidentally walked into businesses where they were not wanted. At other times, they entered knowing that the proprietor would not give them service and that they would protest the affront. Sometimes these protests involved a decision not to pick cotton in the area.[21]

The GNC noted one case in November 1944 when a group of Mexican workers boycotted West Texas farmers. A crew leader and at least two of the workers had traveled with a labor agent from Levelland to nearby Ropesville to examine a farmer's cotton fields and had agreed on the terms of the cotton-picking contract. Before leaving Ropesville, the workers and the agent stopped at a restaurant for a cup of coffee. The proprietor refused to serve the farm workers and reportedly told the agent, "I'll serve you, but I don't serve Mexicans." The agent, obviously worried that the workers would renege on their contract with the farmer, admonished the restaurant owner. Despite his good intentions, the farm workers refused to pick the cotton the next day.[22]

The earlier, well-publicized refusal of service in Levelland may explain why the farm workers reacted so stubbornly at Ropesville. Migratory workers had been coming to Levelland in significant numbers since 1937 when local farmers converted the town's fair park and exposition building into sleeping quarters for them. On a Saturday, October 30, 1943, they began congregating in town to buy supplies, socialize, and rest. A group of them entered a small restaurant and words were exchanged when the proprietor refused them service. According to several reports, T. C. Ticer, the restaurant owner, struck Domingo Vela on the head with a soda bottle. When the injured seventeen-year-old from New Braunfels and his companions walked out, Ticer followed them and shouted threats to other workers who had gathered in front of the restaurant. The disgruntled group quickly grew to one thousand. The frantic county sheriff reportedly called in reinforcements from nearby towns and, according to one observer, averted a more serious conflict.[23]

The Levelland disturbance was one of many conflicts involving farm workers that attracted public and official attention. This time, Mexico took special measures, most probably because of the large numbers of workers involved and the fear that the incident could escalate into a more serious conflict. Mexican officials also used the incident to strengthen their case for the Texas ban, soon after Stevenson's Good Neighbor Policy pronouncements and goodwill tour in northern Mexico. The Mexican Foreign Affairs Office, after receiving initial reports and complaints from consuls at Austin and El Paso, instructed the consulate general from San Antonio to investigate. After his investigation and finding of discrimination, the consulate general informed the Mexican embassy that the U.S. government should conduct its own investigations and that it should place real and effective sanctions on the perpetrators. The Mexican government shared the San Antonio report and other internal official correspondence with the State Department. U.S. diplomats responded with assurances that Texas officials would address the case and continue to monitor the problem of discrimination in the state. The Committee on Mexicans in the Exterior, the agency that the National Chamber of Deputies established to monitor discrimination among its nationals in the United States, was less diplomatic. They concluded that the differences between Mexicans and Anglos "are the result of political propaganda spread by feudal lords of Texas who do not want to believe that slavery is gone."[24]

Most probably at the urging of Washington officials, Stevenson ordered Robert E. Smith, the president of the GNC, and Tom Sutherland, the field representative of the OCIAA, to investigate the case. The governor also instructed the state's attorney general to assign an attorney to assist local authorities in the prosecution of Ticer on charges of assault and disturbance of the peace. A jury eventually found Ticer innocent, but not before the State Department and the office of the governor had demonstrated their concern that discrimination was adversely affecting relations with Mexico. Smith and Sutherland tried, possibly with Stevenson's concurrence, to restore the state's soiled reputation by maintaining that the refusal of service at Levelland was an isolated incident. Mexican officials, however, disputed this view and charged that authorities in the United States could no longer assume that discriminatory practices were infrequent and of little consequence, as Stevenson had noted in his Mexico City press conference.[25]

The Levelland incident also revealed that Mexicans may have provoked such conflicts by entering a business known to refuse service to Mexicans. During the trial, one of the Mexican workers testified that the same restaurant owner refused service to a group of them on a previous occasion. Although the witness and his attorney were seeking to establish a pattern of discrimination, his testimony suggested that the workers entered the place knowing that they would be turned away. State officials did not accuse the complainants of inciting the conflict at Levelland; however, they made the accusation on other occasions. Businessmen who faced charges of discrimination often offered the same defense. They pointed out that Mexicans staged the contentious confrontations to bring public and official attention to discrimination and segregation as social ills of major proportions. The case that emerged in New Gulf, a company town near Houston, suggests that they were not always off the mark.

New Gulf

On September 16, 1943, the operator of the Blue Moon Cafe refused to serve John Herrera, a Houston attorney and state LULAC officer, J. V. Villarreal, a worker with the Texas Gulf Sulphur Company, and Adolfo G. Domínguez, the head of the Mexican consulate in Houston. The owner was adamant, according to a consular report: "not even the consul of Mexico will be served, unless he wants to be served in the kitchen."[26] Herrera and Domínguez had come to participate in the local Sixteenth of September celebration and to investigate complaints that most of the Mexican children from the nearby community of Boling were assigned to a separate Mexican school in New Gulf, a company town owned by the Texas Gulf Sulphur Company. According to their reports to the press and the Mexicans consulate, school officials also refused the few Mexicans who entered the only high school in town to join the football team or participate in other school activities. The Mexican parents from Boling and the town of Goose Creek reacted by refusing to send their children to the school.[27]

Domínguez submitted a report to the Mexican government on the refusal of service and the problems in the schools, and soon after that, on October 15, Mexico issued one of its major wartime protests against the segregation of Mexican children in Texas schools. Mexico gave the case serious attention from the very start. Avila Camacho, for instance, gave official weight to the case when he announced that he would be receiving a personal report on the case from Congressman Alejandro Carrillo, the same official who one month earlier had delivered the speech on behalf of the president during the Sixteenth of September festivities in San Antonio. Mexico's interventions led to condemnations by the State Department and the governor's office. There is no evidence that U.S. authorities took action against the restaurant operator or the local schools. Mexico's complaints, however, added weight to their claims against discrimination and no doubt contributed to the increased official attention given to the Mexican community. The New Gulf families and the Houston leaders, however, deserve the credit for initiating the protest.[28]

The main concern among the families that invited Herrera and Domínguez was school discrimination and segregation. They were also troubled about work-related issues at the New Gulf and Freeport plants of the Texas Gulf Sulphur Company. Herrera would later act as an intermediary between Castañeda and Mexicans from the area who complained of employment discrimination at the sulphur plants. The families obviously thought Herrera and Domínguez, well-known advocates of Mexican rights, could help them by drawing public attention to their grievances. This was a reasonable expectation. They were the best-known advocates for Mexican rights in the area. They also afforded New Gulf Mexicans access to the LULAC and Mexican consulate networks and the possibility that their protest could reach wider audiences and higher authorities. Moreover, the New Gulf families gave important symbolic meaning to their cause when they invited Herrera and Domínguez to participate as honored guests in their celebration of Mexico independence from colonial rule. The symbolism was obvious.[29]

Herrera and Domínguez most probably entered the Blue Moon Cafe knowing that they would be refused service and that this would allow them to call public attention to discrimination and the problem of segregation in the schools. The restaurant had a reputation of refusing service to Mexicans among the locals and Mexican consuls in the area. Luis L. Duplán, the Mexican consul from Austin and a good friend to Herrera and Domínguez, for instance, noted after the incident that Mexicans from the area had previously lodged complaints against the same restaurant. The restaurant owner, according to Duplán, continued to reject Mexicans in 1943, suggesting that he was a well-known segregationist.[30]

Herrera and Domínguez also must have known that a slight against two prominent members of the Mexican community, occurring at the same time that Mexican working-class parents were protesting segregation and celebrating national pride, could accentuate their claim of prejudice and discrimination against all Mexicans. Their quick decision to expand the New Gulf incident into a broad challenge against discrimination suggests that they already had this strategy in mind.[31] While Domínguez sent his confidential report and findings of school segregation to his superiors, Herrera submitted a complaint to the governor and publicized the experience in *La Prensa* and in *Mañana,* a popular newspaper from Mexico. Herrera, less restrained by diplomatic protocol, denounced the restaurant and school from New Gulf. The editors of *Mañana* held back even less when they characterized segregationists in the state as "the Nazis of Texas."[32] Herrera's emphasis, on the other hand, was on discrimination as an offense against Mexicans as a whole: an act that disregarded his citizenship, nativity, membership in a charter community, class background, professional status, leadership experience, and

Domínguez's diplomatic standing. He declared: "I am an American citizen, descendant of the founders of San Antonio, and a member of the Bar. I am also Secretary of the Lulac Council in that city. We were told in this place that I have mentioned that 'it is not important whether you are a doctor, lawyer or consul since not even to the Mexican consul are we able to give service here.' They invited us to go to the kitchen if we desired service."[33]

The incidents at Richmond, El Paso, and Levelland confirm Herrera's view that the denial of service at places like the Blue Moon Cafe denied Mexicans their rights as individuals and as a group. Moreover, Herrera and Domínguez drew on their civic imagination to prompt and publicize cases of discrimination for the purpose of heightening public and official attention on the widespread problem of discrimination and segregation. They also presented themselves as the defenders of what was morally just and constitutionally sound and described segregationists as the cause of racial conflict and wartime disunity. They did not stop there. As in the campaign against segregation in the schools, LULAC members collaborated with Mexican consular officials and helped to join the Mexican cause in Texas with the larger wartime struggle for democracy and justice in the Western hemisphere and throughout the world. Encouraged by the legitimating influence of this association, they also appealed, as we shall now see, for civil rights legislation as a demonstration of official concern and as a lasting solution to the problem of racial discrimination and segregation.

A Civil Rights Law

Mexican civil rights leaders from Texas did not limit themselves to soliciting complaints and bringing them to the GNC or to join with Mexican consuls to report on the continuing problem of discrimination. They also led in efforts to expose the limitations in the state's Good Neighbor Policy. A case in point is the Terrel Wells case. In July 1943, soon after the legislature had passed the Caucasian Race Resolution and the governor had issued the Good Neighbor Policy, a LULAC council from San Antonio set out to test its legal standing. Three prominent LULAC members with close ties to the general consulate office of San Antonio filed a motion for injunctive relief against a local bathhouse known as Terrel Wells. The three plaintiffs, Jacobo I. Rodríguez, a local LULAC officer and editor of *El Pan Americano,* Alberto Treviño, another prominent LULAC member, and Manuel C. Gonzales, had sought admission to the pool. When an attendant refused them because the owner had reportedly "issued orders that Mexican or Spanish people should not be admitted," they sought relief before the Seventy-Third Federal District Court on the grounds that the refusal of service violated the resolution.[34]

The district court granted the injunction citing the resolution as well as the governor's proclamation. The bathhouse owner, however, appealed the decision, and, during the early part of 1944, the Fourth Court of Civil Appeals reversed it. The court noted that, "In the absence of civil rights legislation to the contrary, we believe the proprietors of quasi-public places have a right to exclude whom they want to." They added that, "A mere resolution by the legislature and a proclamation by the governor does not have the effect of a statute." Gonzales announced that he would appeal the case to the Texas Supreme Court, but he was already convinced that the resolution did not have the weight of law and that LULAC and the Mexican consuls were justified in calling for a more effective civil rights law.[35]

LULAC lost no time reminding the public, as well as the governor and other state officials, that official proclamations did not guarantee an end to discrimination. The organization pointed to the failed effort to use the resolution and the governor's decree as well as the continuing cases of discrimination that Mexicans throughout the state were reporting to the GNC. Perales made one of the clearest appeals for action in an earlier interview with a reporter from *La Prensa:* "What we urgently need in Texas is a law by the Texas Legislature or the U.S. Congress that prohibits the humiliation of Mexicans in public establishments like restaurants, theaters, pools, etc., and a good concentration camp to put away for the duration of the war all the owners of such businesses as fifth-columnists, saboteurs of President Roosevelt's Good Neighbor Policy, and traitors to the Nation."[36] The court's verdict and the added pressure that the Mexican leadership exerted may explain why Stevenson and Kibbe abandoned their argument that the resolution had the force of law. This allowed Mexico to continue its claim during the war that Texas was not doing enough to make an appreciable dent on discrimination in the state.

Perales and his allies opened another front in the quest for a civil rights law. He played an especially important role in advancing the cause for civil rights legislation at three international assemblies: the Third Inter-American Bar Association Conference (Mexico City: July 31–August 8, 1944), the Inter-American "Chapultepec" Conference on Problems of War and Peace (Mexico City: February 21–March 8, 1945), and the founding meeting of the United Nations (San Francisco: April 25–June 26, 1945). His aim was to use the Mexican experience in the United States to demonstrate the need for the delegates to prod their respective governments, including the United States, into taking administrative or legal action against discrimination. In all three instances, Perales was able to join with other like-minded delegates and observers to influence the passage of resolutions or proclamations calling on governments to prohibit all forms of racial discrimination.

Perales sought the international stage for several reasons. First, Mexican officials associated with the president's office, the Office of Foreign Affairs, and the Chamber of Deputies had prepared the ground by internationalizing the issue of discrimination against Mexicans in Texas. Periodicals such as *La Prensa* and *Fraternidad,* with their constant attention to racial discrimination as an obstacle to hemispheric and worldwide understanding, also encouraged Perales. The persistence of racial discrimination along with the apparent reluctance by Texas and State Department officials to treat the fight against it in a more forceful manner also caused Perales to seek more receptive audiences. An added factor that explains Perales's actions was his experience as a public figure in Mexican politics and diplomatic circles. Aside from achieving prominence as a spokesman for the civil rights of Mexicans, Perales had participated in thirteen U.S. diplomatic missions to the Dominican Republic, Cuba, Nicaragua, Mexico, Chile, and the West Indies in the 1920s and 1930s. All along, larger encouraging forces were at work. By the early part of 1944, world leaders began to prepare for a postwar period of new political alignments, and they needed safeguards to avert another worldwide conflagration. The Inter-American Bar Association had this purpose in mind.[37]

The association convened delegates representing national and regional legal organizations from American nations. They exchanged views on national legal structures to accommodate more equal international relations and a more integrated system of commercial, political, and social interchange during the postwar period. The overarching concern, according to Padilla's opening speech, was to place limits on "the injudicious sovereignity [sic] of certain nations," meaning that the delegates were to seek ways to curb the excesses that large strong nations visited upon small weak ones. While the delegates mostly concerned themselves with legal and administrative understandings in the areas of trade and political relations, Perales joined with fellow representatives who were more interested in social issues. His closest allies were José Tomás Canales and Manuel C. Gonzales, fellow LULAC founders and officers who were also representing the State Bar of Texas at the conference. Liberal delegates representing the National Lawyers Guild from New York as well as the large Latin American contingent, especially the delegates from Mexico and Panamá, urged the assembly to pass a resolution that condemned racial discrimination and called on countries to adopt administrative or legislative sanctions against its practice. According to Canales and J. Montiel Olvera, a columnist with *La Prensa,* Perales delivered a rousing speech in support of the resolution.[38]

The editors of *Fraternidad* reported that Perales "made concrete reference during his speech to the problem affecting Mexicans in the United States." Soon after that, the delegates adopted the resolution. The resolution's first resolve recommended the protection of the civil rights of all foreigners, and its second and third resolutions called for an inter-American "system" of sanctions against discrimination and segregation based on race, creed, or national origin. The delegates also called on American nations to negotiate international treaties that committed them to institute administrative or legal remedies to discrimination. Although most of the Texas delegation parted with Perales and objected to the two latter opinions on sanctions, the assembly eventually passed the resolution "by enthusiastic acclamation." Latin American delegates had adopted similar declarations at the earlier association meeting in Rio de Janeiro as well as at the recent International Labor Conference held in Philadelphia. The 1944 resolution that emerged at Rio de Janeiro expressed concerns for the civil rights of foreign-born workers who faced discrimination in Germany, an issue that Latin American delegates had raised with the United States in mind during the inter-American meetings of ministers held since the 1930s. This time Perales directed their attention to Mexicans and the United States.[39]

Perales was influential outside the conference as well. He stayed in Mexico City after the meeting and met with members of the Mexican Assembly and President Avila Camacho's cabinet. Francisco P. Jiménez, the new president of the Committee on Mexicans in the Exterior, organized a meeting between Perales and the congressional press corps. Mexico City newspapers such as *Fraternidad* subsequently carried Perales's account regarding discrimination against Mexicans in the United States and the failure of Texas officials to institute effective safeguards against the violation of their civil rights. Soon after the meetings with the Mexican congressmen, Representative Noe Lecona and Senator Jiménez formally proposed that the Texas ban continue.[40]

Perales returned to San Antonio intent on promoting the spirit if not the word of the resolution adopted by the Mexico City conference. After a perfunctory interview with *La Prensa,* Perales wrote Roosevelt on behalf of LULAC and a companion organization, the League of Loyal Americans, with a report on the Mexico City meeting and a request that he instruct Congress to pass a civil rights law. The White House forwarded the letter to the Justice Department. Assistant Attorney General Tom C. Clark asked Perales to substantiate his claim of discrimination and the need for the law. Perales responded with a list of Texas businesses that denied service to Mexicans and a two-part request. He asked the Department of Justice to investigate businesses in thirty towns and cities in Texas known for denying service to Mexicans and to inform the guilty parties that the government would not tolerate discrimination. If compliance failed, Perales followed, the Justice Department was to advise Roosevelt to ask Congress for a legal remedy. Clark responded that Congress could not pass legislation prohibiting discrimination by individuals since the courts had decided in the late nineteenth century that the prohibition was limited to discrimination by the government. Perales tried one more time to convince Clark, but was unsuccessful.[41]

Perales next turned his attention to the Chapultepec conference to give further legitimacy to the appeal for civil rights legislation in the United States. Although Perales did not directly participate in this meeting, he and associates from Texas and Mexico that included Mexico's Comité Contra el Racismo occupied themselves with the idea of influencing the delegates with newspaper articles and a letter-writing campaign. Their underlying argument continued to be that the delegates adopt a resolution for legal sanctions against discrimination in their respective lands. The Chapultepec conference eventually endorsed such a resolution and Perales, along with fellow LULAC leaders, continued to make the case that the Mexican community in the United States and its civil rights cause figured prominently in the larger project for unity and human rights in the Americas.[42]

Mexico had convened the Chapultepec conference in preparation for the United Nations meeting in San Francisco. Its purpose was to strengthen inter-American ties and determine the extent to which the United States was committed to the region's future economic development. The conference was also a rehearsal for the airing of vital issues in the postwar period such as the emergence of small nations in the new world order, cooperative and peaceful relations between nations, and the basic social and economic rights of individuals throughout the world. The United States had convened and organized past inter-American meetings of foreign ministers. This time, Mexico assumed the responsibility, and the assembly elected the eminent Padilla as its permanent president. Mexico's leading role in the proceedings also demonstrated its prominence in the deliberations. The "Declaration of Mexico," for instance, established important guiding doctrines such as the respect for international law, the juridical equality of states, and the nonrecognition of territorial claims resulting from interventions. The foundational document also established the centrality of the rights of the individual and the obligations of states to protect their civil rights. It was within this grand stage of veiled allusions to inequality in the United States that the delegates interpreted discrimination as an obstacle to human rights and a threat to peace in the future.[43]

The delegates to the Chapultepec conference may have offered a united front when they approved their resolution by acclamation, but there were signs of a rift among Mexico's delegation, according to Olvera. The Mexican delegates, mostly representatives from Avila Camacho's administration, especially his diplomatic corps, seemed unwavering in their support of the resolution. Padilla, on the other hand, revealed uncertainty in the ranks. His tongue-in-cheek characterization of the numerous letters that he was receiving on the issue of discrimination as irrelevant to the larger question of postwar relations between nations suggested to Olvera that Padilla was in retreat. Padilla's primary concern was reportedly with general "transcendental" issues such as peace, security, and cooperation between small and big nations in the postwar period. He confirmed this view in speeches and interviews around the time of the Chapultepec and United Nations meetings. With one exception that involved a reference to Mexican complaints of discrimination against the Shell refinery in Houston, Padilla no longer made vigorous public statements that linked discrimination against Mexicans with the application of the Good Neighbor Policy in the United States. This suggests that Mexico was abandoning its alliance with the Mexican civil rights leadership.[44]

Perales nonetheless continued to seek the international recognition of discrimination at the United Nations meeting as the legal counsel for Nicaragua. He had been serving as the general counsel to Nicaragua in Texas, and somehow used his connections to gain a seat with the Nicaraguan delegation.[45] Perales reported in *La Prensa* that he was representing Mexicans from the United States: "The voice of the three million Mexican-origin inhabitants in the United States of America was heard at the Third Inter-American Bar Association Conference held in Mexico's capital in July and August, it was heard at the Conference of Ministers at Chapultepec, and it will be heard at the Conference of the United Nations in San Francisco."[46] Perales served on several committees responsible for formulating foundational documents, including a binding human rights resolution. He made his most notable exhortations on Mexicans in the United States before one of the most important groups, the Social Committee.[47]

Despite the rebuff from the Department of Justice and Padilla's apparent change of heart, Perales expressed great optimism in his reports from San

Francisco. Secretary Stettinuis, the head of the U.S. delegation, according to Perales, had promised that the United Nations Charter would prevent conflicts between nations and promote human rights. Another encouraging development was the creation of the Economic and Social Council and the adoption of the principles of "equal rights and self-determination of peoples," including the "universal respect for, and observance of human rights and fundamental freedoms for all without distinction as to race, language, religion or sex." Perales pointed to other human rights statements in the United Nations Charter as evidence that the fifty participating nations recognized that guaranteeing equality under the law was the best way to ensure peace and security around the world. Racial discrimination and the cause for Mexican rights in the United States, in other words, had been given international importance. All that was needed now was for the signatories to the United Nations Charter to fulfill their promise at home.[48]

The year 1945 would also witness the return of LULAC and its allies to the halls of the Texas legislature to call for the passage of a civil rights bill that could pass legal muster. As far as the LULAC and Mexican consulate activists were concerned, the deliberations at Mexico City and San Francisco had raised the bar at the same time that the Terrell Wells case and the "gradualist" GNC required that the state strengthen its Good Neighbor Policy. The new civil rights proposal of 1945 was called the "Spears bill" after its sponsor, Senator J. Franklin Spears from San Antonio. It disallowed discrimination against Mexicans and placed enforceable sanctions on violators. By the time it reached the Senate floor for a vote, however, it had been stripped of much of its broadly construed language, including references to employment discrimination. Perales, Sanchez, and Castañeda, as well as Horacio Guerra, one of the three recent appointments to the GNC, nevertheless expressed their support for the bill during public hearings and in public statements to the press. The Senate voted for the bill, but the House rejected it. In explaining the defeat of the bill, Anglo members of the GNC who had lobbied against it pointed out that they could not support a measure that dictated behavior. They preferred an educational campaign to promote understanding. Castañeda countered that the governor, the Anglo members of the GNC, and Sutherland opposed the bill for other reasons.[49]

Castañeda stated that the legislators had deleted the employment discrimination provisions of the original bill because they harbored antiworker prejudice. The "pressure from Latin American groups" who obviously believed that the bill was still worth fighting for, however, had helped to place it on the calendar for action by the House on May 16. The GNC officials, according to Castañeda, also led the charge against the bill because they believed that it was a subterfuge that would open the door for major changes in Texas. They reportedly claimed that "if Mexicans were admitted to business places catering to the public or to public places, such as parks, etc., the next step would be admission of negroes." According to Castañeda, GNC officials added that "many Mexicans lived or were married to Negroes and that under the terms of the bill, they would have to be accorded equal rights with whites." Castañeda also concluded that the senators, at the urging of the GNC officials, had also excluded from the bill the term Latin American because they feared claims of civil rights protections by U.S. residents from "the Latin-American countries of the Caribbean, such as Cuba, Haiti, and Santo Domingo, where a large portion of the population is colored."[50]

Matters became all the more discouraging when Congress failed to heed the call for civil rights legislation by the United Nations and even discontinued its support for the FEPC as a postwar agency. A more immediate blow to the civil rights cause was the dismantling of the alliance between Mexican consulates and LULAC in Texas. As noted earlier, Padilla had hinted at the United Nations meeting that he was less than enthusiastic over the issue of discrimination and, as a consequence, cast doubts on his country's advocacy policy. Soon after the United Nations had convened its first meeting and the Texas legislature had rejected the Spears Bill, Padilla moved to undo the wartime pact by removing three of the most active consuls in Texas, Carlos A. Calderón, Ernesto Zorrilla H., and Adolfo G. Domínguez.[51]

Calderón, the consul general from San Antonio who oversaw the Texas consular corps in the South Texas region, and Domínguez, the Houston consul known for his close collaboration with Mexican American leaders, were two of the most vocal critics of discrimination. Zorrilla was not as well known, but he served as the consul of the important San Antonio office, under Calderón. Duplán, the Austin consul, offered an explanation for the removals. In a long letter to Padilla, he noted that his actions announced that Mexico no longer wished to pursue a vigorous campaign against discrimination in Texas. Duplán reminded him that Blocker, the U.S. consul at Ciudad Juárez, who was advising Stevenson and the GNC on orders from the State Department, had asked the U.S. embassy to petition the Mexican government to remove the very same consuls that lost favor with Padilla. The most immediate implication, Duplán added, was that Mexico had agreed with the gradualist approach and was restraining its advocacy work.[52]

Duplán also reviewed the recent history of the fight for a civil rights law.

Texas and GNC officials had entertained the idea of such a law during the early negotiations over the Bracero Program. After the first year of operations, the GNC abandoned it and began to offer a public program of education as the best means to address discrimination. The consuls and Mexican civil rights leaders, meanwhile, had been bringing more and more complaints to the GNC and, in Duplán's opinion, the inadequate attention that the GNC gave the complaints "underscored the obvious necessity of promoting special legislation" to combat the problem. The consuls, according to Duplán, lost faith in the GNC and Kibbe responded by suggesting that the most outspoken ones be removed because they would not cooperate.[53]

The spirited campaigns for civil rights by LULAC exposed the limits that conservative forces would allow in Texas. Mexico's apparent disengagement gave added definition to these boundaries. LULAC, on the other hand, demonstrated its steadfast support for a broad political agenda and determined public discourse. Its work, however, did not end with the campaigns against discrimination in the schools and public establishments and the fight for legally protected rights. LULAC also advanced a labor project that made use of the opportunities offered by the FEPC. LULAC leaders from Texas initiated this relationship when they made the earliest and most concerted effort among Mexicans to bring the FEPC to the Southwest. This early influence explains how the Texas LULAC leadership positioned themselves anew in the cause for Mexican rights.

The Texas Connection

Gonzales, the state LULAC official who also served as a legal counsel to the Mexican consulate from San Antonio, played an especially important role in drawing the FEPC's attention to the Southwest. Others also made important contributions. Perales, for instance, had been waging an impressive article-writing campaign since the 1930s on discrimination and the responsibility of the state to intervene on behalf of Mexicans. José de la Luz Saenz, the author of a World War I diary and one of the founders of LULAC, had also been writing and speaking throughout the state on the subject. Moreover, once Mexico and the United States began to collaborate on the inter-American alliance, leaders like Perales and Saenz, as well as Sanchez and Herrera, made more open use of their cultural and historical ties with their Latin American cousins to broaden their moral and constitutional appeals for justice and equality into a "pan-American" cause. Gonzales, however, stands alone in revealing the early connection between Mexico's advocacy policy and LULAC's attempt to bring the FEPC to Texas.

On November 1941, five months after the FEPC began its operations and soon after the OCIAA had commissioned the Saposs field study, Gonzales offered a broad-based proposal for state action that revealed his dual loyalties. His primary intent was to bring the FEPC to the Southwest. To strengthen his argument, Gonzales pointed out that the government was paying more attention to other groups despite the pervasive nature of the problem and its implications to U.S. relations with Latin American, especially Mexico. His most ambitious claim was that the FEPC should have the authority to investigate the whole range of discriminatory practices and not be limited to the area of employment. Calling for a major assault on social discrimination, of course, was not the intent of the president's executive orders. Gonzales may have seemed naïve to Washington officials, but he was not. He was capitalizing on the discourse over racial discrimination to call for broad-based action as a logical response to the general problem of social discrimination. At the same time, he was strengthening the case for bringing the FEPC to the Southwest.[54]

Gonzales contacted the director of the Office of Production Management (OPM), the FEPC's early parent agency, on behalf of LULAC. He underscored the problem of employment discrimination with a case like many others that periodically reached the Mexican consulate offices and LULAC councils during the war. An unnamed Mexican worker from South Texas had written the editor of the *Valley Evening Monitor* claiming that the painting contractor at the Tri-City Air Base had refused him a job because he was Mexican. The editor subsequently announced that the complaint "was no exaggeration," and that his investigation provided ample evidence of discrimination against Mexican painters. He added that the hiring agent of the local painters' local was also refusing to refer Mexican painters to jobs on the grounds that the contractor and the foreman would not hire them.

Gonzales insisted, as he would continue to do during the lifetime of the FEPC, that Washington was only addressing one part of the larger issue of social discrimination affecting Mexican nationals and U.S.-born Mexicans. His point was that the government was failing to address school segregation and the refusal of service in public establishments with the same energy evident in the work of the FEPC. Gonzales thus cast the issue of discrimination in broader terms, a strategy that allowed him and other LULAC leaders to strengthen their bargaining hand with Washington. FEPC officials could claim that their jurisdiction prevented them from addressing discrimination beyond the war industries, as Gonzales was careful to concede; however, they could not deny that the different forms of discrimination were interconnected and mutually reinforcing.

Gonzales also underscored the problem of government inattention by noting that Mexicans were benefiting less from employment opportunities and government help than African Americans. Although his intent was to demonstrate that the promise of wartime opportunity was not reaching Mexicans to the same extent as other groups, Gonzales's apparent frustration got the best of him when he revealed a breach in his relations with the African American community. In calling for action on behalf of Mexicans, Gonzales pointed out that such discrimination could not be justified as it was with African Americans, that is, Mexicans were not a "colored race" and there was no statutory reason to deny them their rights. Although Gonzales's logic may have left the impression that he was willing to tolerate the segregation of blacks, his major argument that the government was paying less attention to Mexicans was clear. His other point was to demonstrate the special nature of racial discrimination against Mexicans, that is, it lacked the de jure justification normally applied to white-black relations and, as a consequence, was subject to more effective challenges.

FEPC officials may have interpreted Gonzales's remarks as accusatory and racist. They could not deny, however, that the FEPC was failing Mexicans. Nor could they disagree with Gonzales's prodding that it was necessary to say to Latin America that the United States was "the real melting pot where opportunities are not only promised but actually given." The government officials also had to accept, Gonzales added, that the United States was still not living up to its ideals as a Christian nation. Despite the compelling biblical and moral arguments by Gonzales, it was obvious that Mexican workers could not receive the attention that they deserved if the FEPC did not establish offices in the Southwest.[55]

At the same time that Gonzales was communicating with the OPM, LULAC officers from several southwestern states began to coordinate their own messages of concern with the OCIAA and the OPM over the limited handling of Mexican workers' complaints. An OPM official in Texas named W. G. Carnahan subsequently reported to his superiors that LULAC was giving full attention to the problem in their newspaper and that they insisted on seeing that the government address social discrimination with civil rights statutes or administrative remedies, especially since the FEPC restricted its attention to the defense industry and the State Department often confined its own to Mexican nationals. Carnahan added that LULAC representatives from Texas were traveling to Washington to personally communicate their concerns.[56]

> A delegation that included Gonzales, Perales, and Sanchez visited the OPM, FEPC, and OCIAA offices during the second week of December 1941. Although Will Alexander reported that he was not favorably impressed with their demand for a more comprehensive course of action, the LULAC emissaries appeared to have made an impression on him. One day after the meeting, Alexander informed Carnahan that, "There is increased interest here in the Spanish-American situation, particularly because of its bearing on the relations of the nations south of us. I hope you will push this part of your work as vigorously as you have been pushing Negro employment."[57]

This early influence undoubtedly contributed to the decision to establish the previously noted FEPC office in El Paso and begin the assault against the copper industry of West Texas, Arizona, and New Mexico in 1942. The Dallas office opened in July 1943. Within months, the FEPC established another office in San Antonio and the fight against the copper giants began anew. FEPC officials also began to consistently seek the advice of Gonzales, Sanchez, and other LULAC representatives for more efficient and sustained work in Texas. LULAC leaders, believing that they had been instrumental in ending the government's lethargy, were encouraged to redouble their efforts by publicizing the services of the FEPC and soliciting formal complaints of discrimination. The result was a highly energized and well-coordinated fact-gathering and public advocacy campaign that involved most if not all the LULAC councils from Texas and Mexican consular offices from San Antonio, Houston, and Dallas. Gonzales emerged again as the point man in submitting lists of documented cases of discrimination in Texas and in securing for LULAC its new place as a player in the broadened Good Neighbor Policy.[58]

OCIAA officials must have influenced the FEPC into enlisting the assistance of LULAC since they had already established the practice of cooperating with the civil rights organization. The OCIAA funded community projects in the Southwest, financed research projects headed by Sanchez at the University of Texas, and solicited from persons such as Gonzales information regarding employment discrimination. OCIAA officials also made it clear in communications with other agencies that LULAC was the preferred organization in the Mexican community.

The decision by the FEPC to give the Southwest greater attention coincided with the OCIAA findings and the subsequent decision to coordinate the activities of governmental agencies in support of the Good Neighbor Policy. Once Roosevelt reaffirmed his commitment to nondiscrimination in 1943 and the FEPC expanded its operations into Texas and other parts of the Southwest, the fight against employment discrimination resumed in earnest. In the process, the FEPC reflected and reinforced the view that the possible negative international repercussions of discrimination warranted a friendlier public consideration of Mexicans. Moreover, LULAC benefited greatly from this development. The most vocal and moderate political organization in the Mexican community of Texas, LULAC positioned itself well during the initial phase of inclusion, a move which allowed it to claim credit for the change in policy and to strengthen its position as an advocate for Mexican workers' rights.

Conclusion

The wartime cooperation between the Mexican government and the Mexican civil rights leadership faded even further during the postwar period when Mexico agreed to send Braceros to Texas. Historians agree that LULAC leaders also moved away from the alliance as increasing numbers of Mexicans crossed the international border and enlarged the farm labor supply. They became more critical of U.S. immigration policy, especially the government's failure to enforce the law and restrict the immigrant flows. In the process of critiquing the policy and its poor enforcement, they often appeared to be reproaching the immigrants themselves for contributing to a labor surplus and forcing U.S.-born Mexicans to join the highly exploited migratory workforce. Distanced politically from their wartime allies and increasingly alienated from a growing and seemingly threatening immigrant working class, they retreated from their internationalist posture into an ethnic form of activism on behalf of Mexican rights. LULAC leaders also continued to use the language of democracy, although the end of hostilities now denied them the moral weight of wartime aims.

Mexico's interventionist policy on behalf of Mexicans during the war years, however, had energized the civil rights cause. It provided Mexicans with a more focused language of democracy, one that emphasized hemispheric understanding on the basis of equal rights. The decision by the United States to apply the Good Neighbor Policy within its borders also brought official attention to the Mexican community. U.S. officials who directed the focus of federal agencies and state governments to the Mexican community may have been primarily seeking to appease Mexico. Other important changes, however, also occurred. These included reforms in the schools and the extension of federal services into previously isolated Mexican communities. Another result was the emergence of LULAC as the prominent civil rights organization in the Mexican community. The irony for Mexican civil rights leaders was that they benefited more from their alliance with the Mexican government than from their efforts to secure special protections in the United States.

The civil rights campaign dramatized the refusal of service as a racial affront, a violation of democratic principles, and a threat to wartime unity. Any Mexican, including diplomats, soldiers, and migratory workers, faced the possibility of being refused service. It did not matter, in other words, that Mexico was an ally or that Mexicans were officially considered white. It also seemed irrelevant that the United States publicly ascribed to wartime egalitarian principles or that Mexicans were serving honorably in the U.S. military. The civil rights cause, on the other hand, placed far-reaching legislative and administrative remedies before the public, and federal and state officials. All along, they saw in the Roosevelt's nondiscrimination policy in employment and the agency established to enforce it as a model for civil rights legislation. The work of the FEPC, to which we now turn, embodied the government's response to wartime exigencies as well as the hopes and aspirations associated with a LULAC-led cause for equal rights that often spoke in accordance with international norms of democracy and justice.

Chapter 5: The FEPC and Mexican Workers in Texas

After the United Nations meeting, Perales reminded a group of friends welcoming him back to San Antonio that the international assemblies in Mexico City and San Francisco called on nations throughout the world to enact the kind of civil rights statute that President Roosevelt had anticipated with his executive orders against employment discrimination. According to Castañeda, one of the hosts at the function, Perales added that "the principles of the FEPC were irretrievably fused with those of the Charter framed at San Francisco" and Congress was now obligated to retain the agency as evidence of the United States' commitment to the human rights principles enunciated at San Francisco. He reportedly concluded that the world "would question the sincerity of the U.S. in the postulates made at San Francisco" if Congress did not make the FEPC a permanent agency after the war. Perales understood that southern congressmen were intent on ending the life of the FEPC as they campaigned to end the New Deal and preserve the racial order in the South. Nevertheless, he was intent on making use of the San Francisco proclamations on human rights and the nation's nondiscrimination policy to justify civil rights legislation in the United States, or at least in his state of Texas.[1]

Perales saw the agency's work in Texas as more than a response by the state to improve working conditions and to ensure the full and effective use of

Cartoon depiction of Hitler parachuting into a giant cactus, while Uncle Sam and a Mexican laugh and dance, n.d. (Artist: Antonio Arias Bernal, Coordinador de Asuntos Interamericanos. The Holland Collection of World War II Posters, Center for Southwestern Research, University of New Mexico, Albuquerque, New Mexico.)

the available labor supply. It was also part of a larger fight against discrimination, occurring at an important historical juncture in the social incorporation of Mexicans into American society. For him and no doubt many other civil rights leaders, the work of the FEPC represented a galvanizing and transformative moment that joined the cause for Mexican rights with the government's initiative on behalf of war workers. This broadly conceived social history allows us to incorporate Mexicans into the larger discourse over civil and labor rights in the United States. It also permits us to further reconceptualize the history of LULAC and the Mexican civil rights movement. Some historians may prefer to see LULAC largely as a conservative organization collaborating with the state instead of developing an independent critical voice on behalf of Mexican workers. This view, however, would overlook that LULAC leaders recognized the unprecedented opportunities that the war and an activist state offered marginalized communities. The bureaucratic machinery of the FEPC presented them with an untried and undeniable means to give voice to Mexican workers and to participate directly in high-level policy discussions in employment and civil rights. LULAC's intermediary position between the U.S. and Mexican government also allowed its leaders to bring further attention to discrimination, inequality, and Mexicans in the United States.

Our focus in this chapter is not restricted to the instances of collaboration between LULAC and Mexican consuls in support of the FEPC and the larger issue of equal rights. It also treats the FEPC as a place of struggle between contending ideas and projects in Texas. The FEPC, in other words, became a site for the fight between egalitarian and segregationist ideas, much like the California Agricultural Labor Relations Board is said to have functioned as a state-managed site of mediation for political battles migrating from the farms during the 1970s and 1980s.[2] This involved the importation of ideas and causes from a larger political terrain into the internal workings of the FEPC, with LULAC and the Mexican government once again working together for equal Mexican rights. The grievance process, on the other hand, represented a concession by the Mexican social movement much as the U.S. working-class movement subjected itself to a process of labor bargaining that was ultimately beyond their control. African Americans also took part in this give-and-take as both actors and issues of contention. The Mexican cause, especially when set against the hemispheric political setting within which it operated, attracted much official attention in Texas, is lesser known, and, consequently, deserves our concerted attention.

Investigating and Negotiating Complaints

For Mexican workers, the promise of recovery became more believable when the FEPC arrived in the Southwest and began to solicit and investigate their complaints much as it had been doing in other parts of the country. The better-informed workers no doubt found encouragement knowing that the FEPC would try to incorporate them more fully into an expanding economy. The interventions of Mexican government officials and their own use of the language of justice, democracy, and good neighborliness also must have encouraged workers to take their grievances before the FEPC. Lastly, LULAC's campaign for equal rights no doubt emboldened them with their righteous claims of equal rights. Laureano Flores, an FEPC complainant and regular contributor to *La Prensa,* acknowledged what many Mexicans must have understood about the fortuitous circumstance that the war had created, "This is the right time to demand justice."[3]

Mexican workers like Flores often registered their complaints after reading about the FEPC in Spanish-language newspapers or hearing of its services through the vast organizational network of mutual aid societies, Masonic orders, unions, civil rights organizations, and the local consulate-sponsored chapters of the Comisión Honorífica and the Cruz Azul. Well-informed individuals and groups of workers typically submitted the required written complaints with the necessary supporting evidence. Others sought out local community leaders for information about the agency and for help in submitting letters inquiring about the agency's services. FEPC officials typically responded according to established procedure. They docketed a complaint if the alleged act of discrimination occurred in a war industry that was critical to the prosecution of the war. Moreover, if a complainant did not submit the necessary evidence of discrimination or if the FEPC could not corroborate the accusation with information from employers or another government agency, agency officials dismissed the complaint on the grounds that it lacked the necessary evidence and did not constitute a grievance with sufficient merit. On the other hand, if an investigation verified a complaint, the officials issued a favorable finding and began the process of negotiating a settlement with the employer or union. FEPC investigations at times generated far-reaching evidence and settlements that implicated other employers and encouraged additional workers to seek redress. Newspaper coverage also prompted further interest in the FEPC.[4]

Resolving individual and group cases of discrimination had other positive results. In all instances when settlements were reached, FEPC officials insisted that employers adopt a policy of nondiscrimination. Although some employers refused to do so, FEPC records indicate that they often agreed to the nondiscrimination stipulation in their settlements. This meant that employers publicly endorsed and even applied the president's executive orders, further encouraging workers to come forward with their own grievances. Another less measurable change occurred when word spread of a favorable settlement and other employers and unions in the area took corrective measures for fear of facing FEPC investigators and greater public scrutiny.[5]

Most of the Mexican complaints originated in the more industrialized cities of Houston, Dallas, San Antonio, Corpus Christi, Laredo, and El Paso. Workers from Houston, San Antonio, Corpus Christi, and El Paso generated the most complaints. LULAC members, Mexican consuls, and union officers played a key role in publicizing the FEPC's responsibility to enforce the nation's nondiscrimination policy. This kind of support combined with Castañeda's ardent encouragement during his travels throughout the state contributed to the impressive number of complaints that Mexican workers submitted after 1943. South Texas, where Mexicans predominated, submitted fewer complaints largely because the USES did not implement the nondiscrimination policy in agriculture, the principal employer of Mexicans in the area. Its officials were more interested in policing farm workers than in following the FEPC's lead. The Department of Agriculture also failed to apply the president's executive orders when it assumed responsibility over farm labor beginning in January 1944. Moreover, FEPC officials expressed little interest in Mexicans employed in other South Texas industries most probably because they believed that its underdeveloped economy would generate small returns in the form of complaints and far-reaching settlements.[6]

Mexican workers in wartime industries most often complained that employers denied them upgrading opportunities. Employers undergoing FEPC investigations often admitted different forms of discrimination and offered a variety of explanations including a lack of skills, little if any knowledge of English, and union contracts or understandings that set aside the skilled positions for Anglo workers. Employers were most brazen in their admission of discrimination when they explained that Anglo workers were adamant about segregated workplaces to the point of striking if the company cooperated with the FEPC. Castañeda and other field examiners found in favor of the complainants in the majority of cases involving discrimination in hiring, job classification, wages, and upgrading.

Much of the discrimination stemmed from racially defined job classification practices that placed Mexicans as well as blacks in the segregated sections of the plants. Employers usually paid minority laborers less than Anglo laborers and gave them few opportunities for promotion into the higher ranks. Wage discrimination also occurred when minority workers performed skilled jobs but remained classified as laborers. Segregation and the denial of upgrading possibilities, on the other hand, placed a limit on the number of minority workers that an employer would hire. Hiring discrimination thus disregarded the skills and experiences of the minority job applicants and denied them the possibility of filling vacancies above the laboring occupations. Although Mexicans and blacks faced the same types of employment discrimination in Texas war industries, the former submitted a higher number of complaints despite their lower representation in the war industries. This is one reason the FEPC may have paid more attention to their complaints in Texas.[7]

Three field offices handled most of the cases involving Mexicans from Texas. Region X, located in Dallas, had jurisdiction over Louisiana, Texas, and New Mexico beginning in August 1943. The subregional office, which became known as Region XI, was located in San Antonio during the early part of 1944. Castañeda, who served as the director of Region X and special assistant to the FEPC director on Latin American workers, mostly worked out of the San Antonio office. Castañeda's responsibility over all "Latin American Workers" meant that he handled most of the Mexican workers' complaints in Texas, but he also directed the FEPC work in West Texas, New Mexico, Arizona, Colorado, Idaho, Wyoming, Montana, and Utah. Castañeda also worked closely with other regional and subregional offices located in New Orleans, St. Louis, Kansas City, Los Angeles, and San Francisco. Region XIII was established when Castañeda moved to San Antonio and became responsible for East Texas, Mississippi, and Louisiana. Castañeda advised its regional director, W. Don Ellinger, on cases from upper Texas Gulf Coast that he had initiated while in Dallas.[8]

The changing jurisdictional lines of the FEPC offices make it difficult to determine the absolute and proportional numbers of Mexican complaints that the agency processed in Texas. The record in the Dallas office and in the Los Angeles subregional office in Region XII offers the best comparative opportunity to gauge the impressive work that was done among Mexican workers between July 1943 and December 1944. Their emphasis on Mexican workers was evident in the higher number of complaints based on national origin that were submitted to both offices. The national origin complaints originating in the Southwest mostly included immigrant and nonimmigrant

Mexican workers. The complaints submitted on the basis of race included Mexicans but these figures cannot be disaggregated because they also included black complainants. Also, FEPC officials normally docketed Mexican complaints on the basis of national origin. The national origin data consequently represents a reliable source of information for determining the kind of attention that the FEPC gave both U.S.- and Mexico-born Mexicans.

Workers submitted 115 national origins complaints to the Dallas office, an amount that represented 35.7 percent of the total that were docketed. The Los Angeles office received sixty-nine such complaints, or 24.7 percent of its total. Mexicans constituted around 80 percent of the national origin cases in the nation and most probably represented over 90 percent in places such as Dallas and Los Angeles where their numbers were concentrated.[9]

As noted earlier, the FEPC gave much more attention to blacks nationally as well as in Dallas and Los Angeles. Nationally, the agency claimed to have filed 3,298 cases, or 85 percent of the total, involving race, while only 253 of them, or 6.5 percent, noted national origin discrimination. In Dallas, 188 complaints, or 58.4 percent of the total, alleged racial discrimination, while 115, or 35.7 percent, declared national origin discrimination. In Los Angeles 149 complainants, or 53.4 percent, stated race, at the same time that 69, or 24.7 percent, asserted national origin. The trends were unmistakable. The national focus was on blacks while Mexicans drew attention in areas where they predominated. The new offices that opened throughout the Southwest, on the other hand, demonstrated an increased interest in Mexicans. Although this interest must be weighed against the unfortunate decision to give Castañeda such an unrealistic work load, FEPC officials in places like Dallas and Los Angeles, demonstrated great dedication and, especially in the former place, produced impressive results.[10]

Although the Dallas and Los Angeles offices were relatively new and short-staffed, their personnel were effective in soliciting complaints and preparing the cases for satisfactory settlement or dismissal (see table 5.1). They each recorded slightly over three hundred active cases, far below the absolute and proportional numbers recorded in the older and more experienced New York and Philadelphia offices, but well within range of the average caseload of 367 per office. Similar patterns emerged across regional and subregional offices in other areas. The New York and Philadelphia offices, for example, again led in settling cases in favor of complainants with 632 and 424, or 20.9 percent and 14 percent of the national total, respectively. In Dallas and Los Angeles, FEPC officials captured a significantly lower share of the total

Table 5.1. Summary of FEPC caseload activity by regional and subregional offices, July 1, 1943–June 30, 1944

Regions	*Active*[1]	*Closed*[2]	*Settled*[3]	*Withdrawn*[4]	*Dismissed*[5]	*Pending*[6]
Region I						
Boston	89	71	29	8	34	18
	(1.7)	(2.3)	(2.6)	(2.8)	(2.1)	(.9)
		(79.8)	(40.8)	(11.3)	(47.8)	(20.2)
Region II						
New York	912	632	303	37	292	280
	(17.8)	(20.9)	(27.6)	(13.1)	(17.7)	(13.3)
		(68.3)	(47.9)	(5.9)	(46.2)	(30.7)
Region III						
Philadelphia	713	424	134	31	259	289
	(13.9)	(14)	(12.2)	(11)	(15.7)	(13.7)
		(59.5)	(31.6)	(7.3)	(61.1)	(40.5)
Region IV						
Washington	337	206	39	10	157	131
	(6.6)	(6.8)	(3.5)	(3.5)	(9.5)	(6.2)
		(61.1)	(18.9)	(4.9)	(76.2)	(38.9)
Region V						
Cleveland	363	221	67	28	126	142
	(7)	(7.3)	(6.1)	(9.9)	(7.6)	(6.8)
		(60.9)	(30.3)	(12.7)	(57)	(39.1)
Detroit	350	246	133	29	84	104
	(6.8)	(8.1)	(12.1)	(10.3)	(5.1)	(4.9)
		(70.3)	(54.1)	(11.8)	(34.1)	(29.7)
Region VI						
Chicago	564	327	81	22	224	237
	(11)	(10.8)	(7.4)	(7.8)	(13.6)	(11.3)
		(58)	(24.8)	(6.7)	(68.5)	(42)
Region VII						
Atlanta	405	100	22	34	44	305
	(7.9)	(3.3)	(2)	(12.1)	(2.7)	(14.5)
		(24.7)	(22)	(34)	(44)	(75.3)
Region VIII						
Minneapolis	45	30	7	4	19	15
	(0.9)	(1)	(0.6)	(1.4)	(1.2)	(0.7)
		(66.7)	(23.3)	(13.3)	(63.3)	(33.3)
Region IX						
Kansas City	252	121	39	4	78	131
	(4.9)	(4)	(3.5)	(1.4)	(4.7)	(6.2)
		(48)	(32.2)	(3.3)	(64.5)	(52)
Region X						
Dallas	336	213	86	3	124	123
	(6.5)	(7)	(7.8)	(1.1)	(7.5)	(5.8)
		(63.4)	(40.4)	(1.4)	(58.2)	(36.6)
Region XI						
Denver	46	14	7	2	5	32
	(0.9)	(0.5)	(0.6)	(0.7)	(0.3)	(1.5)
		(30.4)	(50)	(14.3)	(35.7)	(69.6)

(*continued*)

Table 5.1. (*continued*)

Regions	*Active* [1]	*Closed* [2]	*Settled* [3]	*Withdrawn* [4]	*Dismissed* [5]	*Pending* [6]
Region XII						
San Francisco	410	261	104	43	114	149
	(8)	(8.6)	(9.5)	(15.2)	(6.9)	(7)
		(63.7)	(39.8)	(16.5)	(43.7)	(36.3)
Los Angeles	311	164	48	27	89	147
	(6.1)	(5.4)	(4.4)	(16.5)	(5.4)	(7)
		(52.7)	(29.3)	(16.5)	(54.3)	(47.3)
Totals	5,133	3,030	1,099	282	1,649	2,103
	(100)	(99.7)	(99.9)	(99.9)	(100)	(99.8)
		(59)	(36.3)	(9.3)	(54.4)	(41)

Source: FEPC, *First Report, July 1943–December 1944* (Washington, D.C.: U.S. Government Printing Office, 1945), 114.
Note: The first row of percentage figures appearing in parentheses offers proportional measures of the total number of cases in the fourteen offices. The second row reflects proportional amounts within each office. Thus, the 213 cases that the Dallas office closed represented 7 percent of the total closed in the fourteen office and 63.4 percent of the total closed within Region X.

[1] The figures represent the cases pending as of July 1, 1943 and the cases docketed between July 1, 1943 and June 30, 1944.

[2] Closed cases refer to settlements, withdrawn cases by workers, and dismissals resulting from a lack of merit, insufficient evidence, a lack of jurisdiction, or "other" reasons.

[3] Settled cases include complaints that resulted in negotiated settlements with employers or unions.

[4] Withdrawn cases involve instances when workers withdrew their complaints.

[5] See note 2.

[6] Pending cases account for unresolved complaints that awaited resolution during the following fiscal year.

settlements (7.8 percent and 4.4 percent, respectively). Both offices, however, managed to register higher proportional figures than six of the other fourteen offices. The Dallas and Los Angeles offices also followed a middle course in dismissing worker complaints on the basis of insufficient merit, inadequate evidence, or jurisdictional problems. On the other hand, workers were less apt to withdraw their complaints at both places, especially in Dallas, where only three workers, or 1.1 percent of the total, were dissuaded from pursuing their complaints. Also, the Dallas office registered a more impressive record in favorable settlements, complaint withdrawals, and dismissals.[11]

The Dallas office was one of the most successful in settling its cases, with a 40.4 percent rate. Only New York and Detroit, offices with large caseloads and more personnel, exceeded this figure. Los Angeles, meanwhile, had the second worst record in negotiating favorable settlements for their complainants. The Dallas staff may have been especially efficient in processing cases because only three complainants, or 1.4 percent of the

Table 5.2. Summary of FEPC caseload activity in Dallas and Los Angeles offices by region, July 1, 1943–June 30, 1944

Regions	*Active*	*Closed*	*Settled*	*Withdrawn*	*Dismissed*	*Pending*
East	1,714	1,127	466	76	585	587
	(37.2)	(33.4)	(42.4)	(27)	(35.5)	(27.9)
Midwest	1,574	945	327	87	531	629
	(30.7)	(31.2)	(29.8)	(30.9)	(32.2)	(29.9)
South	1,078	519	147	47	325	559
Dallas	(21)	(17.1)	(13.4)	(16.7)	(19.7)	(26.6)
	336	213	86	3	124	123
	(31.2)	(41)	(58.5)	(6.4)	(38.2)	(22)
West	767	439	159	72	208	328
Los Angeles	(14.9)	(14.5)	(14.5)	(25.5)	(12.6)	(15.6)
	311	164	48	27	89	147
	(40.5)	(37.4)	(30.2)	(37.5)	(42.8)	(44.8)
Totals	5,133	3,030	1,099	282	1,649	2,103
	(100)	(100)	(100.1)	(100.1)	(100)	(100)

Source: FEPC, *First Report, July 1943–December 1944* (Washington, D.C.: U.S. Government Printing Office, 1945), 114. The percentage figures in parentheses assigned to regions represent the proportions of the national totals noted in each column. The percentage figures in parentheses for Dallas and Los Angeles measure proportions within their respective regions.

total, decided to withdraw their claims. They led all the other offices in this area of work, while Los Angeles again lagged behind with one of the highest withdrawal rates. Neither Dallas nor Los Angeles, however, deviated much from the standard mean of fifty-six in the number of cases dismissed by the fourteen FEPC offices. When examined within each region, the Dallas office thus stood out primarily because its staff was able to settle a larger proportion of its cases while its complainants most often saw the process through to the end.

Case activity in the Dallas and Los Angeles offices appeared more impressive when viewed within their own regions (see table 5.2). The southern and western regions only handled about one-third of all the FEPC cases, while Dallas claimed a 31.2 percent portion in the South and Los Angeles a 40.5 percent share in the West. The Dallas staff also settled more cases than their counterparts in both Washington and Atlanta, the other two offices in the South, while Los Angeles settled less than one-third of the cases in the West, the region that also included the San Francisco and Denver offices. Dallas also continued registering a significantly lower percentage of withdrawn and dismissed cases. The success of the Dallas office can be best appreciated when one considers Castañeda's large caseload and the broad jurisdiction that often drew him away from Texas. In August 1944, he was responsible for fifty-seven cases from Region X, 47.5 percent of the total cases (120), and sixty-five cases from the San Antonio office, the great majority of which involved Mexican workers.

Importing the Mexican Cause

Castañeda's success was largely due to his association with the Mexican civil rights network and his reputation as a civil rights leader in the Mexican community. Soon after assuming his duties as a field examiner, Castañeda made use of his political capital to publicize the purpose of the agency and solicit complaints of discrimination. His September 1943 trip to Austin and San Antonio was one of his earliest and most fruitful. At Austin, he met with Sanchez, the director of the OCIAA-funded Committee on Inter-American Relations. Castañeda also visited the Mexican consulate office and the president of the local LULAC council. In San Antonio, he called on Enrique A. Gonzalez, the Mexican consul general. Castañeda also made contact with Ignacio Lozano, the editor of *La Prensa.* He concluded his trip with a visit to Gonzales who was serving as the editor of the *LULAC News,* the legal counsel to the San Antonio consulate, and the secretary general of the civil rights organization. They promised to encourage workers to seek the help of the FEPC and hosted a reception in his honor. The last three contacts were especially important because they gave Castañeda access to a large Mexican audience and the means to continuously solicit complaints.[12]

While Castañeda was primarily interested in recruiting influential persons to publicize the services of the FEPC and encourage workers to submit complaints, he also used his standing as an established civil rights leader to promote the agency as a partner in the Mexican cause. He made this clear while in San Antonio, in an interview with Lozano. The editor introduced him to the paper's readers as the "champion of Latin American interests" who reportedly said that Roosevelt established the FEPC primarily to "make justice a reality to all persons of Latin American origin who have always been victims of economic discrimination." He added that the FEPC's new focus on the Mexican was part of the president's plan to apply the Good Neighbor policy within the borders of the United States.[13]

Of course, Roosevelt had not established the FEPC with the Mexican primarily in mind. He may not have thought about them at all until Mexico added its weight behind the idea of an expanded Good Neighbor Policy. Castañeda, however, wanted to underscore the historical significance of the federal government's interest in the Mexican and the obvious need to make use of this opportunity: "The Latin American citizen has so long been accustomed to the uselessness of appealing to local authorities for redress of their grievances."[14] His underlying statement was to incorporate the grievance process into the political repertoire of the Mexican cause. Stated differently, he was calling on Mexicans to translate the Mexican vernacular of moralistic and egalitarian ideas into the wartime language of labor utilization within the FEPC.

Although the FEPC presented Mexican civil rights leaders and aggrieved workers a new opportunity to expand their political terrain, their ability to do so depended on a person of Castañeda's stature who could link the network of LULAC councils and Mexican consulate offices with the FEPC. Lozano, a keen observer of the Mexican political scene, understood Castañeda's importance to the civil rights cause as well as to the work of the FEPC. During the reception in Castañeda's honor, Lozano noted that "there is great interest [in the work of the FEPC] because it concerns a person who we all respect and no doubt will help us achieve the vindication that we so deeply hope for."[15]

Castañeda's political pedigree was well established. According to his biographer, Castáneda participated continuously in the civil rights movement, beginning in the late 1920s when he was a doctoral student at the University of Texas. The earliest record of his involvement with LULAC occurred in 1929 when he visited with José T. Canales, then a state representative from the Brownsville area, and other local leaders who were leading a local fight against discrimination in the areas of education and employment. Prior commitments kept Castañeda from joining them at the founding convention of LULAC at Corpus Christi, although he continued his association with the civil rights organization throughout the 1930s and the 1940s. Castañeda made some of his earliest contributions to the civil rights cause while serving as the superintendent of the San Felipe School District, an all-Mexican school along the border.[16] He worked closely with Eleuterio Escobar, the founder of La Liga Pro-Defensa Escolar from San Antonio, in developing the federation of community organizations that supported the legal case against the Del Rio School District in 1930. He was also a member of the inner circle of LULAC leaders that included Canales, Perales, Gonzales, and Sanchez since at least the mid-1930s. Castañeda also served as the state education director for LULAC between 1941 and 1942.[17]

Castañeda was also directly associated with Mexican government officials. This was evident during a meeting called by the Inter-American Relations in Texas Committee in Austin on December 17 and 18, 1943. The committee, operating with OCIAA support at the Latin American Institute of the University of Texas, sought to resolve differences between the surrogates of the Mexican and U.S. governments on the best way to implement the Good Neighbor Policy in Texas, a goal that was meant to repair relations with Mexico and end the Texas ban. No less than Rafael de la Colina, minister counselor of Mexico, led the Mexican delegation, which included the consuls from El Paso, San Antonio, Austin, Houston, and Dallas. U.S. and Texas representatives included members of the GNC, the Inter-American Relations in Texas Committee, the FEPC, the State Department, and the State of Texas, including Governor Stevenson who attended a morning session. The Mexicans supported legislation that outlawed racial discrimination. The U.S. and Texas speakers, on the other hand, maintained that an educational campaign would advance understanding, although they were more concerned with improving relations with Latin American nations than in ending discrimination at home.[18]

Even though Castañeda needed to maintain good relations with U.S. and Texas officials, he seconded de la Colina's resolution for a civil rights law. Parting ways with the gradualists would have ordinarily discredited Castañeda and undermined support for the FEPC; however, his association with the Mexican officials also gave him the political cover to speak openly about discrimination. Castañeda had also been working closely with LULAC and consulate officials in promoting the bill at the legislature that resulted in Resolution 105 and, no doubt, felt sufficiently committed to the idea to proclaim his support before the Austin gathering. He also added the reasonable and conciliatory argument that one would expect from an FEPC official—improved employment opportunities would eventually resolve social inequality and rid society of a major cause of discrimination. Castañeda reportedly stated that "much of the problem of the Latin American is due to his low economic status, and . . . this can be solved by giving him equal opportunity to obtain higher-paid positions; that if this can be done, in a generation or two most of the discrimination will disappear."[19]

The relationships that Castañeda maintained with the Mexican community coincided with another set of affiliations that he nurtured with African American activists and complainants who also imported their cause into the bureaucratic world of the FEPC. Castañeda and his Field Examiners in Dallas, Clay L. Cochran and Virgil Williams, made early contact with African American workers and their communities. Soon after opening the Dallas office, Castañeda sent Cochran on fact-finding and network-building missions into Houston, Galveston, Freeport, and San Antonio. A later trip to the upper Gulf Coast region resulted in a large number of complaints from Mexican and black workers employed by oil refineries. The subsequent meetings that the FEPC officials called with the complainants and representatives of LULAC and NAACP from Houston resulted in a joint strategy against the oil companies. The oil cases, which will be addressed in the next chapter, brought together the representatives of the two social movements in a momentary form of interracial unity.[20] Williams also helped establish a variety of other coalitions involving black activists and unionists in New Orleans, Lake Charles, and other industrial centers in Louisiana.[21]

Linkages with social movements outside the industrial plants that were under investigations provided FEPC officials an opportunity to build community support and improve their chances of success. The cooperation that he received from LULAC and NAACP activists encouraged Castañeda to recommend additional FEPC offices in San Antonio, Houston, El Paso, Albuquerque, and New Orleans. He was especially interested in strengthening his ties with LULAC in Houston and San Antonio. This was evident when he recommended that the agency hire Perales and John J. Herrera, the head of the LULAC council in Houston, as field examiners.[22] They denied his request and reassigned him to the San Antonio office.

Castañeda's importance as a Mexican civil rights leader was also known by his recommenders for the FEPC job. Senator Chavez, San Antonio Archbishop Robert Lucey, and Houston oilman George A. Hill had acknowledged in their letters of recommendation that Castañeda was more than a successful scholar. He was an active member of the LULAC and Mexican consulate networks in Texas and could be expected to use his new position to advance the rights of Mexicans.[23]

Once hired, Castañeda indicated that he would continue his work on behalf of Mexicans within the FEPC. On at least one occasion, Castañeda told Malcolm Ross, the second chairman of the FEPC, that he wished to use the Good Neighbor Policy to bring added weight to FEPC cases involving Mexicans.[24] His superiors were convinced in the approach and encouraged him. He was often told to remind company representatives that Latin American countries would interpret their cooperation on cases involving Mexican complaints as a wartime gesture of goodwill. The encouragement from

Washington eventually resulted in the decision to free Castañeda from some administrative responsibilities and work among blacks. "It might be tragic," Ross explained to Castañeda, to miss the opportunity to wage an effective campaign in defense of Mexican workers "because of a need to divert your attention constantly to the administrative job and to the problems of the Negroes in your region."[25]

Although it was clear that FEPC officials sought a closer relationship with Mexicans, they also cringed when Castañeda tested the limits of his authority by speaking forcefully and at times publicly against social discrimination. At first, he devoted his attention to cases of employment discrimination and forwarded complaints involving social discrimination to the governor's office and to the GNC. Castañeda apparently grew disillusioned with what he believed to be a slow or ineffective response by state agencies and began to boldly speak out, often in concert with fellow LULAC and consulate leaders. FEPC officials did not hesitate to remind him of the boundaries of acceptable behavior for someone in his position, suggesting that he limit his focus to Mexican workers and employment discrimination. In one case Ross cautioned Castañeda to curb his public commentary on controversial issues outside the domain of the FEPC because it could compromise his effectiveness. The trouble began during the spring of 1945 with a conversation between Castañeda and Robert E. Smith, the director of the GNC, and a subsequent letter from Smith to Ross. According to Smith, they had disagreed on the jurisdiction of the FEPC over a case involving the segregation of minority seamen in a Houston hotel. Castañeda was apparently adamant on the issue because he subsequently wrote an article for *La Prensa* in which he critiqued Smith's opposition to the civil rights bill endorsed by LULAC and submitted by Senator Spears from San Antonio in 1945.[26]

Ross informed Castañeda that he agreed with Smith and cautioned him to maintain cordial relations with influential persons so that the FEPC could continue receiving their support. Smith had been helpful in a case against the Shell Oil Company, Ross reminded Castañeda, and "we may need him again." His final admonishment revealed the recurring challenge facing Ross and other FEPC officials: encourage Castañeda to make use of his political stature and connections to bring Mexican complainants to the FEPC but maintain cordial relations with public officials that included segregationists. On one occasion, Ross informed Castañeda, "Your influence in the Southwest is very great, and I think I showed you that I appreciate your enthusiastic use of it for the benefit of FEPC. I must, however, caution you to be exceedingly circumspect in public expressions, confining them to matters directly concerning FEPC of which you are the responsible spokesman in your area."[27]

The balancing act that Castañeda was expected to play reflected the larger concern in the FEPC to tread carefully in light of a potential backlash from conservatives in the South. The FEPC had already expressed this concern in the African American community. During the first two years of its existence, when the agency concentrated its efforts on African Americans in the Northeast, officials had faced noncompliant employers, disagreeable journalists, and white workers' protests in the form of race strikes. Also, when Roosevelt issued Executive Order 9346 and expanded the geographical and budgetary scope of the agency, southern segregationists, including congressional representatives, led a more determined states' rights campaign against the FEPC. This underscored the agency's dilemma of arousing a reaction when they investigated and settled workers' complaints. The FEPC consequently adopted a strategy of only revealing the necessary evidence to prove discrimination and to argue that unfair racial distinctions undermined a basic premise in the war effort, the full and efficient use of the available labor supply.

Clearly, the guarded ways of the FEPC, along with its procedures for settling grievances, defined the parameters that workers and their allies were to observe when they entered the world of mediation and arbitration within the federal government. The FEPC, on the other hand, also had to be attentive to Mexican officials and their LULAC allies who were always ready to point out that discrimination had hemispheric importance. The cautionary notes that Castañeda regularly received from his superiors defined these limits. The public statements against social discrimination by Mexican and black civil rights leaders as well as Mexico's consular staff nevertheless encouraged him to challenge the institutional limits and expand the FEPC's influence beyond the area of labor utilization.

Another limiting factor on the work of the FEPC was legally sanctioned segregation against African Americans and the ingrained antiblack feelings which segregationists on occasion would invoke to resist the authority of the FEPC. This jeopardized and undercut the FEPC's overall effectiveness. On the other hand, the discourse that linked the work of the FEPC with efforts at building unity in the Americas strengthened the hand of the FEPC and brought indirect benefit to black workers. Segregationists, however, understood that a concession to Mexican complainants under any circumstances would encourage black dissidence and place the whole racial edifice in jeopardy. The FEPC-supervised fight for equal rights in the workplace, in other words, could take different turns depending on how the participants analyzed their options and understood the consequences. This was evident in the battle over discriminatory job ads in the *Dallas News* in 1944. The case against the newspaper quickly escalated into a public fight between the governor of Texas and the chairman of the FEPC over the state's segregationist laws directed at African Americans and the agency's right to apply the president's executive orders. Although the focus was on blacks, the quarrel revealed the interdependent nature of racial inequality in Texas, especially when Ross inserted the Good Neighbor Policy into the debate.

The Segregationist Challenge

The 1944 case began with a directive against race-based job announcements, a practice that, according to local FEPC officials, was prohibited by the president's executive orders. Although Leonard Brin, the regional director of the Dallas office, issued a general directive against discriminatory ads in the paper, he based his edict on an advertisement for African American workers. The announcement was bold and clear in its racial intent: "Wanted: Colored man to work at night as paper handler."[28] The paper, characterized elsewhere by its "Olympian arrogance of viewpoint," announced that it would not comply with the FEPC. Its editor reasoned that executive orders and congressional mandates did not trump the authority of the state because local customs and laws were more representative and authentic expressions of the will of the people. He added that the USES, the federalized state agency responsible for handling job placements, approved the discriminatory ads, implying that newspapers did not constitute a critical war industry and that the FEPC had exceeded its authority.[29]

Although the editor claimed that the USES allowed the discriminatory "job specifications," his major defense was that the paper was exercising its freedom of expression while the FEPC was disrupting the natural order of things in Texas. The discriminatory practice, the editor noted, conformed to "embedded social practices" and abided by a southern tradition of segregation that was "widely approved by Negroes and Whites alike as aiding in satisfactory relations between the two races." He propped up his defense by suggesting that the state's segregation laws countered the FEPC at two levels. The laws, like the practice of discrimination, were expressions of the common will in the South while the nation's nondiscrimination policy represented an unpopular imposition by the federal government. The state laws carried greater authority, he implied, because they resulted from a legislative process and underwent judicial review. The FEPC, by contrast, did not have comparable legal weight because an executive order rather than an act by Congress had created it.[30]

Anticipating a debate on the issue, the editor had informed the state attorney general and Stevenson of his intent to disregard the directive. Subsequent public statements by Stevenson suggest that the governor encouraged the editor in his fight with the FEPC. In an open letter to the agency, Stevenson also used a states' rights argument to challenge the directive and the agency's authority. The governor added that he was bound by the Constitution of Texas to faithfully execute the state's fifteen laws that provided for the segregation of "colored races." The state's supreme court, he added, had upheld the laws and provided penalties for anyone who violated them. Stevenson then posed the following questions:

1. By what authority do you conduct your activities in Texas?
2. What is the scope of your operations and what is the objective sought?
3. Does the purpose of your activities include the violation of any of the segregation laws of this state?
4. Is it the purpose to establish policies which are in violation of state laws?[31]

Ross answered with a detailed letter that he also made available to the press. After describing Executive Orders 8802 and 9346 as a basis for the FEPC's work in Texas, Ross noted that the president sought "to promote the fullest utilization of all available manpower, and to eliminate discriminatory employment practices" that undermined "the prosecution of the war, the workers' morale, and national unity." He added that around 40 percent of the complaints that the FEPC found valid were settled in an informal and amicable manner. Only when cases could not be resolved at the regional level, Ross continued, were they referred to Washington.[32]

In response to the third and fourth questions, Ross reminded the governor that the FEPC had solicited from the state's attorney general a list of the segregation laws and determined that none required or countenanced discrimination in employment. The answer was obvious: the committee was not violating the Jim Crow laws nor did it intend to do so. All along, of course, the issue was discrimination against African American workers. Explicit references to Mexicans were missing in the editor's statements and the governor's pointed questions. The editor's refusal to abide by the FEPC directive and

Stevenson's major public challenge, however, hampered the agency's ability to implement the nation's nondiscrimination policy on behalf of both blacks and Mexicans alike. This was evident in the decision by the agency to rescind the directive and encourage the continued use of discriminatory job ads.[33]

The directive had already been retracted when Ross responded to Stevenson's questions. Although Brin and Field Examiner W. Don Ellinger, urged Washington officials to sustain the directive, they capitulated by declaring that newspapers did not constitute a defense industry and that they operated outside the purview of the FEPC. The backtrack allowed newspapers to maintain the discriminatory practice and permitted the USES to continue referring workers to the segregationist employers. Adding to this concession was Brin's unexplained resignation and the suggestion that the Washington leadership did not wish to press too hard, especially after they began receiving news that the directive and the editor's public statements had stirred a segregationist outcry with letters and calls to the editor and the agency's Dallas office.[34]

The capitulation in Dallas undoubtedly emboldened Stevenson as well as the southern congressmen who eventually defeated a proposal to make the FEPC a permanent agency. Texas Senator Tom Connally, for instance, took the cue and warned his colleagues that the FEPC would cause racial conflict if allowed to force employers like the *Dallas News* to abide by the nation's nondiscrimination policy. It did not matter that the issue had already been settled in favor of the segregationists. The point that Connally made was that the FEPC could be expected to continue disrupting local relations if made a permanent agency. According to the senator, "If we intrude the arm of the Government, the mailed fist, into these relationships [between workers and employers], we shall breed dissension, we shall breed trouble."[35]

Stevenson received letters of support that gave fuller expression to the segregationist thinking that condoned discriminatory ads, opposed the FEPC, and threatened social discord. E. D. Wilson, a "vacuum cleaner specialist" from Fort Worth, noted that the federal government was unfairly intruding in the affairs of the people of the South through "these carpet bag Bureaucrats at Dallas." A Texan living in Minnesota added a Jewish conspiratorial note when he told the governor that he had "smoked" out Brin and defended "*our* America" against "what looks like sabotage of American Principle." [36] From Corpus Christi, C. W. Gibson, the president of the Fred Roberts Memorial Hospital, shared concerns over the fragile racial relations in the South and the discord that the federal government was brewing with its unilateral actions.

He was particularly distressed by the challenge against white supremacy and peaceful relations between the races in the South: "We must remember that this free government was established by white men who gave their blood and lives in order that we might have a free government for white folks. These white folks are not going to surrender their government to the alien or colored peoples; at the same time there is in the ear of every white man a desire for peace and justice to exist for all races."[37] S. L. Davis, sales and public relations director for the *Houston Times,* also warned of conflict and condemned the FEPC for usurping states' rights. He was most explicit in defining the battle over states' rights and the FEPC as a fight over personal freedom, that is, southerners had a right to expect the federal government to respect the duly enacted laws that reflected their segregationist will.[38]

The FEPC's reluctance to do battle with segregationists may not have been without foundation. This was made clear by the marked opposition to the proposal to make the FEPC a permanent agency and the directive against the *Dallas News.* The decision to end the FEPC's short-lived challenge against discriminatory ads was also instructive. It demonstrated that the fight, presumably only over black workers, involved the whole system of racial inequality. The FEPC, however, was not without recourse. Ross invoked the state's Good Neighbor Policy as a moral and politically necessary repudiation of all racially discriminatory practices.

In his public response to the governor, Ross drove a wedge in Stevenson's defense of segregation by pointing to the governor's use of the state's Good Neighbor Policy to condemn discrimination against Mexicans. The aim of the FEPC, Ross added, conformed to the policies of the State of Texas as expressed "through your Excellency's expressed concern" over the problem of "race distinction." Although the governor may have disapproved of racial discrimination against Mexicans primarily to mend diplomatic relations with Mexico, Ross was astute in interpreting the state's policy as a theoretical endorsement of the FEPC's purpose. He also recognized that Stevenson would be politically hard-pressed to deny the statement for fear of upsetting the Mexican government.[39]

Despite Ross's impressive stand against employment discrimination, the fight over discriminatory ads represented a segregationist victory in Texas, defined the limits of the president's executive orders, and lent support to the national campaign against the FEPC. Ross, on the other hand, defended the FEPC and the president's executive orders by linking the policy of nondiscrimination with the Good Neighbor Policy and validating the work of the FEPC. This was his most original and compelling move on behalf of the FEPC because it affirmed racial fairness in employment beyond the black-white binary and placed it on a multiracial and international plane.

The Mexican government and Mexican activists in the Southwest had been building their own cause for fairness by stressing the logical and mutually reinforcing connection between the United States' Good Neighbor Policy and the FEPC. This time the chairman of the FEPC used the policy and Stevenson's own reluctant embrace of it to justify a broad FEPC agenda among both Mexican and black workers. The editor of the *Dallas News* and Stevenson, on the other hand, preferred to focus on African Americans, possibly because Castañeda had recently initiated an FEPC informational campaign in the black community of Dallas.[40] The insistence on reducing the issues of race and state authority to black-white relations could also be explained by the preponderance of such a discursive tradition in the South, reinforced as it was, by the existing segregationist laws and the ongoing appeals to antiblack prejudice in the campaign against the FEPC. The focus on the Jim Crow laws also allowed Stevenson to stir up segregationist sentiments against the alleged threat of big government and undermine one of the most important reforms in labor relations that the Roosevelt administration had produced. At the same time, he treated the segregated order in black and white terms, absent the complicating influence of international norms and Mexico's advocacy policy which Mexicans brought to the table. Although Stevenson may not have thought of blocking the broader moral and discursive framework, Ross saw a divisive intent and countered it. The day-to-day operations of the FEPC, to which we now turn, also witnessed this conflict between segregationist and egalitarian ideas that often turned on the internationalist currency with which Mexican workers and their allies negotiated.

Making Common Cause

Mexican and black workers normally submitted separate individual or group complaints despite the fact that they faced the same kind of prejudice, discriminatory treatment, and unequal working conditions. The records of the FEPC do not offer a clear explanation for this, although Castañeda offered a number of suggestive details in his weekly reports. In some cases, the higher representation of a particular group resulted in more complaints from their representatives. Kelly Field in San Antonio, for instance, produced more complaints from Mexican workers, while the Consolidated Vultee Corporation and the North American Aviation Corporation from the Dallas-Fort Worth area generated more from black workers. In other instances, employers seem to have taken unilateral action against persons from one or the other group. The Todd-Houston Shipbuilding Company from Houston, for example, at one point refused to hire black welders on the grounds that whites refused to work alongside them, and the Brown Shipbuilding Company, also from Houston, unfairly discharged a group of Mexican women. The concerted actions of FEPC officials also determined who submitted complaints. Castañeda's previously noted trip to Austin and San Antonio in 1943 and Ellinger's meetings with "a cross section of Negro leadership" in Houston and Austin in 1944 are cases in point.[41]

In still other cases, the number and distribution of complaints may have reflected different measures of resolve among the workers as well as varying amounts and types of experience in seeking redress or the organizational means and support to initiate and sustain their protests. At no time, however, did the workers or FEPC officials indicate in their correspondence and reports that they wished to act independently because of racial antipathies or suspicions. Mexican and black workers no doubt harbored racial ideas which were reinforced by popular group perceptions and their separation in some work sites. Although it is not practical or useful in this study to know the extent to which Mexicans and black ascribed to these ideas, it is worth noting once again that whiteness scholars believe that the former were especially susceptible to them. To the extent that blacks understood this or internalized the prevalent anti-Mexican feelings, they too construed their relationships with Mexicans in racial terms. My preference is to demonstrate that FEPC officials like Castañeda and the minority workers established common ground despite obvious differences.

In numerous cases, Castañeda as well as other officials like Ellinger, who succeeded Brin as the regional director of the Dallas office, used the complaints by Mexican workers as a first step in demonstrating discrimination and convincing employers and unions to adopt a nondiscrimination policy that would benefit all workers including African Americans. This does not mean that the special policy status attached to Mexicans was solely responsible for offering workers and FEPC officials the opportunity to use their own wedge strategy to win settlements. Employers at times seemed to be more disposed to entertain a complaint from a Mexican rather than from a black. At still other times, they were as unsparing with the Mexican as they were with the African American, perhaps because they could see that conceding to Mexican demands invited African American claims. At any rate, Mexican complaints contributed a unique negotiating element, often complicating the process and benefiting the entire minority workforce.

The FEPC's 1944 case against the Shell, Humble, and Sinclair oil refineries—which will be addressed more fully in the following chapter—provides an example of the circumstances surrounding the decision to build a case against discrimination in the workplace with Mexican complaints. Mexican and black workers had submitted complaints of widespread discrimination by management and workers' organizations in 1943. Castañeda and his staff conducted thorough investigations and concluded that the grievances had merit. Since he feared stronger Anglo opposition to African American complaints, Castañeda decided to first establish the existence of racial discrimination with the Mexican complaints and then direct the refineries to adopt a policy of nondiscrimination that would benefit all the minority workers. Castañeda arrived at this decision after a series of meetings with Mexican and black complainants as well as with Mexican consulate officials and African American and Mexican American civil rights leaders from Houston. Although the negotiations with the representatives of the companies and workers' organizations produced mixed results, management at Shell and Sinclair agreed in 1945 to accept the FEPC's directives that involved the settlement of the Mexican complaints and the acceptance of plant policies of nondiscrimination.[42]

The Mexican-based challenge was not free of difficulties, especially since company and union representatives at Shell understood that the African American complainants were waiting in the wings. They knew that Castañeda and Ellinger were maneuvering to end discrimination and segregation with the Mexican complaints, as well as with the more public argument that the company's refusal to settle the Mexican complaints and to accept a nondiscrimination policy undermined wartime unity in the Americas. The public pressure included the widely circulated observation by Padilla during the founding meetings of the United Nations that he welcomed a settlement by Shell as well as the passage of the Spears Bill as expressions of goodwill: "The neighboring nations of Mexico and the United States must cooperate to wipe out discrimination, because the prestige of the United States is involved."[43]

Although the intent of the Mexican-based strategy was obvious and could trigger a wholesale reaction against the FEPC, Castañeda continued to use it in other work sites. This was evident at the Pantex Ordnance Company in Amarillo when a group of Mexican women called on Castañeda alleging hiring discrimination. The eight complainants noted that they had been denied jobs despite the fact that they were all U.S.-born and could claim a total of ten husbands or brothers serving in the military. They informed Castañeda that the company had refused them employment because they were Mexicans. Castañeda apparently agreed with them and decided to use their complaints and the Good Neighbor Policy to negotiate an understanding of nondiscrimination in the plant. After a meeting in which Castañeda and company officials discussed "the under-utilization of Mexicans and Negroes at the plant," Pantex agreed to hire the Mexican workers. The company representatives also promised to hire and classify Mexicans as well as blacks according to their skills and experience when they expanded the plant and to hire eight hundred additional workers in the near future. In order to ensure that the company kept its word, Castañeda solicited the help of the area director of the WMC who was responsible for job announcements and referrals within the local USES offices. He assured Castañeda that his office would monitor Pantex and report any discriminatory activities by the company and other wartime employers in the area.[44]

In contrast to the Pantex official, the owner and publisher of the *San Antonio Express* and *The Evening News* preferred to speak about black workers although Castañeda had called on him to discuss complaints by Mexicans. He may have anticipated that Castañeda intended to use Mexican complaints to negotiate a nondiscrimination policy. The newspaper owner volunteered that he would never permit African Americans to work at the same skill level as Anglos, meaning that he was reserving the better jobs for whites. He reportedly added that he liked a "good Negro who knew how to keep his place." Castañeda reported that his statements were "typical of the prevalent and deep rooted attitude towards minority groups in the south." He concluded that the owner's attitude was directed at minority groups even though he was only expressing views about African Americans. Although the owner did not speak about the Mexican complainants, Castañeda was not deterred from concluding that the owner harbored similar feelings towards them.[45]

Castañeda's conclusion was reasonable since he understood, partly on the basis of his own investigations and conversations with the complainants, that Mexican and African Americans faced similar kinds of prejudice and discriminatory treatment. The owner's inclination to avoid making racial comments about Mexicans, however, suggested an inconsistent view of race relations. The most logical explanation was that he did not feel the same way about them. Castañeda obviously disagreed or he was prone to dismiss individual views that ran counter to the preponderance of evidence of discrimination against Mexicans. The other possibility was that the owner may have been seeking to ingratiate himself with Castañeda by appearing to favor

Mexicans and encourage a sense of racial unity on the basis of their supposed shared loathing towards the liminal "other." Although this may have been the case, Castañeda did not give in to the temptation. He negotiated a settlement of the Mexican complaints and secured from the owner an agreement to implement a nondiscrimination policy in his newspapers. We do not know if the owner kept his word. Castañeda, however, did not abandon the African American workers to the offer of white solidarity.

When seen alongside the imported egalitarian and segregationist ideas associated with ethnic, internationalist and states' rights causes discussed in previous sections, the cases involving ongoing interracial cooperation point to a highly complex political terrain within the FEPC. The FEPC's relationship with other agencies, especially with the USES, complicated matters further. As noted earlier, all federal agencies had the responsibility to promote the president's executive orders. Although the FEPC had the special responsibility of determining the veracity of charges of discrimination and of negotiating settlements, other agencies were minimally responsible for informing employers of the law and reporting violations to the FEPC. The USES, the employment agency operating within the WMC with the responsibility of the placement of workers in urban and rural jobs, created the most difficulties for the FEPC. Although a previous chapter has already addressed the role that the USES played in reinforcing inequality in Texas, its relationship with the FEPC requires some attention at this point in the discussion. The disagreement over the FEPC's authority over discriminatory ads that was discussed earlier in this chapter was one of the most telling problems in the relationship. The USES's practice of directing workers to employers with discriminatory ads and job requests was another. The next section addresses a fight in which FEPC officials demanded cooperation and their USES counterparts either refused to comply with the nondiscrimination policy or claimed that they could not convince employers to reject their discriminatory practices.

The USES

The State of Texas established its first employment agency during the Depression. The outbreak of the war and the pressing concern over the efficient use of the labor supply led the federal government to place all such state agencies under the USES for the duration of the war. Its primary responsibility was to assign available workers to declared job vacancies and, secondarily, provide job training in areas where workers were not readily available. The USES met its responsibility in Texas much like in the rest of the country. The agency was able to contribute significantly to the national task of matching labor supplies with industrial needs. It failed, however, to provide Mexicans and blacks equal access to hiring and training opportunities. The problem was most evident in the Deep South, where USES officials typically acquiesced to the local customs of segregating workers according to race. They usually consented to discriminatory job ads and requests that specified race and went along with exclusionary practices in job training programs.[46]

The USES was in a position to monitor discriminatory job offers and to implement the nation's nondiscrimination policy. It could challenge discriminatory practices in job referrals and training and report uncooperative employers to the FEPC. Although some USES officials tried to abide by these responsibilities, pressure by employers who insisted on racial job specifications weakened the agency's ability to redistribute labor fairly. The problem became so obvious that the WMC was forced to clamp down on the USES during the latter part of 1943 with an interagency agreement that called for greater cooperation in addressing employment discrimination. Some USES officials apparently heeded the instructions. In the Deep South, however, they generally fell short of the pledge of cooperation.[47]

USES offices in the Deep South typically committed three types of unlawful practices. They filled discriminatory job announcements and requests, refused to make nondiscriminatory referrals, and failed to report discriminatory job requests to the FEPC. The transgressions take on greater significance when one considers that USES officials had promised under the WMC agreement of 1943 to report the discriminatory practices and to correct them, independently first and thereafter with the help of the FEPC. In other words, if an employer stipulated a Mexican or African American worker for a job as a laborer, the USES was to advise the employer that his request violated the president's executive orders. If the employer insisted on making discriminatory job requests and hired workers on the basis of their racial background, national origin, or creed, the USES was required to submit reports, known as 510s, informing the regional director of the FEPC of these problems.[48]

The USES offices in Texas followed the same pattern of discrimination evident in the Deep South and even exceeded it in one important way. They outdid their counterparts by refusing to submit reports of discriminatory requests for workers to the FEPC even after the 1943 agreement. The refusal by USES to report violations, according to Ellinger, implicated its staff in more serious ways. Based on an examination of the USES files in the Galveston,

Houston, and Austin offices, he reported that the staff insisted that employers note the race of the workers that they needed. Ellinger and Castañeda became so exasperated with what they considered the major obstacle to their work that they demanded that the WMC intervene. At one point, Castañeda noted, "The chief type of economic discrimination against Latin Americans is being practiced by USES local offices." WMC officials from Washington intervened in November 1944 and, as a result, Jim Bond, the state WMC director, promised that the USES would cooperate. An undetermined number of USES regional offices began to report irregularities to the FEPC, but others still did not.[49]

It is difficult to determine the extent to which WMC and USES officials were prior segregationists or succumbed to local customs because of pressure from racist employers. USES staff often insisted that segregationist customs were too ingrained to challenge and that they were primarily interested in supplying the necessary workers without creating a conflict that would undermine production. To support this contention, they could point to numerous cases in which employers insisted on racial job requests and threatened to stop cooperating with the USES. The state's segregationist laws and Stevenson's open debate with Ross no doubt also encouraged them to accept and even encourage discriminatory job requests. As noted earlier, the racialized process of soliciting workers and servicing these requests contradicted the intent of the nation's nondiscrimination policy. The choice in the bureaucratic environment of the USES, however, did not provide for such a simple decision between a governmental project of fairness or local segregationists practices. Circumstances were more complicated than that.[50]

USES staff, primarily drawn from the local population and most probably reflecting racial prejudices in the area, no doubt realized that government agencies could never actually force employers to adopt a nondiscrimination policy. Consequently, like in other parts of the South, USES officials were apt to heed local expectations. This is corroborated by at least one case involving the Federal Public Housing Authority and the National Housing Agency in Corpus Christi. According to a USES report, the agencies contracted with local Anglo builders to construct housing for workers migrating into the area. Twenty-two six-room houses were constructed for the Anglo workers. Smaller temporary quarters were assigned for the minority families, 172 for Mexicans and 100 for blacks. The local USES staff treated the construction project as a routine matter and never questioned the discrimination that took place.[51]

Noncompliance with the president's executive orders took other forms. Up until the end of 1944, neither the WMC nor the USES were obligated to keep a record of companies that barred minority workers from the better-skilled jobs posted with the USES. Neither were they required to organize their regional reports on unemployment by race, or to identify the racial characteristics of any labor surplus in a particular area. This undercut the ability of the USES to accurately determine the level of utilization of minority labor. It also prevented FEPC officials from identifying special problem areas in the labor market and in the operation of the USES. Although the USES may have corrected some of the reporting and monitoring problems, the agency continued to block the effective application of the nation's nondiscrimination policy. In other words, the dilemma involved more than a social environment of segregation that encouraged local personnel to act independently of the declared policy of nondiscrimination. They were also subjected to the influence of an enabling, if derelict, bureaucratic world that employed them.[52]

The Kelly Exception

Minority employment in military installations provided a strikingly different experience for Mexican workers. Two related trends stand out: workers registered a proportionally smaller number of complaints, and the FEPC usually resolved the complaints quickly and in favor of the complainants. Kelly Field, the training facility that assembled a workforce of approximately twenty thousand from the San Antonio area, is a case in point. The camp employed at least five thousand Mexicans and seventeen hundred blacks, a number that rivaled other large minority workforces at the oil refineries on the Gulf Coast and the airplane assembly plants in the Dallas–Fort Worth area. Despite the significant number of minority workers, no more than forty individual and group complaints reached the FEPC during the war. Also, military and civilian officials generally responded well to inquiries by Castañeda and Ellinger and settled workers' complaints within a short period of time.[53]

The centralized authority of Kelly's military commander made a difference, especially when he affirmed that the president's executive orders were the law of the land and instructed military and civilian personnel to observe them. The camp commander, in contrast to other industrial employers, may have reflected the more meritocratic *esprit de corps* of the military and exercised greater control over the workforce by virtue of his undisputed authority and the chain of command structure that reigned supreme over the military and civilian personnel. Also, despite the availability of an established grievance structure in the camp's personnel office and the Civil Service, Castañeda and Ellinger communicated often and directly with the commander. His regular involvement in the FEPC investigations and negotiations assured a speedy resolution of the complaints and sent a clear message of cooperation throughout Kelly.[54]

One of Castañeda's earliest reports from his San Antonio office left little doubt that the most effective work of the FEPC was occurring in the military camps. Most of the Mexican complaints had been registered against Kelly Field, the Normoyle Ordnance Depot, and the San Antonio Aviation Cadet Center. Castañeda added, however, that almost all of them had been satisfactorily settled. Not content with this impressive record, Castañeda interviewed the complainants to determine if the settlements "had resulted in an improvement of the general condition prevalent in the military posts in San Antonio." The complainants that he interviewed—three from Kelly, one from Normoyle, and three from the Cadet Center—told of marked improvements in their work stations and in the camps. The Kelly workers gave the most glowing report. Kelly promoted them from mechanic helpers to junior mechanics in four months and increased each of their annual earnings by 540 dollars, or 30 percent. They also reported that since their complaints had been brought before the commanding general "there had been a general improvement throughout Kelly Field." This involved the reclassification of "many" other workers who had also received raises and the appointment of a special counselor to the Personnel Office. The special counselor was to review "the record of all Latin-American employees at Kelly Field and see that they receive impartial consideration and are given the proper classification and promotions."[55]

Despite these early settlements, complaints from Kelly workers continued to come in. The camp's commander and staff from the Personnel Office, however, also continued to intercede. This was evident when Castañeda brought a number of complaints before the camp's Personnel Office in April 1945. The workers claimed that several supervisors continued to deny them their rights despite previous settlements that may have involved the same managers. On other such occasions, Castañeda responded immediately by calling on Kelly officials to observe the negotiated settlements and understandings. This time, Castañeda was more relaxed, no doubt confident that they would respond favorably to his entreaties. When he called for a meeting at his San Antonio office, the Personnel Office sent four representatives, including two key individuals, F. L. Tetsch, the chief administrative civilian officer, and Raul Alcalá, the counselor for Latin American workers. The all-morning meeting resulted in additional evidence of a special cooperative relationship.[56]

The Kelly officials promised to visit with the camp's supervisors and other persons in positions of authority to explain the president's executive orders. Tetsch concluded the meeting with a series of statements that reaffirmed Kelly's position regarding minority workers and the FEPC. According to Castañeda, Tetsch explained that the commanding general wished to eliminate all discrimination at Kelly. Tetsch reportedly added that Kelly had established a new grievance procedure and "every effort was being made to prevent the development of conditions or situations that might result in discrimination." Castañeda ended his report on the meeting by quoting Tetsch's statement of understanding on the cooperation that was to govern relations between Kelly and the FEPC. Workers were to continue taking up their grievances with the Personnel Office and seek the help of the FEPC if they were not satisfied with results. Castañeda submitted a report without comment, suggesting that he agreed with the proposed arrangement.[57]

One month after the meeting, Castañeda reported that he was meeting with General G. H. Beverley, the camp's newly appointed commander. The result was a reaffirmation of a policy of nondiscrimination and a resolution of two cases of discrimination, possibly the same ones that had led to the meeting at Castañeda's office. The first one involved a white worker, presumably a driver, who refused to transport black civilian and military personnel in the camp. The second case involved a supervisor with responsibilities over forty workers who boasted that he would never allow Mexicans or blacks to work for him. Beverley, according to Castañeda, restated his predecessor's commitment to rid Kelly of discrimination primarily because he considered it a basic morale problem and "took a personal interest in the matter." He then instructed his personnel officers to resolve the cases. They discharged the white driver and subsequently denied her appeal. They also assigned three Mexican men and one Jewish woman to the offending supervisor. When the supervisor recommended that one of the workers be discharged, the personnel office investigated the case and soon thereafter released him.[58]

The impressive instances of cooperation between Kelly's commander and FEPC officials did not mean that discrimination rarely occurred or that minority workers were always satisfied with the way that camp officials handled their complaints. The very agreements or understandings of cooperation revealed that Anglo workers did not always abide by official policies. This was especially evident in 1943, when FEPC officials publicized the president's executive orders in the local Spanish-language newspapers and urged minority workers to avail themselves of the grievance process. Castañeda made it clear at the time that the FEPC wished to focus on San Antonio because of its large Mexican population. He gave immediate attention to Kelly, in part because of the complaints that had reached his office and the urgings of local leaders like Perales.

One of the early recurring complaints was the use of military discipline on civilian workers at Kelly workers. Typically when workers complained on the job or registered an official complaint with the FEPC, their supervisors would discharge them for insubordination or lack of respect for authority. The commanding officer ordinarily approved the discharge and the FEPC usually found it impossible to obtain a reconsideration of the case. Castañeda's predicament was complicated further by the fact that the executive orders did not give the FEPC the authority over discharges based on insubordination. He faced this problem soon after his appointment to the Dallas office. His superiors in Washington instructed him to docket cases if the complainant charged racial discrimination. Castañeda began doing this during the latter part of 1943 until Kelly's command structure relented and modified its dismissal practice to accommodate informal and official complaints of discrimination.[59]

Minority workers faced another problem associated with the grievance process at Kelly and other military camps in the area. Military camps normally hired minority workers without a civil service examination. According to Castañeda, this practice usually affected the majority of minority workers, especially Mexican nationals, who were hired for the lesser-skilled occupations. The lack of a civil service examination meant that they were without administrative recourse when released from work. In other words, when workers complained, a supervisor could summarily fire them without fear of having to explain his action before a Civil Service Board that would ordinarily investigate such cases on appeal. Once fired, often on charges of insubordination, the workers could no longer avail themselves of administrative remedies available to the rest of the workforce. The FEPC, on the other hand, was limited by the finality that a charge of insubordination and the lack of administrative remedies gave a dismissal of a minority worker.[60]

The U.S. Civil Service Commissions at Kelly and other military camps in the San Antonio area, like Kelly's commander, apparently changed their grievance procedure. By the summer of 1944, Ellinger was reporting that the special representative of the commission at Kelly was "very cooperative and very sincere in his attempts to remove discriminatory treatment of Negroes and Latin-Americans." The change may have extended to other sources of public employment because Ellinger added that the commission had been approving a record number of African Americans for skilled positions in San Antonio.[61] This suggests that the positive relations with the military camps may have led to positive results in other industrial sites in San Antonio, a city in which the FEPC fared much better than in other large urban areas in settling complaints and in securing support for the campaign to make the FEPC a permanent agency after the war.

More research is required before San Antonio can be said to have been a friendlier environment for minority workers. One of the more inviting possibilities was that the large number of military training facilities in San Antonio, with their friendlier response to the FEPC, influenced labor relations throughout the city. The San Antonio political environment, with its long Mexican and labor political traditions, also explains the city's receptivity to the FEPC and causes on behalf of minority workers' rights. The strong Mexican support for the FEPC came from newspapers like *La Prensa,* the local LULAC leadership, the consulate general, and the highly influential Archbishop Robert Lucey.[62]

The single most impressive expression of support occurred on February 27 and 28, 1945, when FEPC Chairman Ross visited the city while on his southwestern tour to promote the Movement for a Permanent FEPC. The visit coincided with the opening of the FEPC office in San Antonio and plans to build support for the National Council for a Permanent FEPC. Perales, Castañeda, and Lucey—a key supporter of the campaign to make the FEPC a permanent agency—planned Ross's visit. On February 27, Ross met with a group of sixteen persons that included industrialists, a GNC official, and representatives of leading organizations from San Antonio. In the evening, he addressed a large meeting at the chancery of the archbishop. The audience included representatives of the Negro Chamber of Commerce, the Baptist Ministers Union, the Negro Democratic Club, the National Negro Congress, the Pullman Porters Brotherhood, the Progressive Women's Club, the Underwriters Association, the Postal Alliance, the NAACP, and the Negro Press. On the following day, Ross met with city and county officials, and in the evening, he spoke to a group of Mexican leaders representing LULAC, the Loyal American Citizens, the Committee of One Hundred, the Federation for Industrial Education and Protection, the Mexican Workers' Union, the Mexican Chamber of Commerce, the Mexican Real Estate Association, and the Mexican consulate. According to Castañeda, "In all these meetings the work and organization of the Committee was explained and the cooperation of local leaders was pledged."[63]

Ross would later recall a dinner during his visit, possibly on the evening of February 28, when the San Antonio leaders honored four Mexican Kelly workers who had negotiated a settlement, most probably with the help of the FEPC. The organizers of the event obviously wanted to underscore the importance of the FEPC and their campaign for workers' rights. If Ross's memory served him right, the victory at Kelly brought more than material benefit to the workers. It affirmed their equality, repaired their injured pride, and opened up new vistas: "The dollars involved were few, the spur to their pride enormous. They were accepted; skilled workers among Anglo skilled workers. A man could go on from there."[64] The FEPC's experience with military camps in San Antonio stood out as such a bright spot in an otherwise bleak horizon that an astute observer such as Ross could feel momentarily inspired and see morally uplifting consequences to the negotiated settlements by Kelly workers.

Conclusion

The close collaboration between Mexican activists and the FEPC in San Antonio suggests that the fight against employment discrimination must be seen broadly. It cannot be treated only in terms of independent or affiliated workers' organizations and their organizing and strike actions. The struggle for workers' rights also occurred in the FEPC, and LULAC stood out in this story. Its leaders were instrumental in drawing the FEPC's attention to the Southwest and in bringing Mexican complainants together with FEPC officials. This influence was especially evident in the selection of Castañeda as a key FEPC operative. His close collaboration with other LULAC leaders and especially his dedication to the Mexican cause, in large part encouraged by the FEPC's focus on Mexicans, meant that Mexican activists had bored into the bureaucratic world of the FEPC.

The work of the FEPC among Mexican workers in Texas reveals yet another layer of meaning. A preoccupation with Mexico and the Good Neighbor Policy clearly drove the FEPC to give emphasis to Mexican workers in the Southwest. This explains the decision to cooperate with LULAC and Mexican consuls. Diplomatic considerations notwithstanding, FEPC officials also discovered that commitments to the Good Neighbor Policy could be used to challenge the segregationist custom of the South. Stevenson could try to paint the racial order according to the limited statutory definition of separate black and white communities, but he could not deny that his pronouncements in favor of the Good Neighbor Policy supported the principle of equal rights. The *Dallas News* got its way, but the governor, like many of the employers that the FEPC investigated, found it more difficult to escape the wedge strategy that the Good Neighbor Policy provided and to deny that the experiences of Mexicans and blacks were interrelated.

The public debate between Stevenson and Ross reflected the daily contentious relations between FEPC officials and segregationist employers, including local USES officials. The opposing forces, gathered as they were in the arena of workers' rights, imported their ideas into the internal workings of the FEPC, often in accordance with prevailing segregationist and egalitarian views. This is an added reason why the FEPC has to be seen as more than a state agency implementing an important nondiscrimination policy. It also functioned as a point of contention between countervailing political-ideological currents originating in local, regional, and international settings. This explains why the USES at times acted according to local custom as it drew its employees from among nearby local residents with segregationist tastes. An employer like Kelly, on the other hand, behaved differently as it tipped the balance against segregationist tendencies with its culture of strict military discipline and accountability.

This chapter has made the underlying argument that Mexicans faced numerous obstacles as they sought entry into wartime industries. Increased wartime production accounted for much of the upward occupational mobility. Discrimination, on the other hand, limited this movement. Official inattention and the government's delay in implementing its nondiscrimination policy in the Southwest added to the problem. Opposition to the work of the FEPC, on the other hand, reinforced white privilege and revealed the depth of the prejudice against minority workers. Despite this opposition the FEPC resolved some disputes in favor of the complainants and encouraged employers to abide by the president's executive orders. The FEPC also contributed in a less perceptible manner. It invigorated the Mexican cause by reinforcing the spirit of resistance and collaboration among workers, Mexican officials, and LULAC leaders. It also strengthened the position of LULAC as a key intermediary between the Mexican community and the state. The work sites that drew the concentrated attention of the FEPC provide us a basis for examining in greater detail the work of the FEPC and the obstacles and possibilities that Mexican workers faced.

Chapter 6: The Slippery Slope of Equal Opportunity in the Refineries of the Upper Texas Gulf Coast

The oil refineries in the upper Texas Gulf Coast region bounded by Texas City, Houston, and Beaumont were not unlike other war industries in the state. They also denied Mexicans, as well as blacks, equal hiring, wage, and upgrading opportunities. The record in oil, however, was also different. The refineries denied workers equal opportunities while they experienced matchless growth and a record number of new well-paying jobs. The response was tightfisted in another way. The refining companies and the predominantly Anglo unions and independent workers' organizations in their plants often pulled out contracts or cited contractual understandings that called for a racial division of labor in the refineries. The segregationists did not restrict themselves to public claims of white supremacy or states' rights arguments to maintain Jim Crow relations in the workplaces. They also made deliberate and formal claims on job control as a form of racial privilege, especially when minority workers solicited the help of the FEPC.[1]

The close collaboration between the refining plants and the Anglo workers gave segregation its enduring quality. AFL, CIO, and independent organizations of Anglo workers typically negotiated contracts with management that dictated the number of minority workers that could be hired, the jobs they were to fill, and procedures that kept them from advancing

Cartoon depiction of a large Mexican man, rolling up his sleeves and grinning down at Hitler and three Nazis, n.d. (Artist: Antonio Arias Bernal, Coordinador de Asuntos Interamericanos. The Holland Collection of World War II Posters, Center for Southwestern Research, University of New Mexico, Albuquerque, New Mexico.)

into better-skilled and better-paying positions. They also came together in their opposition to the FEPC. The workers were even adamant in defending Jim Crow when they suspected that management would accept the agency's findings and proposed settlements. Management, on the other hand, readily admitted discrimination but typically complained that the workers and their unions opposed changes in the segregated order and would react violently if the companies accepted the FEPC directives that favored the minority complainants. Company officials may have exaggerated the segregationist reaction to reject or delay compliance, but Anglo workers and their representatives did openly threaten to stage race strikes. One explanation for the tense relations was that Anglo workers feared losing their hard-won unionist gains of the 1930s. Racial motivations, however, were also obvious in their language and exclusionary activities. Although they may have been primarily concerned over job control, their contracts and open opposition to industrial democracy suggest deeply engrained segregationist ideas as an explanation for unequal wartime recovery.

Soon after its Dallas office began operations, the FEPC waged a two-and-a-half-year challenge against thirteen oil refineries.[2] FEPC examiners focused on group complaints against three refineries (Humble, Sinclair, and Shell), a company union at Humble, the Baytown Employees' Federation, and two CIO unions, Locals 227 and 367. The fight in oil, however, did not occur in isolation of social movements in the Mexican and black communities. FEPC officials collaborated with LULAC and the Mexican consul, as well as with the NAACP from Houston. They also sought favorable settlements in the three refineries as a first step in pushing for a policy of nondiscrimination in the entire regional industry. Anglo worker opposition was so strong, however, that the FEPC was unable to make an appreciable difference in the lives of minority workers. The agency's failure to effectively combat discrimination underscored its powerlessness; it also demonstrated the durable strength of a system of racial inequality.[3]

Although blacks also faced discrimination, the FEPC focused its attention on Mexicans. In some instances, FEPC officials like Castañeda expressed concern that findings in favor of black complainants could trigger a stronger reaction from the companies and the unions. This did not mean that the FEPC abandoned blacks. Field examiners also investigated complaints by black workers and sought to negotiate settlements in their favor. Also, when Mexican and black workers submitted similar complaints from the same refineries, FEPC officials first used Mexican complaints to secure favorable settlements and a policy of nondiscrimination that benefited all workers.

They used this approach on at least one important occasion when, as noted previously, the workers, LULAC, and NAACP representatives met with Castañeda and decided on the strategy. This collaboration had the added benefit of linking discrimination claims and FEPC directives with the Good Neighbor Policy and the larger world of hemispheric politics.

Oil, Mexicans, and the FEPC

The booming oil industry on the upper Gulf Coast generated a growing number of jobs and some of the more attractive wages offered by the state's war industries. Although the industry's growth made this gain possible, successful unionization efforts maximized the employment opportunities. By the mid-1940s the CIO-affiliated Oil Workers' International Union (OWIU) had organized eleven refineries in the region and claimed some of the most favorable labor agreements in Texas, including overtime pay and vacation leave.[4] Economic growth and unionization in oil, however, did not assure equal opportunities. By the time of Pearl Harbor, the refineries employed approximately 2,200 Mexican and black workers, or 6 percent of the total work force of about 36,650. Blacks constituted more than half of the minority workforce, possibly as much as 4 percent of the total. A 2 or 3 percent Mexican figure was appreciably lower than the 5 percent that Castañeda attributed to the Mexican workforce in the state's war industries. The larger representation by blacks was significantly lower than the 6 percent employment rate that they registered in the state's war industries in 1942. Oil refineries also hired Mexican and black workers at a lower rate than their proportional representation in the total population, about 11.5 and 14.4, respectively.[5]

Mexicans and blacks rarely found employment in the pipeline and production branches of the industry, although they are known to have cleared the terrain, including swamp land, for the construction of the refineries in the early 1900s. When the refineries hired them, however, they usually assigned them common laborer jobs, paid them less than Anglos that were similarly classified, and denied them opportunities to train for other jobs or to advance into better-paying skilled occupations. In rare instances when Mexican and African American workers shared skilled jobs with Anglos, their job classification and pay normally remained unchanged, that is, they were categorized as unskilled or semiskilled workers. Management rarely promoted them to such jobs as mechanics, truck helpers, truck drivers, and even bottle washers.[6]

The practice of placing minorities in the common laborer positions and denying them upgrading opportunities created a hiring ceiling that the refining companies often maintained through the previously noted contractual agreements or informal segregationists understandings. Organized labor was thus instrumental in defining the occupational hierarchy, a fact that became clearer when unionists openly pressured the refineries to resist FEPC directives to end discrimination. Popular antiminority feelings that resulted from fears of increased job competition had previously influenced labor's defensive posture and the industry's hiring practices among Mexican workers. The result was a gradual depletion of their Mexican workforce. More importantly, these early tensions and protests coincided with union campaigns and contractual negotiations that shaped the Mexican's bottom position in the industry.[7]

A significant number, perhaps a majority, of the Mexican refinery workers may have been born in Mexico. A survey conducted by the FEPC in one of the refineries in 1943, indicated that 59 percent of them were born outside the United States. According to one observer, the U.S.-born Mexicans were underrepresented because they knew of the discrimination that awaited them in oil and preferred to search for jobs in other more welcoming locations.[8] Mexican nationals apparently had fewer options and were inclined to accept the low-paying jobs. The presence of a large number of Mexican nationals who ordinarily commanded lower wages explains why Anglo workers may have been especially sensitive to the possibility of a wage-cutting threat from below. It also reveals why Adolfo G. Domínguez, the Mexican consul from Houston, played an important role in representing the Mexican complainants before the FEPC. The involvement of the Mexican consul, as well as LULAC, in community struggles was not new. His predecessor, Luis L. Duplán, had joined with numerous community organizations of U.S.- and Mexico-born members from Galveston and Houston to form the statewide federation called La Federación de Sociedades Mexicanas y Latino Americanas.[9]

Mexican oil workers began submitting their complaints in 1941 to the Office of Production Management in San Antonio and the FEPC office in Washington. Domínguez and Manuel C. Gonzales had also contacted officials in Washington and the FEPC offices in El Paso in July and August 1942. These were the complaints and requests for FEPC action that Lawrence Cramer, the executive secretary of the FEPC, and Will Alexander, an OPM official, reported during the previously noted interagency meeting of December

1942. In June 1943, one month before the FEPC opened the Dallas office, Washington officials directed Ernest G. Trimble, the field examiner who had operated the El Paso office, to conduct an investigation in the oil industry. Trimble reported widespread discrimination against Mexicans and blacks. Although Trimble did not report the number of company representatives who admitted that discrimination existed in the industry, he used their admissions to confirm his findings. He also suggested that company officials had disclosed widespread discrimination as part of a strategy to prod the FEPC to take action against the entire industry rather than individual plants. The plan, according to Trimble, was to busy the FEPC with industry-wide investigations, prolong the battle, and place the industry in a position of negotiating strength.[10]

Trimble's report, along with the accompanying workers' complaints and correspondence from Mexican consular officials and LULAC officers, amounted to a call to action when Castañeda opened the Dallas office in July 1943. Soon thereafter, Mexican oil workers submitted four additional complaints of discrimination that gave Castañeda an added reason to act. He immediately sent Clay L. Cochran, a fair practice examiner, to conduct a two-week investigation that focused on the refineries of the upper Gulf Coast. Cochran interviewed Domínguez, Mexican complainants from the Humble, Gulf, and Shell refineries, John E. Crossland, the regional director of the CIO, representatives of the Oil Workers' Organizing Campaign (OWOC), and officers of various CIO locals. Cochran confirmed Trimble's previous findings and found in favor of the new complainants.[11]

The investigations by Trimble and Cochran, and subsequent ones by Cochran, Castañeda, and Don Ellinger, Castañeda's replacement at Dallas in 1944, involved fact-finding meetings with the Mexican consul, local groups of Mexican and black workers and community leaders associated with LULAC and the NAACP. During these meetings, the participants pledged support for the complainants and discussed the previously noted strategy of initiating claims of discrimination on the basis of Mexican workers' complaints. They also urged FEPC officials to act immediately against individual companies. These expressions of support and the overwhelming evidence supporting the claims of discrimination encouraged officials like Castañeda to push for immediate action.[12]

By the end of October, Castañeda, armed with an abundance of evidence, reported to his superiors that conditions needed "immediate action." The head of Shell's Industrial Relations Department openly admitted hiring, job classification, wage, and upgrading discrimination against minority workers. The company representative reportedly stated what he had previously told Trimble "that his company would not change its practice unless all the oil and gas companies in the Gulf Coast Region adopted a similar policy." Castañeda understood, as Trimble had recognized earlier, that the Shell official was admitting discrimination as a "pretext" to influence the FEPC to take action against the industry as a whole. Meanwhile, FEPC officials in Washington were undecided on the course of action. Castañeda, already impatient with the delays in Washington and their requests for additional evidence of discrimination, recommended a plant-by-plant strategy with investigations of the complaints against Shell and Magnolia as well as new ones that Cochran brought back against Humble, Sinclair, and Gulf. A conference between management and labor representatives in each plant, he suggested, could then be called to resolve the complaints and compel the companies to adopt a nondiscrimination policy.[13]

Washington officials eventually decided to pursue the more focused strategy, but not before the internal debate had delayed the negotiations with the individual refineries for about three months. Castañeda expressed much concern over the delay because he felt that it emboldened the refineries. He warned that the individual companies would refuse to comply with FEPC directives until the entire industry was made to observe a policy of nondiscrimination. Castañeda, however, remained confident that issuing directives against individual employers on the basis of substantiated complaints was the more sound approach to the problem.[14] The case against the targeted companies was compelling: "We are not concerned with companies against which no formal complaint has been made, and regardless of what others are doing, if the companies charged admit, as they have, that they are violating the provisions of Executive Order 9346, they must comply with its provisions regardless of the others."[15] Castañeda nevertheless openly feared that the companies were going to hold out as long as possible and worried that the FEPC might not be able to muster the necessary authority to resolve such a standoff.[16]

During the delay between August and November, Castañeda and his staff continued soliciting complaints and investigating the charges made by the workers. During the first week of November 1943, Castañeda reported that the investigation at Gulf, Shell, Sinclair, Texas, and Humble "reveal and confirm the well established discriminatory practices of oil companies and refineries in this area." Cochran conducted at least one more major investigation during a visit to the region between November 8 and 13. His report offered additional substantiating evidence and more complaints. Cochran also noted that the most blatant cases of discrimination were occurring at the Humble, Sinclair, and Shell refineries. Moreover, there were a sufficient number of Mexican workers in each plant willing to formally challenge their employers.[17]

Although the FEPC focused on the three refineries, Castañeda and Ellinger processed Mexican complaints against eight refineries between May 1943 and December 1944. They adopted a dual strategy that first focused on complaints against Humble, Sinclair, and Shell, hoping that favorable adjustments in these refineries would compel the entire industry to enforce the president's executive orders. The second part of the plan involved a decision to challenge the general practice of racial discrimination with complaints by Mexican workers. Since they feared stronger Anglo opposition to African American complaints, Castañeda and Ellinger decided to first establish the existence of racial discrimination on the basis of Mexican complaints. Although the Dallas office recorded a continuous stream of investigations and settlements in other industries throughout the state, the cases against Humble, Sinclair, and Shell kept it occupied until the agency ceased its operations in 1945.[18]

The prolonged fight in oil was in large part due to the opposition by the Anglo rank and file to FEPC directives. The unaffiliated workers' organization at Humble was especially adamant in maintaining racial divisions at the workplace, while the state CIO leadership and the officers of the CIO locals at Sinclair and Shell were unable or reluctant to dissuade the segregationists in their ranks. The CIO unionists may have been the most inconsistent since they sustained Jim Crow locally while their state, national, and even local leadership openly supported the president's executive orders. The inconsistency, however, was not always clear. The OWOC organizers encouraged minority workers to speak out against discrimination at Humble and even joined officers of local unions in the meetings with FEPC investigators, but they were relatively silent at Sinclair and Shell. State CIO leaders, on the other hand, promised to cooperate with FEPC officials, but ultimately refused to dictate "policy" to their rank and file in Houston. The fact remained, however, that CIO locals, like the AFL locals in other plants, negotiated discriminatory bargaining agreements that barred minority workers from the skilled occupations. These agreements as well as informal understandings were negotiated with the knowledge and support of the OWIU. When pressed by the FEPC, the OWIU and local union leaders presumably shared the sentiments of their local membership or preferred not to disturb segregationist customs, especially at Sinclair and Shell.[19]

Although it may be impossible to know to what degree racial thinking colored the attempts at job control, the union leaders freely admitted that their rank and file opposed changes in segregated work sites. Company officials also admitted discrimination when FEPC officials investigated the workers' complaints. Both, however, frequently claimed that they could not agree to resolve the complaints because of the significant opposition among Anglo workers. Castañeda and his fellow FEPC officials noted in their correspondence and reports that they suspected that union leaders and company representatives blamed unionists as a way to forestall the FEPC investigations. They usually agreed that they had supported segregation in the workplace but sidetracked the compliance process by claiming that Anglo workers were determined segregationists and would protest and disrupt production if the FEPC pressed its case. The finger-pointing continued throughout the war as union officers, company officials, and, on some occasions, the unionists themselves resisted FEPC directives.

Castañeda and Ellinger understood that a good number of the rank-and-file Anglo unionists were ardent segregationists, but they also suspected that management and union leaders were concealing their opposition to integration and encouraging dissent to stall the compliance process. Company representatives may have shared racial views with the Anglo workforce. They may have also entertained the idea of promoting racial thinking to curry favor with labor or to encourage divisions among the workers. Their stated position, however, was somewhat credible given the economic losses they could incur as a result of a disruption in production. Although the refineries often publicly complained of FEPC compliance pressures, they usually appeared to be projecting an image of disinterested players rather than actively provoking a reaction. Local union leaders, however, openly encouraged workers to see the intervention of the federal government as a threat to racial privilege and job control. This was evident when union leaders representing the workers' organization at Humble and the CIO locals at Sinclair and Shell openly defied FEPC directives and defended discrimination, particularly against blacks, as the prevailing custom in the South. Moreover, they understood that the FEPC's strategy of focusing on Mexican complaints could unravel the segregationist apparatus. Concessions to Mexicans, they noted, would result in similar claims by blacks, increased competition for jobs, depressed wages, and the displacement of Anglo workers. Mexican workers made their first stand at Humble.[20]

Humble

Humble owned four refineries in Texas, including the one at Baytown that became the center of early controversy for the FEPC. The Baytown plant employed around three thousand workers including about seventy-five Mexicans and four hundred blacks. The complaint against Humble emerged while the CIO-led OWOC was joining the issue of unionization with the cause of minority workers. The CIO's national leadership initially directed the OWOC and thus injected a more progressive view on minority rights than was normally the case in the area. The OWOC leadership endorsed the claim of discrimination by Mexican complainants in part because it was actively soliciting the support of minority workers for the CIO union, Local 333, in the upcoming union election. This touched off a near-violent and racially inspired reaction by the company union, the Baytown Employees' Federation (BEF).[21]

In the middle of this highly controversial organizing campaign, a group of six Mexican workers charged Humble with six forms of discrimination. According to the complaint, Mexican laborers received $0.765 per hour for performing the same tasks as Anglo laborers who were paid $0.895 an hour. While Mexican orderlies in the company hospital received a wage of $137 per month, Anglo janitors received $180 per month. Mexican and Anglo workers doing the same work in and around the acid tanks received $0.795 per hour and $0.925 per hour, respectively. Although Mexicans cut, bent, and tied steel for $0.765 per hour, Anglos working for contractors on refinery property earned $1.34 for the same work. Mexicans were usually assigned to the labor department without opportunities for promotion and Humble had refused to hire Mexicans since at least 1937. FEPC officials substantiated the charges on the basis of their subsequent investigations.[22]

The company superintendent, Gordon L. Farned, responded to the complaint with a lengthy justification of Humble's record with its Mexican workers. He also broached the issue of Anglo worker opposition that was to loom over compliance negotiations in the industry. Farned cautioned the FEPC about disrupting the deep-rooted custom of discrimination against Mexicans in the state and urged a strategy of gradual change to minimize Anglo hostility:

> Unless and until there is a change in public feeling and sentiment, regardless of what we as one employer may do about the matter, it is an undeniable fact that Anglo American workmen and the public generally, exclusive of the

> Mexicans themselves, do set themselves apart and do consider themselves to be superior mentally, physically and socially to the Mexicans. . . . it probably would be to the best interests of the Mexicans "to make haste slowly"; to make social and economic gains gradually, to educate the populace at large gradually, and to promote their acceptance of the principles aimed at, rather than to take action intended to accomplish the ends you seek, which in actuality, if carried out, would most certainly start serious hostilities and lead to a harmful conflagration.[23]

Farned added a second reason for resisting compliance. He suggested that the FEPC seek industry-wide compliance rather than plant-by-plant settlements. Otherwise, each company that complied presumably would be made the focus of the community's wrath with the resulting disruption of production. He added that the company could not have been expected to treat Mexicans better since they did not usually meet educational requirements. Since company officials never defined these requirements in terms of educational attainment levels, they may have meant that they expected a higher fluency in English.

Subsequent investigations revealed a glaring inconsistency in the company's claims. Company officials admitted that Anglos were frequently hired without being subjected to language or educational requirements and that Mexicans were denied employment even when they spoke English fluently and claimed educational experience similar to Anglos. Moreover, the officials failed to demonstrate a lack of ability by the Mexican workers since they often performed the same tasks as Anglos. As a result of the investigation, the FEPC expanded the complaint to include charges of discriminatory skill classifications as well as segregated drinking and toilet facilities.[24]

While Castañeda negotiated with Humble, the company union began to include blacks and the CIO local in their claims of an impending threat to Anglo privilege. BEF officials openly declared that Local 333 was threatening the livelihood of Anglo workers by welcoming Mexicans and blacks into the union and by supporting claims of racial discrimination in the refinery. They stepped up their race-baiting activities against Local 333 and the FEPC during the following weeks through a widely distributed periodical, *The Bulletin.* The paper consistently warned that compliance with the Mexican complaints would lead to complaints by blacks and calls for greater racial equality.[25]

The editors of *The Bulletin* left little doubt about their segregationist tastes when they boldly proclaimed that, "A vote for the CIO is a vote for absolute equality between the white and colored races on every job in the Baytown Refinery from labor gang to Department head."[26] When the FEPC wired the BEF to cease making inflammatory statements, he responded with a red-baiting accusation, much like the *Dallas News* would do the following year. He announced that the Anglo workers did not "intend to be swayed from our purpose by any telegraphed reprimands from any of the C.I.O.-owned and operated Fair Labor Practices Committees in Washington, D.C., so this is a notice to them to save stamps and telegraph costs."[27]

Despite the findings of the initial investigation, the FEPC decided to delay action on the joint complaint and an additional complaint in which Local 333 alleged discrimination in the hiring, tenure, and compensation of Mexican and African American workers. This decision to withdraw from the conflict was made pending the outcome of the union election and FEPC deliberations in Washington on the proposed El Paso hearings. Also contributing to the postponement was the FEPC's continuing indecision on whether to seek compliance on an industry or plant-by-plant basis.[28]

A renewed interest in the oil companies and a plant-by-plant strategy became evident when Castañeda obtained permission for a second investigation at Humble. By this time, the union had failed to secure certification and the FEPC had decided against the El Paso hearings.[29] The investigation generated complaints by three additional Mexican workers alleging wage discrimination. By the time Castañeda met with company officials, Humble had granted the complainants a raise. The settlement, however, involved subterfuge. Humble officials had also signed a contract with the Houston-based Brown and Root Company to shift away the laboring jobs that were filled by Mexican and black workers. In this way, Humble sought to distance itself from any future claims of discrimination.[30]

Company officials had been insistent on adhering to the local custom of denying employment opportunities to Mexican workers on the grounds that to do otherwise would invite trouble. They had also been reluctant to fully admit discrimination or to correct past abuses supposedly because of the feared reaction by Anglo workers. Humble officials, however, may have concluded that compliance was inevitable given the FEPC's belated yet determined decision to consider one refinery at a time. The union election, on the other hand, was probably the single most important factor that opened the way for resolving the impasse.

Humble had kept the FEPC at bay while it did battle with the OWOC on its successful march through the rest of the industry. Once the union lost the election, the company was free to confront the problem that it faced with the FEPC. Although Humble may have appeared overly compliant in granting a raise to the complainants, it had also begun to dispose of its minority workforce. With this move, the company also avoided a conflict with its Anglo workforce and nullified one of Local 333's most important organizational and ideological bases of operation.

Local 333 was the only union in the region known to have cooperated with the FEPC. This was due largely to the influence of the CIO-run OWOC, which embraced the cause of the Mexican complainants. After a successful campaign that resulted in election victories in approximately six refineries, the CIO organizers in the OWOC boldly confronted racial discrimination. Supporting the cause of the Mexican complainants in Humble, however, resulted in the OWOC's only defeat in the early 1940s. The defeat also reinforced local fears of an Anglo workers' reaction to compliance and revealed a serious division between members of the national CIO and local and state leadership around the issue of race.

The OWIU and local CIO leaders had opposed the OWOC's progressive racial policy, including its endorsement of Mexican complaints during the organizing campaign at Humble. Pressure on the national CIO office eventually led to the removal of its organizers and an end to labor's expressed concern for minority workers. The experience at Humble thus demonstrated that the OWIU and local leadership preferred to avoid the race issue for fear of antagonizing Anglo workers, a view that also found expression during the battle at Sinclair.

Sinclair

The Sinclair refinery in Pasadena employed a work force of approximately fifteen hundred that included about one hundred Mexicans and 250 blacks.[31] Mexican workers submitted at least three joint complaints. The local union supported these first complainants. J. O. Gray, secretary-treasurer of CIO Local 227, submitted the first complaint in April 1942 to the Office of Production Management in San Antonio. He indicated that a foreman had unfairly issued warnings to the men and that the union's Workmen's Committee had submitted a request to transfer them to another department.[32] There is no evidence that the FEPC acted on the initial complaint perhaps because around that time a group of Mexican workers from Sinclair was also seeking the assistance of the FEPC with a more comprehensive complaint that charged the company as well as the union with discrimination.

The forty Mexican complainants secured the assistance of Consul Domínguez in alleging a historical pattern of discrimination by the company and Local 227. One of their major allegations was that Sinclair had stopped hiring Mexicans in 1931. The workers also claimed that Sinclair routinely hired blacks to replace departing Mexican workers. They further charged that the company, in collaboration with union leaders, placed Mexicans in the laboring positions at an approximate hourly wage of $0.785. Many performed the same tasks as skilled Anglo workers though they were assigned job classifications as helpers at an hourly wage of $0.985. Four of them received $0.835 an hour. They worked as janitors along with nine African American workers, and they could only transfer to other departments if they kept their classification as common laborers. Moreover, skilled and semiskilled vacancies were never posted, and only Anglo unionists were allowed to bid for these jobs. Only one of the workers had ever been promoted; he was a naturalized citizen who worked as a foreman for a segregated crew of black workers. One of the complainants, Teodosio Gutiérrez, underscored the problem of segregation as a shared experience by noting that almost all the Mexican and black workers were common laborers and that there were "no Anglos in this classification."[33]

The Mexican workers complained about other segregationist practices. They were required to punch the time clock in a separate line shared with African American workers. Also, the company kept separate lockers and bathing facilities for minority workers. During the lunch hour, Mexican workers were given the choice of eating outdoors or joining the African American workers in a segregated section. Lastly, Mexicans and blacks were transported to work in two crowded buses while the Anglos traveled in a separate, less-crowded bus. Once Castañeda had confirmed the allegations through on-site investigations, he submitted the joint complaint to Sinclair officials and Local 227 officers. When neither responded, Castañeda visited the complainants at the Mexican consul's office to further substantiate the charges. On the basis of this inquiry, the FEPC once again forwarded a complaint and requested a response to specific wage and upgrading allegations of discrimination against both Mexican and African American workers.[34]

The superintendent of the refinery, D. A. Young, responded with a denial of the charges. He added that despite the fact that few Mexican and African American workers qualified for the better-paying jobs, Sinclair had upgraded three Mexican workers to semiskilled and skilled positions. Probably because he anticipated a finding in favor of the Mexican complainants, Young resorted to placing the burden of compliance on Local 227. He warned that the union would not "permit the commingling of the different races employed at this plant."[35] To demonstrate that this was not a ploy to evade compliance,

Young furnished Cochran with correspondence in which the union expressly opposed the promotion or reclassification of Mexican workers. During the subsequent meeting with Castañeda, Young expressed a willingness to upgrade Mexican as well as African American workers if the union could be made to guarantee support for compliance. Local 227 representatives, on the other hand, admitted that the union had opposed upgrading but promised to seek the support of the entire membership for a policy of nondiscrimination. Company and union representatives, however, denied that discrimination existed regarding wages, vacancy notices, and transportation facilities.[36]

Two months later Castañeda reported that the upgrading case against Sinclair had been adjusted. The company had kept its word and the union membership had grudgingly decided not to contest what Castañeda admitted were "minor advances given Latin Americans" at Sinclair.[37] A major factor in the settlement was Castañeda's decision to settle the complaint on the basis of the admissions made by the company and union representatives. Castañeda's conciliatory approach was clearly intended to capitalize on the single admission of upgrading discrimination in order to proceed with a directive calling for the adoption of a policy of nondiscrimination. Although Castañeda had initially filed the case alleging discrimination against Mexicans, he sought a settlement that favored the entire minority workforce. Consequently, when he confirmed the settlement, the company entered into a binding agreement that benefited both Mexican and black workers. In a letter to an officer of the union, Castañeda confirmed this understanding: "I am pleased to note that as the result of the meetings held your union has agreed to permit the company to abandon its discriminatory practices and to give all employees an equal opportunity for promotion in accord with their experience, ability and aptitude, regardless of race, creed, color or national origin."[38]

Although the company and the union may have cooperated during the final settlement negotiations, they did not satisfy the Mexican workers who continued to complain of discrimination. One year after Castañeda had settled the cases, the same Mexican complainants again contested Sinclair's discriminatory practices. They claimed that the company was refusing to hire qualified Mexican applicants and denying them upgrading opportunities. The company had allegedly refused employment to three Mexican applicants at the same time that it had been hiring African American and Anglo workers. On the basis of this complaint, Ellinger informed Sinclair that despite the recent settlement, the FEPC had determined that discrimination against Mexicans was continuing.[39]

The company responded to the complaint by denying the charges, while the union simply chose to disregard it. The FEPC, on the other hand, did not press the issue even though additional complaints continued to arrive. This was probably due to the mounting political opposition to the FEPC in Washington that was already signaling the end of the agency and discouraging forthright action. Also, the FEPC was then waging its most trying battle at Shell that may have drawn its resources and attention from the fight at Sinclair.[40]

The case against Sinclair demonstrated the FEPC's difficulty in securing permanent settlements. One obvious problem was the debate over the establishment of a permanent FEPC during the war and the strong opposition that emerged in the South. The continuing deliberation in Washington on how to treat industry-wide discrimination also hampered local efforts to obtain compliance. Other more important factors included the opposition of the union and the refusal of the company to comply until it could be guaranteed that Local 227 would not wage a race strike in protest. Also, the company failed to live up to its promise to comply with the FEPC directives and continued to challenge allegations of discrimination confirmed by the FEPC. The union was generally indifferent to the second complaint, preferring instead to leave the minority workers to fend for themselves against Sinclair.

Reminiscent of the fight at Humble, the FEPC often appeared to back away as if it was facing an opponent too formidable to confront. Despite the large amount of evidence accumulated in support of the complaints, the FEPC exhibited a conciliatory attitude in the settlement process. As noted previously, this prompted Castañeda to seek to correct one case of upgrading discrimination involving a Mexican worker in order to justify a directive calling for nondiscrimination. Rushing into a settlement that conceded ground on key charges, however, no doubt left the impression that the FEPC lacked the confidence and enforcement power to challenge employment discrimination, a perception that plagued the agency in its dealings with Shell.

Shell

The Shell Oil Company maintained a large refinery at Deer Park with a work force of approximately eighteen hundred workers that included at least one hundred Mexican and African American workers.[41] Mexican workers faced the same problems evident in the Humble and Sinclair refineries. Widespread discrimination restricted them as well as African American workers to the lowest-paying unskilled positions. Moreover, both groups of workers were limited to segregated transportation, eating, and restroom facilities. Mexican complaints against Shell resulted in one of the most rancorous fights over the issue of discrimination. It involved open defiance by the union and the continuing embarrassing ineffectiveness of the FEPC.

The FEPC initiated its case against Shell in May 1943 with a complaint submitted by Consul Domínguez on behalf of thirty-four Mexican nationals who had tried unsuccessfully to settle their claims with the company during the previous two years. They had also failed to convince CIO Local 367 to intervene on their behalf. As a result, they quit the union and appealed to the Mexican consul and local LULAC leaders as an act of last resort. The workers made the familiar charges of occupational, wage, and upgrading discrimination, a hiring ceiling, and segregated facilities.[42]

During the meeting at the Mexican consulate that was attended by company, union, and Mexican workers' representatives, an FEPC investigator confirmed the allegations, although he was not able to settle the complaint. When Domínguez asked that Mexican workers should be granted a just wage and the promotional guarantees enjoyed by Anglos, management and union representatives responded that they could not give assurances because of the all too prevalent fear of antagonizing Anglo workers. They claimed that Anglo workers feared that a concession to the Mexicans would encourage complaints by blacks seeking similar guarantees and that this would result in depressed wages and their eventual replacement by minority workers.

The company and the union maintained that the only way to avoid a disruption was if the FEPC held an industry-wide hearing and ordered all the refineries in the area with CIO union contracts to adopt a policy of nondiscrimination. The union offered to communicate the plan to the other locals. Probably seeing no other option, Domínguez expressed his support for the plan and recommended that the FEPC initiate such a settlement in a meeting with O. A. Knight, president of the OWIU, and D. W. Hobey, president of the Gulf Coast Refiners Association.[43]

The FEPC may have allowed Shell and the union to independently implement their proposed plan because there is no evidence that Castañeda participated in the negotiations. When months had passed without any news from Shell, the local union, or the OWIU, Castañeda called on the FEPC to grant him the authority to proceed with the case. He was especially concerned that Domínguez and other Mexican leaders would become disillusioned with the FEPC. Castañeda also restated his view before his Washington superiors that the company and the local union had called for an industry-wide hearing for the sole purpose of delaying the compliance process. He felt that the most reasonable and promising measure to take was individual action based on the findings of discrimination that Shell representatives and Local 367 officers openly admitted.[44]

A worsening situation at Shell underscored the need for immediate action. On November 3, the manager suspended seven Mexican workers for insubordination. According to the workers, he had instructed them to do a temporary job for $0.87 an hour in the segregated pipe-fitting department though the prevailing wage for pipe fitters ranged between $0.97 and $1.39 an hour. When they refused to do the work at the disputed wage, he fired them. The company subsequently advertised vacancies for these same jobs at $0.97 an hour. The workers once again sought the help of Domínguez. This time, however, the Mexican consul dispensed with his regular reporting duties and set out to convince higher-ups in Mexico's diplomatic corps to intercede in the matter. The Mexican ambassador to the United States, Rafael de la Colina, responded immediately by formally expressing his government's displeasure to the chairman of the FEPC. In no uncertain terms, he stated that Shell's continuing defiance violated the Good Neighbor Policy, disregarded the wartime alliance, and undermined the U.S. government's pledge of waging a fight against racial injustice within its borders. The issue of discrimination in oil thus reached international proportions and pressured the FEPC to redouble its efforts.[45]

Meanwhile, to support his contention for a hearing that would address the complaints against Shell, Castañeda called for an additional investigation, which later confirmed the prior findings. He also recommended immediate action, particularly because Shell again admitted practicing discrimination.[46] The conference that Castañeda held with Shell and Local 367 representatives in December ended on a familiar note. The manager of the refinery and the president of Local 367 admitted discrimination but insisted that they would not agree to any changes until an industry-wide hearing was held or a directive was issued by the FEPC ordering the entire industry to implement a policy of nondiscrimination.[47] When FEPC officials requested a formal written response, the union officer answered defiantly and unabashedly, "The Union at this time does not propose to change without first having a hearing or order, as we consider ourselves and the company both in violation of the Executive Order."[48] The company representative added his own challenge to FEPC authority: "The position of the Management of the company is that the consequences of any change in this respect are so far-reaching and would have such detrimental results that we do not see any reason for change."[49]

Shell defended its bid for an industry-wide hearing and directive with the argument that a unilateral settlement would place the company in an unfair position with its competitors. With this argument, Shell placed the burden of change on the union, while the union officers openly admitted that the membership would strike if the company complied.[50] The deadlock seemed unbreakable especially since FEPC officials in Washington once again delayed action while they debated the course of action. They finally decided to proceed with Castañeda's recommendation and to schedule a hearing for December 1944.[51] The public hearing, however, did not occur because Shell officials suddenly decided to cooperate. They requested a private conference and promised to abide by the decision to be rendered by a trial examiner and a committee of four FEPC representatives that included Castañeda.[52]

Although the FEPC agreed to the private meeting, its representatives did not hold back in pointing out the severity of its finding of discrimination. In his opening statement, an FEPC official accused the company and the union of disregarding the skills and experience of Mexican workers and of restricting them to the menial jobs at wages that were lower than those paid to Anglo workers performing the same tasks. This had been accomplished through a formal contract that defined the discriminatory rates of pay, hours of work, and other terms of employment operating in the plant. Since discrimination at Shell had been directed against both Mexicans and blacks, the FEPC called for an end to all forms of discrimination.[53]

The opening statement included other observations that acknowledged the importance that the Shell case had acquired in the international arena.[54] In calling for an end to racial and national origin discrimination, the FEPC described the denial of opportunities as a problem that undermined the war effort because it harmed relations with Latin American nations: "The eyes of our neighbors to the south are watching with keen interest. The denial of equal opportunities for full participation in the war effort, and for advancement to workers of Latin-American extraction, negatives our professions of good neighborliness and reflects upon our moral leadership in the family of nations."[55] The committee appeared to have settled the issue once and for all when it ordered the company and the union to eliminate all forms of discrimination. The company and the union agreed to expunge from their bargaining agreement all language that called for discrimination and to stop denying Mexican and African American workers hiring and upgrading opportunities. The committee also gave specific instructions directing Shell to submit a separate wage complaint to the War Labor Board for adjustment and to upgrade two Mexican complainants to carman's helper and truck driver. The FEPC followed with a decision on January 27 that directed the company and the union to comply with the president's executive order within ninety days.[56] The stage was now set to determine if compliance could proceed without setting off a reaction by Anglo workers.

The compliance process quickly became burdened with difficulties that tested the FEPC's ability to influence the ensuing course of events. When several Mexican workers, including the complainants who had been assured promotions, signed up for available jobs, a foreman and the personnel manager informed them that Shell did not intend to abide by the FEPC directive until the April 27 deadline. FEPC officials rightfully saw this as a direct challenge against the spirit, if not the letter of the settlement. Pressure was again placed on Shell.[57]

In response to the FEPC's requests for support, other government agencies reminded the company that it was obligated to honor the president's executive order or risk losing lucrative federal contracts. The FEPC had mixed results in convincing labor leaders to pressure Local 367. While the national CIO office declared support for a policy of nondiscrimination, state leaders such as O. A. Knight and Timothy Flyn, state CIO director, claimed that the parent organizations did not dictate policy to their locals. Nonetheless, pressure from government agencies finally convinced Shell to cooperate. The first upgrading occurred on March 8 when Shell appointed a Mexican worker to a carman's helper position. A week later, a second Mexican worker was upgraded to a truck driver's job.[58]

Added pressure by the FEPC eventually forced Shell to upgrade additional minority applicants. This, however, did not occur without Shell publicly announcing that the FEPC was forcing the company to integrate the workforce against its will. Two vice presidents of the union added to the growing tensions by resigning from their positions as a sign of disapproval of the FEPC directives. On March 22, the company nevertheless upgraded one Mexican and seven blacks to general helpers in each of the eight separate craft departments. An incident followed that raised the developing conflict to a higher level.[59]

A company foreman added fuel to the fire when he gathered Anglo workers from several departments and asked them to publicly state if they would work alongside the upgraded minority workers. Although some of the Anglo workers may have been inclined to accept the proposition, the fear of reprisals from co-workers was probably too great because none agreed. By opposing the upgrading decision, the Anglo workers were absolving the company of any blame in the ensuing conflict and accepting the major responsibility for defending the status quo. They also encouraged further dissent. Soon after the vote, an undetermined number of Anglo workers and the two union officers that had resigned threatened to stage a strike if the minority workers were placed in their new positions. The company quickly returned the workers to their previous jobs. Emboldened by this immediate response, the protesting Anglo workers demanded that the previously upgraded Mexican workers also be returned to their former jobs. The company again capitulated.[60]

FEPC officials responded by calling a series of conferences with company and union representatives to try to remedy a deteriorating situation. The company maintained that it was forced to concede to the demands of the Anglo workers. Union representatives, on the other hand, expressed an interest in complying with the FEPC directives but requested time to convince some of the members who were opposed to integration.[61] Matters got worse as Shell officials continued to publicly present the company as a helpless victim and as the union membership began to more forcefully express its opposition to integration. Although the union did not guarantee support for compliance, continued FEPC pressure led the company to upgrade two Mexican workers on April 27. The results were predictable.[62]

Anglo workers in the automotive department responded by walking off their jobs. Negotiations followed between the union, Shell, and a conciliator from the Department of Labor. When negotiations failed to produce results, the FEPC brought in the assistant disputes director from the Dallas office of the War Labor Board to help resolve the issue. The result was a six-day hearing that affirmed the FEPC directive and the Smith-Connally Act, which required workers to issue a petition before waging a strike in wartime. As part of the settlement, the workers agreed to remain on the job and not insist on the removal of the upgraded Mexicans without first filing a strike petition with the National Labor Relations Board (NLRB). In granting the union the right to hold a vote on what was essentially a compliance matter, however, the War Labor Board undermined the FEPC directives and provided the segregationists the opportunity to legitimately defy the FEPC at a future date.[63]

The tenuous settlement involved important concessions by FEPC officials who by now seemed to be desperately seeking to regain their influence. First of all, they failed to dispute the decision by the War Labor Board that granted the union the right to challenge the compliance directive. In fact, the FEPC granted Shell and the local a thirty-day extension on the compliance order to accommodate the scheduling of the election. Moreover, a general understanding was reached whereby no more upgrading actions were to be taken until the strike ballot was cast. Although the FEPC was forced to back down, the prospects of losing complete control led Ellinger to declare with some sense of relief, "We have won a tremendous victory by the skin of our teeth in the agreement of the men to work with the Latin-Americans on the job."[64]

Mexican government officials and Mexican civil rights leaders from Texas did not share Ellinger's enthusiasm. They began to more openly view the Shell case as a stark demonstration of deep-rooted racism and ineffective government intervention. It was at this point that Padilla commented to American officials while attending the United Nations Conference at San Francisco that nothing less than the hemispheric prestige of the United States as a democratic nation was at stake. Castañeda added that Mexican leaders from throughout the state expressed "strong resentment" against Shell and felt that the FEPC was not sufficiently aggressive.[65]

Minority workers remained steadfast in support of compliance. Mexican workers called for full integration, while African American workers supported the idea of a segregated work force on a separate but equal basis. In other words, both Mexican and African American workers sought guarantees of equal access to all jobs at the same pay while the latter group did not insist on working side-by-side with Anglo workers. Minority workers also agreed that the FEPC should continue to press the company and the union with claims of discrimination by Mexican workers since they had the best chance of succeeding and setting the necessary precedent for the complete integration of the workforce.[66]

Anglo workers refused to concede despite the urgings of the FEPC and the negative publicity that the case brought the oil industry and the labor movement. This became openly evident when a majority of them voted in favor of a strike on June 6, 1945. The NLRB-sanctioned election not only affirmed the segregationist posture of the union; it also demonstrated the union's newfound talent for legitimately defying the president's executive order. As a result of the election, the FEPC scuttled its compliance directive and endorsed a settlement proposed by the union. The union's plan designated a small number of skilled jobs for minority workers to be set aside in still-segregated departments. Shell representatives, on the other hand, washed their hands of the whole matter. They declared a willingness to adopt whatever plan the FEPC and the union favored.[67]

Mexican workers were indignant over the strike vote and were adamant in demanding that the FEPC not relent in it dealings with the company and the union despite efforts by Anglo workers to divide them. Mexicans were told that if African American workers had not been included in the directive, Anglos would have complied. Blacks, on the other hand, were told that they should not support the Mexicans because they were pretentious and claimed to be better than blacks. With matters still unresolved, the FEPC first restricted and then closed its operations in Texas when Congress decided to deny the agency the needed appropriations for the postwar period. There is no record that the FEPC was able to negotiate a settlement acceptable to the minority workers. Presumably, they were left to fend for themselves against continued occupational and wage discrimination.[68]

The Shell case once again demonstrated the agency's weakness. The case underwent numerous delays primarily because the company and Local 367 refused to comply with the president's executive orders. The Shell local acted much like the Baytown Employees' Federation and Local 227 in reinforcing racial inequality. Local 367 collaborated with management in restricting minority workers to the laboring occupations and in denying them the opportunity to advance into the higher-paying and skilled jobs in the refinery. Unlike Local 227, the Shell union was steadfast in its refusal to support compliance. This refusal, coupled with the FEPC's setbacks at Humble and Sinclair, underscored the significance of discrimination in denying Mexicans equal employment opportunities in the refineries of the upper Gulf Coast.

Conclusion

Mexican oil workers were part of the relatively small yet important wave of upwardly mobile workers making the transition from low-wage employers to high-wage and well-organized firms during the war. Their disproportionate representation in the lesser-skilled and lower-paying jobs, however, defined the limits that discrimination placed on them. The refineries in the upper Gulf Coast generally maintained low hiring quotas for Mexicans, assigned them laborer occupations, paid them a lower wage than Anglos, denied them upgrading opportunities, and restricted them to segregated work, eating, and restroom areas. The race-conscious Anglo workers, including members of CIO-affiliated unions, were a key element in maintaining the racial order. Anglo workers and their representatives also assumed an important role in defending the segregated order by pressuring the companies against complying with FEPC directives. Fearing the loss of their hard-won organizing gains, they claimed job prerogatives and reacted defensively toward the FEPC.

Minority workers, in consultation with FEPC officials and representatives of LULAC, NAACP, and the Mexican consul, devised the strategy of securing settlements with Mexican complaints that included the adoption of nondiscrimination policies. The strategy may seem like a practical arrangement and even an illusory plan against the formidable opposition that it drew, but it was also an intentional act of interracial and intercommunity solidarity against deeply rooted customs of segregation. The international norms and the Good Neighbor Policy that Mexican complainants could contribute to the fight over workers' rights could not be ignored. Nor could minority workers pass up the opportunity to cooperate in this interracial experiment when FEPC officials offered them the statutory basis to unify their demands and strengthen their hand.

Although some improvements for minority workers resulted from the intercession of the FEPC, the agency was not able to effectively challenge discrimination and inequality. Since the FEPC directed most of its attention to three companies and other refineries do not seem to have been compelled to implement nondiscrimination policies, we can conclude that the FEPC did not make an appreciable impact in the oil industry. Its work was a positive yet minor contribution next to the demand for labor that provided Mexican workers the initial limited opportunity for employment. The FEPC's lack of enforcement powers, its short duration in Texas, and internal divisions contributed to the failure of governmental intervention in the oil industry. The most decisive factors in the fight over compliance, however, were the opposition of Anglo workers' organizations and the encouragement of the seemingly impartial company officials. The result was yet another setback in extending recovery opportunities to workers in Texas.

Chapter 7: Negotiating Mexican Workers' Rights at Corpus Christi

Like the refineries in the upper Gulf Coast, the American Smelting and Refining Company and the Southern Alkali Corporation, two of the city's largest war plants in the Gulf port city of Corpus Christi, denied Mexicans equal employment opportunities. The companies hired them at a lower rate than Anglos, assigned them to the lower-wage laborer occupations, and rarely allowed them to move into the skilled jobs. African Americans did not participate in the fight over workers' rights mostly because they did not figure prominently in the plants nor in the region's population. The Mexican workers looked to the FEPC, LULAC, and the Mexican consul for help. The FEPC's ineffectiveness was pronounced in Corpus Christi as well. This time, however, union officers and management adopted new methods for maintaining job control and defending the company's record of discrimination.

The workers had already confronted the companies and the unions when the FEPC arrived in Texas, and they submitted their complaints around the same time that the Mexican and black refinery workers from the Houston area were initiating their own cause. The Mexican consul, Lamberto Obregón, and LULAC officers assisted them in submitting twenty-eight complaints against American Smelting and sixty-seven against Southern Alkali, and their respective unions, the Zinc Workers Federal Labor Union, AFL Local 23245, and the Alkali Workers' Industrial Union, CIO Local 153. Although the workers made similar claims of hiring, classification, wage,

"For the Same Victory! MEXICO," 1944, Secretaría de Gobernación, Mexico. (Franklin D. Roosevelt Presidential Library and Museum, Hyde Park, New York.)

and upgrading discrimination against other employers in the area, their fight against the two manufacturing firms was among the most contentious and involved the largest number of complaints. The grievances were numerous, a virtual "avalanche of cases which practically doubled our case load in one day," noted the overwhelmed Castañeda.[1]

Soon after he opened the Dallas office, Castañeda sent Cochran to interview the complainants and to make a preliminary determination on the merits of their grievances. Once Cochran submitted his report, Castañeda decided that the complaints had sufficient merit to conduct a fact-finding meeting, or hearing, with management, the unions, and the workers. The meeting, however, resulted in a major disappointment for the workers. Although Castañeda had said that he wished to settle the cases in favor of the workers, he grew ambivalent during the hearing as company and union officials accused him of accepting the workers' claims before hearings their side of the story. FEPC officials agreed that Castañeda had mishandled the cases and ordered him to declare the cases closed because of insufficient merit. The Southern Alkali complainants continued their struggle and also expressed reservations about the FEPC's abilities to assist them. The final settlement with Southern Alkali confirmed their doubts. Although the case against American Smelting ended with this 1943 dismissal, there is no evidence that conditions changed in the plant.

American Smelting

Established in 1942, American Smelting was primarily involved in the production of zinc. Its workforce grew steadily between 1942 and 1944, from approximately 350 to 500. Mexican workers constituted less than one-fourth of the workforce throughout the war. By 1943, the workers had organized an ethnically mixed union and obtained a charter from the AFL. Despite an impressive number of Mexican unionists—somewhere between forty and fifty percent of the organization's membership—they were unable to influence the union to challenge the company's practice of racial segregation. According to the company's 1942 reports to the USES, all Mexican workers as well as the two black workers in the plant were classified as unskilled. The company hired less than ten women during the first two years of operation; they were Anglos and most probably worked as secretaries. One black worker worked as a gardener and another as a chauffeur. No appreciable change occurred in the occupational standing of Mexicans at the plant. They remained concentrated in laboring jobs for the duration of the war. A few worked in the next higher category of third class operators. These included semiskilled helpers and skilled workers such as boiler tenders and acid loaders. No more than ten Mexicans worked in the higher-skilled jobs such as tradesmen, clerks, or second- and first-class operators. Mexicans earned the lowest wages largely because they were confined to the laboring class, although the complainants also offered evidence that Anglos earned higher pay in jobs that they shared with Mexicans.[2]

Claiming ineffective union representation, the Mexican workers contacted a member of the Good Neighbor Commission (GNC) about the same time that they were preparing to submit their complaints to the FEPC. They designated Frank Matta, a former union leader, to ask the newly established state agency to help them in addressing the problems that they were facing in the plant. Matta recounted the workers' grievances to Matías de Llano, a Laredo businessman and member of the GNC. He was direct and bold: "We are not getting the same standards of the Anglo American and I have every proof and evidence to back me up, although I have tried to work the problem through our local union but up to date it has not bennifeted at all." Matta added that the company paid lower wages to Mexican workers performing the same jobs as Anglos. Anglo oilers and water tenders received $1.00 an hour while their Mexican counterparts received $0.85 and $0.75 an hour, respectively. De Llano declined to help, noting that the GNC was primarily interested in ending discrimination in public establishments. Once spurned by the GNC, Matta and his companions resumed their collaboration with officers of the local LULAC council and Consul Obregón to submit their complaints to the FEPC.[3]

Adan Cisneroz, a former union member like Matta, had appealed to the Mexican consulate on behalf of twenty-six Mexico-born workers who claimed discrimination. Obregón agreed to support the workers, but suggested that Cisneroz contact Castañeda to secure help for the entire group, which also included U.S.-born Mexicans. Cisneroz and his fellow workers next contacted the local LULAC council and requested its assistance. The complainants continued to be mostly Mexico-born, which explains why LULAC did not play as important a role in American Smelting as in Southern Alkali. Cisneroz and LULAC officers, nevertheless, joined Obregón in informing Castañeda of the problems at American Smelting and committed themselves to work with the complainants.[4]

When Cisneroz wrote to Castañeda, he demonstrated a clear understanding that their claim of widespread wage, classification and upgrading discrimination "is entirely in accordance with the spirit" of the president's executive orders. The workers, according to Cisneroz, alleged wage, classification, and upgrading discrimination and sought payment of back wages and an investigation. Cisneroz used his own case to illustrate the problem. He had worked as a blue print helper for years. Once he moved into the semiskilled position of oiler, the company continued paying him a low wage and denied him other upgrading opportunities. The rest of the group had faced similar problems throughout the plant. Cisneroz noted that the most obvious discriminatory practice involved placing entering Mexicans in laboring occupations at $0.55 an hour and Anglos in temporary unskilled and semiskilled jobs at $0.85 an hour. He added that management always promoted Anglos quickly to better-paying jobs and kept Mexicans in the laboring positions, often by excluding them from in-plant training programs. He eventually quit his job when he was assigned to work under a supervisor who was "unfair to the workers" and "definitely anti-Mexican."[5]

Cisneroz noted in an accompanying affidavit that despite his numerous complaints to superiors, the company continued to pay him and fellow U.S.-born Mexican oilers a lower wage and only entertained requests for promotions by Anglo workers. In order to strengthen his claim, Cisneroz attached yet another affidavit by a worker named Dan Falcón, who spoke of discriminatory practices in another department.[6] Obviously convinced that Cisneroz and Falcón were representing conditions fairly, Castañeda confided in Obregón, an old acquaintance, that he was sending Cochran "to correct this deplorable situation . . . to remedy the discriminatory practices now in force." Once Castañeda received Cochran's report, he decided to schedule the hearings in Corpus Christi. Castañeda and Cochran met with company and union representatives from American Smelting on November 18 and Southern Alkali on November 19. At this point in the FEPC investigation, negotiations began to follow different trajectories for the workers at the two plants. Before we can examine the hearings and the different histories that followed, it is necessary to discuss the complaints from Southern Alkali.

Southern Alkali

Southern Alkali, one of the South's major wartime producers of alkali products, constructed its Corpus Christi plant in 1933. Wartime demands increased its production by 50 percent in 1941. Accompanying this growth was a successful attempt by workers to form a CIO union.[7] Like American

Smelting, the company had a highly segregated workforce. It employed 539 workers in 1945. Mexicans constituted less than one-third, or 27 percent, of the plant's workforce. They were largely classified as laborers while Anglos filled the higher-paying skilled, supervisory, and administrative positions.[8]

Mexican workers at Southern Alkali had established ties with LULAC earlier than their counterparts at American Smelting. A group of them began this working relationship as early as May 1943 when the civil rights organization assisted them in seeking an end to employment discrimination and their segregation alongside the smaller number of African American workers in the dining, shower, and locker areas. Although they claimed their official designation as a white group to call for an end to their segregation in the nonwork area of the plant, it is difficult to determine the extent to which this constituted a strategy to wear down a part of Jim Crow, a reflection of their own racial bias, or both. Regardless of the motivation, the first known Mexican challenge against segregation at Southern Alkali met the same general fate as in the Houston area. The company most probably did not comply with their demands because the workers continued to accuse the company of hiring and classification discrimination.[9]

By November 1943, Mexican workers from Southern Alkali were once again reaching out to LULAC as well as Consul Obregón and making use of the wartime language of justice and democracy. In their "petition" to the local LULAC council, they made almost verbatim reference to policy statements against discrimination found in Executive Order 8802 and to the argument that called for the full utilization of workers. The workers, possibly because of their close connection to LULAC, were fully aware of the general discourse over the Good Neighbor Policy as well as the nation's nondiscrimination policy and the role of the FEPC.[10] The workers also expressed an ethnic consciousness that placed LULAC in an exalted position. LULAC, according to the petition, was "illuminating and paving the way towards a better understanding between the various population groups and of our Latin American citizenry in the United States." They also credited LULAC for participating in a more transcendent cause: "the salvation of our modern civilization and the integrity of the Western hemisphere against the encroachment of subversive doctrines and totalitarian governments."[11]

The LULAC council responded with its own broad sense of unity that made use of the president's executive order and the Good Neighbor Policy. The organization first established a special committee named after its founder, the Ben Garza Memorial Commission, and directed its corresponding secretary, Robert Meza, to work with Obregón and the complainants in preparing a case for an FEPC investigation.[12] Meza no doubt conferred with Obregón and the aggrieved workers because he made specific reference to their claims as well as to the involvement of the Mexican government. Discrimination at Southern Alkali, according to Meza, undermined the war effort, at home and in the Americas: "Incidents of this nature . . . are contrary to public policy and constitute a thorn in the flesh to the President's program of Pan American solidarity. They likewise tend to destroy the morale, the efficiency and the loyalty of our workers and seriously hinder the work of our organization as well as the proper functioning of your Committee as good will ambassadors to the Americas."[13] He added that since Mexico, a co-belligerent in the war, was a party to the petition, the FEPC needed to demonstrate to "the people of the Americas . . . the sincerity of the American Government and of the American people."[14]

As with the American Smelting complainants, Castañeda responded in supportive terms and even identified himself with the struggle at Southern Alkali and the larger cause for Mexican rights: "I am very anxious to do something for the Latin Americans now that I am in position to bring the full weight of the administration to bear on the subject." He added a challenge: "We, Latin Americans, have for a long time been vociferous in our demands for justice, but we have been barking up the wrong trail. Now here's an opportunity for Latin Americans to complain knowing that their complaints will be heard sympathetically and that steps will be taken to secure them redress."[15]

The workers shared their complaints with Cochran during his November visit. They alleged that Mexicans were almost always assigned laboring jobs in the yard at $0.50 an hour, while Anglos entered as skilled workers or as paint gang helpers at $0.755 an hour. They also complained that the company denied Mexicans upgrading opportunities and that the union disregarded these practices as well as their complaints. The only two exceptions to this practice, they noted, were the all-Mexican drum and calcine departments that mostly included laborers. Although most of them were involved in cleaning containers and loading materials for shipping, the segregated status of the departments afforded them some upgrading opportunities. The workers and their LULAC representatives noted that the long-standing practice of assigning Mexicans to the laboring occupations discouraged the more skilled, better-educated, and English-proficient Mexicans from applying for jobs, thus justifying and reinforcing job segregation. Castañeda concluded that the complaints were justified and scheduled his "fact-finding" meetings with company and union representatives from American Smelting and Southern Alkali.[16]

The November Hearings

Castañeda and Cochran met with three complainants and two representatives of American Smelting during the morning session of November 18: C. N. Waterman, the plant manager, and Judge I. W. Keys, a local judge. Since the hearings were intended to ascertain the facts surrounding the complaints, Castañeda asked the complainants to begin the proceedings by stating their case. Matta, Albert T. Castillo, an oiler, and Onofre O. Leal, a second-class operator, followed with testimony that essentially recounted the complaints. Castañeda also made note of the fourth complaint by twenty-five workers who charged that the company maintained a policy of upgrading discrimination and a dual wage system among oilers, water tenders, janitors, weighers, repairmen, and helpers. They also alleged that the company mostly employed Mexicans as laborers and denied them in-plant training.[17]

Waterman and Keys responded with denials and challenges of their own that staggered the usually confident Castañeda. Waterman began by accusing the workers of fabricating their information and then turned to Castañeda with their strongest rebuttal to the charges—supply credible facts to support the workers' contentions. Castañeda and Cochran, of course, mostly had the workers' complaints and information that they had secured through correspondence and on-site interviews with them and their supporters. Keys, obviously familiar with the more formal procedural and evidentiary rules in a court of law, followed with more forceful objections throughout the hearings, accusing Castañeda and Cochran of accepting workers' allegations at face value and without a thorough investigation that gave the company and the union an opportunity to counter the charges with evidence of their own. "Do you expect the Company," argued Keys, "to answer these questions about each one of these employees, just peremptorily, without any kind of investigation, what each one has done or what they haven't done?"[18]

Castañeda and Cochran repeatedly reminded Waterman and Keys that the hearings were intended to collect additional information to determine the veracity of the allegations. But this did not deter Keys. In addition to questioning Castañeda's decision to hold hearings without first substantiating the workers' allegations and prejudicing the outcome, Keys extended his argument and questioned the authority of a federal agency that would commit such procedural errors: "Because a man alleges, after he resigns working for a company, any company, that he wasn't advanced like he thought he ought to have been, then, does the United States Government, through its officials, like you, start an investigation with reference to every company, where a man says he didn't think he was advanced like he ought to be, without stating specifically the reason for it, or giving some facts in connection with it, just because he just didn't get along as fast as he thought he ought to, is that the policy of the Government now or not?"[19]

Keys had hit on a weakness in Castañeda's strategy to use hearings to collect additional information and pressure the company to accede on some of the allegations. Waterman and Keys could reasonably claim that such hearings presupposed a finding in favor of the workers and challenged Castañeda to demonstrate otherwise. The way that Castañeda and Cochran had prepared the case also supported his contention. Cochran had interviewed the workers but Castañeda had only informed the company by mail and telephone of the charges prior to the hearings. Castañeda's communications with Obregón as well as his decision to dispense with a private fact-finding meeting with management suggest that he believed in the merits of the complaints and expected that the hearings would substantiate the allegations. Keys's strong objections, however, may explain why he became conciliatory as the hearings progressed. At one point, for instance, Castañeda underscored his impartiality by characterizing the workers' complaints in questionable terms: "We are going to try to explain to these boys it is just simply their attitude, we are not trying to foster their attitude at all, we are merely trying to obtain the facts in the case."[20]

Waterman, on the other hand, never deviated from his standard response of denying the allegations, and the questions about workplace conditions from Castañeda and Cochran only allowed him to elaborate his defense. Neither Matta, Castillo, nor Leal were denied opportunities, according to Waterman. He added that all entering laborers received the same wages and that the company selected workers for training and promotions according to their demonstrated capacity to advance. Waterman also claimed that some of the complainants were mistaken when alleging a dual wage system because they performed different tasks from Anglos who were similarly classified. Lastly, he pointed to several skilled positions filled by Mexicans.[21]

The afternoon meeting with the union, AFL Local 23245, included its president, Joe Davis, and its secretary, L.W. Smith. Twenty-seven Mexican workers had three general complaints alleging that the union permitted wage and upgrading discrimination by not questioning the practice. They also claimed that the union had negotiated a contract with weak seniority guarantees and without a clause against discrimination, both intended to deny Mexicans upgrading opportunities. Lastly, they noted that union officers used abusive language with them, that no Mexicans served as officers of the union or members of its grievance committee and that the union had excluded Mexicans in the negotiation of a contract.[22]

The dispute with the union had begun during the election of officers and contract negotiations in December, 1942. Although Davis claimed that Mexican unionists had no reason to complain since they had participated in contract deliberations, he admitted that the proposed seniority clause had become a point of contention among them. He pointed out that Mexicans constituted a majority of the membership and that the Anglo officers had tried to accommodate them by holding meetings to discuss the contract at a location on the Mexican side of town. Mexicans outnumbered Anglos at these meetings and at least one of their representatives, Matta, served on the contract committee. Cochran reminded him, however, that Matta resigned from the committee in protest and that large numbers of Mexicans left the union because Anglos controlled it and disregarded their seniority and non-discrimination concerns.

Mexican unionists felt that the seniority clause granted management great latitude and allowed it to arbitrarily decide if a Mexican worker had the necessary abilities to be ranked above an Anglo with an equal amount of service. Given the widespread discriminatory practices evident in the plant, this seemingly neutral position in favor of the best qualified reinforced the racialized status quo, according to the complainants. They claimed that this acquiescence reflected the union's unfriendly attitude toward the Mexicans and was especially glaring when the union refused to negotiate a nondiscrimination clause in the application of seniority rules.[23]

The complainants also alleged that the union disregarded the Mexican-controlled grievance committee when it called for a wage increase for Mexican oilers. Union officers refused to press the demand in their negotiations with the company, preferring instead to concentrate on the election and an eight-cent hourly increase for everyone. Matters worsened, according to the complainants, when the union won the election during the middle of February and consented to a temporary contract pending a War Labor Board (WLB) ruling on three disputed issues: the wage increase, a membership maintenance provision, and a checkoff stipulation. The membership maintenance provision would grant the union the right to claim the existing union members as well as new ones for the duration of the contract. The checkoff stipulation would authorize the company to deduct the union's monthly dues from members' pay regardless of the workers' membership status in the union. The demand for membership maintenance and checkoff guarantees suggests that union officers anticipated a major Mexican exodus during the early negotiation phase and wished to secure the union's position as the sole and unchallenged bargaining unit for the workers. When the disaffected Mexican unionists quit the union, they lost their majority standing in the union and Anglos assumed even greater control of the union and its committees.[24] The WLB decision of August 1943 worsened matters for them. When the board decided in favor of the union, it endorsed the wage demand and approved the two union security provisions which assured the union a stable membership and undisputed recognition as the workers' representative regardless of the large number of disaffected Mexicans and a depleted membership.[25]

Davis and Smith probably conferred with Waterman and Keys prior to the hearings because they responded to the complaints in much the same way. Aside from supporting the company's denials of discrimination, they disputed the charges against the union. They repeated their claim that Mexican workers had participated in union meetings when the contract was discussed and that their representatives had served during the initial negotiations with American Smelting. They added that the decision to shelve the oilers' complaints was reasonable since they were also negotiating a higher wage for the entire workforce. They also defended the seniority clause on the grounds that it was fair and that a nondiscrimination clause was unwarranted. Probably because of the earlier confrontation with Keys, neither Castañeda nor Cochran contested their testimony, choosing instead to express doubts about the workers' claims. Castañeda, for instance, reminded the union officers, "We are trying to ascertain the facts, you see. We don't believe these [the workers'] allegations. We want to know the facts, because our main purpose is to have harmony, both in the administration and among the workers."[26]

Other observations by Davis went unchallenged. When asked to explain why Mexicans had withdrawn from the union, he responded, "The Latin Americans, as we all know, are inclined to be impatient; they want things done in a hurry."[27] A few unscrupulous agitators, according to Davis, encouraged this impatience: "There were some five six or seven that were continually stirring up trouble, inciting the race question—did you get that word 'inciting?'—naturally, the disgruntled ones were easily sold on that question, and, as they quit, one by one, by their own free will, the Latin American number became lesser and lesser in the union."[28] Davis singled out Matta and Cisneroz as two of the most active former union leaders that caused dissension among the Mexican workers. Matta, in particular, "is continually stirring up trouble, inciting the other boys, has always got them boiling, you might say, got them in a turmoil."[29]

Despite the denials by company and union representatives and the mishandling of the cases, Castañeda decided that the complaints had sufficient merit to warrant a settlement in their favor. Not only were the complainants consistent in their allegations, he reasoned, but in some cases company and union representatives unwittingly corroborated their charges. Castañeda, however, had retreated from his original position in favor of the complainants. This encouraged the company and union to refuse a settlement on the grounds that the FEPC had denied them due process. Castañeda compounded the problem when he essentially reversed his view of the workers' complaints. "Later on," promised Castañeda, "we shall call on the individual complainants to further state their case and they will be given a chance to prove whether their contention is correct or not."

The hearings on November 19 did not go any better, as company and union representatives from Southern Alkali also denied the charges of discrimination made by the workers. With one exception, they offered general impressionistic remarks. This exception is worth examining because it demonstrates how the company's defense overwhelmed Castañeda and Cochran, the well-intentioned but by now ambivalent FEPC investigators. To support their contention that the company assigned and promoted workers on the basis of ability rather than race or national origin, the Southern Alkali representatives offered Castañeda and Cochran detailed schooling data on their Mexican and Anglo workers. The significantly lower educational record among Mexicans, according to O. N. Stevens, the company president, explained why Southern Alkali assigned them to the laboring positions and denied them promotions. The company would continue to make this argument throughout 1944 and 1945 without any known challenges from FEPC officials. The argument was clear and persuasive. How could the company disregard differences in educational attributes when placing and upgrading workers, or be blamed for schooling problems that were beyond its control? Moreover, the evidence seemed incontrovertible. A substantive issue, however, seemed to have escaped everyone. Did the educational characteristics of the Mexican and Anglo workers in the plant reflect a comparable distribution among their counterparts in the city's workforce? In other words, did the company show a preference for less-educated Mexicans and more-educated Anglos in the available labor pool?

A distribution analysis of the company's educational data and comparable census figures strongly suggests unequal hiring practices (see table 7.1). One of the most striking characteristics of the Mexican workers at Southern Alkali was that over one-third had not attended school and that more than two-thirds had less than a fifth-grade education. All the Anglo workers, on the other hand, had attended school. They also registered higher education levels, with close to 80 percent claiming to have completed between eight elementary grades and four years of high school. These distributions underscore the significant educational disparity that existed among the workers in the plant; however, they do not explain the possibility that Southern Alkali may have hired disproportionate numbers of Mexicans with less education and Anglos with more. This can be demonstrated by taking into account the workers' educational standing in relation to their corresponding distribution patterns in the census data.

About one-and-a-half times as many Mexicans without an education were represented in the plant than in the city and its vicinity. This means that Southern Alkali was dipping heavily into this sector, a practice that achieved a higher level of inequality in light of the company's failure to hire one single Anglo who claimed less than five years of schooling. Southern Alkali hired Mexicans with an elementary education in numbers that were almost proportionally equal to their larger population (0.93), while it hired Anglos in the same category at a significantly higher rate (1.41). Still, the most impressive Anglo representation occurred among workers who claimed at least eight years of education (2.37).

The hiring disparity was also evident among persons with a high school education. A significantly smaller proportion of Mexican (0.40) than Anglo (1.17) high school graduates worked in the plant. Mexicans improved their relative standing (0.72) as college-educated workers, although only two of them could claim this advantage. The Anglo proportional representation decreased significantly among the college-educated, although they maintained an absolute advantage over the Mexican workers. In sum, there was clear evidence of unequal hiring practices at Southern Alkali.[30]

It is possible, as previously noted, that better educated Mexicans may have been discouraged to apply because of the prospect of being assigned laboring jobs. This self-fulfilling practice may have contributed to the lower educational record of the Mexican workers at the plant. The unequal hiring

Table 7.1. Years of schooling completed by Mexican and Anglo workers in the Southern Alkali Corporation and corresponding figures in the urban area of Corpus Christi

	Mexican Workers			*Spanish Surnamed*		*Anglo Workers*			*Anglo*	
Years	*#*	*%*	*Freq*	*#*	*%*	*#*	*%*	*Freq*	*#*	*%*
None	51	(36.43)	(1.45)	3,785	(25.08)	0			355	(.81)
Elementary										
1–4 Years	43	(30.71)	(88)	5,270	(34.92)	0			1.660	(3.79)
5–6 Years	24	(17.14)	(1.01)	2,550	(16.90)	14	(6.54)	(1.15)	2,480	(5.67)
7 Years	7	(5.0)	(.87)	870	(5.77)	12	(5.61)	(.94)	2,600	(5.94)
8 Years	7	(5.0)	(1.55)	680	(4.51)	50	(23.36)	(2.37)	4.305	(9.84)
High School										
1–3 Years	3	(2.14)	(.07)	970	(6.43)	52	(24.30)	(.99)	10,700	(24.45)
4 Years	3	(2.14)	(.49)	665	(4.41)	70	(32.71)	(1.35)	10,630	(24.29)
College										
1–3 Years	3	(2.14)	(.72)	195	(1.29)	16	(7.48)	(.51)	6.400	(14.62)
4 or More	0			105	(.70)	0			4,640	(10.60)
Totals	140			15,090		214			43,770	

Source: FEPC Hearings, "Investigation of Alleged Complaints Against the Southern Alkali Corporation, Corpus Christi, Texas," November 19, 1943, 15–16, 20; U.S. Bureau of the Census, *U.S. Census of Population: 1950.* Vol. IV, *Special Reports,* Part 3, Chapter C, Persons of Spanish Surname (Washington, D.C.: U.S. Government Printing Office, 1953), 55; U.S. Bureau of the Census, *Census of Population: 1950.* Vol. II, *Characteristics of the Population,* Part 43, Texas (Washington, D.C.: U.S. Government Printing Office, 1952), 99, 120. The census provides comparable years-of-schooling-completed figures for three types of places: standard metropolitan areas, urbanized areas, and urban places.

Note: The table utilizes 1950 census figures in the second and fourth column because the 1940 census report does not provide comparable data for Mexicans. The 1940 census counted Mexicans as either foreign-born or as whites. It is impossible to disaggregate the U.S.-born Mexicans from the white population and thus we are unable to properly calculate the total Mexican population in 1940. The 1950 census, however, provided a special report on persons with a Spanish surname with corresponding educational data. The Anglo population figures in the fourth column were calculated by deducting the Spanish-surnamed and nonwhite from the total of the population for the urbanized area of Corpus Christi. The Spanish-surname report provided aggregate educational data (years of schooling completed) for males and females twenty-five years and older. Comparable figures for Anglos were secured from the 1950 census. The percentage figures measure the proportion of each educational category to the total in each column. The frequency column provides relative distribution figures which were calculated by dividing the percentage figures of Mexican and Anglo workers with their corresponding percentage figures in the Spanish-surname and Anglo columns.

practices evident in the educational data consequently may represent more than an attempt, deliberate or unintentional, to reinforce inequality. Perceptions of general discrimination noted by the complainants also could explain the unequal hiring practices. These perceptions, however, were not without reason.

One of the most convincing pieces of evidence of discrimination at Southern Alkali that emerged during the hearings was a clause in the union contract stipulating that "the ratio of Anglo-American to Latin American employees will remain fixed at the ratio which existed in October, 1937, or 140 Americans to 65 Latin Americans." The contract also stipulated that management could occasionally alter the ratio in the yard department during times of increased construction work. This meant that extra Mexican help would be secured periodically for temporary laboring jobs, however, the basic ethnic arrangement of a 68 percent Anglo and a 32 percent Mexican workforce would be maintained by mutual consent between the company and the union.[31]

Although company and union representatives would not admit that the discriminatory clause maintained a hiring ceiling and a segregated workforce, they announced that it had been removed from the contract in May 1943, and that the numbers of Mexicans employed by the company exceeded the quota stipulated in the contract. The initial complaints that the Mexican workers directed against them during the summer of 1943 probably encouraged them to remove it. The clause may have been removed, but the practice of maintaining a hiring ceiling for Mexicans resurfaced in 1944 and remained at least until 1945. Company records show that Southern Alkali maintained approximate counts of the disputed ethnically defined job ratio (68 percent Anglo and 32 percent Mexican) in 1944 and 1945 (see table 7.2). Castañeda, meanwhile, was apparently satisfied that the discriminatory practice would end once the policy statement was expunged from the contract since he did not bring this issue up again during the November meetings or later negotiations in 1944 and 1945.

Castañeda failed to stand up to the company and union representatives on other occasions when they admitted wrongdoing or offered questionable justifications for discriminatory practices. When Stevens noted on three separate occasions that Anglo workers would not stand for upgrading Mexicans into the skilled occupations, Castañeda did not point out the implicit admission or ask for supporting evidence; nor did he dispute the self-serving logic in his argument. Castañeda also failed to call for the immediate settlement of ten classification and upgrading complaints after Stevens admitted

Table 7.2: Southern Alkali Corporation workforce, by ethnicity, 1943–1945

Year	*Anglo*	*Mexican*	*Black*	*Total*
1943	216 (59)	150 (41)	——	366
1944	421 (75)	137 (24)	6 (1)	565
1945	394 (73)	145 (27)	——	539

Source: Figures calculated from the following: Investigation of Alleged Complaints Against the Southern Alkali Corporation; Southern Alkali Corporation (Corpus Christi, Tex.: Southern Alkali Corporation, 1944); Castañeda, handwritten notes, March 25, 1945.

that the company always appointed and retained Mexicans as laborers in the yard, placed Anglos in higher-paying entering positions, and upgraded them into the higher-skilled occupations. An additional problem was Castañeda's occasional partiality toward the company.

At one point, he suggested that if the company could point to one Mexican hire above the laboring level "that is a refutation of the complaint." Castañeda, apparently pondering the discarded contractual clause, also suggested that the company and the union were correcting their discriminatory practices. In closing the meeting with the union officers, he noted, "We must not allow personal quarrels and prejudices to keep us from using such manpower as is available, and, evidently, this need has been felt already in this plant, and you are now modifying some of this practice that has kept down Latin Americans."[32]

Castañeda may have been eager to elicit the necessary facts to substantiate the existence of discrimination. Reminiscent of the strategy he pursued with the refineries, he was obviously seeking to make the company and union representatives comfortable enough to admit that some discrimination existed. Presumably, he would then build a single airtight case that would warrant a nondiscrimination policy directive. Castañeda also obviously wanted to maintain open and cooperative relations with the company since Stevens had promised to provide him important data that he needed on the company's classification and upgrading practices. A contentious approach would have jeopardized this. These possible strategies notwithstanding, Castañeda was unable to complete his investigation of American Smelting and Southern Alkali. His superiors in Washington grew troubled with his handling of the hearings and decided to abandon the cases against both companies.

According to Stanley Metzger, a legal analyst in the FEPC, the hearings violated the intent of a fact-finding investigation. Field examiners were expected to first discover the facts and attempt to secure an informal adjustment. Hearings were to be held only when all other means of adjusting a case had been exhausted. Metzger added that the informal hearings prejudiced efforts to settle the cases, especially since Castañeda had ostensibly accepted explanations by company and union representatives. FEPC superiors immediately accepted his recommendation that the complaints be dismissed on the grounds that they lacked merit.[33]

Leonard Brin, the field examiner who was to later set off the fight against the *Dallas News*, joined with Castañeda in lamenting the workers' loss: "You and I both know, you especially, that the cases do have merit as far as the facts were concerned." The fact-finding rules, however, reigned supreme. Brin and Castañeda eventually agreed that the agency drop the cases, but asked that Washington provide a "less attackable reason" for dismissal. Otherwise, the company and the union would interpret it as a victory and resist workers' grievances with greater force. The workers from American Smelting may have also anticipated a harder row to hoe. They gave up the fight, while the workers at Southern Alkali continued.[34]

Revisiting Southern Alkali

Eight months after the dismissal of the cases, in August 1944, the embittered Mexican workers from Southern Alkali submitted additional complaints to W. Don Ellinger, Castañeda's replacement as acting regional director of Region X. The workers' representatives included Meza and the president of the Corpus Christi LULAC council, Edmundo E. Mireles. The complaints read essentially the same as before: hiring, wage, classification, and upgrading discrimination. The workers were especially concerned with the company's practice of placing Mexicans in the laboring occupations with few opportunities to move up into the higher-paying and higher-skilled jobs typically reserved for Anglos.[35]

Four workers expounded on the issue of discrimination in interviews with Ellinger. Cristóval Guzmán and Joe Garza, each with ten years experience, noted, "We have observed and know for a fact that all Latin-Americans have been hired as common laborers regardless of trade and that all Anglos have been hired as workers in the paint shop or better." Esteban M. Jiménez, a worker with eleven years service with the company, added that when he inquired about a vacant higher-skilled position, the superintendent in the Production Department told him that he could not have the job because he was Mexican. The assistant to the plant superintendent later informed him that the union contract prohibited such an appointment. Ygnacio Moreno, a worker with nine years experience, recounted a similar story. When the company selected an Anglo applicant with less seniority than him, the union steward explained, "We have nothing against you; we know you can handle the job, but there is nothing we can do about it. They just don't want to mix."[36]

Company and union representatives denied discrimination in their meeting with Ellinger and resurrected the old and tried argument that the lack of educational qualifications explained the almost wholesale placement of Mexicans in the laboring occupations. They added that Anglo workers were opposed to mixed crews and that the company was unable to staff a separate department with Mexicans to circumvent this potentially volatile reaction to integration. Ellinger recognized the evasive nature of the argument. He pointed out in his notes that although Anglo workers may have harbored ill feelings against Mexicans, management was not without its own prejudices. According to Ellinger, Stevens "claimed that he was not prejudiced in any way, but that he would not allow any Mexican with 'too much Indian blood in him' to hold any responsible position."[37]

Ellinger responded to Stevens with a clear statement of the issue and recommendations for the resolution of the problem at Southern Alkali. He reiterated two basic complaints: a differential wage scale and a discriminatory classification system among entering laborers and a denial of upgrading opportunities equal to their Anglo counterparts. Ellinger also questioned the company's practice of denying Mexicans the skilled jobs. This, in his opinion, constituted "different and unequal opportunities." He added that civic leaders whom he had interviewed denied that integration would necessarily result in racial strife. Ellinger concluded that the problem of discrimination could be resolved by guaranteeing everyone entry-level jobs "of equal content and equal wages" as well as an equal upgrading opportunities and a fair grievance procedure to settle future complaints.[38]

Although Ellinger essentially dismissed the claim by Stevens that Anglo workers would react against an FEPC directive, he nevertheless requested John Crossland, a regional director of the CIO in Texas, to seek the cooperation of the local union leadership on the matter. He hoped for a quick resolution "if the local union cooperates." Ellinger followed by calling a meeting with Meza and company and union representatives.[39] Stevens affirmed his support for the president's executive orders. However, he took issue with the view that discrimination existed. In his opinion, Mexican workers were often too quick to claim discrimination when a lack of education or the inability to understand and speak English adequately prevented them from assuming the same jobs as Anglos. "The number of Latin-Americans in the higher class jobs," noted Stevens, "is limited because the number of qualified men is limited and not because of discrimination." An added problem, according to Stevens, was that Mexicans were very unstable, that is, they worked for short periods and quit. Stevens's response, however, was fraught with prejudice. For instance, he described Mexicans as "incapable of handling work which requires intelligence." Also, in a magnanimous attempt to demonstrate that the company discriminated in favor of Mexicans, Stevens admitted the previously noted discriminatory hiring practice: "We have consistently refused to employ illiterate Anglo-Americans while we have made no such policy in regard to Latin-Americans, or colored."[40]

The October meeting had a familiar ending. Management and union officers denied that discrimination existed in the plant and that placing Mexicans alongside Anglos would create conflict and impair production. This time, however, company representatives underscored the unreliability of Mexican workers as a reason for their concentration in the lower-skilled and lower-paying jobs. Their alleged inability to perform skilled jobs without supervision slowed production, created tensions among fellow Anglo workers, and angered supervisors. The company would admit to discrimination only if everyone understood that management alone made decisions about job classifications, promotions, and wages based on merit and not on "propounded theories thrown up as a screen in defense of a discrimination action which to us does not exist in fact."[41]

Ellinger took a hard line against the company. He found in favor of the complainants, and offered suggestions for the satisfactory solution of the problem. Aside from ending discriminatory practices in the areas of hiring, job classification, and wages, Ellinger urged the company to commit to an official policy of nondiscrimination and to give it wide publicity.[42] It finally seemed that the FEPC was taking the company and the union to task. Ellinger, however, also offered a suggestion that granted the company added control over the work process in return for resolving the ongoing complaints of discrimination. He called on the company to adopt a more systematic method of managing its personnel including formal and consistently applied methods for hiring, classifying, and upgrading. Stevens agreed to standardize the process by instituting an examination ostensibly intended to gauge the mental aptitude of workers. Planning, of course, would take "much study and preparation," but the final remedy had been devised.[43]

Aside from offering the company a more scientific method of managing grievances, Ellinger may have unwittingly helped Stevens discover a way to delay and eventually circumvent compliance. He informed Castañeda that Stevens "shows the clearest sort of prejudice," and "had no desire to make adjustment and intends to delay it as long as possible." The delay involved Dr. Otto R. Nielsen, a professor of personnel administration in industrial relations and dean at the nearby Texas College of Arts and Industries, who was contracted to devise a battery of tests on the basis of several visits to the plant and interviews with Mexican and Anglo workers. Although Ellinger and Castañeda pressed Stevens to move more expeditiously on the matter, they nevertheless conceded that a reasonable amount of time was required in order to develop the necessary examinations.[44]

Once the test was completed in January 1945, Stevens informed the FEPC of his plans. The company would retain its practice of classifying its new hires as laborers or painters' helpers although they would now be selected on the basis of an entrance examination. An added understanding was that only the best qualified would be placed as painters' helpers on the assumption that they would be better able to advance into the higher-skilled jobs. Lastly, the company would only promote a worker that demonstrated an ability "to read, write, speak, understand and clearly express himself in English." The justification for the language requirement was that the Anglo workers in supervisory and skilled positions only understood English. This resulted from an alleged lack of skilled workers in the area when the plant opened, the importation of English-speaking supervisors and other skilled workers from the East, and the establishment of English as the necessary form of communication.[45]

The examination involved several steps. First, the worker was to fill out an application form in English. If he could not complete it or required help, he would be offered a job in the labor department. If the applicant completed the form as required, he would be eligible for a position as a painter's helper, but only if he also passed an oral examination. The obvious purpose of the first part of the examination was to determine whether the worker had a basic knowledge of English. Aside from determining to a greater degree the applicant's ability to read, understand, and speak English, the oral portion of the examination allowed for the evaluation of the worker's diction, pronunciation, especially his accent, and "ease of expression."[46]

The oral portion of the examination was in three parts. The worker was first asked to answer questions such as, "Please tell me in your own words the route you traveled from your home to the plant this morning?" or, "Why do you want to go to work for the Southern Alkali corporation?" Next, he had to read a statement of approximately fifty words and discuss its basic ideas. Lastly, the worker was asked to discuss a statement of comparable length that the interviewer read to him. The interviewer evaluated the applicant's performance with numerical scores. For instance, a worker was given a high score of eight if his pronunciation was "clear," a six if he had a "slight accent," a four if he was "faltering," and a two if he was "uncertain." The interviewer also assessed the applicant's general demeanor, confidence, and attentiveness with superior, above average, average, below average, and inferior scores.[47]

The worker who passed the oral portion was eligible to take the third and final part of the examination, a standardized aptitude test that evaluated word meaning, word relations, and numbers. According to Stevens, the test measured aptitude levels among persons with between four and seven grades of schooling. It actually tested language proficiency since the instructions and exercises required a sound grounding in English. The arbitrary method that the evaluators used to determine what constituted a passing grade also worked against the Mexicans, who no doubt scored lower than Anglos. They could raise a score to a passing level "in the event it does not provide men of qualifications sufficient to meet those our past experience indicates are necessary." In other words, management reserved the right to change the minimum score to accommodate workers who may not have passed but that in their estimation were qualified to do the job.[48]

Anyone who passed the examinations was assured a position as a painter's helper. A worker who failed one or two portions, on the other hand, would be given a final opportunity to qualify by taking yet another examination, a nonverbal standardized intelligence test. Passing this examination would allow the applicant to become a painter's helper, although the company again claimed the right to determine what the required score would be. A worker who only passed the "intelligence" examination would be encouraged to "remove his language handicap by self-education" and retake the language tests at a future date.[49]

A final proposal in Stevens's letter undermined the position of Mexican workers that had previously managed to move into the skilled jobs and sought additional advances. According to Stevens, applicants for production or maintenance tradesman's jobs had to be screened with the use of the newly adopted examinations unless they had previously held the painter's helper job. In other words, since none of the Mexicans in skilled jobs had progressed through the painter helpers' group, they too were expected to take the examination. Anglo workers who had entered through their segregated track were exempt. The only Anglo workers required to take the examinations in order to advance occupationally were probably most apt at test-taking since they had come in as higher-skilled workers and presumably with a higher education and better language facility than the rest.[50]

Castañeda supported the testing procedures in his communications with Stevens and Nielsen and encouraged them to continue with their plans. All that was needed now to satisfy the FEPC, according to Castañeda, was a public statement to the press that announced the company's nondiscrimination policy and its new testing procedures.[51] The company dutifully complied. Company officials would no longer discriminate on the basis of race or national origin, but they reserved the right to decide who would be hired and what job they would assume on the basis of their aptitude test.

By March, the company was also reporting the results of the first round of examinations by all new applicants and laborers who sought promotions into the painter's helpers positions. Although FEPC officials were apparently satisfied with the report, the company did not provide sufficiently detailed data to determine the test performance of Mexican applicants. For instance, company officials noted that all "Latin Americans" had passed the examination. However, they failed to provide a total count of Mexican applicants or the number of Mexicans that the company placed in skilled positions as a result of passing the examination. The company's 1945 promotional brochure suggests that a pattern of segregation remained relatively unchanged. Only nine of forty-seven workers in the paint section were Mexicans while they continued to predominate in the yard with forty-one out of forty-eight laborers.[52]

Conclusion

The wartime demand on production at American Smelting and Southern Alkali had increased the number of jobs, but Mexicans continued to work as laborers and were denied opportunities to move into better-paying and higher-skilled jobs. Anglo workers, on the other hand, progressed quickly up the line and received higher pay even in instances when they performed the same jobs as Mexicans. All along management, with the collaboration of local unions, maintained a segregated workforce and turned a deaf ear to the Mexican workers' appeals. This means that although a substantial number of

Mexicans may have improved their prior occupational standing as a result of improved opportunities, they nevertheless lagged significantly behind their Anglo counterparts.

Aside from facing the familiar discriminatory practices and an inefficient and impotent FEPC, Mexicans at Southern Alkali encountered a formidable barrier to mobility not evident anywhere else in the state. This involved a plan by the company's personnel office to implement English proficiency examinations as a basis for employment, job placement, and promotions. According to Castañeda, the company's plan would "remove all grounds for charges of discrimination on account of race, creed, color or national origin in the future employment or promotion of all employees."[53] He was probably right. The tighter bureaucratic control over the workforce that resulted from the "intelligence" tests gave a semblance of impartiality and discouraged further complaints. However, a language proficiency examination left management's prerogatives and segregation intact, particularly with regards to the Mexico-born Mexicans. The FEPC nevertheless felt justified in closing the case in favor of the company and the union.

The FEPC's dismissal of the complaints against American Smelting and the settlement that finally resolved the almost two-year fight at Southern Alkali must have deeply disappointed Mexican workers especially since the FEPC and the wartime rhetoric of equality had encouraged them to believe that they could expect some improvements in their condition. The workers from American Smelting understood relatively quickly that they could not change things, even though their defeat may have been due to the stubborn reaction of management and the union as much as to the ineffectiveness of the FEPC. The workers at Southern Alkali continued their fight only to find out later that, despite the abundance of evidence, the FEPC's manner of negotiating settlements left them vulnerable to the machinations of the company and union representatives. The lack of resources may have established important limiting parameters in the work of the FEPC; however, the appeasing approach to the application of the nation's nondiscrimination policy contributed mightily to the losses in Corpus Christi.

Attempts by Castañeda and Ellinger to reach settlements on minimal admissions and demonstrations of culpability or more rational and accountable forms of labor-industrial relations did not necessarily reflect a lack of negotiating ability or poor understanding of the issues that were at stake. Their work in Corpus Christi, as well as Castañeda's in the upper Gulf Coast, reflected a clear sense of the limitations that ingrained segregationist ideas and practices placed on the FEPC's ability to negotiate settlements in favor of the aggrieved workers. FEPC negotiators may have been overly compliant and Castañeda may not have been sufficiently mindful of established negotiating procedure, but it was the companies and unions that ultimately dictated the outcome of the investigations with their obstinate and unprincipled behavior. Under these circumstances, the FEPC's general inability to enforce the nation's nondiscrimination policy can be said to reflect the play of the local relations of power as much as the battles in Congress over budgetary and statutory issues.

Chapter 8: Conclusion

I began this study by following a research trail that included provocative and suggestive primary texts, and I proceeded according to the evidence and research questions that came into sight. Traveling back and forth between primary and secondary sources allowed me to verify tentative discoveries, broaden my research agenda, and reorder the unfolding narrative structure into my presentation of findings, interpretations, and conclusions. Castañeda's articles in Perales's book provided an initial point of departure. His position as a civil rights activist, historian, and, most importantly, a former FEPC official, gave significant credibility to his basic observation that widespread discrimination denied Mexicans equal wartime opportunities.

My first examination of Mexican workers in the refineries of the upper Texas Gulf Coast confirmed Castañeda's view and encouraged me to recast my study in broader terms to determine how discrimination affected the movement of Mexican workers out of agriculture and into wartime industries. Focusing on the two "ends" of the mobility stream provided a sound basis for measuring the significance of discrimination in the Texas labor market. This approach also allowed me to understand how the federal government promoted and hindered geographical and occupational mobility. The FEPC sought to implement the nation's nondiscrimination policy mostly in wartime industries, while the USES collaborated with segregationist farmers and urban employers to maintain an uneven rate of mobility between Mexican and Anglo workers and to undermine the work of the FEPC. In

"Las Americas Unidas Para La Victoria y el Progreso Humano." (World War II Poster Collection, Minneapolis Public Library, Minneapolis, Minnesota.)

sum, discrimination and segregation interacted with an expanding wartime economy and an activist state in shaping the recovery experience among Mexicans in Texas.

Since LULAC officers and Mexican consuls were prominent in the battle over workers' rights in the refineries and other contested workplaces, I used an even broader framework that incorporated other major political actors, including Mexican officials and civil rights leaders. Contrary to the general consensus in the history of Mexicans in the United States, LULAC has not always confined itself to civil rights. Castañeda and Perales noted in no unclear terms LULAC's close association with the Mexican government and the FEPC over the Good Neighbor Policy and the implementation of the president's executive orders.

Castañeda's weekly reports and newspaper articles, along with the correspondence among LULAC officers, demonstrated that LULAC collaborated with Mexican consuls in assisting workers secure the assistance of the FEPC as well as in elevating the issue of racial discrimination to a hemispheric level of importance. The records of the FEPC and the Mexican Foreign Affairs Office also suggested that the workers often appealed for the help of the FEPC, LULAC, and Mexican consulate offices as an act of last resort because of the strong segregationist opposition to change in the workplace. This required an even more extended framework that included workplace struggles against discrimination and segregation as well as the larger political agendas of LULAC and the Mexican government, especially their use of the court of public opinion and the wartime language of justice, democracy, and good neighborliness to intervene on behalf of Mexicans in the United States.

While labor market experiences, an activist state, labor-community relations, and hemispheric politics define the general parameters of the study, discrimination serves as a point of binding emphasis. It explains the lag in Mexican mobility, the activism of LULAC, the opening of FEPC offices in the Southwest, the complaints by Mexican workers, their ties with their communities, and the decision by Mexico to intervene. The importance that I give discrimination and the unequal relations that it sustained, however, may give the impression that Mexicans experienced little in the way of occupational advancement. To restate the obvious, Mexican workers made important gains. This is reflected in the occupational data from the U.S. Bureau of the Census, as well as in the FEPC and USES occupational reports that identified work sites such as Kelly Field as relatively welcoming places. Moreover, the concept of the unequal rate of mobility and attendant levels of recovery—evident between Mexicans and Anglos, and among Mexicans—

acknowledge, rather than negate, the experience of upward mobility. It also reinforced group inequality and intensified internal class differentiation.

Despite the problem of unequal access to new wartime jobs, Mexicans made unprecedented improvements in their lives. One only has to consider the road that immigrants traveled from destitute places in Mexico to better-paying cotton-picking areas in Texas to appreciate this change. Although they assumed the lowly position of farm workers, Mexican immigrants made appreciable gains in farm jobs that doubled and even tripled the earnings they had received in Mexico. A similar assessment could be made of change over time in the lives of many, if not most, of the Mexican workers who lived in the state's urban areas. They saw noticeable and, often, sudden improvements in their living and working conditions as they journeyed from the impoverishment of the Depression to the improved job opportunities made available by the war. Clearly, Mexicans improved their occupational standing, earned more, and lived better than before. As telling and significant as these measures of change may have been, however, they did not equal the experiences of Anglo and, in some instances, black workers in Texas.

Discrimination was significant because it explains much of the social inequality in Texas, especially when segregationists inside and outside government openly admitted it and even codified it in union contracts that specified race along with other terms and conditions for employment. Discrimination assumes greater significance when one considers the degree of prejudice that sustained it. Deeply ingrained in society, it persisted despite unprecedented job opportunities, the Good Neighbor Policy, workers' challenges, and an unprecedented initiative that called for equal access to jobs in government employment, unions, and wartime industries. An added piece of evidence is the classification of workers by race in the files of numerous USES offices and their discriminatory job announcements and placements. The persistent concentration of Mexican workers in the lower-skilled jobs evident in the census reports of 1950, 1960, and 1970 also underscores the long-lasting significance of discriminatory practices.

The trend of inequality in the labor market deserves added attention at this point in the discussion. In 1971, the labor economist Fred H. Schmidt described a "stair step" minority employment pattern in which the number of Mexicans "descends as the occupational hierarchy ascends."[1] Barrera added that farm workers only moved up slightly on the occupational ladder, typically into the semiskilled occupations and that the semiskilled workers moved up as well, but at an even slower rate. The Mexicans who entered the skilled or white collar occupations, according to Barrera, usually filled the lower segments in each occupational category. This was especially evident among the majority if not most of the Mexicans who became lawyers, restaurant owners, and farm owners but did not attain the status or earning power of their Anglo counterparts. The skilled and semiskilled workers were also segmented throughout the 1950s and 1960s.[2]

The census-based occupational data for Mexican farm workers offered the clearest case of a lower rate of upward mobility as Anglos moved out of agriculture between 1930 and 1970. Mexican nationals probably escaped farming to a lesser extent than the U.S.-born Mexicans. USES labor market reports and interviews conducted by the Latino and Latina World War II Oral History Project, on the other hand, strongly suggest that Mexican women in urban areas entered the skilled ranks in fewer numbers and at a slower rate than Anglo and black women.

FEPC reports and investigations rarely acknowledged the presence of Mexican women, suggesting that they did not usually obtain employment in war industries. Mexican nationals, on the other hand, had a difficult time securing jobs in some war industries, like airplane construction and repair, because of security concerns among employers and military officials. FEPC records indicate, however, that Mexican males, including Mexican nationals, secured jobs in war industries, albeit at a slower rate than Anglos and blacks. This mostly occurred after 1943 when military conscription had depleted the labor supply of Anglo males enough to allow for added numbers of minority workers to move into the higher-skilled and better-paying jobs.

Labor participation and mobility patterns can be described in general terms by revisiting the figures that measured their movement out of the farms and into the war industries. Two-thirds of the entire Mexican workforce in 1930 worked in the farms. By 1970, this figure dropped to one-third, suggesting that they were leaving the farms and, presumably, getting better-skilled and better-paying jobs in urban areas. The exit figures for Anglo and black farm workers, however, were higher. As a result, Mexicans were more likely to be farm workers during the same period of time.

In urban areas, Mexicans represented around 5 or 6 percent of the total workers in war industries in 1944 and 1945, while blacks increased their representation to approximately 10 percent by 1944, a figure almost equal to their proportion in the overall population. Anglo females registered the fastest rate of entry into the war industries that resulted in over 20 percent representation by 1944. Anglo male participation in war industries remained high throughout the war, hovering somewhere between 60 and 70 percent.

The slower movement of Mexicans out of agriculture and into the urban-based manufacturing plants, especially the critical war industries, strongly suggests that white privilege remained largely intact during the war years. The unprecedented occupational gains that they made and would continue to make during the 1950s and 1960s nevertheless pointed to important changes in social relations. The upwardly mobile Mexicans—especially the increasing numbers of them who benefited from wartime employment opportunities and entered the skilled, professional and white collar sectors—contributed to the blurring of racialized divisions. Although segmentation isolated them from their white cohorts, they nevertheless moved into white society and made possible the greater acculturation of their children.

Upward mobility and acculturation also distanced them from the rest of the working-class population and no doubt contributed to an emerging ethnic and even "whitened" political identity and strategy in the postwar period. The solidarity that LULAC expressed across the emerging class and racial lines also suggests that the upwardly mobile Mexicans were not above using moral, constitutional, and strategic considerations to build an encompassing cause for equal rights.

Political Actors

In this section, I borrow from a framework by the Swedish scholar Bent Flyvbjerg to better explain the behavior of the different actors in my study. Flyvbjerg's "phronetic" approach calls for an examination of the socially and historically conditioned contexts that explain the values and interests motivating social actors in their public commentary and social action. Flyvbjerg recommends that researchers first analyze behavior on the basis of the Aristotelian concept of *phronesis,* or the prudent and ethically practical judgments that cannot always be reduced to a theoretical axiom or an ideological precept. He suggests that we disregard, if only for a moment, the rightness or wrongness of a political action but determine the motivations and justifications of historical actors with the following questions: Where are we going? Is this desirable? What should be done?[3]

I have amended these questions to provide an account that approximates the political terrain that my study has revealed. The actions of actors such as Mexican workers, segregationists, LULAC officers, FEPC officials, USES staff, and Mexican consuls can be best understood by asking what goals they sought, the impulse that drove them to seek these goals, the actions that they took, the results of their actions, and who benefited in the end. Moreover, the political landscape in which they thought and acted involved a racially segregated order that was at once reinscribed by the labor utilization work of the USES, interrupted by the nondiscrimination policy of the FEPC, and recast as a human rights issue of hemispheric importance by the interventions of the Mexican government and LULAC.

Local segregationists placed their weight behind the USES with arguments in favor of racial custom and the recurring warnings that nondiscriminatory policies antagonized whites and jeopardized production. Mexican and black workers stood by the FEPC with the hope that a federal nondiscrimination policy could correct the abuses in the workplace. Both camps claimed organized supporters in their communities. The Mexicans, however, brought a singular element to the political mix; the influence of the Mexican government and its internationalist claim for equality. Although U.S. government officials did not always welcome Mexico's intervention, the need for wartime unity in the Americas required that they at least tolerate it. LULAC, meanwhile, energized and broadened its cause for equal rights by working with the Mexican consulate and adopting the egalitarian language of the Good Neighbor Policy.

Large-scale government initiatives gave major impulse to the segregationist and egalitarian values doing battle in wartime work sites, but it was the workers who gave them immediate meaning. Although workers must have understood that the interference of military service, insufficient or inadequate skills, and the lack of job experience would affect their ability to make full use of home front opportunities, they expected significant improvement in their lives. Poor Mexican workers, like their black and white counterparts, also most probably understood that they did not have the same access to better jobs and training opportunities as others. Mexican and black workers, on the other hand, had to contend with the possibility that discrimination would continue to marginalize them on racial grounds. A growing wartime economy nevertheless maintained the possibilities for occupational advancement.

The expansion of the wartime economy and the efforts by workers to make use of unprecedented opportunities explain many of their gains in the form of new, better-paying, and even permanent jobs. The government's labor distribution and training programs, as well as federal policies that promoted industrial democracy, also brought significant improvements. Workers contributed to their new conditions by joining the rural-to-urban migration, seeking the job-placement, training, and advocacy services offered by government agencies, and tying their political fortunes to organizing activities in new bureaucratic terrains regulated by agencies like the FEPC. Since Mexicans and blacks faced limited recovery experiences, their conditions, as well as collective actions, often looked the same.

In rural areas like South Texas, Mexicans made use of opportunities circumscribed by the labor-repressive measures that government agencies and farmers took to control the farm labor supply. Many of them responded to the immobilizing campaigns by the Farm Bureau, the USES, and the Farm Labor Program by taking to the road in search of higher wages and often settling in urban areas where job opportunities were better. This informal labor initiative represented a bargaining act intended to maximize the opportunities offered by a wartime economy. More formal responses included the establishment of unions and mutual aid societies, some of which sought and obtained affiliation with AFL and CIO federations. Other actions included appeals to government agencies like the GNC and requests for assistance from local LULAC Councils. Despite these efforts and some occupational gains, Mexican rural workers remained concentrated as agricultural laborers during the war years and beyond.

The USES reports present a similar picture for African Americans. They faced the same kind of labor repressive measures and, although the immobilizing pressures kept many of them in the farms of Southeast Texas, increasing numbers also escaped into nearby and distant urban centers. Unlike Mexicans who predominated in the less industrialized region of South Texas, blacks seem to have secured jobs in war industries situated near their places of concentration like the highly industrialized Houston and Dallas metropolitan areas. Blacks, however, also faced discrimination and segregation in the major manufacturing plants. Mexican and black workers were hampered by racial thinking and no doubt internalized prejudices about each other. The documentary, archival, and oral history materials consulted for this study, however, do not provide evidence of racial animus among them that might have undermined their entry into the war industries or impaired their FEPC-supported claims against segregationist employers and unions.

Mexican workers also made use of the relatively better opportunities in urban areas despite the formidable obstacles that they faced. They capitalized on the limited access to the higher-skilled and better-paying jobs through government training programs and the job placement services of agencies such as the USES. They also benefited by joining the larger number of organizations in their communities, including the Masonic orders, mutual aid societies, LULAC councils, and the predominantly Mexican and mixed labor unions.

These organizations provided their members status as community leaders, a safe environment for cultural adjustment, basic services such as death and illness insurance benefits, and more focused assistance like job seeking services. In many instances, members and nonmembers also sought the help of these organizations to negotiate changes in their workplaces. LULAC councils, however, were the single most important organizations that brought workers and the FEPC together, most probably because the civil rights organization promoted this kind of action and presented itself as culturally adept at negotiating rights in the English-speaking and bureaucratic world of the U.S. government. The LULAC membership, comprised largely of upwardly mobile workers, also may have been strategically inclined to assist workers in war industries as their natural constituency. It is also important that LULAC had fashioned a close relationship with Mexican consuls and the Mexican government's campaign on behalf of Mexicans in the exterior.

The ability of the state leadership of LULAC to place itself in the cultural and political middle owed much to its adaptation of the wartime language of justice and democracy to the discourse of good neighborliness in the Americas. Joining the cause of hemispheric solidarity with a campaign for more neighborly behavior at home encouraged a more just and humane treatment of all Mexicans. Although moral arguments abounded to justify the Good Neighbor Policy at home and abroad, it was the more mundane arguments of wartime cooperation that gave utilitarian meaning to its application. In any event, the cause for civil and labor rights obtained greater importance and legitimacy when it was incorporated into the larger political project of hemispheric unity.

LULAC leaders appropriated the wartime language to give their social movement the moral force of a crusade. They cast themselves as the true Americans because they consistently supported the grand egalitarian principles of the war at the same time that they described the segregationists as the disloyal opposition at home. Saenz, Perales, Castañeda, Sanchez, and Gonzales regularly invoked an American, or hemispheric, identity as a way to insert themselves into a larger neighboring community and share in the broader application of democratic principles. Americanism, Saenz declared, "can no longer be the birthright of only one nation, but must be applied and bring benefit to all and every one of the nations in the Western hemisphere."[4]

The egalitarian language permeated the discourse over equal rights in the Mexican community. LULAC leaders, however, may have been especially drawn to it because they had already been interpreting their cause as "loyal citizens" since the founding of their organization. Their rhetorical strategy as well as their patriotic stance may have also reflected an attempt to gain favor with government officials who were clearly searching for "acceptable" representatives of the Mexican community. On the other hand, the decision by U.S. and Mexican government officials to collaborate with LULAC could have reinforced these inclinations. Other organizations like La Liga de Habla Española, La Alianza Hispano-Americana, and the International Union of Mine, Mill, and Smelter Workers of America also used the egalitarian language and participated in the fight for equal rights. LULAC's preferred status, however, placed it in a better position to influence official and public opinion during the war, especially in Texas where the organization was born and dominated politics in the Mexican community.

LULAC leaders may have focused their attention on workers and their appeals before the FEPC, but they insisted on a broad political agenda, much like the workers reached out to the larger social movement in their communities. This was evident in Perales' unrelenting call for civil rights legislation at home and endorsements of the human rights cause in national and international forums. The inability of civil rights leaders to enact an effective law in Texas and influence the president, Congress, or the attorney general to consider the passage of a civil rights law, drove him and his contemporaries to seek the support of influential Mexican officials and intellectuals as well as delegates to three important international meetings.

This effort, taken mostly in collaboration with the Mexican government, did not result in a legal victory in the United States, but it did allow LULAC to help maintain the issue of discrimination in the discourse over the Good Neighbor Policy and the inter-American system of unity and cooperation. Maintaining a public and diplomatic focus on discrimination brought added benefit to LULAC and the causes that it promoted, including the FEPC-supported fight against discrimination in war industries.

LULAC's rhetorical engagement with the larger discourse over human rights may have given its leaders and the workers that they represented before the FEPC and other agencies a stronger and more compelling hand, but it also brought them into conflict with policy limitations and the bureaucratic bargaining process. This was evident when Gonzales and Perales were told time and time again that the FEPC and the GNC would not look beyond their prescribed areas of work. Castañeda, on the other hand, was constantly reminded of the statutory limits of the FEPC. The policy clarifications, snubs, and even reprimands that they received represented the limits that officials dictated to the more broadly minded and aspiring Mexican activists.

Mexican activists always tested policy limits; however, they also accommodated to the terms of the relationship with the FEPC, a relationship that carried a double-edged sword. On the one hand, they strengthened their claims against employment discrimination with the use of the president's executive orders and the government's call for the rational use of all available workers. On the other hand, they accepted the basic premise of a nondiscrimination policy that sought limited negotiated settlements on individual or group cases of discrimination as a solution to a pervasive structural problem in society. They also agreed to subject their claims of discrimination to a highly bureaucratic process directed by an agency that was unable to mount an effective challenge against the deeply ingrained segregated order.

Despite its bureaucratic limitations, the FEPC and its advocacy for nondiscrimination in the workplace represented a counterpoint to the USES and its policy of containing farm labor and promoting discriminatory job ads and referrals. The state was obviously pursuing multiple and seemingly contradictory functions when it purported to deliver the wartime promises of recovery and industrial democracy to Mexican urban workers at the same time that it prevented many of them as well as their counterparts in the farms from escaping their low-wage and low-skilled jobs. The USES's refusal to report employers who insisted on maintaining a system of discriminatory job ads and referrals brought it into direct conflict with the FEPC. USES officials thus defied the federal mandate that called on all federal agencies to report violators to the FEPC. They did this at the same time that the government was proclaiming the wartime aim of providing full and equal employment opportunities according to the dictates of the labor market.

The inconsistent and often contradictory behavior of government agencies was also evident in the State Department as it responded to pressure from the Mexican government to extend the Good Neighbor Policy into the home front. State Department officials declared publicly after the summer of 1942 that it would apply the president's executive orders in the copper industry but cancelled the hearings that would have brought public attention to discrimination and strengthened the bargaining position of the FEPC. U.S. government officials wanted to assure Mexico of their inter-American intent but were concerned that exposing discrimination would anger Mexican citizens and pressure Mexico to become even more openly critical of the United States. Added complications included security concerns among State Department officials who feared that the added attention to discrimination could provide grist to the Axis propaganda mill. They also worried that the increasingly public diplomacy over discrimination would agitate Mexican political leaders in the United States and that the work of the FEPC would trigger a reaction among Anglo segregationists.

Some U.S. government officials may have been sincerely concerned about discrimination and the marginalized position of the Mexican community. They broadened policy arenas to maintain cooperative relations with Mexico and to reconcile the declared principles of democracy and justice with the unjust realities of the home front. Stubborn segregationists in public establishments and workplaces as well as the protests that they generated, however, also forced State Department and OCIAA officials to publicly defend their actions as reasonable and sufficient. In response to the ever-watchful Mexico, U.S. officials usually claimed that they were doing enough despite some public opposition and the ever-present fear of a segregationist reaction. This interpretation suggested that policy could not guarantee equal rights under the law but could encourage the Anglo public to gradually adopt a more considerate view of Mexicans and that changing attitudes could improve their social standing. A civil rights law, in other words, was out of the question. Mexico, as well as LULAC, typically expressed less faith in the perfectibility of the Anglo public through moral suasion. They possessed instead an abiding confidence in the notion that equal rights could be legislated and that segregationists in the work place could be made to adopt a nondiscrimination policy.

Segregationist thinking explains much of the inequality that USES officials often reported and that FEPC investigators noted as they took action against employers, unions, and the USES itself. Evidence of racial prejudice was also evident among business owners who refused to give service to Mexicans, state officials who maintained separate and unequal schools, and employers from rural and urban areas who openly used racial language to immobilize farm workers and defy the spirit and the letter of the nation's nondiscrimination policy. This did not mean, however, that some Texans did not question racial prejudice. Legislators passed a nondiscrimination law; Stevenson granted the GNC its weak but encouraging investigative authority; state education officials introduced Spanish and inter-American education into the public school curriculum; and business leaders called for a better understanding of Mexicans. Much of this newfound interest in Mexicans, however, was directed at improving political and commercial relations with Latin American nations. These initiatives also made the dissenters appear overzealous since Texans like Stevenson could claim that they were doing as much as could be expected with a public that viewed segregation as the natural order of things.

Either subterfuge, or a convenient form of self-delusion, was evident in the civil rights bills before the Texas legislature and the establishment of the GNC. According to Stevenson, state leaders wished to extend the benefits of the state's Good Neighbor Policy to Mexicans. The bills, however, were stripped of their broad intent, including the strategic possibility of extending it to African Americans. Also, the GNC members and Stevenson always minimized the seriousness of discrimination and the originally supportive Kibbe even questioned the integrity of Mexican civil rights leaders by suggesting that they were exaggerating the problem and falsely accusing officials of not doing enough. The employers and union officers in the refineries as well as in other work sites were also conveniently inconsistent. Many of them joined in the effort to make the world safe for democracy but practiced racial discrimination against fellow workers and resisted the work of the FEPC, including the adoption of a nondiscrimination policy.

Mexican civil rights leaders and their consulate allies who called for a broad civil rights law did not always speak in inclusive terms, but they still expressed opposition to all forms of racial discrimination and they sought remedies for all of its victims. In his statements before the delegates at the Mexico City and San Francisco conferences, Perales used the issue of discrimination against Mexicans to make common cause with other critics of racial discrimination and to call for national and international policies that prohibited the practice in its entirety.

LULAC and consulate leaders also demonstrated broad vision when they framed a bill to open the door for a civil rights law, but legislators recognized the intent and passed a resolution that only promised protections to Mexicans. Castañeda and his staff also promoted interracial unity in the oil cases and negotiated the adoption of nondiscrimination policies on numerous occasions with the idea of extending protections to all workers. And although newspapers from Texas and Mexico like *La Prensa, El Pan Americano,* the *Lulac News,* and *Fraternidad* would, as expected, focus their concern on Mexicans and a Mexican civil rights law, their writers would also condemn discrimination as a whole and declare it a central issue in uniting nations for peace after the war.

Recent studies on "Whiteness" as a political impulse would have us believe that Mexican civil rights leaders undermined the possibility for interracial unity because they used the government's designation of Mexicans as white to conceal and manipulate for self gain a sense of white privilege over African Americans. There is no doubt that some LULAC leaders harbored racial prejudice against blacks and that this animus reinforced racial thinking and undermined the possibility of interracial unity. Their official paper, *LULAC News,* and some private correspondence occasionally offer evidence of prejudice and distance from the African American social movement. The historical evidence, however, does not support the view that the Mexican civil rights agenda of the 1940s was only concerned with Mexicans or that the leadership deliberatively and spitefully excluded African Americans from their fight for equal rights. On the contrary, activists like Perales, Castañeda, and Herrera consistently agitated against racial inequality inside and outside the FEPC and joined in building collaborative ties with African American workers and their civil rights leaders.

The Mexican government focused on Mexican nationals, but its campaign for equal rights also included U.S.-born Mexicans with a critique that condemned racial discrimination as a whole. Mexico remained distant from Mexicans in the United States during the First World War because of its preoccupation with the Mexican Revolution, but renewed its interest during the 1920s and 1930s with material and moral support that promoted a Mexican identity and strengthened the connection with the homeland. Mexican consuls directed the policy of advocacy that involved basic legal and informational services and the formation of networks of affiliated self-help organizations like La Cruz Azul and Comisiones Honoríficas. Consuls also intervened publicly or quietly with local, state, and federal authorities to settle cases of discrimination, mostly involving businesses who refused to serve Mexicans and employers who violated contractual understandings. In some instances, Mexican officials took a more active ideological interest in Mexican politics by supporting one group over another and antagonizing segments of the local population. One of its most dramatic interventions involved the failed colonization project that encouraged untold numbers of Mexicans to return to Mexico during the Depression.

Mexico reaffirmed its concern for Mexicans in the exterior during the Second World War at the same time that it promoted other national interests and purposes. Its primary interest was to contribute to hemispheric defense and capitalize on its favored status as the United States' principal ally in the hemisphere to improve relations with its northern neighbor. The wartime need for cooperation in the Americas catapulted Mexico into an important position of leadership and further enhanced its relations with the United States. The hope for assistance in the development of Mexico's economy during the postwar period may not have reached some expectations in Mexico, but Mexican officials were able to negotiate numerous wartime agreements of military and economic cooperation, settle the difficult oil crisis, secure contractual guarantees for Braceros, and strengthen the right to speak for their nationals and U.S.-born Mexicans in the United States.

It is impossible to determine how much Mexico's campaign on behalf of Mexicans in the United States defined its overall foreign policy, but it clearly predominated and acquired added importance as it coincided with security concerns in the State Department and regional issues like the alleged shortage of agricultural workers in Texas. Mexico's opposition to racial discrimination had always been important in its advocacy work, but it obtained greater importance during the war years. This was evident in the expansion of the consular cause for human rights, the development of more cooperative relations with the United States, and the elaboration of the inter-American system of cooperation. In all these instances, Mexican officials raised their diplomatic standing with an unassailable position: discrimination was a global affront to human dignity and a violation of the morally inviolable right to be treated equally. Their fight against discrimination and an expectation for cooperation from the U.S. government logically followed.

Mexican officials understood that the U.S. government was reluctant to wage a frontal assault on discrimination but was compelled to address it as an expression of hemispheric solidarity, especially if they called for it openly and in concert with LULAC. Less clear, however, is whether Mexican officials were motivated primarily by their concern over Mexicans in the United States or the national goal of improving relations with the United States. The complex world of wartime diplomacy did not necessarily offer such neatly drawn choices. The initiatives were so interrelated that it may be enough to state that they were mutually reinforcing during the war. On the other hand, the decision by Padilla to replace his more outspoken consuls around the time of the United Nations meeting indicates that the advocacy policy, in its wartime form, became an expendable corollary to Mexican diplomacy.

Mexican consuls from San Antonio, Austin, Houston, and Dallas left little doubt that they were concerned over the discrimination that Mexicans faced in public establishments, schools, and workplaces. The open association that they maintained with LULAC leaders, their public critiques of discrimination, and especially the private correspondence with their superiors and fellow LULAC activists strongly suggest that they were largely committed to Mexico's advocacy policy. In the end, however, Mexico City determined how and to what end the policy would be pursued. During the war, Mexican consuls were encouraged to speak openly and loudly about discrimination. For reasons that are not yet known, Padilla removed the most active consuls and effectively ended their relationship with LULAC immediately after the United Nations meeting in San Francisco.

Mexico's intervention on behalf of Mexicans may have been short-lived, but it waged a vigorous and well-coordinated campaign that influenced the U.S. government to give its attention to the Mexican community. This was evident in the decision to open FEPC offices in the Southwest and to solicit the help of Mexican consulate offices and LULAC councils in the work of the agency. The most determined diplomatic move by Mexican officials was the Texas ban and the State Department's most telling response was its support for the Good Neighbor Policy in Texas. Although the public discussion over the ban and numerous cases of discrimination brought before Mexican and U.S. authorities seemed to place the alliance in crisis, intergovernmental relations remained stable throughout the period of the war.

The treaties and agreements of cooperation and the public affirmations of inter-American unity solidified relations between Mexico and the United States to such a point that the public negotiations over discrimination could become heated and even acrimonious without impairing intergovernmental relations. Padilla's hard bargaining on the ban and Mexico's broader advocacy project, in other words, were possible because overarching considerations—the U.S.'s Good Neighbor Policy, Mexico's favored status, and the region's inter-American alliance—dictated cooperation. Avila Camacho's 1943 decision to extend to the OCIAA the country's highest honor, the Order of the Aztec Eagle, for instance, reinforced the diplomatic standard of cooperation at the same time that Padilla and Mexican consuls were challenging Stevenson's sincerity.

Mexico's pressure on the United States and the alliance between Mexican consuls and LULAC councils produced important results. The open denunciations, the calls for improved racial understanding, and the recurrent use of the language of democracy and justice advanced more considerate views of Mexicans and no doubt encouraged Mexicans to expect a better deal from an activist state. Although the work of the USES and the GNC must have reminded them that government agencies could not be entirely trusted to make major changes in society, the official policies of improved racial understanding and the full use of the available work force reinforced egalitarian principles that Mexican activists used to justify their demands for change. Indefatigable FEPC officials like Castañeda, Ellinger, and Brin also showed them that the state could be made to arbitrate local differences in a fair and just manner. The number of individual and group settlements that the FEPC was able to negotiate may have been small, but the victories often included the adoption of a binding nondiscrimination policy and other positive changes in the workplace. On the other hand, government officials could not assume full credit for these gains. A tightening labor market as well as pressure by groups such as LULAC and the NAACP also contributed to the fuller and more efficient utilization of minority labor.

The Mexican and the U.S. government benefited as well. The Mexican government was able to demonstrate, though briefly, that it could lobby on behalf of Mexicans in the United States and that they could capitalize on their favored ally status to improve relations with the United States. Avila Camacho and Padilla were also able to use their advocacy work to demonstrate that Mexico had forged a new role for itself as a truly independent ally that could defend Mexicans in the exterior and negotiate a favorable set of postwar relations. The U.S. government, on the other hand, managed its wartime relations deftly and established, with Mexico's help, a reliable inter-American system of unity and cooperation. The issue of discrimination could have hampered these efforts. State Department officials, however, extended the Good Neighbor Policy into the United States and although the problems of discrimination and inequality remained relatively unchanged, the United States was able to maintain close cooperative relations with Mexico.

Perales's discouraging note regarding the persistence of discrimination and inequality soon after the defeat of the Spears Bill in the Texas legislature suggests that resentments would continue to feed the cause for human rights during the postwar period. The victims of discrimination, he added, would have to wait patiently until "the bad Texans are educated." Perales reserved a measure of sarcasm for Mexico by pointing out that discrimination against Mexican nationals would end in the United States "the day that Mexico decides to take the necessary action towards that end." This statement underscored the fact that Mexico, as a signatory of the Act of Chapultepec and the United Nations Charter, was in a position to negotiate a treaty to protect the rights of their nationals on foreign soil and to give added weight to the general cause for human rights. It also affirmed a view by Perales and possibly many of his companions that little could be expected from Mexico when it could not even do right by its own nationals. He added that Mexicans in the United States had to rethink the idea of pursuing a civil rights law and suggested that they had to continue their cause without Mexico at their side.

Perales's disenchantment with the Mexican government was well-founded. This does not mean that Mexico ended its relationship with Mexi-

Persons associated with the 1948 *Minerva Delgado v. Bastrop Independent School District:* Robert C. E. Eckhardt, esq., standing by the microphone, Carlos C. Cadena, esq., sitting, third from the left, Dr. George I. Sanchez, sitting fourth from the left, Gustavo C. García, esq., sitting fifth from the left, all others are unidentified. (Nettie Lee Benson Latin American Collection, University of Texas at Austin.)

can struggles in the United States. The financial and diplomatic support that they gave the still largely unexamined 1948 legal fight against segregation in the Bastrop Independent School District, for instance, points to a continuing advocacy policy and cooperation with Mexican groups in Texas. Mexico, however, seems to have retreated to a back-channel form of diplomacy during the postwar period.[5]

The failure to convince state and federal officials in the United States to pass a civil rights law, according to Perales, left "no other option" but to pay the poll tax and elect fair and just persons to public office. Mexicans in the United States, in other words, had to consider other strategies for change during the postwar period. The emphasis on a politics of persuasion and a civil and labor rights campaign would have to make room for other methods, including the election of friendly candidates as well as legal challenges against discrimination and segregation in the schools.[6]

LULAC probably benefited the most from the struggles of the war years. With a depleted membership and a small cadre of leaders, they managed to bring greater attention to discrimination and, in the process, assume a leading public position as intermediaries in intergovernmental relations. They also strengthened their ties as a favored Mexican ally in U.S. governmental circles and further improved its reputation as effective political actors who could travel the distance between local political terrains and national seats of power with cultural and political ease. Regarding interracial unity, LULAC officers and their members could also claim to have promoted unity and equal rights in the fight over a civil rights law, the work of the FEPC, and the battles that raised racial discrimination to a level of hemispheric importance. Moreover, LULAC's use of the public egalitarian language, with its patriotic undertones and its reputation as a major advocate of a civil rights statute reinforced its claims for constitutional rights. The upwardly mobile Mexicans, including the returning veterans, many of whom were U.S.-born, would find this experience attractive and useful as they entered the conservative period of the 1950s.

The attention that the U.S. and Mexican governments, as well as LULAC, brought to the work of the FEPC figured prominently in the way that this narrative was structured. U.S. officials were drawn to the wartime challenge of regulating the labor supply and in insuring that racial thinking did not disrupt wartime production. Their Mexican counterparts and LULAC members understood that the war emergency offered Mexicans unprecedented employment opportunities to recover from the Depression and possibly alter the structure of inequality. The history of discrimination and Mexico's intervention, however, required that the U.S. government intervene to allow the wartime economy to provide full and equal opportunities. Mexican workers, on the other hand, struggled on a daily basis in work sites throughout the state, mostly informally and largely without the help of labor unions or government agencies.

The workers that reached the wartime industries met the same obstacles to recovery as elsewhere. Roosevelt's executive orders, however, provided them the legal means to claim their rights. Their struggle from within the government bureaucracy brought them limited gains, while the wartime economy, with all its obstacles to equal opportunity, provided them with most of the improvements that they were able to achieve. The war years delivered less than promised, but hope still lay ahead in new economic and political opportunities, an activist state, and the Mexican will to continue claiming rights and righting wrongs in the postwar years.

The Swedish scholar Bent Flyvbjerg would agree that Mexican history at the Texas home front represents the kind of "rich ambiguity" in life that is difficult at first blush to organize into "neat scientific formulae, general propositions, and theories." This study began as a broadly construed concern over the unmet promise of equal wartime recovery for Mexicans. It became a multilayered account and analysis of discrimination as an obstacle to upward occupational mobility situated against a larger, unfolding drama of international norms, wartime concerns over hemispheric unity, the multivariate state, and the Mexican cause against inequalities. The "thick" narrative that emerged from my largely empirically-driven approach both disentangles and complexifies the history of Mexicans in the United States.

Appendix 1: Demographic and Social Patterns among Mexicans in the United States, 1930–1945

Immigration from Mexico contributed significantly to changing demographic and social patterns in the Mexican community of the United States during the first half of the twentieth century. Ernesto Galarza, noted author and activist in the Mexican community, acknowledged this on the eve of the United States' entry into the Second World War when he observed that it represented "one of the most significant mass movements of population between two republics of the Western Hemisphere." The back-and-forth movement involved an increasing number of families who decided to settle permanently in the United States. Between one and two million people, or about 10 percent of the total population of Mexico, had settled in the United States by 1940. This increased the Mexican population, added to its dispersion, and contributed to urbanization. Moreover, as Mexican nationals gave birth to children in the United States, the overall Mexican birth rate grew dramatically.[1]

The Depression and the war years offered starkly contrasting demographic and social experiences for the Mexican community in the United States. Mexicans experienced a population decline during the Depression but recovered demographically during the Second World War. This pattern corresponded with the ebb and flow of Mexican migration and the low and high levels of production during the same periods. The significant population drop during the Depression, for instance, resulted from the major exodus of destitute working families and the shrinking number of Mexican immigrants. Improved job opportunities beginning in the late 1930s, on the other hand, reversed the downward spiral. Despite important variations in the downward and upward demographic movements in the Southwest, the trends in the Mexican populations of California and Texas offer suggestive similarities as they moved from the Depression to the war years.

The U.S. Bureau of the Census estimated a noticeable Mexican population increase in 1940 and a significant one in 1950 in the southwestern states of Arizona, California, Colorado, New Mexico, and Texas. Their numbers increased by 22.4 percent between 1930 and 1940, and by 45.3 percent between 1940 and 1950 (see table A.1). Clearly, the years of the Depression

Table A.1. Population figures for Mexicans in five Southwestern states, 1930–1950

Region/State	*1930*[1]	*% of total*	*1940*	*% of total*	*% incr/decr*	*1950*	*% of total*	*% incr/decr*
Southwest								
Total	13,396,647		15,254,846		13.9	20,804,720		40.8
Mexican	1,282,883	9.6	1,570,740	10.3	22.4	2,281,710	11	45.3
Arizona								
Total	435,573		499,261		14.6	749,587		50.1
Mexican	114,173	26.2	101,880	20.4	–11	128,580	17.2	26.2
California								
Total	5,677,251		6,907,387		21.7	10,586,223		53.3
Mexican	368,013	6.5	416,140	6	13.1	758,400	7.2	82.3
Colorado								
Total	1,035,791		1,123,296		5.4	1,325,089		18
Mexican		5.6	92,540	8.2	60.5	118,715	9	28.3
New Mexico								
Total	423,317		310,078		–27	432,627		39.5
Mexican	59,340	14	221,740	71.5	274	248,560	57.5	12.1
Texas								
Total	5,824,715		6,414,824		10.1	7,711,194		20.2
Mexican	683,681	11.7	738,440	11.5	8	1,027,455	13.3	39.1

Sources: Paul Bullock, "Employment Problems of the Mexican American," *Industrial Relations* 3, no. 3 (1964), 37–50; Campbell Gibson and Kay Jung, "Historical Census Statistics on Population Totals by Race, 1790 to 1990, and by Hispanic Origin, 1970 to 1990, for the United States, Regions, Divisions, and States," U.S. Bureau of the Census, Population Division, Working Paper Series No. 56, September 2002 (http://www.census.gov/population/www/documentation/twps0056.html); Carey McWilliams, *Ill Fares the Land* (Boston: Little, Brown and Company, 1944), 247; Seth Shepard McKay, *Texas and the Fair Deal, 1945–1952* (San Antonio: The Naylor Company, 1954), 2–3; Lyle Saunders, "The Spanish-Speaking Population of Texas," Inter-American Education Occasional Papers No. 5 (Austin: University of Texas Press, 1949).

[1] The rate of increase for the Mexican population in 1930 cannot be computed because the corresponding population figures for 1920 are not available.

interrupted a regional trend of significant growth extending from the late 1800s to the early 1900s, while the war years reestablished it during the rest of the twentieth century. The two historical periods spawned another related set of markers involving California and Texas, the states with the largest number of Mexicans in the Southwest. Mexicans were primarily concentrated in Texas until 1930. Beginning in 1940, California became the state with the largest number of Mexicans, and it led the entire Southwest with the most impressive growth rates. Also, a striking decline-recovery pattern in California and Texas diverged in a significant way from the overall trend in the Southwest of a slight population increase in the 1930s and a major one in the 1940s.[2]

The Mexican portion of the overall population in California and Texas declined by 1940 and recovered by 1950. The unusually higher proportional figures in states with fewer Mexicans such as New Mexico skewed the data in the Southwest with slow and steady increases. The proportional losses by California and Texas in 1940 can be best appreciated when one considers that the census included the numerical gains that occurred as the region began recovering from the Depression in the late 1930s. The improved conditions triggered a return migration from Mexico that offset to some extent the losses of the early 1930s. The slight proportional increases recorded in 1940, in other words, obscure the lower figures of the early 1930s, during the middle of the hard times of the Depression. Significant migrations from Mexico as well as from rural to urban areas in the United States were already evident by 1939. The census count of 1950, on the other hand, included the significant demographic growth of the war years as well as the less impressive population figures of the postwar period. The appreciable proportional levels that Mexicans reached in California and Texas in 1950 consequently also represent conservative estimates.

Population growth rates further illustrate the importance of the hard times of the Depression and the economic recovery of the 1940s. Here again, New Mexico stood out by skewing the data in the Southwest in the direction of significant population increases in both 1940 and 1950 that exceeded the corresponding figures among the total population in the Southwest. Mexicans from California and Texas only increased their respective numbers by 13.1 percent and 8 percent in 1940. In 1950, however, they exceeded the overall state rates as well as the increases in all the other southwestern states.

The more impressive Mexican and overall increases in California in 1940 and 1950 require added explanation. The state population grew at a faster rate in California during the 1930s, thanks largely to the "Okies" and Dust Bowl migrants who were lured by the possibility of escaping the difficult conditions in their home areas. The earlier start and higher rate of wartime production in California accounted for a significant movement of workers and their families into the state beginning in the late 1930s. California's general and Mexican populations continued to register the highest growth rates in the Southwest in the 1940s (53.3 and 83.3 percent, respectively). The less impressive increases among Mexicans in Texas (39.1 percent), but especially in Arizona (26.2 percent), New Mexico (12.1 percent), and Colorado (28.3),

Table A.2. Mexico and U.S.-born Mexican population in five Southwestern states in censuses of 1930, 1940, and 1950

Region/State	*Mexico-born*	*U.S.-born*		*Total*
		Mexico/mixed parentage	*U.S.-born parentage*	
Southwest (total)				
Mexicans, 1930	530,672	498,770	253,441	1,282,883
Percentage of total	41.4	66.3	33.7	9.6
Spanish mother tongue, 1940	323,440	619,300	628,000	1,570,740
Percentage of total	20.6	49.6	50.4	10.3
Percentage increase	–39.1	25.2	147.8	22.4
Spanish surname, 1950	392,500	775,530	1,113,680	2,281,710
Percentage of total	17.2	33.9	48.8	11
Percentage increase/decrease	21.4	25.2	191.6	45.3
Arizona				
Mexicans, 1930	47,855	47,363	18,955	114,173
Percentage of total	41.9	71.4	28.6	8.9
Spanish mother tongue, 1940	24,140	50,140	27,600	101,880
Percentage of total	23.7	64.5	35.5	6.5
Percentage increase	–49.6	5.9	45.6	–10.8
Spanish surname, 1950	23,235	51,965	53,380	128,580
Percentage of total	18.1	49.3	50.7	5.6
Percentage increase/decrease	–3.8	3.6	93.4	26.2
California				
Mexicans, 1930	191,346	147,529	29,138	368,013
Percentage of total	52	40.1	7.9	28.7
Spanish mother tongue, 1940	136,700	215,740	63,700	416,140
Percentage of total	32.9	51.8	15.3	26.5
Percentage increase	–28.7	46.2	118.6	13.1
Spanish surname, 1950	166,860	324,705	266,835	758,400
Percentage of total	22	42.8	35.2	33.2
Percentage increase/decrease	22.1	50.5	318.9	82.3
Colorado				
Mexicans, 1930	12,816	11,904	32,956	57,676
Percentage of total	22.2	26.5	73.5	4.5
Spanish mother tongue, 1940	6,640	14,100	71,800	92,540
Percentage of total	7.2	16.4	83.6	5.9
Percentage increase	–48.2	18.5	117.9	60.5
Spanish surname, 1950	4,965	15,000	98,750	118,715
Percentage of total	4.2	13.2	86.8	5.2
Percentage increase/decrease	–25.2	6.4	37.5	28.3

(*continued*)

Table A.2. (*continued*)

Region/State	*Mexico-born*	*U.S.-born*		*Total*
		Mexico/mixed parentage	*U.S.-born parentage*	
New Mexico				
Mexicans, 1930	15,983	17,771	25,586	59,340
Percentage of total	26.9	41	59	4.6
Spanish mother tongue, 1940	7,820	21,100	192,820	221,740
Percentage of total	3.5	9.9	90.1	14.1
Percentage increase	–51.1	18.7	653.6	273.7
Spanish surname, 1950	10,520	21,235	216,805	248,560
Percentage of total	4.2	8.9	91.1	10.9
Percentage increase/decrease	34.5	.6	12.4	12.1
Texas				
Mexicans, 1930	262,672	274,203	146,806	683,681
Percentage of total	38.4	40.1	21.5	53.3
Spanish mother tongue, 1940	148,140	318,220	272,080	738,440
Percentage of total	20.1	43.1	36.8	47
Percentage increase	–43.6	16.1	85.3	8
Spanish surname, 1950	186,920	362,625	477,910	1,027,455
Percentage of total	18.2	35.3	46.5	45
Percentage increase/decrease	26.2	3.9	75.7	39.2

Source: U.S. Bureau of the Census, 1950 Population Census Report P-E, No. 3C, Persons of Spanish Surname (Washington, D.C.: U.S. Government Printing Office 1953), 7.

suggest that California benefited most from interstate as well as international migrations. This further indicates that the census in large part recorded the effects of significant migrations in and out of regions and between Mexico and the United States in the 1930s and 1940s.

A generational analysis of the census data offers yet another way to explain the striking demographic mark that the Depression and the war years left on the Mexican community. The well-documented anti-immigrant campaigns and the deportations and expatriations that occurred during the 1930s suggest that the first generation, that is, the Mexico-born persons of Mexican parentage, experienced more suffering and recovered more slowly than the second, third, or later generations. The most consistent finding in the five southwestern states was a major population decline among the first generation in 1940 (see table A.2). New Mexico claimed the most significant decline (–51 percent), California registered a significant one (–28.7 percent), while the region as a whole also reported an important drop (–39.1 percent). The first generation did not recover these losses in 1950 in large part because it felt the brunt of the deportations and repatriations. Moreover, they do not seem to have shared equally in the economic recovery of the war. While the first generation recorded significant population losses in 1930, the second and third generations demonstrated impressive growth in 1940 and significant increases in 1950.

The third generation more than doubled its numbers in the Southwest by 1940. California contributed most significantly to this growth, especially during the war years. The striking figure of 318.9 percent strongly suggests that California, with its more robust wartime economy, attracted a disproportionate number of U.S.-born Mexicans from the other southwestern states. Although many of them may have ended up working in agriculture, some of them secured jobs in urban-based wartime industries and consequently benefited from the recovery opportunities of the war to a greater extent than in Texas.

Mexicans who lived in Texas, regardless of generational status, outnumbered their counterparts in each of the southwestern states in 1930, 1940, and 1950. They also maintained a higher share of their state population than in California in the 1930s and 1940s. This meant that Mexican immigrants continued to select Texas as their favored destination. The higher number of U.S.-born Mexicans of U.S.-born parents in Texas also underscores a long-term presence by a community with Spanish colonial roots. Denials of opportunity, especially during a period of accelerated production, must have chafed deeply among Mexicans with this kind of historical presence. The first and second generation Mexicans, on the other hand, most probably suffered more social deprivation as well as denials of job opportunities.

Appendix 2: Partial List of Mexican FEPC Complainants in Texas, 1943–1945

The following list of complainants is not exhaustive, although it does include all the names and addresses that appeared in the FEPC records examined for this project. Accents did not appear on all the personal names, but common usage makes their pronunciation evident. The list is an act of recovery; it recognizes many of the names of the heretofore unknown workers who defended their rights against discriminatory employers and unions.

AMARILLO

Pantex Ordnance Plant

Cleo M. Garcia, 1306 South Arthur St.
Marie Ramos, 1518 South Arthur St.
Tony L. Velez, 1316 South Arthur St.
Jesse Losoya, 1517 South Garfield St.
Concha Losoya
Janie Vitela, 1904 South Arthur St.
Magdalene Quintero, 1214 South Arthur St.
Mary Cuellar, 1401 South Arthur St.
Juanita Molina, 1306 South Arthur St.
Lina Jimenez, 1515 South Arthur St.

BROWNSVILLE

Brownsville Ship Building Corporation

Mrs. Jose A. Besteiro, 742 NW. Charles Street
Maria R. Salinas

CORPUS CHRISTI

American Smelting and Refining Company

Frank Matta Jr., 1505 Howard Street
Adan C. Cisneroz, 1214 Leopard Street
Dan Falcon
Albert T. Castillo, 1514 Howard Street
Onofre O. Leal, 1514 Kennedy Street
Margarito Silva
Porfirio Guerra
Henry Canchola
Primitivo Gonzalez, c/o National Club, 1009 Leopard Street
J. C. Navarro, c/o National Club
Manuel Cruz, c/o National Club
Victor Gonzalez, c/o National Club
C. S. Sanchez, c/o National Club
Antonio Davila, c/o National Club
John Ramirez, 802 12th Street
Alfredo Castro, 824 Mesteña
Simon Gonzalez
John H. Salazar
Guadalupe Marroquin
Victor S. Suarez
Jesus Hinojosa
Manuel Baldez
Manuel Gonzalez
Philip E. Barrera
Damacio Guerra
R. F. Rico
G. M. Quintana
Chato Garza

Naval Air Base

Mrs. Geneva A. Gonzalez, 2018 Howard Street
Jose B. Aguilar, 437 Vera Cruz St.
Berta Hinojosa, 1014 E. Yoakum, Kingsville

Southern Alkali Corporation

Robert Meza, LULAC Council #1, 2318 Agnes
Esteban M. Jimenez, 2513 Mary Street
Santiago Sibrian
Manuel D. Prado
Jesus Muro, 2921 Margarite
Frank O. Guerra
Ernesto Flores Lopez
Pablo Galvan
Ramon Gonzalez
Mauricio Gonzalez
Felipe Alaniz
Jose Valadez
Sonciano S. Fresina
Francisco Guzman
Andres Masedo
Jose Carrera
Santiago Perez
Reynaldo Martinez
Ben Guerra
Geronimo Banda
Alfredo Garcia
Guadalupe Martinez
Victoriano M. Rojas
J. L. Coitz
E. Rodriguez
Jesus Lopez
Luis U. Hernandez
Abelardo Perez Jr.
Jose Reyez
Saragosa Reyez
Jose Perales
Thomas R. Flores
Juan Santana
Juan Martinez
Pascua Ledesma
Remigio Gomez

Camilo Vela
Alfredo C. Gutierrez
Valentin Tijerina
Reynaldo Loa
Louis Hernandez, 760 Cheyene
Richard Garcia, 1600 Water Street
Sebastian Ramirez, 1502 Margarite
C. B. Mauricio, 2011 Mussett
Ygnacio Moreno, 3005 Buford
Frank O. Guerra, 205 Josephine
Mauricio Gonzalez, 513 18th
Frank G. Escalero, 1818 Lipan
Jose T. Alvarado, 1630 Laredo
Jose Valadez, 207 Bluntzer
Alfredo G. Gutierrez, 2628 Sonora
A. G. Rivera Jr., 1560 18th
Jose Garza, 807 Waco
Chris Guzman, 807 Waco
Gabe Lozano
Elias Licona

MATHIS

UCAPAWA Local 87

Telesforo Oviedo, Secretary Treasurer
Gregorio Hernandez, President
Espindioni Paez, Vice President
Augustin Coronado, Recording Secretary
Luis Castillo
Leandro de Leon
Espiridion Leal
Juan S. Reyes
Calistro Padron
Jose Huerta
Dorotea Padron

DALLAS

Housing Authority

Matias Villarreal

North American Aviation

Jesus C. Castro
Everardo Lozano
Rodolfo Castro, 2819 N. Harwood

Pure Food Products

Jovita Hernandez
Amelia Hernandez

DUMAS

American Zinc

Santos Muñiz Ibarra
Encarnacion Ramos

HOUSTON

Brown Shipbuilding Company

Mary Treviño, 7527 Avenue J
Victoria Ruiz, 606 Northrup
Innocencia G. Ortiz. 7713 Avenue K
Hortencia Reyes, 4049 Cortney
Caroline Castro
J. R. Torres
P. C. Hernandez
C. A. Sanchez
P. O. Vela
P. M. Calvo

Gulf Portland Cement Company

Jose Rodriguez, 7509 Avenue K
Miguel Gonzalez-Taush, Member of Mexican Consulate staff
Manuel V. Velasquez

Texas Employment Office

Fernando R. Ypina, 2721 Engelke

UCAPAWA, CIO Local 75, Cotton Compress and Oil Workers Union

L. G. Camacho, Vice President
Antonio Garcia, Financial Secretary
Claudia G. Suarez, Contract Negotiator, Terminal Warehouse
Bennie Nava, Contract Negotiator, Terminal Warehouse
Sam Costilla, Contract Negotiator, Houston Compress
Roy Rodriguez

USES

Fernando R. Ypina

Company Unknown

Mike Luna, 2517 Garron
Antonio Schnur, 306 Charles St
Ramon P. De La Garza, 2605 Navigation
Federico S. Jimenez, 2514 Sallus

PASADENA

Shell Refinery

J. Casas
R. R. Flores
J. R. Alba
Reynaldo Armendariz

Cpl. William Sanchez
J. J. Herrera

Sinclair Refinery

Julio R. Flores, 7533 Avenue H (complaint against Local 227)
J. H. Gonzales
J. Belman
Jesse Lozano Caballero
Henry S. Mendez, 8405 John St.
Napoleon. De La Garza, 7102 Avenue L
Juan "John" Robledo, 7626 Avenue L
S. Rodriguez, 7334 Avenue I
A. V. Salinas, 7936 Sherman
A. S. Sanchez, 7936 Sherman, 7615 Avenue E.
Teodosio Gutierrez, 7623 Avenue F
P. Jaramillo, 1918 Franklin
N. Gomez, 904 McKee

BAYTOWN

Humble Refinery

Macedonio Rincon
J. Santana
Andres Contreras
C. Beltran
Onofre Gonzalez
L. Herrera
G. N. Ponce

NEW GULF

Texas Gulf Sulphur Company

Israel G. Vera
Cruz R. Amaro

Crispin Guajardo Campos
Refugio Rodriguez
Herculano F. Rios
Gustavo S. Garcia
Cruz de los Santos
Donaciono Bustos
Bonifacio Sanchez Guzman
Daniel Vega Garcia
Daniel Rubio
Vicente Rangel

FREEPORT

Ethyl-Dow Chemical Company

Felix V. Vara

Staufer Chemical Company

Lalo R. Garcia
Benito Fuentes
Jose G. Delgado
Rosalio Hernandez
Julian Gutierrez
Alfredo Lara
Fernando Salinas
Manuel P. Leiba
Francisco "Frank" Cabrera
Victor Aviles
Don Asiano Lopez
Manuel E. Braun
Severo E. Braun
Pablo Gasso
Pedro Perez
Abelino Rodriguez
Francisco Rodriguez
Julio Ramirez

Gonzalo T. Garcia
Cesilio Aguilar
John Rodriguez
Jose Martinez
Maximiliano Castillo
Salvador Garcia
Isidoro Cisneros
Jose O. Perez
Jose Aguilar
Mateo Mosqueda
Enrique Estrada
Guadalupe Gonzalez
Refugio Gonzalez
Ezequiel Martinez

PALACIOS

UCAPAWA Local 192, 1939–1940

C. Valdez, President
Mrs. Ethel Peres, Secretary Treasurer
Felipe Rodriguez, Guard
Alex Sanchez, Executive Board
Felipe Rodriguez

VELASCO

Dow Magnesium Plant

Mike Luna
Antonio Schnur
Ramón P. de la Garza
Federico S. Jiménez

SAN ANTONIO

Ed Frederich Inc.

Angelita Almanza, 427 Gould St.

IGN Railroad

Henry Gutierrez
Manuel Martinez, BRP Member
Ernest Marroquin

Kelley

Alfredo Flores
Toribio Gonzales
Manuel Lopez
Jose Ismael Perez
Tomas Guede Jr., 118 Montezuma St.

Office of Censorship, Post Office

Laureano Flores

Southwestern Bell Telephone

Lydia Newman
Rosa de los Santos

UCAPAWA Local 172, 1939–1945

Santos G. Vasquez
Ramon Chavarria
L. G. Vasquez
Telesforo Oviedo
Alexandre Gonzalez
Lucille Mondragon
Margarita Almarez

Benigna Guardarrama
Juan Alejos

USES (Sunshine Manufacturing Co.)

Pola Flores, 137 Burbank
Josephine Alaman, 42 Leal, Fannin 4808

Notes

Chapter 1

1. Throughout this book, I use the term Mexican to identify persons of Mexican origin, except where it is necessary to note their nativity or citizenship. In those instances, I use Mexican national and Mexico-born for people born in Mexico, or U.S.-born Mexican for people born in the United States. I prepared all the translations from Spanish-language sources that appear in the text and notes.

2. The historical literature on the varied experiences at the U.S. home front is extensive. The following selected works address the subject, including the idea that workers, minorities, and women did not always enjoy full and equal recovery from the hard times of the Depression: John Morton Blum, *V Was for Victory: Politics and American Culture during World War II* (New York: Harcourt Brace Jovanovich, 1976); Elizabeth Cohen, *Making a New Deal: Industrial Workers in Chicago, 1919–1939* (New York: Cambridge University Press, 1990); John W. Jeffries, *Wartime America: The World War II Home Front* (Chicago: Ivar R. Dee, 1996); Ruth Milkman, *Gender at Work: The Dynamics of Job Segregation by Sex during World War II* (Champaign: University of Illinois Press, 1987); William O'Neill, *A Democracy at War: America's Fight at Home and Abroad in World War II* (New York: Free Press, 1993); Richard Polenberg, *America at War: The Home Front, 1941–1945* (Englewood Cliffs, N.J.: Prentice-Hall, 1968); Ronald Takaki, *Double Victory: A Multicultural History of America in World War II* (Boston: Little, Brown and Company, 2000); Allan M. Winkler, *Home Front U.S.A.: America during World War II* (Wheeling, Ill.: Harlan Davidson, 2000); Emilio Zamora, "The Failed Promise of Wartime Opportunity for Mexicans in the Texas Oil Industry," *Southwestern Historical Quarterly* 95, no. 3 (1992): 23–50; Robert H. Zieger and Gilbert J. Gall, "Labor Goes to War, 1939–1945," in *American Workers, American Unions, The Twentieth Century,* (Baltimore: The Johns Hopkins University Press, 2002), chapter 4.

3. The literature on the New Deal is also extensive. The following is a selective list of useful general surveys, critical interpretations, and focused studies on labor, agriculture, and the state: Cletus E. Daniels, *Bitter Harvest: A History of California Farmworkers, 1870–1941* (Ithaca, N.Y.: Cornell University Press, 1981); Suzanne Forrest, *The Preservation of the Village: New Mexico's Hispanics and the New Deal* (Albuquerque: University of New Mexico Press, 1989); Steve Fraser and Gary Gerstle, *The Rise and Fall of the New Deal Order, 1930–1980* (Princeton, N.J.: Princeton University Press, 1989); Barry D. Karl, *The Uneasy State: The United States from 1915 to 1945* (Chicago: University of Chicago Press, 1983); Irene Ledesma, "The New Deal Public Works Program and the Mexican Americans in McAllen Texas, 1933–36" (master's thesis, The University of Texas-Pan American, 1977); William E. Leuchtenburg, *Franklin D. Roosevelt and the New Deal, 1932–1940* (New York: Harper and Row, 1963); Rhonda Levine, *Class Struggle and the New Deal: Industrial Labor, Industrial Capital, and the State* (Lawrence: University Press of Kansas, 1988); Harvard Sitkoff, *A New Deal for Blacks: The Emergence of Civil Rights as a National Issue* (New York: Oxford University Press, 1978).

4. The following works address the history of LULAC and in some cases they include its leadership's use of the wartime language as a tool to advance its civil rights

agenda: Thomas H. Kreneck, *Mexican American Odyssey: Felix Tijerina, Entrepreneur and Civic Leader, 1905–1965* (College Station: Texas A&M University Press, 2001); Benjamín Márquez, *LULAC: The Evolution of a Mexican American Political Organization* (Austin: University of Texas Press, 1993); Cynthia E. Orozco, "The Origins of the League of United Latin American Citizens (LULAC) and the Mexican American Civil Rights Movement in Texas with an Analysis of Women's Political Participation in a Gendered Context, 1910–1929" (PhD diss., University of Texas at Austin, 1992); Guadalupe San Miguel Jr., "The Struggle against Separate and Unequal Schools: Middle Class Mexican Americans and the Desegregation Campaign in Texas, 1929–1957," *History of Education Quarterly* 23, no. 3 (1983): 343–59; Oliver D. Weeks, "The League of United Latin American Citizens; A Texas-Mexican Civic Organization," *The Southwestern Political and Social Science Quarterly* 10 (1929): 257–78; Emilio Zamora "Fighting on Two Fronts: José de la Luz Saenz and the Language of the Mexican American Civil Rights Movement," in *Recovering the U.S. Hispanic Literary Heritage,* vol. 4, eds. José F. Aranda Jr. and Silvio Torres-Saillant, 214–39 (Houston: Árte Público Press, 2002). Other authors have given prominence to LULAC in their studies on related subjects. These include: Mario García, *Mexican Americans: Leadership, Ideology and Identity, 1930–1960* (New Haven, Conn.: Yale University Press, 1989); Gilbert G. Gonzalez, "Interamerican and Intercultural Education and the Chicano Community," *The Journal of Ethnic Studies* 13, no. 3 (1985): 31–53; Guadalupe San Miguel Jr., *"Let Them All Take Heed": Mexican Americans and the Quest for Educational Equality in Texas, 1918–1981* (Austin: University of Texas Press, 1987).

5. See the following for calls to internationalize U.S. history: Gordon A. Craig, "The Historian and the Study of International Relations," *American Historical Review* 88, no. 1 (1983): 1–11; Akira Iriye, "The Internationalization of History," *American Historical Review* 94, no. 1 (1989): 1–10. Scholarship in Mexican history anticipated the call to go beyond national limits for a fuller understanding of U.S. history. They include Américo Paredes's early work on the transnational area of "Greater Mexico" and Juan Gómez-Quiñones's study of the Mexican revolution and the exiled Partido Liberal Mexicano in this same region. Paredes, *With His Pistol in His Hand* (Austin: University of Texas Press, 1958); Paredes, *A Texas-Mexican Cancionero: Folksongs of the Lower Border* (Urbana: University of Illinois Press, 1976); Gómez-Quiñones, "Toward a Perspective on Chicano History," *Aztlán* 2 (1972): 1–49; Gómez-Quiñones, *Sembradores, Ricardo Flores Magón y El Partido Liberal Mexicano: A Eulogy and Critique,* monograph no. 5 (Los Angeles: UCLA Chicano Studies Research Center, 1973).

6. Home front studies noted in note 2 address the subject of industrial mobilization, including the role played by government agencies like the USES and the FEPC. The literature on the FEPC is vast owing primarily to the agency's work in the area of employment discrimination and its association with the beginning of the modern black civil rights movement. Some of the latest publications on the FEPC include: Clete Daniel, *Chicano Workers and the Politics of Fairness: The FEPC in the Southwest, 1941–1945* (Austin: University of Texas Press, 1991); Merl Reed, *Seedtime for the Modern Civil Rights Movement: The President's Committee on Fair Employment Practice, 1941–1946* (Baton Rouge: Louisiana State University Press, 1991); Zamora, "The Failed Promise of Wartime Opportunity for Mexicans in the Texas Oil Industry." Although class, racial, and sexual bias accounted for much of the unequal access to wartime opportunities, the following notable critiques of industrial mobilization argue that the state did not seek structural changes in U.S. society and that state actors generally retreated from the reform agenda of the Depression years: Alan Brinkley, *The End of Reform: New Deal Liberalism and War* (New York: Alfred A. Knopf, 1995); Gregory Hooks, *Forging the Military-Industrial Complex: World War II's Battle of the Potomac*

(Champaign: University of Illinois Press, 1991); Daniel Kryder, *Divided Arsenal: Race and the American State During World War II* (Cambridge: Cambridge University Press, 2000); Brian Waddell, *The War Against the New Deal, World War II and American Democracy* (DeKalb: Northern Illinois University Press, 2001).

7. The following recent studies demonstrate how African American civil rights influenced U.S. foreign policy during the postwar period: Mary Dudziek, *Cold War Civil Rights: Race and the Image of American Democracy* (Princeton, N.J.: Princeton University Press, 2000); Azza Salama Layton, *International Politics and Civil Rights Policies in the United States* (New York: Cambridge University Press, 2000). Although the "emerging" field of civil rights and U.S. foreign policy is generally associated with African Americans and the postwar period, scholars from Mexico and the United States have demonstrated the participation of Mexicans in the internationalization of U.S. and Mexican history dating back to the middle of the nineteenth century. María Rosa García and David R. Maciel, "El México de afuera: políticas mexicanas de protección en Estados Unidos," in *Al Norte de La Frontera: El Pueblo Chicano,* eds. David R. Maciel and José Guillermo Saavedra, 375–413 (México, D.F.: Consejo Nacional de Población, 1988); Juan Gómez-Quiñones, "Mexican Immigration to the United States and the Internationalization of Labor, 1848–1980: An Overview," in *Mexican Immigrant Workers in the United States,* anthology no. 2, ed. Antonio Ríos Bustamante, 13–34 (Los Angeles: UCLA Chicano Studies Research Center Publications, 1981); Gonzalez, "Interamerican and Intercultural Education and the Chicano Community"; Blanca Torres, *Historia de la Revolución Mexicana, Periódo 1940–52: México en la Segunda Guerra Mundial* (México, D.F.: El Colegio de México, 1979); Emilio Zamora, *The World of the Mexican Worker in Texas* (College Station: Texas A&M University Press, 1993); Emilio Zamora, "Mexico's Wartime Intervention on Behalf of Mexicans in the United States," in *Mexican Americans and World War II,* ed. Maggie Rivas-Rodríguez (Austin: University of Texas Press, 2005); Luis Zorrilla, *Historia de las Relaciones Entre México y Los Estados Unidos de America, 1800–1958,* Tomo II (México, D.F.: Editorial Porrúa, 1966).

8. The following historiographies make evident the gaps as well as the important contributions in Mexican home front history: Juan Gómez-Quiñones and Luis Leobardo Arroyo, "On the State of Chicano History: Observation on Its Development, Interpretations, and Theory, 1970–1974," *Western Historical Quarterly* 7, no. 2 (1976): 155–85; David G. Gutiérrez, "Significant for Whom? Mexican Americans and the History of the American West," *The Western Historical Quarterly* 24, no. 4 (1993): 519–39; Alex M. Saragoza, "Recent Chicano Historiography: An Interpretive Essay," *Aztlán* 19, no. 1 (1988–1990): 1–77.

9. Juan Gómez-Quiñones, *Roots of Chicano Politics, 1600–1940* (Albuquerque: University of New Mexico Press, 1994); Juan Gómez-Quiñones, *Chicano Politics: Reality and Promise, 1940–1990* (Albuquerque: University of New Mexico Press, 1990); David Montejano, *Anglos and Mexicans in the Making of Texas, 1836–1986* (Austin: University of Texas Press, 1987); George N. Green, *The Establishment in Texas Politics: The Primitive Years, 1938–1957* (Norman: University of Oklahoma Press, 1979); Ben Proctor, "Texas from Depression through World War II, 1929–1945," in *The Texas Heritage,* ed. Ben Proctor and Archie P. McDonald, 165–86 (Arlington Heights, Ill.: Harlan Davidson, 1992); Randolph B. Campbell, "The 'Prosperity Decade' and the Great Depression, 1921–1941," and "World War II and the Rise of Modern Texas, 1941–1971," in *Gone to Texas: A History of The Lone Star State* (New York: Oxford University Press, 2003), 360–95, 396–437; Ernest Obadele-Starks, *Black Unionism in the Industrial South* (College Station: Texas A&M University Press, 2000). Also see the following book on the postwar period and one of the latest studies on the Depression for some commentary on the World War II

years: Seth Shepard McKay, *Texas and the Fair Deal, 1945–1952* (San Antonio: The Naylor Company, 1954); Walter L. Buenger, *The Path to a Modern South: Northeast Texas between Reconstruction and the Great Depression* (Austin: University of Texas Press, 2001).

10. San Miguel Jr., *"Let All of Them Take Heed": Mexican Americans and the Campaign for Educational Equality in Texas, 1910–1981;* García, *Mexican Americans: Leadership, Ideology and Identity, 1930–1960;* George J. Sanchez, *Becoming Mexican American: Ethnicity, Culture, and Identity in Chicano Los Angeles, 1900–1945* (New York: Oxford University Press, 1993); Matt García, *A World of Its Own: Race, Labor, and Citrus in the Making of Greater Los Angeles, 1900–1970* (Chapel Hill: University of North Carolina Press, 2001); Carlos K. Blanton, *The Strange Career of Bilingual Education in Texas, 1836–1981* (College Station: Texas A&M University Press, 2004); Arnoldo de León, *Ethnicity in the Sunbelt: A History of Mexican Americans in Houston* (Houston: Center for Mexican American Studies, University of Houston, 1989); Vicki Ruiz, *Cannery Women, Cannery Lives: Mexican Women, Unionization, and the California Food Processing Industry, 1930–1950* (Albuquerque: University of New Mexico Press, 1987); Vicki Ruiz, *From out of the Shadows: Mexican Women in Twentieth-Century America* (New York: Oxford University Press, 1998).

11. Luis Zorrilla, *Historia de las Relaciones Entre México y Los Estados Unidos de America, 1800–1958;* Blanca Torres, *Historia de la Revolución Mexicana, Periódo 1940–52, México en la Segunda Guerra Mundial.* Other representative works with perspectives from Mexico that this study has incorporated include the following: Jorge Castañeda, *Mexico and the United Nations* (New York: Manhattan Publishing Company, 1958); Luis F. Gonzalez-Souza, "La política exterior de México ante la protección internacional de los derechos humanos," *Foro Internacional* 18, núm. 1 (1977): 108–38; Lourdes Arizpe, "El éxodo rural en México y su relación con la migración a Estados Unidos," *Estudios Sociológicos* 1, no. 1 (1983): 9–33; Robert A. Pastor and Jorge G. Castañeda, *Limits to Friendship: The United States and Mexico* (New York: Vintage Books, 1989); Manuel García y Griego, "El Comienzo y el Final: La Interdependencia Estructural y Dos Negociaciones Sobre Braceros," in *Interdependencia, ¿Un Enfoque Útil Para el Análisis de las Relaciones México-Estados Unidos?,* ed. Blanca Torres (México, D.F.: Colegio de México, Centro de Estudios Internacionales, 1990); Remedios Gómez Arnau, *México y La Protección de Sus Nacionales en Estados Unidos* (México: Centro de Investigaciones Sobre Estados Unidos de América, Universidad Nacional Autónoma de México, 1990); Josefina Zoraida Vázquez and Lorenzo Meyer, *México Frente a Estados Unidos: Un Ensayo Histórico, 1776–1988,* 2d ed. (México, D.F.: Fondo de Cultura Económica, 1992); Emelia Violeta Domínguez López, "El Programa Bracero 1942–1947: Un Acercamiento a Través de los Testimonios de Sus Trabajadores," Tésis, Facultad de Filosofía y Letras, Universidad Nacional Autónoma de México, 2001.

12. Juan Gómez-Quiñones made early important contributions to transnational scholarship as the director of the Chicano Studies Research Center and as the editor of its journal, *Aztlán,* at the University of California at Los Angeles during the 1970s and 1980s. David Maciel authored and arranged publications, including dissertations and anthologies, by university and government presses in Mexico during the 1980s and the 1990s. The following works by Gómez-Quiñones, Maciel, and others inform this study: Emilio Zamora, *El movimiento obrero Mexicano en el Sur de Texas, 1900–1920* (México, D.F.: Secretaría de Educación Pública, 1986); Maciel and José Guillermo Saavedra, eds., *Al Norte de la Frontera: El Pueblo Chicano* (México, D.F.: Consejo Nacional de Población, 1988); Gómez-Quiñones, "Piedras Contra la Luna, México en Aztlán y Aztlán en México: Chicano-Mexican Relations and the Mexican Consulates, 1900–1920," in *Contemporary Mexico: Papers of the IV International Congress of Mexican History,* eds. James W. Wilkie, Michael C. Meyer, and Edna Monzón de Wilkie, 494–527 (Los Angeles: University of California Press, 1976); Antonio

Ríos-Bustamante, ed., *Mexican Immigrant Workers in the U.S.* (Los Angeles: UCLA Chicano Studies Research Center Publications, 1981); Carlos Vásquez and Manuel García y Griego, eds., *Relations between the Mexican Community in the United States and Mexico* (Los Angeles: UCLA Chicano Studies Research Center Publications, 1983).

13. Walter Fogel, *Mexican Americans in Southwest Labor Markets,* Advance Report 10, Mexican-American Study Project (Los Angeles: UCLA Graduate School of Business Administration, 1967); Mario Barrera, *Race and Class in the Southwest: A Theory of Racial Inequality* (Notre Dame, Ind.: University of Notre Dame Press, 1979).

14. García, "Americans All: The Mexican-American Generation and the Politics of Wartime Los Angeles, 1941–1945," *Social Science Quarterly* Vol. 68 (June 1987): 278–89; Richard Santillán, "Rosita the Riveter: Midwest Mexican American Women during World War II, 1941–1945," in *Mexicans in the Midwest,* eds. Juan R García, Ignacio M García, and Thomas Gelsinon (Tucson: Mexican American Studies & Research Center, University of Arizona, 1989); Gerald D. Nash, "Spanish-Speaking Americans in Wartime," in *The American West Transformed: The Impact of the Second World War* (Bloomington: Indiana University Press, 1985), chapter 7; George N. Green, "The Good Neighbor Commission and Texas Mexicans," in *Ethnic Minorities in Gulf Coast Society,* eds. Jerrell H. Shofner and Linda V. Ellsworth (Pensacola, Fla.: Gulf Coast History and Humanities Conference, 1979); Zamora, "The Failed Promise of Wartime Opportunity For Mexicans in the Texas Oil Industry"; Zamora, "Mexico's Wartime Intervention On Behalf of Mexicans in the United States." Consult works in the anthology by Maggie Rivas-Rodríguez and the following dissertations for examples of recent studies that make contributions to Mexican history during the Second World War: Rivas-Rodríguez, *Mexican Americans and World War II* (Austin: University of Texas Press, 2005); Elizabeth R. Escobedo, "Mexican American Home Front, The Politics of Gender, Culture, and Community in World War II Los Angeles" (PhD diss., University of Washington, 2004); Robert Rodriguez, "A Survey of Texas Gulf Coast Area Mexican-American World War II Veterans" (PhD diss., University of Houston, 1997).

15. Daniel, *Chicano Workers and the Politics of Fairness: The FEPC in the Southwest, 1941–1945.* A dissertation on Mexicans and the FEPC by Lou Ella Jenkins also provides important insights on the subject: Jenkins, "The Fair Employment Practice Committee and Mexican-Americans in the Southwest" (PhD diss., Georgia State University, 1974).

16. Morín, *Among the Valiant: Mexican-Americans in WW II and Korea* (Los Angeles: Borden Publishing Company, 1963); McWilliams, *North From Mexico; The Spanish-Speaking People of the United States* (New York: Greenwood Press, 1948); Kibbe, *Latin Americans in Texas* (Albuquerque: University of New Mexico Press, 1946); Perales, *Are We Good Neighbors?* (San Antonio: Artes Gráficas, 1948). Related publications include: McWilliams, *Ill Fares the Land; Migrants and Migratory Labor in the United States* (Boston, Little, Brown and Company, 1942); and Perales, *En defensa de mi raza,* 2 vols. (San Antonio: Artes Gráficas, 1936–7).

17. Few studies have examined the World War II period in Mexican American history and even fewer have assessed this history within the context of Mexico-U.S. relations. Book-length studies that address this period include: García, *Mexican Americans: Leadership, Ideology, and Identity, 1930–1960;* Gómez-Quiñones, *Chicano Politics: Reality and Promise, 1940–1990*; Montejano, *Anglos and Mexicans in the Making of Texas, 1836–1986*; San Miguel Jr., *"Let All of Them Take Heed": Mexican-Americans and the Quest for Educational Equality in Texas, 1918–1981.* Essays that treat the history in an international context include: Mario García, "Americans All: The Mexican-American Generation and the Politics of Wartime Los Angeles, 1941–1945," *Social Science Quarterly* 68 (1987): 278–89; Gilbert G. Gonzalez, "Culture, Language, and the Americanization of Mexican Children," in *Latinos and*

Education: A Critical Reader, eds. Antonia Darder, Rodolfo D. Torres, and Henry Gutierrez (New York: Routledge, 1997); Nash, "Spanish-Speaking Americans in Wartime"; Zamora, "Mexico's Wartime Intervention on Behalf of Mexicans in the United States."

18. Two prominent contributors to the book, Carlos Castañeda and José de la Luz Saenz, are discussed in this chapter. Others contributors include Robert Lucey, the archbishop of San Antonio; Malcolm Ross, the executive director of the FEPC; and Dennis Chavez, the U.S. senator from New Mexico who served between 1935 and 1962. For works on or by these authors, see: Saenz, *Los México-Americanos en La Gran Guerra y Su Contingente en Pró de la Democracia, La Humanidad y La Justicia* (San Antonio: Artes Gráficas, 1933); Ross, *All Manner of Men* (New York, Reynal and Hitchcock, 1948); Saul E. Bronder, *Social Justice and Church Authority: The Public Life of Archbishop Robert E. Lucey* (Philadelphia: Temple University Press, 1982); Roy Luján, "Dennis Chavez and the Roosevelt Era, 1933–1945" (PhD diss., University of New Mexico, 1987); Stephen A. Privett, *The U.S. Catholic Church and its Hispanic Members: The Pastoral Vision of Archbishop Robert E. Lucey* (San Antonio: Trinity University Press, 1988); Félix D. Almaraz, *Knight Without Armor: Carlos Eduardo Castañeda, 1896–1958* (College Station: Texas A&M University Press, 1999); Zamora, "Fighting on Two Fronts: José de la Luz Saenz and the Language of the Mexican American Civil Rights Movement."

19. Castañeda, a historian and archivist of the Borderlands, built a remarkable reputation as a scholar in the United States and Mexico. He primarily gave Mexican meaning to his success in the predominantly Anglo world of academia by specializing in Catholic Church history as well as by recovering the still largely Spanish colonial history and promoting it before scholarly and popular audiences in both English and Spanish. Moreover, his acclaimed revisionist scholarship and unparalleled archival collection work resonated with the ongoing popular claim of self-worth that Mexican activists often made as a minority response to the disparaging Anglo prejudice. Castañeda coupled the symbolic meaning of his work with a record of direct participation in the civil rights cause to become a respected leader in the Mexican community. Consult Castañeda's excellent biography by one of Texas' most distinguished scholars: Almaráz, *Knight Without Armor: Carlos Eduardo Castañeda, 1896–1958.*

20. War industries, according to the often imprecise use of the term, meant businesses contracted by the government to supply critical goods, services, and supplies. Airplane construction and repair operations, oil refineries, smelters, and munitions factories were included. The less critical, but important areas of production were often called essential industries. These often included agriculture, meat packing, garment, and construction. Roosevelt established the FEPC on June 25, 1941, with Executive Order 8802. Executive Order 9346, issued on May 26, 1943, reorganized the agency and strengthened its effectiveness with an improved budget and regional offices in such places as Dallas and San Antonio. Early book-length studies of the FEPC include: Louis C. Kesselman, *The Social Politics of FEPC: A Study in Reform Pressure Movements* (Chapel Hill: University of North Carolina Press, 1948); Louis Ruchames, *Race, Jobs, and Politics: The Story of FEPC* (Westport, Conn.: Negro Universities Press, 1953); Herbert Garfinkel, *When Negroes March: The March on Washington Movement in the Organizational Politics for FEPC* (Glencoe, Ill.: The Free Press, 1959).

21. Almaraz, *Knight Without Armor: Carlos Eduardo Castañeda, 1896–1958;* García, *Mexican Americans: Leadership, Ideology, and Identity, 1930–1960.*

22. See the following examples: Orozco, "The Origins of the League of United Latin American Citizens (LULAC) and the Mexican American Civil Rights Movement in Texas with An Analysis of Women's Political Participation in a Gendered Context, 1910–1929"; San Miguel Jr., *"Let All of Them Take Heed": Mexican Americans and the Campaign for*

Educational Equality in Texas, 1910–1981; Márquez, *LULAC: The Evolution of a Mexican American Political Organization.*

23. García was especially interested in demonstrating that the LULAC leadership represented a new political generation of upwardly mobile Mexicans who were bold and culturally adept reformers rather than compliant and naïvely conservative, or accomodationist, leaders. García, *Mexican Americans: Leadership, Ideology, and Identity, 1930–1960.* Also see the other work by García that addresses the way that the "Mexican American generation" used citizenship to negotiate acceptance into American society: "Mexican-Americans and the Politics of Citizenship: The Case of El Paso, 1936," *New Mexico Historical Review* 59, no. 2 (1984): 187–204.

24. Ian F. Haney Lopez, "White Latinos," *Harvard Latino Law Review* 6 (2003): 2. Also see the following excellent study by the same legal scholar on the role of law in the social construction of race in the United States: Haney Lopez, *White by Law: The Legal Construction of Race* (New York: New York University Press, 1996). I witnessed Mexican civil rights leaders respond to an even more serious charge than a lack of moral concern during the World War II Conference held at the University of Texas in May 26–27, 2000. A "Whiteness" scholar charged the leadership with racism by focusing on the well-known and highly respected Ed Idar, a major civil rights leader in Texas and former state officer of the American G.I. Forum. Idar, who was sitting in front of the presenter, vehemently denied the charge and pointed out that the civil rights leadership did not limit itself to the other white strategy and even cooperated with the African American civil rights cause. Another past officer of the American G.I. Forum, who was equally offended, defended the memory of Dr. Hector P. García, a founder of the American G.I. Forum and his former mentor. He claimed that García never stated publicly or privately that he used whiteness to gain favor with Anglos or to place himself above African Americans. He too noted that Mexican civil rights leaders sought cooperative links with their black counterparts. The scholar, who had obviously failed to interview the civil rights leaders or share his conclusions with them, did not respond to the criticism. One might think it unreasonable to expect a racist to admit his fault or that the lack of a racist motivation does not preclude attempts to maintain a racial edifice with the other white strategy. On the other hand, the scholar demonstrated little interest in differing opinions and in the need to contextualize and balance his observations with possible countervailing evidence, a problem that is also evident in the article by Haney Lopez. See the following article (and the responses to it) in a special issue of a journal that acknowledges important contributions by whiteness studies, including the call for the expansion of the black/white paradigm of civil rights and the more rigorous application of the concept of race in historical analysis: Eric Arnesen, "Whiteness and the Historian's Imagination," *International Labor and Working-Class History* 60 (2001): 3–32. The following article makes a notable contribution to the issue of whiteness in labor relations during the 1930s and 1940s: Eric V. Meeks, "Protecting the 'White Citizen Worker': Race, Labor, and Citizenship in South-Central Arizona, 1929–1945," *Journal of the Southwest* 48, no. 1 (2006): 91–113.

25. Foley, "Becoming Hispanic: Mexican Americans and the Faustian Pact with Whiteness," in *Reflexiones 1997: New Directions in Mexican American Studies,* ed. Neil Foley (Austin: University of Texas at Austin, Center for Mexican American Studies, 1998): 53–70; Blanton, "George I. Sanchez, Ideology, and Whiteness in the Making of the Mexican American Civil Rights Movement, 1930–1960," *The Journal of Southern History* 72, no. 3 (2006): 569–604. In a more recent essay, Foley laments that Mexican and black litigants almost reached common ground in their cases against segregation in the schools in the 1930s and 1950s. However, the former argued for integration as whites while blacks sought rulings

that invalidated the separate but equal doctrine of the 1896 Supreme Court decision in *Plessy v. Ferguson.* Foley faults the Mexican strategy because it "complicated, and in some ways compromised . . . a promising start to interracial cooperation." Foley, "Over the Rainbow: Hernandez v. Texas, Brown v. Board of Education, and Black v. Brown," in *"Colored Men" and "Hombres Aqui": Hernandez v. Texas and the Emergence of Mexican-American Lawyering,* ed. Michael A. Olivas, 111–21 (Houston: Arte Público Press, 2006).

26. See the following essay in which the historian Neil Foley relies mostly on a single letter to generalize about racism among the LULAC leadership in Texas: Foley, "Becoming Hispanic: Mexican Americans and the Faustian Pact with Whiteness." The 1936 correspondence was from Gregory R. Salinas, the secretary of LULAC Council #16 from San Antonio, to Louis Wilmot, the president of LULAC Council #1, from Corpus Christi. Salinas, speaking on behalf of his council, told of a group of "Negro musicians" from his city that had "illicit relations" with "certain ignorant and ill-informed Mexican girls." He warned Wilmot that a Mexican promoter from Corpus Christi had hired the musicians and recommended that his council "tell these Negroes that we are not going to permit our manhood and womanhood to mingle with them on an equal social basis." The LULAC members from Corpus Christi discussed the letter in one of their meetings and decided to ask the local promoter to abide by the segregationist recommendation. Foley argued that the leadership harbored racist ideas and that the membership embraced them. Although this may have been the case, more research is necessary to determine the extent of racial thinking in Mexican communities like Corpus Christi, its translation into varied political actions, and its influence on Mexican-black relations. Also, Salinas's letter requires a fuller analysis that takes into account the embedded paternalistic and sexist views that motivated him to call for a separation of the races. Salinas to Wilmot, August 13, 1936, Andres de Luna Papers, LULAC Collection, Mexican American Library Program, Nettie Lee Benson Collection, University of Texas at Austin.

27. Merl E. Reed, "FEPC and the Federal Agencies in the South," *The Journal of Negro History* 65, no. 1 (1980): 43–56; William J. Collins, "Race, Roosevelt, and Wartime Production: Fair Employment in World War II Labor Markets," *The American Economic Review* 91, no. 1 (2001): 272–86; Daniel Kryder, "The American State and the Management of Race Conflict in the Workplace and in the Army 1941–1945," *Polity* 26, 4 (1994): 601–34; Roger W. Lotchin, "The Historians' War or The Home Front's War?: Some Thoughts for Western Historians," *The Western Historical Quarterly* 26, no. 2 (1995): 185–96;

28. The following are selected works that address the subject: William H. Harris, "Federal Intervention in Union Discrimination: FEPC and West Coast Shipyards During World War II," *Labor History* 22, no. 3 (1981): 325–47; Merl E. Reed, "Black Workers, Defense Industries, and Federal Agencies in Pennsylvania, 1941–1945," *Labor History* 27, no. 3 (1986): 356–84; Reed, *Seedtime for the Modern Civil Rights Movement: The President's Committee of Fair Employment Practice, 1941–1946*; and Ernest Obadele-Starks, *Black Unionism in the Industrial South.*

29. See the following for a recent survey of the literature on African Americans that focuses on the issue of privilege and inequality during the war and postwar periods: Ira Katznelson, *When Affirmative Action Was White: An Untold History of Racial Inequality in Twentieth-Century America* (New York: Norton, 2005). Obadele-Starks also examines discrimination and inequality among African Americans in the South and provides a focused treatment of their relationship with the FEPC in Texas: Obadele-Starks, *Black Unionism in the Industrial South.*

30. Zamora, "The Failed Promise of Wartime Opportunity for Mexicans in the Texas Oil Industry."

31. For studies that underscore interventions by Mexican consular officials on behalf of its citizens as well as their collaborative ties with local Mexican leaders, see the following: Francisco E. Balderrama, "México de afuera y los consulados Mexicanos, 1900–1940," *Revista Mexicana de Ciencias Políticas y Sociales* 27, núm. 10 (1981): 175–86; Balderrama, *In Defense of La Raza: The Los Angeles Mexican Consulate and the Mexican Community, 1929 to 1936* (Tucson: University of Arizona Press, 1982); María Rosa García and David R. Maciel, "El México de afuera: políticas Mexicanas de protección en Estados Unidos"; Francisco Arturo Rosales, *Pobre Raza!: Violence, Justice, and Mobilization among México Lindo Immigrants, 1900–1936* (Austin: University of Texas Press, 1999).

32. Chapter 3 is based on a revised version of my previously noted essay entitled "Mexico's Wartime Intervention on Behalf of Mexicans in the United States."

33. The following work provides one of the more recent examinations of the Bracero Program against the backdrop of a state-mediated conflict involving farm workers and agribusiness in the United States: Linda C. Majka and Theo J. Majka, "The State as Labor Contractor: The Bracero Era," in *Farm Workers, Agribusiness, and the State,* (Philadelphia: Temple University Press, 1982), chapter 8.

34. García, *Mexican Americans: Leadership, Ideology and Identity, 1930–1960.* The "Mexicanist" designation which denotes an inclusive and internationalist political orientation, according to Zamora, was prominent prior to the Second World War. Zamora, *The World of the Mexican Workers in Texas.* Some of the leftist organizations included the CIO-affiliated local union of pecan shellers from San Antonio and smelters' workers from Laredo, as well as the Dallas, Austin, and San Antonio affiliates of the Mexico-based Confederación de Trabajadores Mexicanos en Norte América and the local representatives of the Spanish-Speaking People's Congress in San Antonio. The pecan shellers were affiliated with the CIO through the United Cannery, Agricultural, Packing, and Allied Workers of America and the smelters workers through the Mine, Mill, and Smelter Workers' Union of America. Historians have not yet given the Confederación the attention that it deserves. It was a leftist-leaning national labor federation from Mexico with locals throughout the United States. The national leadership of the Congress was associated with the Communist Party and focused on workers' rights. The best available history on Mexican politics in the United States is the two-volume work by Juan Gómez-Quiñones: *Chicano Politics: Reality and Promise, 1940–1990*; *Roots of Chicano Politics, 1600–1940.*

35. Refer to previously noted sources, including works by Montejano, San Miguel, and Zamora. Also consult the following for one of the most recent works on the Mexican civil rights movement after the Second World War: Zaragosa Vargas, "In the Years of Darkness and Torment: The Early Mexican American Struggle for Civil Rights, 1945–1963," *New Mexico Historical Review* 76, no. 4 (2001): 383–81.

36. Saenz, *Los México-Americanos en La Gran Guerra y Su Contingente en Pró de la Democracia, La Humanidad y La Justicia.* See the following, for an analysis of Saenz's writings: Zamora, "Fighting on Two Fronts: José de la Luz Saenz and the Language of the Mexican American Civil Rights Movement." A translated and revised version of this paper is available as: "La guerra en pro de la justicia y la democracia en Francia y Texas: José de la Luz Sáenz y el lenguaje del movimiento mexicano de los derechos civiles," *ISTOR, Revista de Historia Internacional* 4, Núm. 13 (2003): 9–35.

37. For histories that include these organizations, see aforementioned works by Gómez-Quiñones, García, and Sanchez and the following ones: David G. Gutiérrez, *Walls and Mirrors: Mexican Americans, Mexican Immigrants and the Politics of Ethnicity* (Berkeley: University of California Press, 1995); Emilio Zamora, "Labor Formation, Identity, and Self-Organization, The Mexican Working Class in Texas, 1900–1945," in *Border Crossings:*

Mexican and Mexican-American Workers, ed. John Mason Hart, 139–62 (Wilmington, Del.: Scholarly Resources, 1998); Zaragosa Vargas, *Labor Rights are Civil Rights: Mexican American Workers in Twentieth Century America* (Princeton, N. J.: Princeton University Press, 2005).

Chapter 2

1. Daniel L. Schorr, "'Reconverting' Mexican Americans," *The New Republic,* September 30, 1946, 412.

2. Schorr interviewed a number of persons in the San Antonio area. A "principal source" was Henry B. Gonzalez, the future U.S. congressman who was working with the city's health office in 1946 (Daniel Schorr to Emilio Zamora, electronic mail, August 10, 2004). At the time of the interview, Gonzalez was about to initiate an impressive political career as a city councilman, state representative, and U.S. congressman. During the postwar period, he attained special recognition for being the first Mexican American to seek the governorship and for participating in a filibuster at the Texas legislature against racial bills that were intended to undermine the Supreme Court ruling in *Brown v. Board of Education.* Eugene Rodríguez, Henry B. Gonzalez: A Political Profile (New York: Arno Press, 1976); Julie Leininger Pycior, "Henry B. Gonzalez," in Profiles in Power: Twentieth-Century Texans in Washington, eds. Kenneth E. Hendrickson, Michael L. Collins, and Patrick Cox, 295–308 (Austin: University of Texas Press, 1993).

3. Historians rarely distinguish between essential and critical industries, preferring instead to focus on the critical industries and to group them under the heading of war industries. This study also uses the general descriptive category of wartime industries except when it is necessary to make a distinction or note the difference between employment in critical industries like oil, munitions, or aircraft construction and repair and essential industries like agriculture.

4. David Brody, *In Labor's Cause: Main Themes on the History of the American Worker* (Oxford: Oxford University Press, 1993), 175–76. The following works treat the development of the wartime economy in the Southwest: Odie B. Faulk, *Land of Many Frontiers: A History of the American Southwest* (New York: Oxford University Press, 1968), 290–96; Nash, *The American West Transformed: The Impact of the Second World War;* Arthur C. Verge, "World War II and the Metropolis, 1941–1945: The Impact of the Second World War on Los Angeles," 234–54, in *The American West, The Reader,* eds. Walter Nugent and Martin Ridge (Bloomington: Indiana University Press, 1999).

5. U.S. Employment Service, *Texas Labor Market Report,* August 1946, American History Center, University of Texas, Austin, Texas [hereafter cited as Texas Labor Market Report]. The principal industrial areas included: Austin, San Antonio, Corpus Christi, Brownsville, El Paso, Abilene, Amarillo, Lubbock, Fort Worth, Wichita Falls, Waco, Dallas, Longview, Texarkana, Beaumont-Port Arthur-Orange, Houston-Baytown, and Galveston-Texas City. The total population in these areas was 3,264,425. The nonagricultural, civilian workforce in April 1940 was 878,357 and in July 1946 it totaled 1,209,117.

6. See the following for descriptions of major army posts, forts, camps, and air fields in Texas during the early part of 1941: Dallas Morning News, *1941–42 Texas Almanac and State Industrial Guide* (Dallas: A. H. Belo Corporation, 1942), 316–18.

7. Corpus Christi Caller-Times, *Corpus Christi: 100 Years* (Corpus Christi, Tex.: The Corpus Christi Caller-Times, 1952), 123–25.

8. Ibid., 126–29.

9. J. Lee Stambaugh and Lillian J. Stambaugh, *The Lower Rio Grande Valley of Texas* (San Antonio: The Naylor Company, 1954), 262–64.

10. Green Peyton, *San Antonio: City in the Sun* (New York: McGraw-Hill Book Company, 1946), 97–99, 104.

11. Ibid., 104–105; Texas Labor Market Report, February 15–March 15, 1943, 21–22.

12. Unless otherwise noted, wage and occupational information on Mexican workers in agricultural and nonagricultural employment is culled from the Records of the U.S. Employment Service, the Records of the War Manpower Commission, and the Records of the Fair Employment Practice Committtee, National Archives and Records Administration, Washington, D.C. [hereafter cited as Records of the USES, Records of the WMC, and Records of the FEPC].

13. Victor H. Schoffelmayer, "Texas Employment Service Does Excellent Job of Handling Migratory Labor Problem," *Dallas Morning News,* March 11, 1940, Online Clipping Service, Texas Legislative Reference Library, Texas Capitol Building, Austin, Texas. USES reports on the Texas labor market, cited elsewhere, confirm the conservative figures that officials representing the Texas State Employment Service provided Schoffelmayer, the agricultural editor of the Dallas newspaper. According to the Farm Security Administration, approximately 80 percent of the migratory laborers in Texas were of Mexican descent by 1940 (Farm Security Administration, "Migrant Farm Labor," 40, cited in Perry Morris Broom, "An Interpretative Analysis of the Economic and Educational Status of Latin-Americans in Texas, With Emphasis upon the Basic Factors Underlying an Approach to an Improved Program of Occupational Guidance, Training, and Adjustment for Secondary Schools" [PhD diss., University of Texas at Austin, 1942], 25). For studies on Mexican immigration, see the following: Lawrence A. Cardoso, *Mexican Emigration to the United States, 1897–1931: Socio-Economic Patterns* (Tucson: University of Arizona Press, 1980); Gómez-Quiñones, "Mexican Immigration to the United States and the Internationalization of Labor, 1848–1980: An Overview."

14. Unless otherwise noted, observations regarding Mexican farm labor and migratory work are based on the following sources: Carey McWilliams, *Ill Fares the Land: Migrants and Migratory Labor in the United States*; McWilliams, *North from Mexico: The Spanish-Speaking People of the United States;* Selden C. Menefee, *Mexican Migratory Workers of South Texas,* Works Project Administration, Division of Research (Washington, D.C.: Government Publications Office, 1941); Montejano, *Anglos and Mexicans in the Making of Texas, 1836–1986;* Paul S. Taylor, "Migratory Farm Labor in the United States," *Monthly Labor Review* 44 (March 1937): 537-49 ; Dennis Nodín Valdés, *Al Norte, Agricultural Workers in the Great Lakes Region, 1917–1970,* Mexican American monograph no. 13, Center for Mexican American Studies (Austin: University of Texas Press, 1991); Stanley A. West and Irene S. Vásquez, "Early Migration from Central Mexico to the Northern United States," in *The Chicano Experience,* eds. Stanley A. West and June Macklin, 17–31 (Boulder, Col.: Westview Press, 1979); Zamora, *The World of the Mexican Worker in Texas.*

15. Mexicans attracted much public attention during the 1920s as periodicals like the *Readers' Guide* began to increasingly speak about immigration as "the Mexican Problem." This occurred at the same time that agriculture in Texas, according to Carey McWilliams, was undergoing a "revolution," as Mexican migratory "free" labor was replacing the ethnically mixed sharecropper and tenant workforce. McWilliams, and later David Montejano, explained that the "Mexican Problem" involved a racialized debate over immigration between restrictionists who complained about the farmers' inability to keep the immigrants from settling in urban areas and the antirestrictionists who insisted on uninterrupted immigration. Charles F. Marden, *Minorities in American Society* (New York: American Book

Company, 1952), 128; McWilliams, *Ill Fares the Land: Migrants and Migratory Labor in the United States,* 208; Montejano, *Anglos and Mexicans in the Making of Texas.*

16. For an early examination of the onset of migratory labor and striking rural poverty among Mexican farm workers in Texas between 1900 and 1940, see McWilliams, *Ill Fares the Land,* 208–29.

17. Studies by Francisco Balderrama, Raymond Rodríguez, and Abraham Hoffman on the repatriation experience offer a comprehensive treatment of the subject: Balderrama and Rodríguez, *Decade of Betrayal: Mexican Repatriation in the 1930s* (Albuquerque: University of New Mexico Press, 1995); Hoffman, *Unwanted Mexican Americans in the Great Depression: Repatriation Pressures, 1929–1939* (Tucson: University of Arizona Press, 1974). For other important studies on the history of immigration and the experience of the Depression, see the following: Julia Kirk Blackwelder, *Women of the Depression: Caste and Culture in San Antonio, 1929–1939* (College Station: Texas A&M University Press, 1984); Gómez-Quiñones, "Mexican Immigration to the United States and the Internationalization of Labor, 1848–1980: An Overview," 13–34; Ralph Guzmán, "La repatriación forzosa como solución política concluyente al problema de la inmigración ilegal, Una perspective histórica," *Foro Internacional* 18, núm. 3 (1978), 494–513; Douglas Monroy, *Rebirth: Mexican Los Angeles from the Great Migration to the Great Depression* (Berkeley: University of California Press, 1999).

18. The colonization projects promised the returning Mexican families farm land, seeds, equipment, fertilizer, and small loans. The government provided recently cleared land, but reneged on most of its other promises. The few, possibly two, colonization ventures that succeeded were due to the determination and hard work of the émigrés. Mercedes Carreras de Velasco, *Los Mexicanos que devolvio la crisis, 1929–1932* (México, D.F.: Secretaría de Relaciones Exteriores, 1974).

19. Texas Labor Market Report, April 15–May 15, 1942, 4. The earnings registered in the 1930s were substantially less. A 1938 TSES report, for instance, noted that Texas cotton pickers earned an average of $37.50 during a six-month season. That same year, the FSA reported Mexican weekly incomes of less than two dollars a week. Figures appear in McWilliams, *Ill Fares the Land,* 238.

20. Fogel, *Mexican Americans in Southwest Labor Markets,* 26. Barrera expanded on Fogel's findings with occupational data from the U.S. Bureau of the Census. He underscored the difference in mobility rates as well as the continuing concentration of Mexicans as farm workers. According to Barrera, Mexicans were three times as likely to be farm workers in 1950, almost four times as likely in 1960, and four-and-one-half times as likely in 1970. Mexicans, in other words, remained in the farms to a greater extent while Anglos moved with greater ease into nonagricultural employment. Barrera, *Race and Class in the Southwest: A Theory of Racial Inequality,* 132.

21. Meyer, "Child Workers in Valley: Wet-Backs are Here, There, Everywhere," *The Spectator,* June 7, 1946, 8.

22. Selden C. Menefee and Orin C. Cassmore, *The Pecan Shellers of San Antonio: The Problem of Underpaid and Unemployed Mexican Labor* (Washington, D.C.: U.S. Government Printing Office, 1940); Helen Wood Warburton and Marian M. Crane, *The Work and Welfare of Children of Agricultural Laborers in Hidalgo County, Texas,* U.S. Department of Labor Children's Bureau publication 298 (Washington, D.C.: U.S. Government Printing Office, 1943), 2–3.

23. The WMC, established in 1942, headed an interagency manpower program that included the Department of Agriculture, the War Department, the Department of Labor, the Civil Service Commission, the FEPC, the USES, the National Youth Administration,

and several job training programs. Its primary responsibilities were to oversee the recruitment of labor for critical and essential civilian industries, train workers for jobs that were necessary for the war effort, analyze manpower utilization practices, and gather labor market information. Although the WMC continued to work closely with farm labor through the USES and other departments and agencies, the Department of Agriculture assumed greater responsibility over farm labor activities beginning in 1943. See electronic descriptions of the Records of the WMC, the Records of the Extension Service, and the Records of the Office of Labor in the Department of Agriculture, National Archives and Records Administration, Washington, D.C.

24. The Records of the WMC includes numerous documents written by federal and state officials that describe the "freezing" policy as an initiative designed to discourage the movement of workers out of agriculture. The head of the WMC, Paul McNutt, offered the following assurance to U.S. Representative Richard Kleberg from Kingsville: "The War Manpower Commission, in cooperation with the United States Employment Service, the Department of Agriculture, and other agencies, is developing recruiting programs for agricultural workers which we hope will attain as adequate a supply of this type of labor as possible. At the same time the United States Employment Service, under the Commission's instructions, is emphasizing the recruitment of industrial workers from sources other than essential farm areas." McNutt to Kleberg, July 2, 1942, Records of the WMC.

25. Montejano, *Anglos and Mexicans in the Making of Texas, 1836–1986,* especially chapter 9, "The Web of Labor Controls," 197–219; Teresa Palomo Acosta, "The Farm Placement Service of Texas," *The Handbook of Texas Online,* http://www.tsha.utexas.edu/handbook/online/articles/FF/aafcm.html.

26. Caeser Hohn, "The Farm Labor Situation in Texas," *Papers Presented at Annual Meeting of Texas Agricultural Workers' Association,* Fort Worth, Texas, January 11–12, 1944, 63–64.

27. Prior to the war, the Department of Agriculture oversaw all government activity related to agriculture except matters related to the regulation of the farm labor, which was the purview of the USES. The USES, operating under the War Manpower Commission, continued with this responsibility in Texas during the war until the Department of Agriculture's Extension Service at Texas A&M University assumed it in January 1944. The USES began the war period with a central administrative office in Austin, twelve district offices, and local programs in 184 of the 254 counties in the state. The agency expanded throughout the war. In 1942, the USES cooperated with other agencies in the farm labor field through USDA War Boards, a state board, and 254 county boards that were composed of representatives of ten USDA offices such as the Agricultural Adjustment Administration, the Bureau of Agricultural Economics, and the Farm Security Administration. Reflecting the predominance of Mexicans in agriculture, the USES mostly regulated the Mexican farm labor supply. In 1941, for example, 75 percent of the agency's placements, or successful referrals, were "Other non-whites," or Mexican. Fifteen percent were "Whites" and ten percent were "Negroes." "Working Agreement by and between United States Department of Agriculture War Board and United States Employment Service in Connection with Labor Supply and Labor Demand Problems in the State of Texas," signed by B. F. Vance, chairman, USDA War Board for Texas, and J. H. Bond, director for Texas Employment Service, April 21, 1942, Records of the WMC; "Questionnaire Concerning Farm Placement Activities of the United States Employment Service for Texas," February 6, 1942, Records of the WMC. For an early and recent work on the labor importation program that introduced more than 5 million Braceros, see Richard B. Craig, *The Bracero Program: Interest Groups and Foreign Policy* (Austin: University of Texas Press, 1971; Wayne A. Grove, "The Mexican Farm Labor

Program, 1942–1964: Government-Administered Labor Market Insurance," *Agricultural History* 70, no. 2 (1996): 302–20.

28. Hohn, "The Farm Labor Situation in Texas," 64; Texas A&M, College Extension Service, *Annual Report, 1942,* 3–5.

29. Texas A&M, College Extension Service, *Annual Report, 1942,* 3–5.

30. Fred Bailey, legislative consultant to the National Grange and a member of the Secretary of Labor's Migratory Farm Workers Board, confirmed that the USES at times recruited workers on the border despite the availability of U.S.-born workers. Fred Bailey testimony, U.S. President's Commission on Migratory Labor, Stenographic Report of Proceedings, July 13–October 18, 1950, vols. 1–4, microfilm 1 (of 4) (Washington, D.C: Ward and Paul, 1950), 150.

31. Texas Labor Market Report, April 15–May 15, 1942, 4; Texas Labor Market Report, May 15–June 15, 1942, 22, 57. For a discussion of the state laws that regulated out-of-state labor recruiters, see McWilliams, *Ill Fares the Land,* 254–55; Montejano, *Anglos and Mexicans in the Making of Texas,* 190, 208, 210–213.

32. Texas Labor Market Report, July 15–August 15, 1942, Area III, Brownsville, 84–85. The agricultural agents were precise in their record-keeping. According to this report, 4,451 cotton pickers passed through the check points during the thirty-day period. Most of them, 4,022 persons, rode in 380 trucks. The rest, 429 workers, traveled in 144 passenger cars. The great majority, 3,425, had jobs waiting for them, while 1,026 did not.

33. Kibbe to members of the Good Neighbor Commission, December 29, 1944, Records of the Good Neighbor Commission, Texas State Library and Archives Commission (hereafter cited as Records of the GNC).

34. Gonzales to Lulac councils of the League in Texas, February 20, 1945, Manuel C. Gonzales Papers, Mexican American Library Program, Nettie Lee Benson Latin American Collection, University of Texas at Austin (hereafter cited as Gonzales Papers).

35. The records of the USES provide much anecdotal evidence to suggest that the draft boards from South Texas preferred to target Mexicans outside of agriculture. A survey conducted among Mexican nationals in the U.S. military by Mexico's Office of Foreign Affairs corroborates this observation. According to the survey of approximately eight hundred Mexican nationals, few farm workers received the call to military service. The great majority of the inductees had been urban nonagricultural workers prior to the war. Aside from the possible influence by farmers, the exempt status that the Selective Service and Training Act of 1940 gave farm youth also may explain why the draft boards may have overlooked them. The analysis of the data from Mexico's Foreign Affairs Office appears in the following: Emilio Zamora, "Mexican Nationals in the U.S. Military during World War II," paper presented at the Latino Latina World War II Forum, Washington, D.C., September 12, 2004.

36. Kleberg to McNutt, June 19, 1942, Records of the WMC.

37. McNutt to Kleberg, July 2, 1942, Records of the WMC.

38. Release forms, the formal wartime equivalents of the pass documents that Montejano found in the 1920s and 1930s, were part of a system of accountability that the USES mostly used to control the movement of workers between urban-based industries. The Extension Service did not always use the standard USES form, although they did provide equivalent documents.

39. The following USES report from Brownsville suggests that government agencies used rationing to immobilize farm workers and the truck drivers who transported them: "All Rationing Boards in this area have issued letters to all gins and had the letters publicized in all the papers to the effect that all local truckers who migrate out before cotton picking is generally regarded as being completed, forfeit all future eligibility for tire relief. This stand

by the Rationing Boards is getting desired results." Texas Labor Market Report, June 15–July 15, 1942, 87.

40. Eugene Butler, "The Effect of the War on Farm Labor," *Papers Presented at Annual Meeting of Texas Agricultural Workers' Association,* Fort Worth, January 11–12, 1944, 51. Despite important challenges, Texas farmers were able to maintain a labor supply that, according to Montejano, often exceeded their needs. Montejano made this finding when he compared the declared labor needs in a South Texas farm with the actual number of workers required, according to a calculated per acre yield of cotton and an average number of pounds that could be picked in a season. The excessive labor supply allowed the farmers to maintain low wages and to deny workers the necessary leverage to bargain for change. Martha Menchaca and Matt García note that farmers from Southern California used Braceros in the same way. Montejano, *Anglos and Mexicans in the Making cf Texas,* 177–78; Menchaca, *The Mexican Outsiders: A Community History of Marginalization and Discrimination in California* (Austin: University of Texas Press, 1995), 90–91; García, *A World of Its Own: Race, Labor, and Citrus in the Making of Greater Los Angeles, 1900–1970* (Chapel Hill: The University of North Carolina Press, 2001), 119.

41. Agricultural Extension Service, Report 1943, 4; Butler, "The Effect of the War on Farm Labor," 51.

42. For an examination of rural communities of Mexican workers in California, including temporary and permanent "company town" quarters that resembled the ones that predominated along the Texas migratory trail, see Gilbert G. Gonzalez, "Labor and Community: The Camps of Mexican Citrus Pickers in Southern California," *The Western Historical Quarterly* 22, no. 3 (1991): 289–312. Although historians have not yet produced a comparable study for Texas, Gonzalez's work suggests that a wide variation in rural settlement patters emerged in agricultural areas throughout the Southwest in the 1930s and 1940s. My focus in this section is on the temporary quarters that farmers built during the 1930s and 1940s and the government-sponsored labor camps that supplanted them during the 1940s.

43. The following sources address the subject of labor camps in Texas: Lewis T. Nordyke, "Mapping Jobs for Texas Migrants," *Survey Graphic* 29, no. 3 (1940): 152–60; Agnes E. Meyer, "A Look at Labor Camps," *The Spectator,* June 30, 1947, 6–7, 11. Also, see the historical designation narrative for the Lamesa labor camp in the Texas Historical Commission web page: "Lamesa Farm Workers' Community Historic District," Texas Historical Sites, Texas Historical Commission, http://www.state.tx.us. Farming communities had established private "concentration camps" for migratory workers beginning in 1936. Large numbers of workers moved in and out of these camps. According to McWilliams, the camps in Lubbock, Sinton, and McLennan accommodated between three thousand and four thousand workers during a six-week period in 1937. McWilliams, *Ill Fares the Land,* 237–38.

44. By the end of the war, the program had built nine labor camps, at Weslaco, Raymondville, Robstown, Sinton, El Campo, Levelland, Lubbock, Lamesa, and Plainview. Kibbe to members of the Good Neighbor Commission, December 29, 1944

45. Although the labor camps accommodated mostly Mexican migratory workers, some camps housed a majority of out-of-state Anglo farm workers. The Harlingen camp, for example, included mostly Anglos. According to some recent interviews, the Harlingen camp and possibly others with Anglo residents may have administered a different program for them. At Harlingen, the staff may have given its Anglo residents more permanent quarters and assistance in making a transition out of agriculture. A forthcoming dissertation by Verónica Martínez-Matsuda at the University of Texas at Austin examines this possible racial

difference in the administration of the Texas labor camps, which is beyond the scope of this study. Randy Davidson, the author of the following series of articles on the Harlingen camp that appeared in the *Valley Morning Star* (Harlingen), interviewed camp residents and staff members: "Our Heritage," November 27, 2003; "Rangerville Road Site of Labor Camp," December 11, 2003; "Farm Labor Camp Was Located Near Where Milam School Now Stands," December 18, 2003; "Primitive Conditions Order of the Day at Farm Labor Camp," December 25, 2003; Martínez-Matsuda, "The Making of the Modern Migrant: Labor, Community, and Resistance in the Federal Migratory Labor Camp Program, 1935–1947" (PhD diss., University of Texas at Austin, forthcoming).

46. Meyers, "A Look at Labor Camps," 11. Meyers was not alone in critiquing the Farm Labor Program. Robert Eckhardt, for instance, wrote a scathing report on the impoverished condition of Mexican farm labor and the indifference of farmers and state officials. Eckhardt, "Economic Crisis in the Southwest," *The Texas Spectator,* June 9, 1947, 3–4.

47. Meyers, "A Look at Labor Camps," 11.

48. Ibid.

49. See the following for a discussion of the use of welfare provisions in California as a method for sustaining a racialized and spatial division of labor in the 1920s and 1930s: Jess Walsh, "Laboring at the Margins: Welfare and the Regulation of Mexican Workers in Southern California," *Antipode* 31, no. 4 (1999): 395–420. The discussion that follows is primarily based on the available monthly USES Labor Market Reports, or "501s," for Texas between September 1940 and November 1946. Between two hundred and fifty thousand and three hundred thousand persons, or one-third of the total number of agricultural workers, moved continuously between agriculture and industry. There are no available estimates according to ethnic background. Mexicans, however, represented around 80 percent of the migratory workforce in the state. William C. Holley, Division of Farm Population and Rural Welfare, U.S. Department of Agriculture, Bureau of Agricultural Economics, "The Farm Labor Situation in Texas," presented before the Senate Committee of Education and Labor, May 1940, Records of the WMC.

50. The migratory work force reached a peak of three hundred thousand workers during the fall as the crop reached maturity in the Panhandle area. Fourteen construction projects in San Antonio military establishments alone reported hiring as many as twenty-two thousand workers during the fall of 1942. Texas Labor Market Report, September 15–October 15, 1942, 59.

51. McWilliams's early description of the "Big Swing," or the movement of workers that originated in Texas, remains one of the most vivid and moving accounts of migratory work and their journey in search of work: McWilliams, *Ill Fares the Land,* 230–56. The USES office at Corpus Christi may have formalized the process of labor transfers to a greater extent. When faced with an intensification of construction work, especially at the local Naval Air Station, USES officials established a "Construction Office" to ensure the "effective and orderly" identification and placement of skilled, semiskilled, and unskilled workers. Texas Labor Market Report, September 1940, 7.

52. Texas Labor Market Report, January 15–February 15, 1942, 34–35. The following is a typical report from Houston that reflected the significant influence of unions of construction workers: "Much of hiring of unskilled is through United States Employment Service and preponderance of skilled hiring is through union. Although the latter practice might conceivably result in importation of skilled union workers prior to exhaustion of local skilled non-union workers, no specific instance of such practice can be cited." Texas Labor Market Report, May 15–June 15, 1942, 179.

53. Texas Labor Market Report, February 15–March 15, 1942, 27; Texas Agricultural

Experiment Station, *Report of the Farm Labor Situation in Texas,* May 20, 1942, Coke Stevenson Papers, Texas State Library and Archives Commission, Archives Division, Austin, Texas (hereafter cited as Stevenson Papers).

54. Texas Labor Market Report, February 15–March 15, 1942, 37.

55. Texas Labor Market Report, April 15–May 15, 1942, 63.

56. Texas Labor Market Report, September 1940, 2; August 15–September 15, 1942, 66. According to a study conducted in Corpus Christi, predominantly Anglo unions of construction workers continued to discriminate against Mexicans after the war. The author, Marjorie Brookshire, found that the unions barred Mexicans from the skilled occupations through a discriminatory apprentice system. Although the union's apprentice system was theoretically intended to match new workers with all the jobs in the industry, the union restricted Mexicans to the laboring occupations. Brookshire, "The Industrial Pattern of Mexican American Employment in Nueces County, Texas" (PhD diss., University of Texas, Austin, 1954), 197–99.

57. Texas Labor Market Report, December 15, 1941–January 15, 1942, 38.

58. The USES reports were issued on a weekly and monthly basis and they either provided general statewide information on the labor market or focused on an industry or groups of industrial plants in a particular region. In addition to conducting surveys and interviews among the workers and employers, the USES reviewed employer records and secured recruitment, training, and utilization reports from industrial establishments. My commentary on minority and women participation in wartime industries is based primarily on statewide reports and on the following industries: ordnance, aircraft, machinery, chemicals, synthetic rubber, iron and steel, shipbuilding, petroleum refining, and nonferrous metals. War Manpower Commission, "Informational Report on the Texas Labor Market and Activity Reports, November 1944," prepared by War Manpower Commission for Texas, December 1944, 38.

59. Texas Labor Market Report, May 1941, 13.

60. Texas Labor Market Report, June 15, 1943–July 1943, State Summary, 1–2.

61. The USES reported numerous cases of discrimination against Mexicans in war industries. The following representative ones involved industrial sites on the Gulf Coast, including the American Smelting and Refining Company at Corpus Christi: Texas Labor Market Report, February 15–March 15, 1943, 18, 51; Texas Labor Market Report, December 15, 1943–January 15, 1944, 11.

62. Texas Labor Market Report, January 15–February 15, 1942, 1. The decision to incorporate women into war production was especially impressive when one considers the kind of obstacles that hindered their employment. First of all, stereotypes underscored frailty among women and the possible disruption of family life. Also, in some instances, the construction of new bathroom facilities and even nurseries represented a special cost to employers that some of them did not want to incur. Lastly, some government officials and employers expressed concern that male workers would object and possibly disrupt production. Texas Labor Market Report, February 15–March 15, 1943, State Summary, 4; Texas Labor Market Report, May 15–June 15, 1943, State Summary, 1.

63. Texas Labor Market Report May 15–June 1943, State Summary, 50–51; Texas Labor Market Report, October 15–November 15 1943, State Summary, 1–2. Michael R. Botson Jr., in his study of the Hughes Tool Company in Houston, also found that the oil drill producer turned to white women during the early years of the war. Their representation in the plant's workforce increased from 1.4 percent to 26.6 between May 1942 and September 1943. Botson, *Labor, Civil Rights, and the Hughes Tool Company* (College Station: Texas A&M University Press, 2005), 135.

64. Texas Labor Market Report, July 15–August 15, 1943, State Summary, 50; Texas Labor Market Report, August 15–September 15, 1943, State Summary, 53–54; Texas Labor Market, October 15–November 15, 1943, State Summary, 2, 23; Texas Labor Market Report, June 15–July 15, 1942, Area V, Amarillo-Abilene, 113.

65. Testimony of Carlos E. Castañeda, U.S. Congress, Fair Employment Practices Act Hearings, Subcommittee of the Committee on Education and Labor, United States Senate, 79th Congress, 1st Sess., March 12, 13, and 14, 1945. Castañeda's testimony also appears in Perales, *Are We Good Neighbors?,* 92–104.

66. A 5 percent share of the workforce in wartime industries represented approximately twenty-five thousand Mexican workers. This calculation is based on the conservative estimate of the Mexican population in Texas to be one million and on the also conservative estimate of the proportion of the total number of gainfully employed persons over fourteen years of age to be one-half. This figure, when compared with the total state population of six million, renders a 16.6 percent for the entire Mexican population in the state. Joe Belden, the head of a research office in Texas, noted that Mexicans represented 17 percent of the total population in 1950. Little, *Spanish-Speaking Children in Texas* (Austin: University of Texas Press, 1944); Eckhardt, "Economic Crisis in the Southwest," *The Texas Spectator,* June 9, 1947, 3–4; Joe Belden to Albert Evans, June 5, 1951, Records of GNC.

67. Testimony of Castañeda, 1945.

68. Ibid.

69. War Manpower Commission Report (Texas), "Qualitative Analysis and Case Histories of Utilization Activities Reported on Utilization Recommendations and Actions Slips," March 1944–September 1944, 1–2.

70. Ibid., 9–13. The noted cases were drawn from a listing in the WMC/USES report. The listing includes seven types of cases involving 225 employers from throughout the state that had accepted utilization recommendations. The cases, with the corresponding number of companies, included Aliens (2), Army Wives (7), Part-Time Workers (12), Soldiers (16), Mexican and African American workers (17), Youth (51), and Women (120).

71. Castañeda's entry in Perales's publication provided added useful descriptions of Mexican participation in various wartime industries. Castañeda, "Statement on Discrimination Against Mexican-Americans in Employment," in Perales, *Are We Good Neighbors?,* 59–63.

72. Interviewees by the Latino and Latina World War II Oral History Project from the University of Texas at Austin corroborate the view that Mexican American men and women entered war industries at a lower rate than Anglos. A recent study by Joanne Rao Sanchez, based on a sample of twenty-one Latinas, provides personal accounts of upward mobility that mostly involved a movement from the unskilled to the skilled ranks, but rarely into the wartime industries. She did not find exceptions to the pattern in Texas. Shipbuilding in places like the Kaiser Shipyard in Richmond, California, did provide Mexican women better opportunities. This explains the movement of Mexican workers from Texas to California during the war. Joanne Rao Sanchez, "Latinas of World War II: From Familial Shelter to Expanding Horizons," paper presented at the Latino Latina World War II Forum, Washington, D.C., September 12, 2004.

73. Texas Labor Market Report, July 15–August 15, 1943, 47; Texas Labor Market Report, April 15–May 15, 1942, 111; Texas Labor Market Report, May 15–June 15, 1942, 62; Texas Labor Market Report, June 15–July 15, 1942, 25; Texas Labor Market Report, September 15–October 15, 1943, 78. Although the largest number of Mexican women in agriculture worked in the fields, some of them moved from farm labor to canneries and packing sheds and back to farm labor or domestic work while a still smaller group managed

to get jobs in the larger towns and cities. Some of them found employment in wartime industries, although in significantly lower numbers than Anglo and black women.

74. Security concerns were expressed in the Beaumont-Longview shipbuilding industry. In 1941, a USES official reported that shipbuilding employers required a birth certificate as a prerequisite for employment. He added, "Aliens are not employed as long as a citizen can be found." Security concerns also may have prevented the Laredo Gunnery School from Laredo from filling 120 unskilled positions with local workers. According to a 1943 USES report, civil service restrictions against the hiring of aliens had forced the school to request the agency's help in recruiting the laborers from outside the area. The report measured the extent of local opposition by noting that the local labor supply would have been adequate if the restrictions had not been observed. Texas Labor Market Report, September 15–October 15, 1941, 120; Texas Labor Market Report, July 15–August 15, 1943, 71.

75. Castañeda, Weekly Reports, October 9, November 6, 1945. Foreign-born persons were required by joint agreement of the War, Navy, and Maritime Commission to submit applications for permission to work in security sensitive industrial plants. The clearance process involved the submission of an application to a plant security officer who in turn sent it to a military agency for final approval. Castañeda complained to the regional director of the WMC and the staff of local USES offices, as well as to Col. Paul G. Bell, chief of the Continuous Security Branch, Internal Security Division, Eighth Service Command.

76. Texas Labor Market Report, May 15–June 15, 1942, 51.

77. Texas Labor Market Report, August 1–September 15, 1941, 35; Texas Labor Market Report, October 15–November 15, 1942, 14.

78. Texas Labor Market Report, December 1943, 33; Texas Labor Market Report, August 15–September 15, 1941, 35.

79. Texas Labor Market Report, September 15–October 15, 1942, 71.

80. Texas Labor Market Report, October 1943, 25, 51.

Chapter 3

1. Sumner Welles, *The Time for Decision* (New York: Harper & Brothers Publishers, 1944), 192–93. See the following for works on the United States' Good Neighbor Policy: Fredrick B. Pike, *FDR's Good Neighbor Policy: Sixty Years of Gentle Chaos* (Austin: University of Texas Press, 1995); Richard V. Salisbury, "Good Neighbors? The United States and Latin America in the Twentieth Century," in *American Foreign Relations: A Historiographical Review,* eds. Gerald K. Haines and Samuel J. Walker, 311–33 (Westport, Conn.: Greenwood Press, 1981); Marquard Dozer, *Are We Good Neighbors? Three Decades of Inter-American Relations, 1930–1960* (Gainesville: University of Florida Press, 1959). Also, consult the following for opposing views: Peter Smith, *Talons of the Eagle: Dynamics of U.S.-Latin American Relations* (New York: Oxford University Press, 1996), 65–67, 85–87; Bryce Wood, *The Dismantling of the Good Neighbor Policy* (Austin: University of Texas Press, 1985). Smith argues that despite the United States' open proclamations of a new wartime era in hemispheric relations, the intent was to maintain U.S. hegemony in Latin America and the Caribbean through diplomatic, financial, and economic means. Wood, on the other hand, notes that the policy successfully promoted unity and discouraged military interference during the war.

2. Castillo Nájera, "Relaciones Culturales Entre México y Los Estados Unidos de América," Discurso Pronunciado en la "Academia Norteamericana de Ciencias y Artes," Boston, April 6, 1943. Castillo Nájera also expressed the following related view in a confidential report as early as May 1941 that essentially justified Mexico's eventual formal alliance

with the United States: "Our current international policy is already defined; our position is in line with our ideology and with our interests, which coincide with that of the United States." Castillo Nájera, "Los Estados Unidos y la situación internacional, consecuencias para Mexico," May 3, 1941, Archivo Francisco Castillo Nájera, Archivo Histórico Genaro Estrada, Secretaría de Relaciones Exteriores, México, D.F.

3. The following are selected works on Mexico-U.S. relations by Mexican and U.S. authors that have treated the subject since the 1950s: Howard F. Cline, *The United States and Mexico* (Cambridge, Mass.: Harvard University Press, 1953); Zorrilla, *Historia de las Relaciones Entre México y Los Estados Unidos de América, 1800–1958;* Mario Ojeda, *México, El surgimiento de una pólitica exterior activa* (México: Secretaría de Educación Pública, 1986); Pastor and Castañeda, *Limits to Friendship: The United States and Mexico;* W. Dirk Raat, *Mexico and the United States: Ambivalent Vistas* (Athens: The University of Georgia Press, 1992); Zoraida Vázquez and Meyer, *México Frente a Estados Unidos (Un Ensayo Histórico, 1776–1988).* The hope for friendlier ties and the modernization of Latin American economies did not materialize after the war. The United States, according to historians Zoraida Vázquez and Meyer, thought less of its wartime promise of support for the development of Latin American economies and more about encouraging Latin American countries to conform to a cold war policy intended to avert the influence of the Soviet Union in the Western hemisphere (Zoraida Vázquez and Meyer, *México Frente a Estados Unidos,* 10–12).

4. Mexico and the United States came close to severing diplomatic relations when Lázaro Cárdenas expropriated foreign-owned oil companies operating in Mexico and the United States took an aggressive posture in defense of the U.S. oil companies. The Mexican Supreme Court had intervened in a national labor dispute by ordering the oil companies on March 1, 1938, to accept a plan arbitrated by a federal agency. When the oil companies refused to abide fully by the court order, Cardenas, on March 18, announced the expropriation. Clayton R. Koppes, "The Good Neighbor Policy and the Nationalization of Mexican Oil: A Reinterpretation," *Journal of American History* 69, no. 1 (1982), 62–81; C. Neale Ronning, *Law and Politics in Inter-American Diplomacy* (New York: John Wiley and Sons, 1963), 33–34, 38–41; Zoraida Vázquez and Meyer, *México Frente a Estados Unidos,* 172–75. See the following for speeches by Padilla before foreign ministers meetings and other venues between 1940 and 1945: Padilla, *Three Speeches at Río de Janeiro* (México: Department of State for Foreign Affairs, The International Press Service Bureau, 1942); *En el Frente de la Democracia, Discursos* (México: Cía. Editora y Librera ARS, S.A., 1945).

5. On several occasions, Padilla responded to critics by noting that old resentments could undermine the wartime opportunity to build equal relations. He also pointed out that egalitarian ideas associated with Pan Americanism had "passed beyond the individual countries of America to spread [their] concepts of equality and social justice throughout the continent" (Padilla, *Free Men of America* (New York: Ziff-Davis Publishing Company, 1943), 169). For an examination of the Mexican press's critique of discrimination against minorities in the United States, see Hensley C. Woodbridge, "Mexico and U.S. Racism, How Mexicans View our Treatment of Minorities," *The Commonweal,* June 22, 1945, 234–37. The Comité en Contra el Racismo, or the Committee Against Racism, included "the most prominent persons in the world of science, finance, art and politics," according to the editors of *Fraternidad.* The organization's members included: Vicente Lombardo Toledano, Gustavo Baz, Roberto Lopez, Antonio Castro Leal, José Clemente Orozco, Esperanza Balmaceda, Matilde Rodríguez Cabo, Ermilo Abreu Gómez, Ing. Camilo Arriaga, Raul Noriega, Dolores del Río, Antonio Ruiz, Juan Manuel Elizondo, Emilio Fernandez, Eduardo Villaseñor, Jaime Torres Bodet, Alfonso Caso, Isidro Candia, Carlos Chavez, Ernesto Hidalgo, Alfonso Reyes, Arturo B. de la Garza, Félix F. Palavicini, María Asunsulo,

Manuel R. Palacios, Celestino Gasca, Heriberto Jara, and Gabriel Leyva Velazquez. Between 1944 and 1945, the Comité published *Fraternidad,* Mexico's best well-known periodical devoted to critiquing racial discrimination throughout the world. The publication gave focused attention to discrimination against Mexicans in the United States, especially in Texas. "Editorial, nuestra finalidad," *Fraternidad: Organo del Comité Mexicano Contra el Racismo,* Junio de 1944, Año 1, no. 1, 3; "Se formó un comité contra el racismo, combatirá todo brote de discriminación que surja en México," *La Prensa,* April 7, 1944.

6. Padilla, *Free Men of America,* 1; J. Lloyd Mecham, *A Survey of United States–Latin American Relations* (New York: Houghton Mifflin Company, 1965), 372–73. Also see the following for an examination of Avila Camacho's successful campaign to build national and continental unity in cooperation with the United States' own hemispheric designs: Michael Nelson Miller, *Red, White, and Green: The Maturing of Mexicanidad, 1940–1946* (El Paso: Texas Western Press, 1998).

7. Jesús Silva Herzog, *Una vida en la vida de México* (México, D.F.: Secretaría de Educación Pública, 1986), 285.

8. Zoraida Vázquez and Meyer, *México Frente a Estados Unidos,* 185–87.

9. Zorrilla, *Historia de las Relaciones Entre México y Los Estados Unidos de América;* Luis F. Gonzalez-Souza, "La política exterior de México ante la protección internacional de los derechos humanos," *Foro Internacional,* 18 (Julio–Septiembre 1977), 108–38; Sanchez, *Becoming Mexican American; Ethnicity, Culture and Identity in Chicano Los Angeles, 1900–1945.* Zorrilla offers the most compelling argument that the war gave Mexico the opportunity to challenge discrimination against Mexicans in the United States. Gonzalez-Souza reminds us that Mexico has a tradition of advocating human rights in international arenas. Sanchez includes the Mexican state in a history of Mexicans in the United States.

10. McWilliams, *North from Mexico: The Spanish-Speaking People of the United States,* 269; Zorrilla, *Historia de las Relaciones Entre México y Los Estados Unidos,* 506–507. Also see the following works that have examined the Bracero negotiations: Johnny McCain, "Contract Labor as a Factor in United States-Mexican Relations, 1942–47" (PhD diss., University of Texas at Austin, 1970); and Manuel García y Griego, "El Comienzo y el Final: La Interdependencia Estructural y Dos Negociaciones Sobre Braceros," in *Interdependencia, ¿Un Enfoque Útil Para el Análisis de las Relaciones México-Estados Unidos?.* Padilla's general response to the critics of Mexico's foreign policy, particularly the alliance with the United States, appears in the following: "Nuestra Política Internacional," in Padilla, *En El Frente de la Democracia, Discursos* (México: Cía. Editora y Librera ARS, 1945), 281–93.

11. "Draft of Memorandum to be Attached to Annual Report Relating to Spanish-Speaking Minority Project," December 15, 1942, 1. The OCIAA was established by executive order on July 20, 1941, under the Office of Emergency Management. This order superseded a previous one, on August 16, 1940, that had organized the Office of the Coordinator of Commercial and Cultural Relations. The new agency gave the initiative a clearer focus on "the foreign policy of cooperation laid down by the President and the State Department." According to an OCIAA report, the agency sought "to build up a strong mutual respect and understanding between the Americas, in order that the nations of the Western Hemisphere might better be prepared to meet jointly emergency war-time demands and plan jointly for a sound post-war structure." Soon after the United States declared war on the Axis powers, the Latin American delegates to the Conference of Foreign Ministers which met at Rio de Janeiro in January, 1942, formally endorsed the idea of continental unity. OCIAA, "Summary of the Activities of the Office of the Coordinator of Inter-American Affairs," March 1, 1942, Records of the OCIAA. The following sources also provide the basis for the commentary on the history and operations of the agency:

"Objective and Plan of Operation of Inter-American Activities in the United States," May 1, 1942, Records of the OCIAA; Office of the Coordinator of Inter-American Affairs, "Report, Division of Inter-American Activities in the United States, December 1941–December 1942," in U.S. Bureau of the Budget, *Administrative Histories of World War II Civilian Agencies of the Federal Government,* research publication of the Second World War History Program of the Bureau of the Budget, microfilm 41 (New Haven, Conn.: Research Publications, 1974), 1–43.

12. Nelson Rockefeller, director, OCIAA, to W. C. Longan, executive secretary, Coordination Committee for Mexico, March 7, 1942, Records of the OCIAA.

13. Will Alexander, consultant on minority groups, WMC, to Isabel Leonard, secretary, Foundation for the Advancement of the Spanish Speaking People, February 19, 1942, Records of the WMC.

14. Rockefeller to W. C. Longan, executive secretary, Coordination Committee for Mexico, March 7, 1942, Records of the OCIAA. Rockefeller served as the director of the OCIAA between 1940 and 1944 and thereafter, between 1944 and 1945, as assistant secretary of state for Latin American affairs.

15. The Minorities Section received approval from the State Department on May 15, with a temporary budget of $105,233 that was to keep the office operating until July 1. The Bureau of the Budget disallowed all appropriations in June on the grounds that its activities came under the jurisdiction of other offices. The bureau retracted the decision by the end of 1942 and made available the necessary appropriations. Walter H. C. Laves, director of the Division of Latin-American Activities in the United States, to Arthur Jones, September 8, 1942, Records of the OCIAA; Program for Cooperation with Spanish-Speaking Minorities in the United States, "Progress Report of Resident Latin American Unit," July 1, 1942, Ernesto Galarza Papers, Department of Special Collections, Stanford University, Stanford, Calif. (hereafter cited as Galarza Papers).

16. McWilliams, *North from Mexico,* 275–79. McWilliams included the following in his list of critics: Dr. Joaquín Ortega, the University of New Mexico; Dr. George Sanchez, the University of Texas; Dr. W. Lewis Abbott, Colorado College; Dr. Ben Cherrington, the University of Denver; and Mr. C. J. Carreon, a member of the Arizona legislature. McWilliams's proposal was one of the most comprehensive. Aside from proposing studies to determine ways to address social problems affecting the Spanish-speaking, McWilliams asked that the OCIAA sponsor public programs on Mexican history and culture, encourage long-term Mexican residents to become citizens, and support local reform efforts especially in the areas of education and health. McWilliams to Nelson Rockefeller, October 15, 1941, Galarza Papers.

17. Craig, *The Bracero Program: Interest Groups and Foreign Policy,* 40–42; Robert D. Tomasek, "The Political and Economic Implications of Mexican Labor in the United States Under the Non Quota System, Contract Labor Program, and Wetback Movement" (PhD diss., University of Michigan, 1957), 50–52. The following discussion on the Bracero Program also draws on Wayne D. Rasmussen, *A History of the Emergency Farm Labor Supply Program, 1943–1947,* agricultural monograph no. 13, U.S. Department of Agriculture, Bureau of Economics (Washington, D.C: U.S. Government Printing Office, 1954); Otey M. Scruggs, "Texas and the Bracero Program, 1942–1947," *Pacific History Review* 32, no. 3 (1963): 251–64; Peter N. Kirstein, *Anglo over Bracero: A History of the Mexican Worker in the United States from Roosevelt to Nixon* (San Francisco: R and E Research Associates, 1977); *Boletín Del Archivo General de la Nación, México* (Special Documentary Issue on the Bracero Program), IV, Núm. 4 (Octubre–Diciembre, 1980); Barbara A. Driscoll, *Me voy pa' Pensilvania por no andar en la vaganzia* (México: D.F.: Consejo Nacional Para la Cultura

y Las Artes y Universidad Nacional Autónoma de México, 1996); Domínguez López, "El Programa Bracero 1942–1947: Un Acercamiento a Través de los Testimonios de Sus Trabajadores."

18. Report by Jaime Torres Bodet, attached to letter from Cordell Hull, secretary of state, to McNutt, director, War Manpower Commission, June 30, 1942, Records of the WMC.

19. Zorrilla, *Historia de las Relaciones Entre México y Los Estados Unidos,* 490–92. Consult the following book-length study on the repatriations of the 1930s: Hoffman, *Unwanted Mexican Americans in the Great Depression: Repatriation Pressures, 1929–1939.*

20. Leland M. Goodrich and Maried J. Carroll, *Documents on American Foreign Relations* 5 (July 1942–June 1943) (Boston: World Peace Foundation, 1944), 395. According to the Bracero Agreement, "Mexicans entering the United States as a result of this understanding shall not suffer discriminatory acts of any kind in accordance with the Executive Order No. 8802 issued at the White House, June 25, 1941."

21. Gómez Arnau, *México y La Protección de Sus Nacionales en Estados Unidos,* 148–63. Avila Camacho gave equal prominence to both agreements before the Mexican Congress: "El Gral Manuel Avila Camacho, al abrir el Congreso sus sesiones ordinarias, el 10 de septiembre de 1942," *Los Presidentes de México Ante La Nación, Informes, Manifiestos y Documentos de 1821 a 1966* (México: Imprenta de la Cámara de Diputados, 1966), 205.

22. The State Department commissioned the first study in December 1941, when it ordered William P. Blocker, U.S. consul general at Ciudad Juarez, to conduct an investigation of discrimination in the United States against Mexicans. Although this study has not yet been located, the field studies and reports prepared between January and April, 1942, by the Office of Facts and Figures, the OCIAA, and the FEPC are available and provide official views of discrimination. Lawrence Duggan, advisor on political relations, to Sumner Welles, undersecretary of state, December 31, 1941, U.S. Department of State, Records of the U.S. Department of State Relating to Political Relations Between the United States and Mexico, 1930–1944; Paul Horgan, "United States Latins in the Southwest, A Domestic Wartime Responsibility with Foreign Overtones," January 1942, Records of the OCIAA; David J. Saposs, "Report on Rapid Survey of Resident Latin American Problems and Recommended Program," April 3, 1942, Records of the FEPC; and Vincenso Petrullo, "Report on the Spanish-Speaking Peoples in the Southwest," field survey, March 14–April 7, 1942, Records of the FEPC.

23. Numerous observers had previously pointed out the government's findings and had even described the conditions facing the Mexican community as comparable to and at time worse than that of African Americans. See the following for some representative government and academic studies: Victor S. Clark, *Mexican Labor in the United States,* U.S. Bureau of Labor Bulletin no. 78 (Washington, D.C.: U.S. Government Printing Office, 1908); Selden C. Menefee and Orin C. Cassmore, *The Pecan Shellers of San Antonio: The Problem of Underpaid and Unemployed Mexican Labor,* U.S. Work Projects Administration, Social Research Section, Division of Research (Washington, D.C.: Government Printing Office, 1940); Menefee, *Mexican Migratory Workers of South Texas,* U.S. Work Projects Administration, Social Research Section, Division of Research (Washington, D.C.: Government Printing Office, 1941); Manuel Gamio, *Mexican Immigration to the United States: A Study of Human Migration and Adjustment* (Chicago: The University of Chicago Press, 1930); Paul S. Taylor, *Mexican Labor in the United States: Imperial Valley,* University of California Publications in Economics, vol. 6, no. 1 (Berkeley: University of California Press, 1928); Taylor, *Mexican Labor in the United States: Dimmit County, Winter Garden District, South Texas,* University of California Publications in Economics, vol. 6, no. 5 (Berkeley:

University of California Press, 1930); Taylor, *Mexican Labor in the United States: Chicago and the Calumet Region,* University of California Publications in Economics, vol. 7, no. 2 (Berkeley: University of California Press, 1932); Taylor, *An American-Mexican Frontier, Nueces County, Texas* (Chapel Hill: The University of North Carolina Press, 1934).

24. Saposs Report, 2.

25. Ibid., 2–3.

26. The following are the dates and points of origins of reports sent by Saposs on his field study between February 19 and March 27, 1942: Saposs to John M. Clark, February 22 (Texas), 23 (Texas), 24 (Texas), March 5 (Texas), 7 (New Mexico), 17 (Arizona), 20 (Los Angeles), 30 (Colorado), 1942.

27. Saposs Report, 2.

28. Ibid, 3.

29. Ibid., 4–6, 14.

30. Sanchez, *Becoming Mexican American,* 264–67. The riot involved a rampage by hundreds of servicemen in downtown Los Angeles and in the predominantly Mexican community. The police watched as the rioters targeted Mexicans, particularly youth who dressed in the popular Zoot-Suit tradition. The local media, meanwhile, once again demonized the Mexicans and encouraged the violence. Consult the following, for more complete treatments of the ethnic tension in Los Angeles, the Sleepy Lagoon case, and the so-called "Zoot Suit Riots of June, 1943": Luis A. Alvarez, "The Power of the Zoot: Race, Community, and Resistance in American Youth Culture, 1940–1945" (PhD diss., University of Texas at Austin, 2001); Mauricio Mazón, *The Zoot-Suit Riots: The Psychology of Symbolic Annihilation* (Austin: University of Texas Press, 1984); McWilliams, *North From Mexico,* 228–58; Eduardo Obregón Pagán, *Murder at the Sleepy Lagoon: Zoot Suits, Race, and Riot in Wartime L.A.* (Chapel Hill: University of North Carolina Press, 2004).

31. Laves to William G. McLean, divisional assistant, Division of American Republics, Department of State, November 7, 1942; Laves to Arthur Jones, September 8, 1942, Records of the OCIAA. Although the OCIAA established the Minorities Section with the idea of implementing a broad plan of action, it remained focused on local projects of "social rehabilitation" prior to the Los Angeles troubles. The Office of the Budget, the agency for approving operating funds, had determined that the Office of War Information, instead of the Minorities Section, would assume the primary responsibility of leading a public information campaign to promote understanding across the racial divide. The effort was to give primary emphasis to Mexican contributions to the war effort in order to discourage Anglo prejudice and facilitate the social incorporation of the Mexican community. The troubles in Los Angeles changed this. It was now necessary to address the issue of discrimination and to give the OCIAA a primary responsibility in this effort. Cranston to Laves, May 28, 1942, September 17, 1942, Records of the OCIAA.

32. Laves to Robert Redfield, November 3, 1942; Laves to Arthur Jones, September 8, 1942, Records of the OCIAA. Also see the following for a discussion of Mexican political activity surrounding the Sleepy Lagoon case and its use of the wartime rhetoric of democracy: Gutiérrez, *Walls and Mirrors; Mexican Americans, Mexican Immigrants, and the Politics of Ethnicity,* 126–30.

33. For examples of private consultations and public denials on the "Zoot-Suit riots," see the following: Francisco Castillo Nájera, "Memorandum," June 1943 and "Answers to Questions Asked in Your Letter of July 3, 1943," Archivo Castillo Nájera. Castillo Nájera reported in the memorandum that the troubles in Los Angeles were a topic of discussion in his regularly-held meetings with Sumner Welles, the U.S. subsecretary of state. He also reported the following response to a question from an African American reporter on the riot: "This is entirely a domestic issue concerning which I do not wish to express any opinion."

34. Mexican officials most probably informed Texas authorities of the forthcoming ban prior to the establishment of the Bracero Program. In February 1942, John D. Reed, the director of the Texas Bureau of Labor Statistics, informed President Avila Camacho that Texas was "doing everything possible to end the exploitation of these kinds of workers [farm workers]." Reed also may have been appealing for the relaxation of Mexico's policy against illegal immigration to the United States during the war. Reed to Avila Camacho, February 11, 1942, *Boletín Del Archivo General de la Nación,* 5–6.

35. "Los quintacolumnistas provocan la discriminación racial en E.U., declaración del ministro E. Padilla, exhorta a los compatriotas en contra de los nazi-fascistas, el cónsul de México en Houston explica la situación del mexicano," *La Prensa,* June 24, 1943, 1.

36. Federal Bureau of Investigation, "Survey of Spanish Activities in the San Antonio Field Division," July 22, 1942, Department of Justice, National Archives and Records Administration, Washington, D.C. See other FBI reports with similar observations for San Antonio and the surrounding area: "League of United Latin American Citizens," September 4, 1942; "Survey of Spanish Activities in the San Antonio Field Division," October 20, 1942; "Survey of Spanish Activities in the San Antonio Field Division," November 20, 1942; "League of United Latin American Citizens," January 8, 1943; "League for United Latin American Citizens," February 3, 1942; "Survey of Spanish Activities in the San Antonio Field Division," February 27, 1943. The FBI reported investigations of LULAC and fellow organizations in the Rio Grande Valley, Houston and Dallas between 1942 and 1943.

37. McWilliams, *North From Mexico,* 240–44; Kibbe, *Latin Americans in Texas,* 252–54.

38. Cullen W. Briggs to Stevenson, July 8, 1943; Messersmith to Stevenson, June 29, 1943, Stevenson Papers. According to Luis L. Duplán, Mexican consul at Austin, the State Department had unofficially designated Blocker as diplomatic advisor to Governor Stevenson. Duplán credited Blocker with suggesting the idea of a Good Neighbor Commission. Duplán to Ezequiel Padilla, September 29, 1945, Galarza Papers.

39. Thomas A. Guglielmo, "Fighting for Caucasian Rights: Mexicans, Mexican Americans, and the Transnational Struggle for Civil Rights in World War II Texas," *The Journal of American History* 92 no. 4 (2006): 1212–36. Guglielmo covers some of the same topics addressed in my two previous publications on the Texas home front as well as in this chapter. He focuses on the legislative fight for Mexican rights in wartime Texas to demonstrate how the Mexican civil rights movement became a transnational concern. Guglielmo also points to a "complicated" yet not fully explained Mexican attachment to whiteness as a political strategy and as an expression of racial preference and privilege. The Texas legislature rejected a "Racial Equality Bill" in 1941 and the Spears Bill in 1945, two legislative initiatives that also sought to extend protections to Mexicans in Texas. The legislative cause in support of these two bills also included LULAC leaders and Mexican government officials.

40. The legislators also anticipated the 1954 Supreme Court decision in *Hernandez v. Texas* that declared Mexicans a class apart from the majority white population and affirmed that discrimination against them constituted a violation of the equal protection clause of the Fourteenth Amendment. The resolution excluded African Americans despite immediate protestations that pointed to the blatant problem of discrimination against blacks and the apparent inconsistency of the legislature's action. The following are sample letters of protest received by Stevenson shortly after the passage of Resolution 105: E. H. F. Jones to Stevenson, June 28, 1943; B. E. Howell, President, and G. F. Porter, secretary, National Association for the Advancement of Colored People, Dallas Branch, to Stevenson, August 3, 1943; Eloísa Galán to Stevenson, September 18, 1943, Stevenson Papers. See the following essay for a general treatment of legal strategies that Mexican-American activists took between 1930 and 1960: Steven H. Wilson, "Brown over "Other White": Mexican-Americans'

Legal Arguments and Litigation Strategy in School Desegregation Lawsuits," *Law and History Review* 21, no. 1 (2001).

41. Although Governor Stevenson may have decided to exclude African Americans from the purview of the GNC and Resolution 107 because he was primarily interested in placating Mexico, his use of racial language indicated animosity toward them. When Sutherland advised Governor Stevenson to establish the GNC, he reportedly said, "Meskins is pretty good folks. If it was niggers, it'd be different." "Meskins" somehow measured up to his racist expectations. His contempt for African Americans was obvious and probably shared by some of the legislators who framed the resolution. Green, *The Establishment in Texas Politics: The Primitive Years, 1938–1957,* 81.

42. Stevenson, "Proclamation by the Governor of the State of Texas No. 7039," June 25, 1943; Draft of Letter, Stevenson to Padilla, June 25, 1943; Briggs to Stevenson, July 8, 1943; Telegram, Briggs to Ernest Boyette, Governor's Secretary, July 9, 1943; Messersmith to Stevenson, August 12, 1943; "Remarks Made by Licenciado Ezequiel Padilla, Mexican Minister of Foreign Affairs, to the Press on Wednesday Evening, August 11, 1943," Enclosure to Letter, Messersmith to Stevenson, August 12, 1943; Stevenson to Padilla, August 12, 1943, Stevenson Papers.

43. Padilla to Stevenson, August 20, 1943, in *The Good Neighbor Policy and Mexicans in Texas,* National and International Problems Series (México, D.F.: Department of State for Foreign Affairs, Bureau of International News Service, 1945). It is not clear if Messersmith or Stevenson wrote the August 12 letter attributed to the governor. Messersmith refers to it as "your letter," although he also acknowledges Stevenson's handwritten comments on a typed draft, suggesting that the letter may have been initially prepared at the U.S. embassy. At any rate, they both worked on the letter. Moreover, it is clear that Ambassador Messersmith was a driving force behind the Texas experiment in face-saving diplomacy. Discrimination in Texas, in other words, did not merely represent an obstacle to the immigrant labor flow. It also impaired relations between Latin America and the United States.

44. Messersmith to Stevenson, June 29, 1943, Stevenson Papers.

45. Goodrich and Carroll, *Documents on American Foreign Relations,* 441–45; *Buenos Vecinos, Buenos Amigos,* Discursos Pronunciados por los Presidentes de México y de los Estados Unidos de América, en Monterrey, N. L., El 20 de Abril de 1943 (México: Secretaría de Gobernación, 1943); José G. Morales, *Unión de dos pueblos, la entrevista de Monterrey* (Monterrey, México: Unknown Publisher, 1943). See the following for Avila Camacho's report before the Mexico Congress on the meeting and the negotiated agreements that demonstrated "mutual regard": "El Gral. Manuel Avila Camacho, al abrir el Congreso sus sesiones ordinarias, el 10 de septiembre de 1943," *Los Presidentes de México Ante La Nación, Informes, Manifiestos y Documentos de 1821 a 1966,* 247–48.

46. Goodrich and Carroll, *Documents on American Foreign Relations,* 444.

47. Ibid., 443.

48. Ibid., 442.

49. McWilliams, *North from Mexico,* 240–44; Kibbe, *Latin Americans in Texas,* 252–54. Duplán to Sanchez, April 23, 1943, Stevenson Papers. Duplán continued to publicize his views. In July, he published a shorter, but equally critical letter on discrimination that he had written to Sanchez: Duplán, "Un jugoso documento del Cónsul de México en Austin, Luis L. Duplán, en una carta dirigida como respuesta a otra del profesor Jorge I. Sanchez, le señala casos concretos de discriminación racial," *La Prensa,* July 12, 1943.

50. See note 34.

51. "Padilla dice que protege a los mexicanos, asegura que protestó por los incidentes de Los Angeles, Calif., y que se le ataca debido a interéses políticos personales de por medio," *La Prensa,* June 23, 1943, 1.

52. "Los quintacolumnistas provocan la discriminación racial en E.U., declaración del ministro E. Padilla, exhorta a los compatriotas en contra de los nazi-fascistas, el consul de México en Houston explica la situación del mexicano," *La Prensa,* June 24, 1943, 1; Elithe Hamilton Beal, "Good Fences Make Good Neighbors," *Southwest Review* 30, no. 1 (1944), 42. Sources for other public comments by Padilla are noted elsewhere. Hamilton Beal made note of the Calderón observation.

53. "Los quintacolumnistas provocan la discriminación racial en E.U., declaración del ministro E. Padilla, exhorta a los compatriotas en contra de los nazi-fascistas, el consul de México en Houston explica la situación del mexicano," 1. Domínguez may have been expressing an understanding with U.S. officials that Mexico's advocacy work could include U.S.-born Mexicans. This understanding was evident in a Washington meeting between officials from the Mexican embassy and the U.S. Department of Justice in July 1943. When Vicente Sanchez Gavito announced that "it is intolerable that Mexicans born in this country should be victimized because they are Mexicans," Victor Rotnen reportedly assured him that "the Department of Justice is not interested in technicalities in international law," and proposed that Mexican authorities should report to his office any violation of "individual rights." "Memorandum sobre la intervención de la embajada de México en Washington, en el caso de Jesús Silvas y otros," July 28, 1943, document attached to letter from Rafael de la Colina, minister counselor, Mexican embassy, July 28, 1943, Archivo Rafael de la Colina, Archivo Histórico Genaro Estrada, Secretaría de Relaciones Exteriores, México, D.F.

54. Mexican embassy to State Department, July 23, 1943. See the following articles in *La Prensa* for coverage of the negotiations, including copies of diplomatic correspondence and articles from newspapers in Mexico: Pertinax, "No mas discriminación," *La Prensa,* August 11, 1943; J. Montiel Olvera, "La odiosa segregación de Mexicanos en Texas," August 14, 1943; J. Montiel Olvera, "México-Americanos y no Latino-Americanos," August 25, 1943; "No vendrán a Texas obreros Mexicanos a levantar cosechas debido a las distinciónes raciales," September 14, 1943. The following chapter discusses how LULAC tested the Caucasian Race Resolution.

55. The following articles that appeared in *La Prensa* reflect the public interest in Stevenson's trip and in relations with Mexico: "C. Stevenson brindó por México," September 10, 1943; "Es necesario conocer mas a México, dijo el gobernador del estado de Texas, Coke Stevenson," September 9, 1943; "El ejecutivo de Texas ante Chihuahua," September 10, 1943; "Coke Stevenson llegó ayer a la metrópoli," September 13, 1943; "Recepción a Stevenson en C. Victoria," September 13, 1943; "Coke Stevenson participa en las fiestas patrias," September 15, 1943; "Situación de los Mexicanos en Texas," September 15, 1943; "Es necesario conocer mas a México," September 17, 1943; "Los festejos patrios en la capital tuvieron inusitada trascendencia para México," September 17, 1943; "En la exposición de Tamaulipas," September 19, 1943. Stevenson's entourage included Duplán who accompanied him to Mexico, and two representatives from the office of the San Antonio mayor. The mayor's envoys, Ramón Galindo, a member of the Realtors' Association, and José Olivares, president of the Mexican Chamber of Commerce, joined the governor on the return trip.

56. "Coke Stevenson participa en las fiestas patrias, ayer asistió al desfile de los bomberos y cuerpos policiácos, presenciará desde el Palacio Nacional la ceremonia del 'Grito'," *La Prensa,* September 15, 1943. See the following for the role of the CTM and its famed leader, Vicente Lombardo Toledano, in building leftist support for the Avila Camacho administration and the U.S.'s Good Neighbor Policy: Torres, *Historia de la Revolución Mexicana, Periódo 1940–52; México en la Segunda Guerra Mundial.*

57. "Avila Camacho dirígese al México de afuera, en cordial y cálido mensaje, sigue con interés la vida de los Mexicanos que residen en EE. UU.," *La Prensa,* September 17, 1943.

58. Ibid.

59. Allen to Sanchez, September 21, 1943, Stevenson Papers.

60. For a recent examination of the end of the Texas ban, see the following study: Cristina Salinas, "A Border in the Making: The INS and Agricultural Relations in South Texas during the Mid-Twentieth Century," (master's thesis, University of Texas at Austin, 1948, University of Texas at Austin, 2005).

61. Laves to Rockefeller, December 28, 1942, Records of the OCIAA.

62. Daniel, *Chicano Workers and the Politics of Fairness,* 6–13.

63. Morton Blum, *V was for Victory: Politics and American Culture During World War,* 198–99; Trimble to Lawrence W. Cramer, executive secretary, FEPC, September 1942, Records of the FEPC. According to Lou Ella Jenkins, Trimble complained that "workers knew little of FEPC and its work" because of the FEPC previous inattentiveness. This negligence had led to protests by the Committee for Americanism and Inter-American Solidarity, a Mexican organization from an undetermined location in the area. The organization had critiqued the OCIAA and the FEPC for ignoring Mexican complaints of discrimination. Jenkins suggests that these kinds of protests contributed to the establishment of the El Paso office and to collaboration with the Committee for Americanism and LULAC in publicizing the agency's services and soliciting complaints from Mexican mine workers. Jenkins, "The Fair Employment Practice Committee and Mexican-Americans in the Southwest," 68.

64. State Department officials had consistently expressed concerns about drawing attention to discrimination. This was evident during the first official expressions of interest in discrimination and the need for governmental action evident by December 1941, as well as during the establishment of the OCIAA's Latin American Division and the Minorities Section between March and April 1942. The State Department, however, endorsed these initiatives including the decision to establish the FEPC office at El Paso. The prospects of a full airing of widespread discrimination in the Southwestern copper region, coming in the wake of the well-publicized troubles in Los Angeles and the understanding associated with the Bracero Program that encouraged Mexico to more actively intervene on behalf of Mexicans in the United States, no doubt made the State Department more concerned about impairing relations with Mexico.

65. Most of the work that the OCIAA supported involved "public educational programs," including Spanish-speaking fiestas, or celebrations, exchange programs that brought Mexican intellectuals and artistic talent to local areas, and scholarly conferences. The OCIAA also established a scholarship fund for Spanish-speaking college students, and promoted programs in radio and other media outlets that publicized Spanish-speaking contributions to the war effort. Laves to Wallace K. Harrison, April 14, 1942, Records of the OCIAA.

66. The Barelas Community Center worked with government agencies to provide important services including a health clinic, adult education classes, and recreational activities. The center also cooperated with the University of New Mexico to establish a training school for Spanish-speaking social workers. The Taos County Project involved the University of New Mexico as well as a number of federal agencies. The project offered its mostly rural constituency assistance in agricultural methods and marketing practices as well as advice and help on diets, schooling, and recreation. The OCIAA established another community center in Chicago modeled after the Barelas and Taos projects. For a study on the expansion of LULAC into New Mexico and its role in founding and administering the Barelas Community Center, see Cynthia Orozco, "Regionalism, Politics, and Gender in Southwest History: The League of United Latin American Citizens' Expansion into New Mexico from Texas, 1929–1945," *The Western Historical Quarterly* 29, no. 4 (1998): 459–83.

67. Louis T. Olom, untitled report, November 17, 1942; Olom to Laves, November 18, 1942; "Memorandum for Files," November 16, 1942, Records of the OCIAA.

68. Saposs, "Memorandum for the Files," November 17, 1942. Besides the agencies already mentioned, the others that were represented at the November meeting included the War Production Board, the War Labor Board, the Board of Economic Warfare, and the Office of Price Administration.

69. "Second Inter-Agency Meeting on Problems of Spanish Speaking Peoples Held December 10, 1942, in Mr. Walter H. C. Laves' Office," December 11, 1942, Records of the OCIAA. Besides the six agencies already noted, the following had representatives at the December 10 meeting: the WMC, Bureau of the Budget, the War Department, the Office of Civilian Defense, the Office of Defense Health Welfare Services, the Bureau of Public Assistance, and the Labor Department. The following discussion on the December 10 meeting is also based on two other reports by the staff of the Children's Bureau of the Department of Labor: Pauline Miller, "Report on the Meeting Called by the Coordinator of Inter-American Affairs on Problems of Spanish Speaking Peoples," December 11, 1942; Memorandum, "Report of Meeting on Spanish-American Minorities," December 15, 1942, Records of the OCIAA.

70. "Second Inter-Agency Meeting on Problems of Spanish Speaking Peoples Held December 10, 1942, in Mr. Walter H. C. Laves' Office," December 11, 1942, Records of the OCIAA; Zamora, "The Failed Promise of Wartime Opportunity for Mexicans in the Texas Oil Industry," 323–50.

71. Green and Smith, *Foreign Policy in U.S.-Mexican Relations,* Dimensions of U.S.-Mexican Relations, vol. 5 (San Diego: Center for U.S. Mexican Studies, University of California, San Diego, 1989), 5.

72. The following survey identifies many of these organizations in the first half of the twentieth century: Zamora, "Labor Formation, Community, and Politics: The Mexican Working Class in Texas, 1900–1945," 139–62.

Chapter 4

1. San Miguel Jr., *"Let All of Them Take Heed": Mexican Americans and the Campaign for Educational Equality in Texas, 1910–1981,* 74–81, 117–34. LULAC waited until 1948 to file its next suit against segregation, after a federal court had ruled in *Mendez v. Westminster School District* that the segregation of Mexican children by California schools had violated the equal protection clause of the Constitution. The Texas case, *Delgado v. Bastrop Independent School District,* involved LULAC and the new Mexican veterans' organization, the American G. I. Forum. The court ruled that the segregation of Mexican children was, according to San Miguel, "arbitrary, discriminatory, and illegal," and that all educational agencies should seek to eliminate it. San Miguel points out that school officials disregarded this ruling as well as the more famous 1954 Supreme Court decision in *Brown v. Board of Education* by failing to dismantle segregation in the public schools. Other legal challenges as well as the piecemeal approach to change continued in the 1950s and 1960s. The wartime years thus stand out for the lack of major legal challenges by LULAC or independent attorneys.

2. Ibid., 81–87. LULAC and other community organizations were also successful in convincing the city councils in San Antonio and Corpus Christi to approve ordinances prohibiting discrimination against Mexicans in public establishments.

3. Ibid., 94–108. See the following for a review of the extensive inter-American educational activities that U.S. governmental agencies, in cooperation with public schools,

colleges, and universities, sponsored in both domestic and hemispheric arenas during the war: Harold E. Davis, "Practicing the Good-Neighbor Policy," *The Journal of Higher Education,* 17 (1946): 196–200, 226. The following offers a general examination of the "propaganda" campaign by the State Department and the OCIAA to influence public opinion in Latin America with the use of radio programs, news releases, movies, exchanges of professors, teachers, and students, and technical and scientific assistance programs: Edward O. Guerrant, *Roosevelt's Good Neighbor Policy* (Albuquerque: University of New Mexico Press, 1950), 117–134.

4. Myrtle Tanner, "The Study of Spanish in Texas Schools," *The Texas Outlook* 28, no. 5 (1944): 38-39; Thurmond Krueger, chairman of the Inter-American Cooperative Committee of the Texas Junior Chamber of Commerce, to Marvin P. Baker, superintendent of the Corpus Christi Schools, February 24, 1942, Edmundo E. Mireles Papers, Mexican American Library Program, Nettie Lee Benson Latin American Collection, University of Texas at Austin. The Tanner article, written by an official with the State Department of Education, describes the three-year Spanish language program in eighty-one schools throughout the state. The Krueger letter demonstrates that the campaign to promote hemispheric understanding and the teaching of Spanish in Texas elementary schools, especially in Corpus Christi, drew significant support from influential citizens. The Mireles Papers also includes other evidence in the form of correspondence and clippings that points to this support. Edmundo Mireles was a Spanish teacher and active member of LULAC from Corpus Christi. Mireles and his wife, Jovita González, built a reputation as ardent supporters of Spanish-language instruction in Texas.

5. The leading journal on Texas education contains articles like the following that describe teacher-training programs in colleges and universities: "Latin-American Workshop," *The Texas Outlook* 27, no. 7 (1943): 46; "Latin American Workshop Education Workshop," *The Texas Outlook* 28, no. 4 (1944): 62; Jesse J. Villarreal, "Short Cuts in Teaching English As a Second Language," *The Texas Outlook* 28, no. 7 (1944): 11; "Inter-American Workshop," *The Texas Outlook* 29, no. 3 (1945): 48. The following sources contain a conference program, speeches, and essays by leading educators and a teaching guide involving teacher preparation activities in Texas sponsored by state and federal agencies: John G. Flowers, ed., *Report of Conferences on Professional Relations and Inter-American Education* (San Marcos: The Southwest Texas State Teachers College, 1944); George I. Sanchez and Henry J. Otto, *A Guide for Teachers of Spanish Speaking Children in the Primary Grades* (Austin, Tex.: State Department of Education, 1946).

6. Although federal and state officials described the inter-American campaign broadly, they acted narrowly, in part because they feared that a public airing of discrimination would negatively affect relations with Mexico and other Latin American countries. San Miguel Jr., *"Let All of Them Take Heed": Mexican Americans and the Campaign for Educational Equality in Texas, 1910–1981,* 91–96, 106–108.

7. "Pan-Americanism Must Begin at Home, Sanchez Tells Parent-Teacher Congress," *Albuquerque Journal,* May 6, 1942. The newspaper article reported on one of the earliest public critiques that Sanchez leveled against inter-American activities in the schools. James W. Young to Nelson Rockefeller, May 6, 1942, OCIAA Records. Also see the following work for an example of the continuing influence that Sanchez had on the discourse over inter-American education: Sanchez and Otto, *A Guide for Teachers of Spanish Speaking Children in the Primary Grades,* 10. The coauthored publication, which addressed the challenges of ending school segregation and improving the education of Mexican children in Texas schools, also credited Sanchez with saying that Mexicans in Texas were facing a "test case," that is, an opportunity to challenge school segregation with the use of the Good Neighbor Policy.

8. As noted earlier in the study, LULAC and Mexican government officials typically investigated the complaints of discrimination, confirmed the charges, and asked the business owners, usually in writing, to stop the practice on the grounds that discrimination negated important moral principles, violated constitutional rights, contradicted the Good Neighbor Policy, and undermined the war effort in the Americas. They also submitted reports of their investigations to local and state authorities and the Mexican embassy, especially when the denial of service involved Mexican nationals. Of all the LULAC leaders, Perales gave the greatest attention to discrimination in public places. His already noted articles in *La Prensa* and three book-length publications are replete with personal statements, primarily in the form of notarized affidavits that he used to substantiate the charge of discrimination "in two hundred and forty nine out of the two hundred and fifty four Counties of the State" (Perales to Franklin Delano Roosevelt, March 31, 1944, in Perales, *Are We Good Neighbors,* 278–80). Also see the following: "Some of the Places Where Mexicans Are Discriminated against in Texas Either by Denying them Service or by Segregating Them from Anglo-Americans," *Are We Good Neighbors?,* 213–23.

9. José de la Luz Saenz, a LULAC founder, a World War I veteran and the author of the previously noted war diary, was one of the most ardent critics of discrimination against Mexicans. For samples of his work, see the following: "Racial Discrimination, a Number One Problem of Texas Schools," in *Are We Good Neighbors?,* 29–33, and "Racial Discrimination," *The Texas Outlook* 30, no. 12 (1946): 12, 20.

10. Perales to Congressman Paul J. Kilday, November 24, 1944, appearing with the title, "Record of Mexican-Americans in World War II," in Perales, *Are We Good Neighbors?,* 283–84. *La Prensa,* the popular San Antonio daily, offered much news, information, and opinion regarding the war and Mexican participation in it. The following are sample headlines from 1943: "Un joven México-Americano ha recibido medallas por su heróico comportamiento en seis batallas, Se trata de Victor A. Egger Trejo, quién tomó parte en las batallas de Midway, Mar del Coral, Islas Salomón y Santa Cruz; El heroe ingresó a la marina de guerra hace cuatro años y a la fecha, en premio a sus servicios cursa materias especiales en la Texas Christian University," August, 15; "Dos soldados Mexicanos condecorados, Prisciliano Cruz y Vicente Rivera, del Estado de Texas," September, 18; "Un alto elogio a los soldados americanos de habla española; Mexicanos, México-Americanos y gentes de otro origen, que hablan nuestro idioma, se han distinguido en todos los frentes de batalla," October 17. Numerous videotaped interviews collected by the U.S. Latinos and Latinas and World War II Oral History Project at the University of Texas at Austin also contain much information on the contributions of Mexican Americans to the war effort, at home and on the battlefield. See the following examples: Aurora Estrada Orozco, "Testimonio," U.S. Latinos and Latinas and World War II: Changes Seen, Changes Wrought Conference, May 29, 2000, Austin, Tex.; interview with Aurora Estrada Orozco by Desireé Mata, October 17, 2003, Austin, Tex., in Archives of the U.S. Latinos and Latinas and World War II Oral History Project, University of Texas at Austin; Desireé Mata, "A Time When all the Young Men Disappeared," *Narratives* 4, no. 2 (2004): 102.

11. Salvador Guerrero, *Memorias; A West Texas Life,* ed. Arnoldo de León (Lubbock: Texas Tech University Press, 1991), 101.

12. George M. Villarreal to Stevenson, November 19, 1943, Stevenson Papers. Among the previously noted diplomats, migratory workers, and servicemen who may have accidentally walked into businesses that did not welcome them, the latter may have occasionally done it to plan a protest or to test the extent to which the war had changed old practices. This is especially evident in cases involving servicemen protesting discrimination against businesses in their hometowns or in the vicinity of their hometowns. Although servicemen may have most often done this, there is ample evidence in Perales's affidavits as well as in

archival collections such as the Stevenson Papers and the Galarza Papers to suggest that many other Mexicans also acted in this manner. Perales, *Are We Good Neighbors?,* 139–213.

13. Castañeda, monthly report, September 15, 1945, Records of the FEPC; "LULAC Pays Homage to Sugar Land War Hero," *Houston Post,* Sept 7, 1945, (copy of article in John Herrera Papers, Houston Metropolitan Library, Houston, Texas); affidavit by Macario García, October 5, 1946, in Perales, *Are We Good Neighbors?,* 156–57; Morín, *Among the Valiant; Mexican-Americans in WWII and Korea,* 143–48. Also see the front-page coverage of the incident by *Fraternidad,* the newspaper of the Mexico-based Comite Mexicano Contra el Racismo: "Golpean en Texas a un Mexicano, soldado y héroe," October 1, 1945, 1.

14. This discussion on the diplomatic exchanges and the following one on the increased travel of Mexican officials into the United States are based on the numerous records in the form of correspondence and reports found in the Archivo de Relaciones Exteriores, México, D.F. (herafter cited as Relaciones). Cases of discrimination typically triggered correspondence from the local consulate office to the Office of Foreign Affairs and the Mexican consulate with an occasional copy of a response from the State Department. Local newspapers such as *La Prensa* also printed reports on the involvement of various agencies representing both governments as well as their own descriptions of cases of discrimination involving Mexican officials. Outhwaite to Will Alexander, April 13, 1942, Records of the FEPC.

15. "News From Mexico City, Discrimination," *Pan American* (San Antonio), May 1945, 9. The editors of the *Pan American* reported, "Every paper in Mexico City carried a story this week telling of the refusal of service to the Federal Senator Eugenio Prado, president of the Mexican Senate and Arturo Chavez, Mayor of the City of Juarez." Another observer reported that the Pecos incident was "One of the most striking discriminatory acts that received practically universal publicity" in Mexico City. Hensley C. Woodbridge, "Mexico and U.S. Racism: How Mexicans View Our Treatment of Minorities," *The Commonweal,* June 22, 1945, 236.

16. Enrique Gonzalez Martínez, president of the Mexican Committee against Racism, to Alonso S. Perales, March 26, 1945, in Perales, *Are We Good Neighbors?,* 177. Although it is not known if Prado's complaint to U.S. and Mexican government officials caused the restaurant owner to apologize or end his discriminatory practices, it did bring international attention to the issue of discrimination. Such cases also gave Mexico the opportunity to test the United States' wartime pledge to promote a Good Neighbor Policy of equality and understanding within its own borders as well as in the Americas.

17. "El incidente de Pecos," *La Prensa,* March 27, 1945, 3; Gonzalez Martínez to Perales, March 26, 1945, in Perales, *Are We Good Neighbors?,* 177 and in *La Prensa,* March 28, 1945, 1; J. Montiel Olvera, "La discriminación racial, fue abolida en la Conferencia de Chapultepec," 5, 6; "Por una sociedad sin clases," *La Prensa,* March 24, 1945, 5; Castañeda, "Ley antidiscriminatoria," *La Prensa,* March 24, 1945, 5.

18. "El incidente de Pecos," 3; Gonzalez Martínez to Perales, March 26, 1945; Orozco to Stevenson, no date, in "Protestan los méxico-americanos de Pecos, Texas, con motivo de la discriminación racial," *La Prensa,* March 28, 1945. Gonzalez Martínez, a renowned poet in Mexico, headed the Comité en Contra el Racismo, or the Committee against Racism. As previously noted, the Comité included some of the most prominent persons in Mexico. Its periodical, *Fraternidad,* directed much of its attention to discrimination against Mexicans in the United States, especially in Texas.

19. U.S. House, Interstate Migration Hearings, 76th Congress, 3rd Sess, September, 1941, 1800, 1923. The figures for the size of the migratory workforce originate in a report, "Migratory Farm Labor in Texas Agriculture," prepared in September 1940, by Texas A&M University researchers at the request of Governor W. Lee O'Daniel. The report appeared

in the published hearings. The percentage figures were part of a joint statement submitted to the congressional committee by J. H. Bond, director for the Texas Employment Service, Robert M. M'Kinley, assistant director for the Texas Employment Service and farm placement supervisor, and E. H. Banks, farm placement supervisor, Texas Employment Service

20. Kibbe, "Report of the Executive Secretary to the Members of the Good Neighbor Commission," December 29, 1944, 3, Galarza Papers.

21. Montejano, *Anglos and Mexican in the Making of Texas,* 235-42. Montejano addresses the "flexibility of salesmanship" whereby merchants who catered to migrant customers sometimes relaxed their segregationist habits and even spoke out against segregationist practices in otherwise inhospitable areas like West Texas.

22. Kibbe, "Report of the Executive Secretary to the Members of the Good Neighbor Commission," 5–6. A verbatim copy of the Ropesville story appears in the following: Ross, *All Manner of Men,* 272. Ross recounted the story to demonstrate the extent of discrimination in Texas and to call for improved understanding.

23. Kibbe, *Latin Americans in Texas,* 231–32; Texas State Employment Service, "Statement on Employment Problems of Migratory Farm Workers Originating in Texas," 1821; "Mexico Asks Probe of Incident in Texas," Associated Press, November 1, 1943, Herrera Papers; Memorandum, San Antonio Consul to Mexican Embassy, November 3, 1943, Relaciones; "Continúa en Texas la discriminación racial," *La Prensa,* November 2, 1943.

24. "Mexico Asks Probe of Incident in Texas," Associated Press, November 1, 1943, Herrera Papers; Memorandum, San Antonio Consul to Mexican Embassy, November 3, 1943, Relaciones.

25. "Protección a nuestros compatriotas," *La Prensa,* November 3, 1943, 2; "Fue clausurado el café de Levelland y su encargado sera juzgado por lesiones," November 5, 1943, 1, 2; "Tom Sutherland, de la Comisión del Buen Vecino aclara que no hubo motín," November 7, 1943, 1, 2; "Declara el señor R. E. Smith," November 10, 1943, 1; "Ticer será llevado ante un jurado," December 16, 1943, 1; "El autor del incidente racial ocurrido en Levelland, Absuelto," December 17, 1943, 8; "State to Have Part in Mexican Row Trial," *Fort Worth Star-Telegram,* December, 12, 1943, Stevenson Papers.

26. Luis L. Duplán, Consul of Mexico, Austin, to Stevenson, September 30, 1945.

27. "Newgulf is Charged with Discrimination against Persons of Mexican Descent," *Houston Post,* September 19, 1943; Jesús Sosa, "Carta Abierta, al C. Coke R. Stevenson, Gobernador del Estado de Texas," *El Popular,* October 27, 1943, Copy in Ernesto Galarza Papers, Stanford University. A Good Neighbor Commission report prepared in 1951 described New Gulf as a company town, a "private corporation town devoted to the mining of sulphur." The Texas Gulf Sulphur Company employed between one and two thousand Mexico- and U.S.-born Mexicans. "Report to the Good Neighbor Commission, A Survey of Wharton County," February, 1971, Records of the GNC.

28. McWilliams, *North from Mexico, The Spanish-Speaking People of the United States,* New Edition, Updated by Matt S. Meier (New York: Greenwood Press, 1990), 240–41. The consul general of San Antonio was responsible for Texas, Oklahoma, Florida, Arkansas, Louisiana, Georgia, Alabama, and Mississippi. "Tomó posesión de su cargo de Consul General de México en San Antonio el Sr. Carlos A. Calderón, viene resuelto a enfrentarse y resolver los problemas globales de la colonia, desarrollando patriótica y noble labor," *La Prensa,* May 9, 1944, 1.

29. Herrera to Castañeda, no date, Herrera Collection; Castañeda, Weekly Report, March 3, 1945; Castañeda, Weekly Report, March 31, 1945; Castañeda, Weekly Report, May 16, 1945; Castañeda, Weekly Report, May 31, 1945. Approximately one thousand, or

30 percent, of the workforce in the New Gulf and Goose Creek plants were Mexican. After a contentious process of negotiation, Castañeda settled at least four complaints by Mexican workers alleging widespread discrimination in the plants.

30. Duplán to Stevenson, September 30, 1945. New complainants may have staged their own rejection and subsequent protest. One of them, Juan Lara, went into the Blue Moon Cafe with a friend. Once they were denied, his son, Fred Lara, asked for service and was also denied. Obviously sensitive to popular justifications for discrimination against Mexicans in public place, Juan noted that "neither my companion nor I were under the influence of intoxicants nor dirtily attired." Fred, on the other hand, was careful to note in his complaint that he was wearing his military uniform, suggesting that he had tested the owner's prejudice and determined that it was directed at all Mexicans: "I was wearing the uniform of the United States Army." Juan Lara, Notarized complaint, November 6, 1943; Fred Lara, Notarized complaint, November 6, 1943, Documents attached to Duplán to Stevenson, December 1, 1943.

31. Herrera offered one of the strongest denunciations of Wharton County as a place rife with discrimination when Castañeda informed him that he was investigating complaints against the Texas Gulf Sulphur Company. "This will be your toughest fight," noted Herrera; discrimination "is bred into the Anglo-American from the cradle until the grave. They glory in it and they don't care who doesn't like it." The previously cited report by the Good Neighbor Commission reported that although social relations had improved, a resident of the county aptly noted, "We need some new headstones in our cemetery before we can realize our moral, civic, and economic ambitions inherent in better human relations." Herrera to Castañeda, undated letter (circa September 1944), Herrera Papers; "Report to the Good Neighbor Commission."

32. As quoted and reported by Curtis Vinson, "Race Issue Arouses Ire of Mexicans," *Dallas Morning News,* October 24, 1943, Online Clipping Service, Texas Legislative Reference Library, State Capitol, Austin, Texas. A copy of the article appeared in Perales, *Are We Good Neighbors?,* 269–70. The article, written by the Mexico City correspondent of the *Dallas Morning News* reported that the press in the Mexican capital, especially *Mañana,* was giving more attention to the issue of discrimination in Texas than to previous conflicts such as the Zoot-Suit troubles in Los Angeles and the public debate over discrimination against Mexican workers in the United States. The Mexican press had also been addressing Padilla's critique of discrimination as "fifth columnism" in the United States and Governor Stevenson's Good Neighbor Policy response. According to Vinson, the New Gulf incident and the reports by Domínguez and Herrera were "climaxing all reports" in Mexican periodicals.

33. The quote is from a translated article originating in a Mexican newspaper. The article, "Grievous Racial Discrimination Case Denounced in Texas," appeared in a Mexican newspaper, *El Continental,* September 17, 1943. The article was attached to a letter from Jesus Sosa to Coke Stevenson, September 24, 1943, Stevenson Papers. William P. Blocker, the American consul general in Ciudad Juarez, may have translated the article for Stevenson. He transmitted the article and the letter from Sosa, a strong supporter of improved relations between Mexico and the United States who "represents the labor unions in Ciudad Juarez." Blocker to Stevenson, October 2, 1943, Stevenson Papers.

34. "Mexicans Ask for Court Aid, Want Judge to Order Owners of Pool to Let Latin-Americans Swim," *San Antonio Express,* July 22, 1943; "Caso de prejuicio racial denunciado por un Mexicano, pide la intervención de la ley a efecto de que cesen tales actos, cita un bochornoso incidente en el que fue protagonista," *La Prensa,* July 23, 1943; "Decisión que

sienta tesis legal, el juéz de distrito W. B. Terrell condena una discriminación racial, la sufrida por el señor Jacobo Rodríguez y otras dos personas mas," *La Prensa,* August 4, 1943.

35. "Court Upholds Pool in Ban on Latins," February 2, 1944, Clipping without name of newspaper, Gonzales Papers. The following article contains some of Perales's critical observations, including a copy of the court decision: "Alonso S. Perales, el reciente fallo de la cuarta corte de apelaciónes civiles y la doctrina del buen vecino," *La Prensa,* February 6, 1944.

36. "El comité creado por Roosevelt es el mas eficáz para acabar con los prejuicios raciales, esta comisión tiene las facultades necesarias para obrar con prontitud y eficacia en los campos industriales, solo falta un comité en el campo social," *La Prensa,* September 12, 1943.

37. Perales had extensive experience in diplomatic missions. After receiving his law degree in 1925, he completed thirteen diplomatic missions to the Dominican Republic, Cuba, Nicaragua, Mexico, Chile, and the West Indies. Perales was a cofounder of LULAC in 1929 and helped write the LULAC constitution, along with José Tomás Canales, Eduardo Idar, and possibly José de la Luz Saenz. He served as the organization's third president and formed Council 16 in San Antonio, a rival to Council 2 and Manuel C. Gonzales.

38. Padilla, *Paz Permanente y Democracia Internacional* (México: Secretaría de Relaciones Exteriores, Departamento de Información Para El Extranjero, Serie Cultural, 1944), 18; Montiel Olvera, "La segregación racial condenada por la Conferencia Inter-Americana de Abogados," *La Prensa,* August 22, 1944, 3; "Breve entrevista con el abogado José T. Canales," *La Prensa,* September 25, 1944, 2. For a report on the conference and a copy of the resolution, see Manuel S. Canyes, "The Third Conference of the Inter-American Bar Association," *Bulletin of the Pan American Union* (November 1944), 613–16; Federación Interamericana de Abogados, *Memoria de la Tercera Conferencia de la Federación Interamericana de Abogados,* 3 vols. (México: Talleres Tipográfico Modelo, S. A., 1945), 58–59.

39. Montiel Olvera, "La segregación racial condenada por la Conferencia Inter-Americana de Abogados"; "El Lic. Perales propugnó por una legislación antidiscriminatoria, en el Congreso de Abogados," *La Prensa,* August 3, 1944, 2; "La cuestión racial en la Conferencia de Abogados," *Fraternidad,* September 1, 1944, 3; "Como llegó a su final el Congreso de Abogados," *La Prensa,* August 20, 1944. There is no evidence that the American Bar Association promoted the resolution in the United States. George A. Finch, a member of the American Bar Association who attended the Mexico City meeting, even denied that the delegates had approved such a resolution: "Through faulty regulations, a few subjects of a political and diplomatic nature, which had no place on the program of a private law association, were given undue prominence, and, although the resolutions on these subjects were finally overwhelmingly defeated, for the time being the consideration of them overshadowed the real work of the meeting." Finch, "Mexico Meeting of the Inter-American Bar Association," *The American Journal of International Law* 38, no. 4 (1944), 684.

40. "Antes de salir de la capital de México, El Lic. Alonso Perales concede una entrevista a 'La Prensa,'" *La Prensa,* August 3, 1944; "Que no se envíen braceros Mexicanos al estado de Texas," *La Prensa,* August 11, 1944.

41. "Los Lulacs y la Liga de Leales Americanos se dirigieron al Depto. de Justicia de los Estados Unidos," *La Prensa,* November 1, 1944; "Con el propósito de insistir en que se legisle respeto a la injusta discriminación en contra de los de origén Latino Americano," *La Prensa,* November 1, 1944; Perales, "Un informe acerca del estado de las gestiones encaminadas a acabar con las discriminaciones," November 12, 1944; Perales, "Sobre la discriminación

racial," *La Prensa,* November 22, 1944. The relevant archival sources (Tom C. Clark Papers, Law Library Archives, University of Texas at Austin; Harry S. Truman Presidential Papers, Independence, Missouri; Records of the Department of Justice, National Archives and Records Administration, Washington, D.C.) do not contain the letters from Perales. He included major portions of them, however, in *La Prensa.* Clark offered his interpretation on the civil rights law of 1875 and the Supreme Court's ruling of 1883 against state-sponsored discrimination. Clifford M. Lytle, "The History of the Civil Rights Bill of 1964," *The Journal of Negro History* 51, no. 4 (1966), 275–96; Valeria W. Weaver, "The Failure of Civil Rights, 1875–1883, and Its Consequences," *The Journal of Negro History* 54, no. 4 (1969), 368–82; "An Act to Protect all Citizens in their Civil Rights," Public Acts of the Forty-Third Congress of the United States (March 1875), *The Statutes At Large,* December 1873–March 1875 (Washington, D.C.: Government Printing Office, 1875).

42. Perales, "Informe núm. 8 acerca del estado de las gestiones encaminadas a terminar con la discriminación," *La Prensa,* March 11, 1945, 4; Montiel Olvera, "La discriminación racial fue abolida en la Conferencia de Chapultepec," *La Prensa,* March 16, 1945, 5. The following, according to Perales, had written letters to the Texas legislature (in support of the Spears Bill) and delegates to the Chapultepec Conference by February 25: the Federación de Sociedades Mexicanas de Dallas; the Frente Unico Latino Americano de Taylor; Sociedad Mutualista Obrera, de San Antonio; "a group of citizens from El Dorado"; the Liga de Leales; the Alianza Hispanoamericana, the Club Roual and Campamento No. 3327 of the Leñadores del Mundo of New Braunfels; Fortino Treviño of Alice; Matilde Chapa of New Braunfels; Liborio Cadena of Benavides; José A. Gonzalez of Taylor; Francisco V. Juárez of San Angelo; Francisco Múzquiz of Moore; Aurelio Díaz of Del Rio; the Sociedad Mutualista Vicente Guerrero and the Sociedad Mutualista Melchor Ocampo of New Gulf; and the Reverend Salvador Rodríguez, "on behalf of 5,000 parishioners." "Informe núm. 6 acerca del estado de las gestiones encaminadas a terminar con la discriminación," February 25, 1945, 6.

43. For reports on the conference, see L. S. Rowe, "The Inter-American Conference on Problems of War and Peace," *Bulletin of the Pan American Union* 79 (1945), 249–59; Pan American Union, *Inter-American Conference on Problems of War and Peace,* Report Submitted to the Governing Board of the Pan American Union by the Director General (Washington, D.C.: Pan American Union, 1945).

44. Montiel Olvera, "La próxima conferencia de cancilleres y la discriminación racial," *La Prensa,* February 2, 1945, 5; Montiel Olvera, "La conferencia inter-americana," *La Prensa,* March 3, 1945, 3. During the United Nations meeting Padilla seemed to be more conciliatory than before. Most probably in response to the letters that Mexican civil rights leaders sent him, Padilla reportedly stated, "Cases of discrimination about which I have been recently informed are of an individual nature and do not represent the attitude of our neighbors." Armando del Moral, "El ministro de relaciones exteriores de México define la actitud del país en relación a los problemas mundiales," *La Prensa,* May 6, 1945, 1, 2.

45. "El lic. Perales objeto de gran distinción," *La Prensa,* April 18, 1945, 2;

46. Perales, "Informe núm. 10 del Estado en que se hallan las gestiones encaminadas a terminar con la discriminación," *La Prensa,* April 22, 1945, 6.

47. Castañeda advised Perales on behalf of the FEPC. According to Castañeda, the FEPC had furnished Perales "all the information at our disposal to enable him to present his case against discrimination and to promote the adoption of a positive resolution by the Committee." Aside from seeking higher standards of living and full employment around the world, the FEPC recommended that the United Nations seek "universal respect for, and

observance of, human rights and fundamental freedoms for all without distinction to race, language, religion or sex." Castañeda, Bi-Weekly Report, June 16, 1945, 6.

48. United Nations, *Documents of the United Nations Conference on International Organization, San Francisco, 1945,* vol. X, Commission II, General Assembly (United Nations: United Nations Information Organizations, 1945), 280; Perales, "La conferencia de San Francisco," June 15, 1946, 5; Perales, "La conferencia de San Francisco y el porvenir de nuestros pueblos," June 7, 1945, 6; Perales, "La conferencia de San Francisco," June 29, 1945, 5. Perales was assigned to the Preamble, Purposes, and Principles Committee, and the Committee on Economic and Social Cooperation. He claimed to have also done some work in the other ten committees during the conference. Perales, "La carta mundial," *La Prensa,* July 9, 1945, 2.

49. Castañeda, Bi-Weekly Report, May 31, 1945; "El rechazo de la ley Spears," *Fraternidad,* July 25, 1945, 5. See the following articles and reports in *La Prensa* for opinions and a running account of the work by LULAC and other organizations from throughout Texas on behalf of the Spears bill: Perales, "Informe núm. 6 acerca del estado de las gestiones encaminadas a terminar con la discriminación," February 25, 1945, 6; Perales, "Informe núm. 7 acerca del estado de las gestiones encaminadas a terminar con la discriminación," March 4, 1945, 2; "Primer triunfo de los latinos en el estado de Texas," March 7, 1945, 1; "Se verificó la audiencia sobre el proyecto de ley Spears," March 7, 1945, 2; Perales, "Informe núm. 8 acerca del estado de las gestiones encaminadas a Terminar con la Discriminación," March 11, 1945, 4; Perales, "El proyecto de ley antidiscriminatorio será discutido y votado por el senado de Texas muy en breve," March 28, 1945, 8; "Informe núm. 9 acerca del estado de las gestiones tendientes a terminar con la discriminación," April 1, 1945, 3; Laureano Flores, "La discriminación racial debe analizarse para comprender lo que busca con la legislación que pedimos," April 15, 1945, 3; "El senado de Texas aprobó la ley anti-discriminatoria," May 9, 1945, 2. Horacio Guerra, "the Czar of Starr," was a political boss and large landowner from Roma in Starr County. The other two Mexican members of the GNC were Matias de Llano, a businessman from Laredo, and Andrés Rivera, a banker from San Antonio. Elithe Hamilton Beal, "Good Fences Make Good Neighbors," *Southwest Review* 30, no. 1 (1944), 43–44.

50. Castañeda, Bi-Weekly Report, May 31, 1945; Bi-Weekly Report, September 5, 1945.

51. Duplán may have been one of the most circumspect consuls. His careful diplomatic style, for instance, at times contrasted with the more aggressive style that consuls such as Domínguez demonstrated with the New Gulf incident. The differences may have reflected varying political orientations and strategies. Duplán showed his guarded manner when he reported to Kibbe that Luis Perez Abreau, the Mexican consul from Dallas, had submitted a complaint, "with the purpose of finding a satisfactory solution to these unfortunate cases and avoid at the same time any publicity which could jeopardize the good relations that happily exist between our two great governments and people." Duplán to Kibbe, December 30, 1943, Stevenson Papers; Duplán to Padilla, September 29, 1945, Galarza Papers.

52. Duplán to Padilla, September 29, 1945.

53. Ibid.

54. Gonzales to Sidney Hillman, director, Office of Production Management, November 17, 1941, Records of FEPC.

55. Cramer to Gonzales, November 26, 1941, Records of the FEPC. The full text of Gonzales's remarks is as follows: "You might conclude that racial segregation and racial discrimination in National Defense projects are totally different subjects. We know that one

is the outgrowth of the other, and that if we are to be the Christian, democratic and truly Americans that we want to be, we must, in keeping with the heritage of our forefathers, fight religious intolerance, [and] the mistaken theory of the existence of racial superiority, so that we can point with pride, in referring to the Latin American Republics, to America as the real melting pot where equal opportunities are not only promised but actually given."

56. W. G. Carnahan to Will W. Alexander, Minority Groups Branch, Labor Division, OPM, December 9, 1941, Division of Field Operations, Records of the FEPC.

57. Alexander to Carnahan, December 16, 1941, Division of Field Operations, Records of the FEPC.

58. The records of the FEPC contain numerous letters from Gonzales and other Texas LULAC representatives. The following are some early samples: Gonzales to Ernest G. Trimble, FEPC field representative, July 29, 1942; George I. Sanchez to Cramer, July 31, 1942; Gonzales to Trimble, August 10, 1942; Gonzales to Cramer, August 18, 1942. The collection also contains letters from at least forty-six Texas LULAC councils.

Chapter 5

1. Castañeda, Bi-Weekly Report, June 31, 1945, Records of the FEPC. Perales expressed similar views in a meeting called by San Antonio Archbishop Robert Lucey, a major proponent of a permanent FEPC, a founding member of the Bishops' Committee for the Spanish-Speaking, and a member of President Truman's Civil Rights Commission. According to Castañeda, Perales noted that the Charter bound the United States to adopt legislation "that will guarantee and protect equal economic opportunities for all workers regardless of 'race language, sex, or religion.'" Castañeda, Bi-Weekly Report, July 15, 1945, FEPC; Kibbe, *Latin Americans in Texas,* 268–70.

2. Margarita Arce Decierdo, "The Struggle Within: The California Agricultural Labor Relations Board, 1975–1990," in *Chicano Politics and Society in the Twentieth Century,* ed. David Montejano (Austin: University of Texas Press, 1999); Levine, *Class Struggle and the New Deal: Industrial Labor, Industrial Capital, and the State.*

3. Laureano Flores, "La discriminación racial debe analizarse para comprender lo que busca con la legislación que pedimos," 3.

4. In some places, Mexican workers made contact with the FEPC through well-known leaders in their communities such as Houston Consul Adolfo G. Domínguez. At other times, Castañeda would ask a friend like John J. Herrera, the president of LULAC Council #60 from Houston, to publicize FEPC services and solicit complaints from Mexican workers. Castañeda also maintained contact with Lozano, the editor of *La Prensa.* Domínguez to Castañeda June 8, 1943, Castañeda to Domínguez, September 16, 1943 to Herrera, October 7, 1943, Records of the FEPC. See the following for a description of the official procedures on handling of FEPC complaints: FEPC, *First Report, July 1943–December 1944* (Washington, D.C.: U.S. Government Printing Office, 1945), 18–22; U.S. House, *Hearings Before the Committee on Labor,* H.R. 3986, H.R. 4004 and H.R. 4005, Bill to Prohibit Discrimination in Employment Because of Race, Creed, Color National Origin, or Ancestry, 78th Cong., 2nd Sess., vol. 2, November 16, 1944 (Washington, D.C.: U.S. Government Printing Office, 1944), 138–39.

5. John A. Davis, "An Analysis of Satisfactory Adjustments Effected by the Committee for October 1944," Records of the FEPC.

6. Brin, Weekly Report, February 12, 1944; Don Ellinger, Weekly Report, June 26, 1944, Records of the FEPC.

7. See the following for a report on the types of discriminatory practices that Mexican workers usually faced: Castañeda to Clarence M. Mitchell, Associate Director of Field Operations, March 9, 1945, Records of the FEPC.

8. FEPC, *First Report, July 1943–December 1944,* 106–107; FEPC, *Final Report, June 28, 1946* (Washington, D.C.: U.S. Government Printing Office, 1947), 118; Will Maslow, director of field operations, to Castañeda, December 17, 1943, Records of the FEPC.

9. FEPC, *First Report, July 1943–December 1944,* 119–20.

10. Ibid. See Appendix E in the report for thirty tables that compare the caseloads of the various offices between July 1, 1943 and June 30, 1944. The regional and subregional offices were organized as follows: East (Boston, New York, Philadelphia); Midwest (Cleveland, Detroit, Chicago, Minneapolis, Kansas City); South (Washington, Atlanta, Dallas); West (Denver, San Francisco, Los Angeles). The following are the jurisdictional areas for each region: Region I, Boston (Connecticut, Maine, Massachusetts, New Hampshire, Rhode Island, Vermont); Region II, New York (New York); Region III, Philadelphia (Delaware, New Jersey, Pennsylvania); Region IV, Washington, D.C. (Washington, D.C., Maryland, North Carolina, Virginia, West Virginia); Region V, Cleveland, Detroit (Kentucky, Michigan, Ohio); Region VI, Chicago (Illinois, Indiana, Wisconsin); Region VII, Atlanta (Alabama, Florida, Georgia, Mississippi, South Carolina, Tennessee); Region VIII, Minneapolis (Iowa, Minnesota, Nebraska, North Dakota, South Dakota); Region IX, Kansas City (Arkansas, Kansas, Missouri, Oklahoma); Region X, Dallas (Louisiana, New Mexico, Texas); Region XI, Denver (Colorado, Idaho, Montana, Utah, Wyoming); Region XII, San Francisco, Los Angeles (California, Nevada, Oregon, Washington).

11. Although administrative effectiveness and staff dedication may account for the impressive amount of work conducted in the regional offices, the size and professional status of their staff also made a difference. The New York office, for instance, recorded the largest number of cases during the latter part of 1943 at the same time that it employed a regional director, three examiners, an assistant examiner, two consultants, and three clerks. Philadelphia reported a regional director, two examiners, and two clerks. Atlanta, one of the offices with the lowest number of settlements in 1944, reported a regional director, an examiner, and a clerk. Dallas, on the other hand, had a better settlement record than the other southern FEPC office in Atlanta with a regional director, two examiners, and two clerks. "Schedule of Personnel, December 27, 1943," U.S. House, *Hearings Before the Committee on Labor,* November 16, 1944, 258–59.

12. Castañeda, Weekly Report, September 11, 1943; "Por acuerdo del Presidente Roosevelt se creó el Comité Sobre Prácticas Justas de Empleo, hácese cargo de el, el Dr. Carlos E. Castañeda, ex-catedrático y bibliotecario de la Universidad de Texas, jugosa entrevista con el reputado literato, y campeón de los intereses latinoamericanos," *La Prensa,* September 8, 1943.

13. "Por acuerdo del Presidente Roosevelt se creó el Comité Sobre Prácticas Justas de Empleo," *La Prensa,* September 8, 1943.

14. Castañeda, Weekly Report, September 11, 1943. Lozano himself had a reputation as a civil rights leader, especially on behalf of Mexican nationals. A local journalist called him "a potent force for good." Peyton, *San Antonio: City in the Sun,* 174.

15. "Prominente Latino-Americano viene a San Antonio, *La Prensa,* February 16, 1944.

16. Almaraz, *Knight Without Armor: Carlos Eduardo Castañeda, 1896–1958,* 67–68, 131–32.

17. Manuel C. Gonzales, national executive secretary, to Dan Osuna, president general of LULAC, Albuquerque, June 16, 1942, Andrés de Luna Papers.

18. Report, "The UT Conference on Inter-American Relations in Texas," Stevenson Papers.

19. Ibid.

20. See the following for accounts on African Americans and the FEPC in the Texas Gulf Coast: Obadele-Starks, *Black Unionism in the Industrial South.* According to Obadele-Starks, the NAACP activists also saw their work on behalf of African American complainants as an extension of their civil rights struggle and understood that cooperation with the FEPC was a major part of their fight for workers' rights.

21. Castañeda, Weekly Report, October 16, 1943; FEPC, *First Report, July 1943–December 1944,* 11, 106–107. For Castañeda's association with the Pan American Round Table and the Texas Federation of Women's Clubs, see the following representative documents: Ruth Coit, director, San Antonio Pan American Round Table, to Castañeda, April 4, 1943; Florence J. Scott, state chairman, Department of International Relations, to Castañeda, August 3, 1942, Carlos E. Castañeda Papers, Mexican American Library Program, Nettie Lee Benson Latin American Collection, University of Texas at Austin (hereafter cited as Castañeda Papers).

22. Castañeda, Weekly Reports, September 11, 18 1943.

23. Hill to Senator Tom Connally, June 2, 1943, Castañeda Papers.

24. Castañeda to Ross, December 18, 1943, Records of the FEPC.

25. Ross to Castañeda, November 27, 1943; Haas to Castañeda, July 27, 1943; Haas to Castañeda, July 17, 1943, Records of the FEPC. The records of the FEPC offer different titles for Castañeda's appointment, including assistant director for Spanish Speaking persons, assistant director for Latin Americans, and assistant director for Latin American workers. I use the latter term because it was used most frequently.

26. Ross to Castañeda, May 10, 1945, Records of the FEPC. On an earlier occasion, Will Maslow, the director of field operations for the FEPC, also counseled caution: "Be careful to take no official action or even to express an opinion about matters not within our jurisdiction. While you should always try to be helpful to all complainants, remember that our jurisdiction is limited to discriminatory employment practices" (underlined in original). Castañeda mostly observed this stricture in 1943, although he continued his association with LULAC and served as the honorary consultant to the GNC. By the middle of 1944, Castañeda, like his counterparts in LULAC, became disillusioned with the grievance procedure of the governor's Office and the GNC and became more outspoken. Maslow to Castañeda, October 6, 1943; Castañeda Weekly Report, October 23, 1943, Records of the FEPC.

27. Ross to Castañeda, May 10, 1945, Records of the FEPC.

28. U.S., House, *Congressional Record,* 78th Congress, 2nd Sess., Vol. 90, Part 4, May 12–June 12, 1944, 5035.

29. George Sessions Perry, *Texas, A World in Itself* (New York: McGraw-Hill Book Company, 1941), 78. U.S. House, *Congressional Record,* 78th Congress, 2nd Sess., Vol. 90, Part 4, May 12–June 12, 1944, 5034–5037. The *Congressional Record* includes most of the material used in this section. Brin had worked in the Dallas office of the War Labor Relations Board when Castañeda brought him on board as a field examiner. Rafael de la Colina, minister counselor, Mexican embassy, to the San Antonio consulate, December 4, 1943, Relaciones.

30. The state laws, known as the Jim Crow laws or black codes, explicitly prohibited intermarriage and allowed segregation in public schools, colleges and universities, libraries, railroads, busses, boxing matches, washrooms in mining operations, and some hospitals.

Milton R. Konvitz, "The Extent and Character of Legally-Enforced Segregation," *The Journal of Negro Education* 20, no. 3 (1951), 425–35.

31. Brin, Weekly Reports, May 27, 29, 1944, Records of the FEPC; Stevenson to Brin, June 7, 1944, Records of the FEPC; "Stevenson Asks FEPC to Prove Rights," *Dallas News,* June 8, 1944, Stevenson Papers. Brin resigned as regional director immediately after the governor's letter appeared in the newspaper. Although the resignation may have had nothing to do with the letter, there was much speculation that it did. W. Don Ellinger, his successor, prepared the office's weekly reports beginning during the second week of June, although Brin's name continued to appear on them.

32. Ross to Stevenson, June 14, 1944, Stevenson Papers.

33. Ibid.

34. Brin, Weekly Report, June 10, 1944, Records of the FEPC.

35. U.S. House, *Congressional Record,* 78th Congress, 2nd Sess., Vol. 90, Part 5, June 13–August 24, 1944, 6262. For additional entries in the *Congressional Record* on the case against the *Dallas News,* also see: 6263, 6341–44.

36. Wilson to Stevenson, June 10, 1944; Mr. Frances to Stevenson, June 11, 1944. These as well as the other cited letters to Stevenson are in the Stevenson Papers.

37. Gibson to Stevenson, June 10, 1944.

38. Davis to Stevenson, June 14, 1944

39. Ross to Stevenson, June 14, 1944, Records of the FEPC. Ross's reference to the governor's comments on Mexicans referred to communications between Stevenson and Ezequiel Padilla, Mexico's secretary of foreign affairs, in July 1943 when the former initiated the campaign against discrimination to convince the Mexican government to send Braceros to Texas. Castañeda may have informed Ross and other FEPC officials at Washington about the governor's statements regarding Mexican workers and the agency. He reported that Stevenson had expressed support for the work that the FEPC was doing among Mexicans during a Good Neighbor Commission meeting that they attended.

40. Castañeda kicked off the FEPC campaign, much like he did in Mexican communities, by conferring with members of the African American civil rights leadership. In September, for instance, he conferred with Maceo Smith, a civil rights leader from Dallas who had achieved regional prominence, and Clarence R. Johnson, an African American field representative from the Los Angeles office of the WMC. Castañeda followed with an article that appeared in the *Dallas Express,* a weekly with a circulation of at least twelve thousand in the African American community. The article contained an interview with Castañeda by the paper's editor in which he expounded on the purpose and work of the FEPC. Other actions included a recommendation to hire an African American field examiner "at as early a date as possible, as it will soon become essential to the work of this office." The FEPC eventually hired L. Virgil Williams who assisted Castañeda incorporate black complainants from East Texas and Louisiana into the world of the FEPC. Williams was especially helpful in investigating and settling complaints by African American workers in the aircraft construction plants of the Dallas–Fort Worth area, the Consolidated Vultee Corporation, and the North American Aviation Corporation. Castañeda Weekly Reports, September 25, 1943, October 9, 1943, Records of the FEPC.

41. Examples abound in Castañeda's Weekly Reports. See the following, for references to the cited cases, Weekly Reports, November 4, 14, and December 9, 1944, Records of the FEPC.

42. Castañeda's strategy can be gleaned from the weekly reports that he submitted between May 1943, and December 1944, the period when he and other FEPC officials

conducted an investigation of the refining industry in the lower Texas Gulf Coast. See chapter 6 for a more thorough treatment of this campaign and the action against the Shell, Humble, and Sinclair refineries.

43. *San Antonio Light,* May 9, 1943, as quoted in Castañeda, Weekly Report, May 16, 1943, Records of the FEPC.

44. Ellinger, Weekly Report, December 23, 1944, Records of the FEPC; Mrs. Cleo M. García to Castañeda, December 7, 1944, Records of the FEPC; Ellinger, Weekly Report, January 13, 1945, Records of the FEPC; Castañeda, Weekly Report, February 17, 1945, Records of the FEPC.

45. Castañeda, Bi-Weekly Report, April 30, 1945, Records of the FEPC.

46. John A. Davis, "An Analysis of Satisfactory Adjustments Effected by the Committee for October 1944," Records of the FEPC. FEPC and WMC records indicate that Mexican and black workers most often complained of discriminatory job referrals. Complaints against job training programs were less evident. FEPC investigations of the large aircraft plants, North American Aviation Corporation and Consolidated Vultee Aircraft Corporation, in the Dallas–Fort Worth area suggest some explanations: private industry in many cases operated the programs in a somewhat independent fashion and beyond the purview of manpower officials; the programs often moved workers in a lateral or upward fashion from skilled positions where minority workers were underrepresented; minority workers may not have been well informed about training opportunities; and African Americans were afforded some participation through segregated programs. A third and less frequent complaint involved job releases. Minority workers occasionally complained that employers refused to give them the required release so that they could obtain employment elsewhere. Castañeda, Weekly Reports, October 2, November 22, 1943, December 6, 1943, April 30, 1945, Records of the FEPC; Leonard M. Brin to J. M. Hassler, director, Industrial Relations, Consolidated Vultee Aircraft Corporation, January 15, 1944, Records of the FEPC; Chronological "Summary" of Case Against Consolidated Vultee, January 17, 1944, Records of the FEPC; Brin, Weekly Report, April 22, 1944, Records of the FEPC; Ellinger, Weekly Report, March 3, 1945, Records of the FEPC.

47. Kryder, *Divided Arsenal: Race and The American State During World War II,* 111–13. Kryder does not explain the extent to which the USES complied with the WMC order nor the effects of this change on other minority workers besides African Americans. He does state that the USES failed to follow the WMC orders in the Deep South.

48. Lawrence A. Appley, deputy chairman and executive director, WMC, to all regional, state, and area manpower directors, August 1943, Records of the WMC; Francis J. Haas, chairman, FEPC, and Paul V. McNutt, chairman, WMC, "Operating Agreement Between FEPC and WMC on Non-Discrimination Program," August 1943, Records of the WMC.

49. Castañeda, Monthly Report, September 11, 1943, Records of the FEPC; Brin, Weekly Reports, April 24, 1944, May 13, 1944, Records of the FEPC; Castañeda, Weekly Reports, December 25, 1943, August 5, 1944, Records of the FEPC; Ellinger, November 4, 1944, Records of the FEPC. Ellinger reported a "continuing lack of information regarding 510s, the acceptance of discriminatory hiring orders as a matter of course, and the lack of information on the part of subordinate personnel with any phase of the discrimination program."

50. FEPC officials from Texas regularly reported that the WMC was lax in monitoring the USES and that the USES staff systematically classified and referred workers in a racial manner. Although the staff was following regular procedures, they often assumed responsibility for the discriminatory practices. In some cases, they justified the discrimination

by noting that Mexicans and blacks had no reason to complain about discrimination in wartime industries because they were earning more money than ever before. Brin reported one case in which a USES official stated that his office "did not discriminate any more than the rest of the industries," and that it would be unfair to single them out for filling discriminatory employment orders. Castañeda, Weekly Report, December 25, 1943, Records of the FEPC; Brin, Weekly Report, April 24, 1944, Records of the FEPC. WMC officials in Texas reportedly admitted that its placement and training divisions also discriminated against Mexicans and that this discrimination was "more or less" due to "local conditions in this area." Castañeda to Francis J. Haas, FEPC chairman, August 27, 1943, Records of the FEPC.

51. Federal agencies, especially in the South, were known to regularly deny blacks equal employment opportunities. The USES was especially negligent in encouraging discriminatory job requests. Merl E. Reed explains that the agencies employed persons from the region who brought their antiblack prejudice into their work. Reed, "FEPC and the Federal Agencies in the South," *The Journal of Negro History* 65, no. 1 (1980): 43–56; Texas Labor Market Report, February 15–March 15, 1943, 51. Also see an FEPC complaint from Fernando R. Ypina, a worker from Houston who claimed that a USES official used a loudspeaker to pull Anglos from among workers who were waiting for job assignments. According to Ypina, officials regularly sent Anglos to the skilled jobs and disregarded Mexicans fresh out of defense training programs (Ypina to Walter Laves, no date, "List of Cases of Discrimination" (November 1941–May 1942, Records of the FEPC).

52. A study of the files of the Austin USES office for the period between June 1, 1947, and June 1, 1948, offers overwhelming evidence of continuing discriminatory practices. According to the author, the USES regularly assigned Mexicans and blacks to the lower-skilled positions in the construction, railroad, food processing, agricultural, and service industries regardless of their education, training, skills, or prior job experience. His major finding was that the staff did not do this in an arbitrary fashion and that the Austin case reflected a larger statewide trend. The staff followed regular established procedures that called for the systematic classification and referral of workers on a racial basis. Forest Burr Crain, "The Occupational Distribution of Spanish-Name People in Austin, Texas" (master's thesis, University of Texas at Austin, 1948), 20–21, 41, 49–59, 75.

53. There are numerous pieces of evidence in the records of the FEPC suggesting that military camps cooperated with the agency more than any other industrial site in the state. In one of these, Perales praised Castañeda on behalf of Mexican workers who had obtained satisfactory settlements to their complaints: "I have spoken to some of the boys at Kelly Field and your good work has already made itself felt. They are delighted, and feel grateful to you. Keep up the good work, my friend, you are doing a lot of good to our people" (Perales to Castañeda, November 22, 1943, Records of the FEPC).

54. Castañeda, Weekly Report, September 25, 1943, Records of the FEPC. Castañeda offered numerous examples to demonstrate how a cooperative command structure could contribute to the elimination of discrimination. A representative case appeared at the Naval Air Station from Corpus Christi. A worker named Ernest Herrera had been assigned to work in a supervisory capacity. Twelve Anglo women in the department immediately threatened to resign because they did not want to work under a Mexican. Personnel officials promptly informed them that the military camp would accept their resignations on the condition that they state they were refusing to work under a Mexican foreman. The twelve women apparently agreed to accept the Mexican foreman and not risk giving just cause for their removal; none resigned or were released (Castañeda, Bi-Weekly Report, May 31, 1945, Records of the FEPC).

55. Castañeda to Will Maslow, director of field operations, January 21, 1944, Records of the FEPC.

56. Castañeda, Bi-Weekly Report, April 30, 1945, Records of the FEPC.

57. Ibid.

58. Castañeda, Bi-Weekly Report, June 15, 1945, Records of the FEPC.

59. Castañeda, Weekly Reports, September 25, 27, 1943, Records of the FEPC. A case in point involved a junior aircraft engine mechanic named Andrés Canales, who was discharged in 1943. A Kelly Field representative reported that he had shown a lack of respect to his superior officer. Castañeda, Weekly Report, September 18, 1943.

60. Castañeda, Weekly Report, October 30, 1943, Records of the FEPC.

61. Ellinger, Weekly Report, July 31, 1944, Records of the FEPC.

62. Works that address minority politics in San Antonio and the emerging liberal urban-based coalition of labor and minorities in Texas, include Blackwelder, *Women of the Depression: Caste and Culture in San Antonio, 1929–1939*; García, *Mexican Americans: Leadership, Ideology, & Identity, 1930–1960;* Richard García, *Rise of the Mexican American Middle Class: San Antonio, 1929–1941* (College Station: Texas A&M University Press, 1991); Green, *The Establishment in Texas Politics; The Primitive Years, 1938–1957;* Kenneth Mason, *African American and Race Relations in San Antonio, Texas, 1867–1937* (New York: Garland Publishing, 1998); Montejano, *Anglos and Mexicans in the Making of Texas, 1836–1986;* Rodolfo Rosales, *The Illusion of Inclusion: The Untold Political Story of San Antonio* (Austin: University of Texas Press, 2000); and Vargas, *Labor Rights Are Civil Rights; Mexican American Workers in Twentieth-Century America.*

63. Mitchell to Castañeda, March 3, 1945; Castañeda, Weekly Report, March 3, 1945, Records of the FEPC.

64. Ross, "Those Gringos," *Common Ground* 8 (1948), 9.

Chapter 6

1. Three basic texts inform this chapter. They include an unpublished manuscript by a CIO organizer involved in the Oil Workers' Organizing Campaign of 1942–43. It describes the successful attempt by the CIO to enter the oil industry in the Texas Gulf Coast. (Johnson, "The Battle for Baytown," June 1984, Copy of book-length manuscript in author's possession). A study by the labor economist Ray Marshall examines racial discrimination against black workers in the Texas Gulf Coast oil industry and the successful 1955 challenge against it by the government and the NAACP: "Some Factors Influencing the Upgrading of Negroes in the Southern Petroleum Refining Industry," *Social Forces* 42 (1963), 186–95. The recent study by Obedele-Starks on workers studies the larger African American social movement in the Gulf Coast: Obadele-Starks, *Black Unionism in the Industrial South.*

2. The thirteen refineries were Sinclair (Houston), Shell (Houston), Humble (Baytown), Texas Company (Houston), Republic (Texas City), Pan American (Texas City), Southport (Texas City), Texas Company (Port Neches), Pure Oil (Port Neches), Texas Company (Port Arthur), Gulf (Port Arthur), Magnolia (Beaumont), and Humble (Ingleside). FEPC, *Final Report,* 23; W. Don Ellinger, "Complete Report on Shell Situation, May 1, 1945," 1–5, Records of the FEPC.

3. The FEPC conducted preliminary investigations in the Southwest in 1942 that resulted in the discovery of widespread discrimination against Mexican workers in the oil

companies of the Texas Gulf Coast. The cases against the refineries and the workers' organizations lasted until the closing of the Dallas office in 1945. Report of Clay Cochran to Castañeda, October 25, 1943, Records of the FEPC; Morton Blum, *V Was for Victory: Politics and American Culture During World War II,* 198; Lawrence W. Cramer to Manuel C. Gonzales, November 26, 1941, Records of the FEPC; Will Alexander to W. G. Carnahan, December 26, 1941, Records of the FEPC; Castañeda to Will Maslow, January 26, 1944, Records of the FEPC.

4. For readings on the oil industry, see Carl Coke Rister, *Oil: Titan of the Southwest* (Norman: University of Oklahoma Press, 1949); Joseph A. Pratt, *The Growth of a Refining Region* (Greenwich, Conn.: JAI Press, 1980); Warner, "Texas and the Oil Industry"; and Warner, "The Oil Industry in Texas Since Pearl Harbor." Other studies that treat the subject of labor organizing in Texas, include Harvey O'Conner, *History of the Oil Workers' International Union* (Denver: Oil Workers' International Union, 1950); F. Ray Marshall, *Labor in the South* (Cambridge, Mass.: Harvard University Press, 1967), 194–99, 230–33; Herbert Werner, "Labor Organizations in the American Petroleum Industry," in *The American Petroleum Industry: The Age of Energy, 1899–1959,* ed. Harold F. Williamson, Ralph L. Andreano, Arnold R. Daum, and Gilbert C. Klose, 827–45 (Evanston, Ill.: Northwestern University Press, 1963).

5. The figure for the Mexican workforce was estimated based on a total of about 36,650 workers in the Gulf Coast refineries. Pauline Kibbe also suggests a low Mexican figure of less than 3 percent. Obadele-Starks proposes an even smaller number of Mexicans in the industry when he cites the total of twenty-two hundred minority workers, or 6 percent of the total workforce, with African Americans constituting a larger portion. Kibbe, *Latin Americans in Texas,* 159–61; Obadele-Starks, *Black Unionism in the Industrial South,* 79–80.

6. One important FEPC finding in the Texas Gulf Coast oil industry involved the use of a dual classification system. According to one FEPC report, all refineries in the area with the exception of the Texas Company maintained a wage differential that segregated two types of common laborers. The first group was composed of Anglos who received the higher rate of pay, which was approximately $0.89 an hour. The second group was made up of Mexican and African American workers who received around $0.795 an hour (Ernest G. Trimble to Francis J. Haas, July 9, 1943, Records of the FEPC).

7. This summary of conditions has been gleaned from numerous FEPC documents cited throughout the paper.

8. Golightly, "Wartime employment of Mexican-Americans," 2, Records of the FEPC; G. L. Farned to Cramer, January 26, 1943, 4–5, Personal collection of Clyde Johnson, Berkeley, California (hereafter cited as Johnson Collection). The nativity figures suggested by the survey differ substantially from the census-derived ratio of one Mexico-born to six U.S.-born Mexicans in the state.

9. De Leon, *Ethnicity in the Sunbelt: A History of Mexican Americans in Houston,* 71–76. According to Emilio Zamora, the federation was active as late as the early 1940s and joined other community organizations to establish of the famed Congreso del Pueblo de Habla Española (Zamora, "Labor Formation, Community, and Politics: The Mexican Working Class in Texas, 1900–1945," 159).

10. Castañeda, Weekly Report, October 23, 1943, Records of the FEPC.

11. Cochran to Castañeda, October 25, 1943, Records of the FEPC. Cochran's "Review of Previous Developments Affecting This Industry," accompanied Cochran's "Report" to Castañeda that was also dated October 1944. Although Mexican workers from various refineries submitted complaints, the workers from Humble, Sinclair, and Shell registered the

most and best-documented ones. Also, these Mexican workers were consistent in resubmitting complaints through the Mexican consul's office when the FEPC periodically requested additional evidence in support of the complaints.

12. Manuel C. Gonzales to Sidney Hillman, November 17, 1941, Records of the FEPC; Cramer to Gonzales, November 26, 1941, Records of the FEPC; Carnahan to Alexander, December 1, 1941, Records of the FEPC; Carnahan to Alexander, December 9, 1941, Records of the FEPC; Gonzales to Trimble, July 29, 1942, Records of the FEPC; Stanley D. Metzger to Clarence M. Mitchell, July 11, 1944, Records of the FEPC.

13. Castañeda, Weekly Report, October 23, 1943, Records of the FEPC.

14. The division in Washington on the strategy to pursue with the oil industry had at least two origins. On the one hand, the concern that revealing widespread discrimination would damage relations with Latin America had not died down since the cancellation of the El Paso hearing of 1942. Lawrence Cramer, the executive secretary of the FEPC, on the other hand, supported a general hearing in oil, but feared that it could provoke a reaction by segregationists much like the one that occurred after the 1943 FEPC hearings on racial discrimination in Alabama coal mining. Cramer and other FEPC officials in Washington may have also feared that, unlike in Birmingham, Alabama, local political elites could whip up emotions among Houston segregationists. John Beecher, a federal official associated with job training programs, credits Jesse Jones, one of the most influential political leaders from Houston, with blocking an unidentified government hearing in 1943. Kesselman, *The Social Politics of FEPC,* 17–18; Edwin Smith to Clyde Johnson, November 6, 1942, Johnson Collection; Castañeda to Maslow, September 1, 1944, Records of the FEPC; Interview with John Beecher by Jack Rabin, November 16, 1974, Jack Rabin Collection on Alabama Civil Rights and Southern Activists, University Libraries, The Pennsylvania State University, Special Collections Department, Historical Collections and Labor Archives.

15. Castañeda to Maslow, September 1, 1944, Records of the FEPC.

16. Castañeda, Weekly Report, October 23, 1943, Records of the FEPC.

17. Castañeda, Weekly Report, November 6, 1943, Records of the FEPC.

18. Ross, *All Manner of Men,* 273–74; Castañeda, Weekly Report, December 25, 1943, Records of the FEPC. Castañeda's strategy can be gleaned from his Weekly Reports.

19. See Johnson, "The Battle for Baytown," for a critique of the union leadership that acknowledges racial prejudice and discrimination. Johnson was especially critical of the inconsistent support that the OWIU gave the CIO-backed Oil Workers' Organizing Campaign (OWOC) between 1941 and 1943. Much of the conflict that occurred between the staff of the OWOC and the OWIU hinged on the general reluctance of the latter organization to support the OWOC's strong civil rights plank that called for an end to discrimination in the refineries. Johnson, "The Battle for Baytown," June, 1984; interview with Clyde Johnson by the author, February 9, 1988; Clyde Johnson, "CIO Oil Workers' Organizing Campaign in Texas, 1942–1943," in *Essays in Southern Labor History: Selected Papers, Southern Labor History Conference, 1976,* ed. Gary M. Fink and Merl E. Reed, 173–87 (Westport, Conn.: Greenwood Press, 1977). See the following for copies of these contracts or references to them: Castañeda to Will Maslow, May 24, 1944, Records of the FEPC; Leonard M. Brin to Will Maslow, May 24, 1944, Records of the FEPC; "Application of Seniority for Selecting Men for Jobs in New Operating Units Not Replacing Other Units," July 23, 1943, Records of the FEPC; "Mechanical Seniority," October 1, 1936, Records of the FEPC; and President Committee on Fair Employment Practice, Stipulation, In the Matter of Shell Oil Company, Incorporated, and Oil Workers' International Union, Local 367, CIO, December 30, 1945, 3–4, Records of the FEPC.

20. The leadership of the OWIU freely admitted widespread discrimination by its

locals in the Gulf Coast, although they claimed that it was for the most part "company inspired" and, to an extent, reflective of local prejudices (Oil Workers' International Union, Report of the Oil Workers' International Union Concerning Experiences in the Field of Racial and Religious Discrimination, 1944, Records of the FEPC). There were exceptions to the general rule of discrimination by the unions. CIO Local 449 from Southport refinery in Texas City is a case in point. When the refinery refused to end its practice of wage discrimination, the union successfully challenged the company before the War Labor Board in 1943. The WLB ordered the company to end its dual classification system and pay African American workers equal wages. Another example occurred at the Gulf refinery of Port Arthur in 1945. When 250 members of the black CIO union, Local 254, went on a wage strike, the president of the white CIO union announced the support of his membership. National War Labor Board, In the Matter of Southport Petroleum Company of Delaware and Oil Workers' International Union Local 449, Case No. 2898-CS-D, June 5, 1943, Johnson Collection; Castañeda Weekly Report, June 16–31, Records of the FEPC.

21. "Humble Oil and Refining Company, Baytown, Texas," typed summary of FEPC case against Humble, November 1943, Records of the FEPC. For information on early discriminatory practices, see Henrietta M. Larson and Kenneth Wiggins Porter, *History of Humble Oil and Refining Company: A Study in Industrial Growth* (New York: Harper and Brothers, 1959), 200–201.

22. Statement on Discrimination Against Mexican Workers at the Baytown Refinery, Humble Oil and Refining company, Baytown, Texas, Signed by Andrés Contreras, C. Beltrán, J. Santana, Onofre Gonzalez, L. Herrera, and G. N. Ponce, November 25, 1942, Johnson Collection.

23. Gordon L. Farned to Cramer, January 26, 1943, Johnson Collection. The summary of Farned's response is drawn from his letter to Cramer, as well as from the following: Clyde Johnson to Ernest G. Trimble, March 15, 1943, Johnson Collection; and "Humble Oil and Refining company, Baytown, Texas," November, 1943, Records of the FEPC.

24. Farned to Cramer, January 26, 1943, Records of the FEPC.

25. "Humble Oil and Refining Company, Baytown, Texas," 4, Records of the FEPC; Victor Rothen, memorandum for the solicitor general, 1–2, Records of the FEPC. See issues of the *CIO Campaigner,* the OWOC's organ in the Gulf Coast, for critiques of discrimination in the industry. Also, see copies of *The Bulletin* for examples of the Federation's criticisms of the union. Both are in the Johnson Collection.

26. *The Bulletin,* May 6, 1943.

27. Ibid., April 27, 1943.

28. Castañeda, Final Disposition Report, Humble, February 9 and 10, 1944, Records of the FEPC; Rothen, memorandum for the solicitor general, 1–2, Records of the FEPC; "Humble Oil and Refining Company, Baytown, Texas," 2–3.

29. Castañeda to Maslow, October 16 and October 23, 1943, Records of the FEPC.

30. Castañeda, Final Disposition Report, Humble, February 9 and 10, 1944; Castañeda to Maslow, January 26, 1944, Records of the FEPC.

31. Brin, Final Disposition Report, Sinclair, February 11, 1944, Records of the FEPC.

32. Gray to Carnahan, April 15, 1942, Records of the FEPC; Affidavit, A. S. Sanchez, February 15, 1945, Records of the FEPC.

33. The discussion on the complaint is based on the following documents from FEPC Records: Minutes of the Conference Held with Management and Labor of Sinclair Refinery, Houston, Texas, December 28, 1943, 2–6, Records of the FEPC; Adolfo G. Domínguez, Memorandum on Discrimination of Mexican Workers at the Refinery of the Sinclair Refining company in Houston, Texas, June 8, 1943, Records of the FEPC; Affidavits of J. R.

Flores and Teodosio Gutiérrez, November 20, 1943, Records of the FEPC; and Cochran to Sinclair Refining Company, November 26, 1943, Records of the FEPC.

34. Castañeda to Maslow, December 25, 1943, 3–4, Records of the FEPC; Minutes of the Conference, December 28, 1943, Records of the FEPC.

35. Young to Cochran, December 7, 1943, 1–6, Records of the FEPC.

36. Minutes of the Conference, December 28, 1943, 1–6, Records of the FEPC.

37. Castañeda, Final Disposition Report, Sinclair, February 11, 1944, Records of the FEPC.

38. Castañeda to Clyde Ingram, March 1, 1944, Records of the FEPC.

39. Ellinger to Sinclair Refining Company, March 15, 1945, Records of the FEPC; Affidavits dated February 1945 and signed by A. S. Sanchez, A. V. Salinas, Juan Robledo, S. Rodríguez, Jesse Lozano Caballero, Henry S. Mendez, and M. de la Garza, Records of the FEPC.

40. Ellinger to Sinclair Refining Company, March 15, 1945.

41. Summary of Shell Oil Case, May 5, 1945, 1, Records of the FEPC. A precise figure for the number of Mexican workers at Shell is not available.

42. Domínguez, memorandum on racial discrimination at the Shell Refining Co., Houston, Texas, April 26, 1943, and Memorandum on Conference Held Friday, May 14, 1943, at Mexican Consulate in Houston, Texas, Relative to Discrimination of Mexican Workers at Shell Oil and Refining Company, May 15, 1943, Records of the FEPC. The discussion that follows on the complaint is based on the Domínguez documents.

43. Trimble to Haas, July 9, 1943, 1–2, Records of the FEPC.

44. Castañeda to Maslow, September 18, 1943, Records of the FEPC.

45. Castañeda to Maslow, December 4, 1944, Records of the FEPC; Castañeda to Domínguez, September 16, 1943, Records of the FEPC; Castañeda to John J. Herrera, October 7, 1943, Records of the FEPC; Castañeda to Domínguez, October 7, 1943, Records of the FEPC.

46. Castañeda to Maslow, October 16, 23, 1943, Records of the FEPC.

47. Castañeda to O. A. Knight, January 1, 1944, Records of the FEPC.

48. Castañeda to Maslow, December 31, 1943, Records of the FEPC.

49. Ibid.

50. Castañeda to Maslow, December 31, 1943, January 1, 1944, Records of the FEPC.

51. Castañeda to Maslow, January 26, 1944, , Records of the FEPC; Castañeda to Brin, May 17, 1944, Records of the FEPC.

52. Opening Statement, December 28, 1944, Records of the FEPC; Ellinger to Maslow, December 30, 1944, Records of the FEPC.

53. Opening Statement, December 28, 1944, Records of the FEPC. Also see President's Committee on Fair Employment Practice, Statement of Charges and Order for Hearing, In the Matter of Shell Oil Company, Incorporated, and Oil Workers' International Union, Local 367, CIO, December 11, 1945, Records of the FEPC; Statement of the Case, January 27, 1945, Records of the FEPC; and FEPC, Stipulation, December 30, 1945, Records of the FEPC.

54. Opening Statement, December 28, 1944, 1, 9, Records of the FEPC.

55. Ibid.

56. Statement of the Case, January 27, 1945, Records of the FEPC; Stipulation, December 30, 1945.

57. Castañeda to Maslow, March 24, 1945, 5, Records of the FEPC; Mitchell to Ellinger, April 11, 1945, Records of the FEPC.

58. Summary of Shell Oil Case, May 5, 1945, 1, Records of the FEPC.

59. Ibid., 1–2.

60. Ibid.; Ellinger to Ross, May 1, 1945, 1–5, Records of the FEPC. The following description of events is based on information from these two reports.

61. Also see Mitchell to Emanuel Bloch, April 12, 1945, Records of the FEPC.

62. Ellinger to Ross, Re: the Attached Memorandum, May 1, 1945, 1–3, Records of the FEPC; Ellinger to Ross, Re: Complete Report on Shell Situation, May 1, 1945, 1–5, Records of the FEPC.

63. Ibid.

64. Ellinger to Ross, Re: The Attached Memorandum, May 1, 1945, 2, Records of the FEPC.

65. Castañeda to Maslow, May 16, 1945, 4, Records of the FEPC.

66. Ellinger to Knight, May 24, 1945, Records of the FEPC; Knight to Ellinger, June 2, 1945, Records of the FEPC.

67. George Weaver to Ellinger, June 19, 1945, Records of the FEPC; Ellinger to Mitchell, July 14, 1945, Records of the FEPC; J. J. Hickman to Ellinger, July 24, Records of the FEPC; Castañeda to Maslow, June 1–15, 1945, 4–5, Records of the FEPC. See Ellinger to Ross, May 20, 1945, Records of the FEPC, for proposal by union on segregated workforce.

68. Castañeda to Maslow, June 16–30, 1945, 4, Records of the FEPC.

Chapter 7

1. Castañeda to Maslow, November 29, 1943, Records of the FEPC. Corpus Christi, the largest city on the lower Texas Gulf Coast, had approximately one hundred and fifty thousand inhabitants, including about fifty thousand Mexicans and four thousand African Americans. The area's economy had depended heavily on the area's agricultural industry with vast amounts of acreage devoted to cotton and cattle. The Second World War marked the beginning of impressive growth in industrial production with a newly opened port facilitating the development of oil refinery, chemical production, and trade. Tourism, as well as the local naval air station, also emerged as important new employers during the 1940s and 1950s. See the following promotional publication for a history of the Gulf Coast town: Corpus Christi Caller-Times, *Corpus Christi: 100 Years.*

2. Cochran, Table of Work Force ("constructed on the basis of data supplied by the American Smelting and Refining Company"), November 1943, Records of the FEPC. Workforce figures appeared in Castañeda's weekly reports, as well as in the following transcription of the hearing discussed in this chapter: FEPC, *Investigation of Alleged Complaints Against the American Smelting and Refining Company,* Corpus Christi, Texas, November 18, 1943, 11, 29, 44, 46, Records of the FEPC.

3. Matta to Matias de Llano, August 12, 1943, Records of the FEPC; de Llano to Matta, August 25, 1943, Records of the FEPC; de Llano to Matta, September 10, 1943, Records of the FEPC. Matta had worked in the Texas Harvest Hat Company, a business owned by de Llano, and no doubt was encouraged to seek help from his former employer when he read of his appointment to the GNC.

4. Cisneroz to Castañeda, October 27, 1943, Records of the FEPC.

5. Ibid.

6. Notarized statement of Adan Cisneroz, Nueces County, Texas, November 5, 1943, Records of the FEPC; Notarized statement of Dan Falcón, Nueces County, Texas, November 6, 1943, Records of the FEPC; Castañeda to Cisneroz, November 2, 1943,

Records of the FEPC. The notarized statements were resubmitted by Cisneroz in response to a request by Castañeda that they be signed and dated. This is the reason why these documents appear dated after Cisneroz refers to them.

7. The company was a subsidiary of Pittsburgh Plate Glass Company and American Cyanamid and Chemical Company. It produced lime, soda ash, caustic soda, and chlorine from the large supply of limestone, oyster shell, water, salt, brine, and natural gas available in the Corpus Christi area. The union negotiated a contract with the company as the Alkali Workers Industrial Union, Local No. 12078 of District 50, United Mine Workers of America, in May 1, 1942. By 1943 it was affiliated with the United Gas, Coke, Chemical and Allied Workers, a CIO federation, as the Alkali Workers Industrial Union Local No. 153. Contract, Southern Alkali Corporation (Corpus Christi, Tex.: Southern Alkali Corporation, 1944), 1–2, 4, 6–10, 14, 19–22, 35, 38, 41, Records of the FEPC; The Alkali Workers Industrial Union, United Gas, Coke and Chemical Workers of America, Constitution and By-Laws, (Corpus Christi, Tex.: Local No. 153, 1943), Records of the FEPC; Alkali Workers Industrial Union, 1943–44 Agreement Governing Wages and Working Rules (Corpus Christi, Tex.: Local No. 153, 1944), Records of the FEPC.

8. Castañeda, handwritten notes, March 25, 1945, Records of the FEPC. Castañeda noted the following workforce figures: 145 Mexican hourly workers; 241 Anglo hourly workers; and 153 Anglo salaried workers.

9. FEPC, Investigation of Alleged Complaints Against the Southern Alkali Corporation, Corpus Christi, Texas, November 19, 1943, Records of the FEPC.

10. Jimenez, et al., to League of United Latin American Citizens, Council Number One, no date, Records of the FEPC.

11. FEPC, Investigation of Alleged Complaints Against the Southern Alkali Corporation, Corpus Christi, Texas, November 19, 1943, Records of the FEPC.

12. Meza to President's Committee on Fair Employment Practice, July 17, 1943; Jimenez, et. al., to League of United Latin American Citizens, Council Number One, no date, Records of the FEPC.

13. Meza to President's Committee on Fair Employment Practice, July 17, 1943, Records of the FEPC.

14. Ibid.

15. Castañeda to Meza, October 2, 1943, Records of the FEPC; Clarence Mitchell to Meza, August 23, 1943, Records of the FEPC.

16. Investigation of Alleged Complaints Against the Southern Alkali Corporation; Investigation of Alleged Complaints Against the Alkali Workers' Industrial Union, Local No. 153, Corpus Christi, Texas, November 19, 1943, Records of the FEPC.

17. *Investigation of Alleged Complaints Against the American Smelting and Refining Company,* 3–5, Records of the FEPC.

18. Ibid., 7.

19. Ibid., 20.

20. Ibid., 33.

21. Waterman's testimony appears throughout the transcribed copy of the hearing.

22. FEPC, *Investigation of Alleged Complaints Against the Zinc Workers Federal Labor Union, Local 23245, A.F.L.,* Corpus Christi, Texas, November 18, 1943, 3–4, Records of the FEPC.

23. *Investigation of Alleged Complaints Against the Zinc Workers Federal Labor Union, Local 23245, A.F.L.,* 22–25.

24. *Investigation of Alleged Complaints Against the American Smelting and Refining Company,* 25–26; *Investigation of Alleged Complaints Against the Zinc Workers Federal Labor*

Union, Local 23245, A.F.L., 6, 8–9, 16–17, 31, 36. Complete Anglo control of the union occurred when the predominant Anglo membership elected their own to the grievance committee and officer positions during elections in October and November 1942. This continued the following year. Only six Mexicans attended the November 1943, election for union officers.

25. The first provision read: "All employees who, 15 days after the date of mailing of the Directive Order of the Regional War Labor Board in this case, are members of the Union in good standing in accordance with the constitution and by-laws of the Union, and those employees who may thereafter become members shall, during the life of the agreement as a condition of employment, remain members of the Union in good standing." The second noted: "When the Union, or any of its individual members, presents to the company an authorization for deduction of the Union dues of any employee from his pay during the contract period, the Company will honor the same and pay monthly to the Union the amount of dues which such authorization direct" (Eighth Regional War Labor Board, *Directive Order,* Case No. 8-D-101, American Smelting and Refining Company and Zinc Workers Federal Labor Union No. 23245, AFL, August, 1943, Records of the FEPC).

26. *Investigation of Alleged Complaints Against the American Smelting and Refining Company,* 28.

27. Ibid., 26.

28. Ibid.

29. Ibid., 38.

30. The company may have overlooked schooling in Mexico in their calculations, which may explain the Mexican workers' poorer educational record. Although it is difficult to determine the number of Mexico-born in the plant, the complainants made several references to their presence and even claimed discrimination on the basis of national origin, suggesting that there were a substantial number of them. Some of these workers may have claimed schooling in Mexico. The possible exclusion of these data, however, does not lessen the significance of the findings since the figures supplied by management reflect the operating perception in their hiring and job classification decisions.

31. Investigation of Alleged Complaints Against the Southern Alkali Corporation; Alkali Workers Industrial Union, Local No. 12078 of District 50, United Mine Workers of America, 1942, Contract Between The Southern Alkali Corporation and the Alkali Workers Industrial Union (Corpus Christi: Local No. 12078, 1943), 18–19; Alkali Workers Industrial Union Local 153, C.I.O, 1943–44 Agreement Governing Wages and Working Rules Between the Alkali Workers Industrial Union Local 153 and The Southern Alkali Corporation (Corpus Christi, Tex.: Local No. 153, 1944), Records of the FEPC.

32. Investigation of Alleged Complaints Against the Alkali Workers' Industrial Union, p. 28; Investigation of Alleged Complaints Against the Southern Alkali Corporation.

33. Metzger to Maslow, January 12, 1944, Records of the FEPC; Clarence M. Mitchell to Brin, January 21, 1944, Records of the FEPC.

34. Brin to Castañeda, January 24, 1944, Records of the FEPC; Brin to Mitchell, January 26, 1944, Records of the FEPC; Castañeda to Brin, January 26, 1944, Records of the FEPC.

35. Ellinger to Castañeda, August 24, 1944, Records of the FEPC; Ellinger's handwritten notes, August 15, 1944, Records of the FEPC. Mireles was also a member of the school board. He subsequently appointed Meza, his organization's vice-president, Gabriel Lozano, and secretary, Elias M. Licona, to work as a committee with Ellinger. Meza to Ellinger, October 23, 1944, Records of the FEPC.

36. Ellinger to Stevens, October 21, 1944, Records of the FEPC; Ellinger's handwritten

notes of interviews with the workers, August 15, 1944. The company's promotional brochure identifies Cristoval Guzmán as the highest ranking Mexican worker in the plant, the foreman of the Drum Shop Department. He was also the Latin American Vice President and Recording Secretary of the union. Jiménez and Moreno worked in the Calcine Department as semiskilled workers. The brochure does not identify Garza. Southern Alkali Corporation, Southern Alkali Corporation (Corpus Christi, Tex.: Southern Alkali Corporation, 1944), 21, 41, 47, Records of the FEPC.

37. Ellinger to Stevens, October 21, 1944, Records of the FEPC.

38. Ellinger to Stevens, September 5, 1944, Records of the FEPC.

39. Ellinger to Crossland, September 5, 1944, Records of the FEPC; Ellinger to Meza, September 27, 1944, Records of the FEPC; Ellinger to W. P. Harrington, October 21, 1944, Records of the FEPC.

40. Stevens to Ellinger, September 28, 1944, Records of the FEPC.

41. Stevens to Ellinger, November 10, 1944, Records of the FEPC; B. B. Biddle, President, Alkali Workers Industrial Union, Local 153, to Ellinger, November 11, 1944, Records of the FEPC.

42. Ellinger to Stevens, November 9, 1944, Records of the FEPC.

43. Stevens to Ellinger, November 10,1944.

44. Ellinger to Castañeda, November 13, 1944, Records of the FEPC; Otto R. Nielsen to Castañeda, December 13, 1944, Records of the FEPC; Ellinger to Stevens, January 13, 1945.

45. Stevens to Ellinger, January 25, 1945, Records of the FEPC.

46. Ibid.

47. Ibid.; "Oral Test (Instructions for Interviewer)," Records of the FEPC; "Oral Examination for Job Applicant," Records of the FEPC

48. H. T. Manuel, James Knight, J. A. Floyd, and R. C. Jordan, *Word-Number Test of Scholastic Aptitude for Grades 4 to 7* (Austin, Tex.: The Steck Company, 1939).

49. *Pruebas Interamericanas de Habilidad General, Prueba Avanzada; Inter-American Tests of General Ability, Advanced Test, Part I, II, III* (Washington, D.C.: The American Council on Education, 1943), Records of the FEPC.

50. Stevens to Ellinger, January 25, 1945, Records of the FEPC.

51. Castañeda to Stevens, January 30, 1945, Records of the FEPC; Castañeda to Stevens, February 13, 1945, Records of the FEPC.

52. Ellinger's handwritten notes on the company's report, March 28, 1945, Records of the FEPC.

53. Castañeda to Stevens, January 30, 1945, Records of the FEPC; Castañeda Final Disposition Report, April 27, 1945, Records of the FEPC.

Chapter 8

1. Some of Schmidt's other findings for the 1960s underscore the durability of occupational inequality: 1) Mexicans received little official attention; 2) they were still concentrated in the lower-skilled and lower-wage jobs; 3) they faced barriers as they climbed the occupational ladder, especially as they tried to enter white collar occupations; 4) training programs did not facilitate their upward mobility; and 5) racism contributed to occupational disparities. Fred H. Schmidt, *Spanish Surnamed American Employment in the Southwest,* Prepared for Equal Employment Opportunity Commission (Washington, D.C.: U.S. Government Printing Office, 1971), 2.

2. Barrera, *Race and Class in the Southwest,* 130–38. Also see the following study based on 1950 census data for further corroboration of Fogel and Barrera: Robert H. Talbert, *Spanish-Name People in the Southwest and West,* Prepared for the Texas Good Neighbor Commission (Fort Worth, Tex.: Leo Potishman Foundation, 1955).

3. Bent Flyvbjerg, *Making Social Science Matter: Why Social Inquiry Fails and How it Can Succeed Again* (New York: Cambridge University Press, 2001).

4. Saenz, "Americanismo deductivo," *La Prensa,*" April 21, 1944, 5. Castañeda and Sanchez shared Saenz's view on Pan Americanism. Unlike his contemporaries, however, Saenz did not emphasize citizenship distinctions. In true Pan Americanist spirit, he believed that equality should exist between American nations as well among their representatives within the United States.

5. See the following reports and correspondence involving Gustavo C. García, the attorney for the plaintiff in *Minerva Delgado v Bastrop Independent School District,* Miguel G. Calderón, the counsel general from San Antonio, and Vicente Sanchez Gavito, an official in Mexico's embassy, for information on the case and Mexico's relationship with it: García, "Informe que rinde el jefe del Departamento Legal, Licenciado Gustavo C. García, al C. Cónsul General de México en San Antonio, Texas, sobre la demanda en contra de la segregacion escolar de los niños de origen mexicano," 18 de noviembre de 1947, García to Calderón, undated, Calderón to Sanchez Gavito, Junio 25 de 1948, Archivo Manuel Avila Camacho, Archivo de la Nación, México, D.F. Calderón attached the undated letter from García in his own letter to Sanchez Gavito, indicating that García penned it earlier.

6. Perales, "El rechazo de la Ley Spears," July 25, 1945, *La Prensa,* 5, "Estado de la gestiones encaminadas a acabar con la discriminación," *La Prensa,* July 29, 1945, 6.

Appendix 1

1. Galarza, Hearings Before the Select Committee to Investigate the Interstate Migration of Destitute Citizens, U.S. House, 76th Congress, 3rd. Sess, Part 10, December 11, 1940, and February 26, 1941 (Washington, D.C.: U.S. Government Printing Office, 1941), 3883.

2. The census population data is most reliable when analyzed comparatively and across time to construct general demographic trends. Its unreliability is due primarily to a failure by the Bureau of the Census to identify Mexican-origin persons in a consistent manner at every decennial count. The 1930 census, for example, identifies Mexicans primarily in racial and foreign terms. The 1940 census, on the other hand, used a 5 percent sample of the entire population to determine the mother tongue, or the language other than English spoken in the home. Mexican data have been extracted from this section of the tabulation. Lastly, the 1950 census used a 20 percent sample to identify persons of Spanish surname. According to the Bureau of the Census, the different referents were also inefficient indicators of Mexican-origin persons and underestimated their numbers, especially in New Mexico and South Texas where communities with colonial roots were more apt to be U.S.-born and English-speaking. U.S. Bureau of the Census, 1950 Population Census Report P-E, No. 3C, *Persons of Spanish Surname* (Washington, D.C.: Government Printing Office, 1953), 4–6.

Bibliography

Government Sources

Boletín del Archivo General de la Nación, Mexico. (Special Documentary Issue on the Bracero Program). Tomo IV, Núm. 4 (Octubre–Diciembre, 1980).

Clark, Victor S. *Mexican Labor in the United States.* U.S. Bureau of Labor Bulletin No. 78. Washington, D.C.: Government Printing Office, 1908.

"El Gral Manuel Avila Camacho, al abrir el Congreso sus sesiones ordinarias, el 10 de septiembre de 1942." *Los Presidentes de México Ante La Nación, Informes, Manifiestos y Documentos de 1821 a 1966.* México: Imprenta de la Camara de Diputados, 1966.

Menefee, Selden C. *Mexican Migratory Workers of South Texas, Works Project Administration, Division of Research.* Washington, D.C.: Government Publications Office, 1941.

Menefee, Selden C., and Orin C. Cassmore. *The Pecan Shellers of San Antonio; The Problem of Underpaid and Unemployed Mexican Labor.* Washington, D.C.: U.S. Government Printing Office, 1940.

Mexico. Archivo de Secretaría de Relaciones Exteriores. México, D.F.

Mexico. *Buenos Vecinos, Buenos Amigos, Dicursos Pronunciados por los Presidentes de México y de los Estados Unidos de América, en Monterrey, N.L.,* El 20 de Abril de 1943. México: Secretaría de Gobernación, 1943.

Pruebas Interamericanas de Habilidad General, "Prueba Avanzada; Inter-American Tests of General Ability," Advanced Test. Part I, II, III. Washington, D.C.: The American Council on Education, 1943.

Rasmussen, Wayne D. *A History of the Emergency Farm Labor Supply Program, 1943–1947.* Agricultural Monograph No. 13. U.S. Department of Agriculture, Bureau of Economics. Washington, D.C: U.S. Government Printing Office, 1954.

Stevenson, Coke R., and Ezequiel Padilla. *The Good Neighbor Policy and Mexicans in Texas.* National and International Problems Series. México, D.F.: Department of State for Foreign Affairs, Bureau of International News Service, 1945.

Texas. Agricultural Experiment Station. *Report of the Farm Labor Situation in Texas.* May 20, 1942. Governor Coke Stevenson Papers.

Texas. Good Neighbor Commission. Records of the Good Neighbor Commission. Texas State Library and Archives Commission, Archives Division, Austin, Texas.

Texas. "Lamesa Farm Workers' Community Historic District," Texas Historical Sites, Texas Historical Commission, http://www.state.tx.us.

U.S. Bureau of the Budget. *Administrative Histories of World War II Civilian Agencies of the Federal Government.* Research Publication of the Second World War History Program of the Bureau of the Budget. Microfilm 41. New Haven, Conn.: Research Publications, 1974.

U.S. Congress. House of Representatives. *Congressional Record.* 78th Cong., 2d sess., Vol. 90, Part 4, May 12–June 12, 1944. Washington, D.C.: U.S. Government Printing Office, 1944.

U.S. Congress. House of Representatives. *Congressional Record.* 78th Cong., 2d sess., Vol. 90, Part 5, June 13–August 24, 1944. Washington, D.C.: U.S. Government Printing Office, 1944.

U.S. Congress. House of Representatives. *Hearings Before the Committee on Labor, H.R. 3986, H.R. 4004 and H.R. 4005, Bills to Prohibit Discrimination in Employment Because of Race, Creed, Color National Origin, or Ancestry.* 78th Cong., 2d sess., Vol. 2, November 16, 1944. Washington, D.C.: U.S. Government Printing Office, 1944.

U.S. Congress. House of Representatives. Hearings Before the Select Committee to Investigate the Interstate Migration of Destitute Citizens. 76th Cong., 3rd. sess., Part 10, Washington Hearings, December 11, 1940 and February 26, 1941. Washington, D.C: Government Printing Office, 1941.

U.S. Congress. Senate. *Hearings Before the Subcommittee of the Committee on Education and Labor,* 79th Cong., 1st sess., March 12, 13, 14, 1945. Washington, D.C.: Government Printing Office, 1945.

U.S. Department of Agriculture. Records of the Extension Service. Record Group 33. National Archives and Records Administration, Washington, D.C.

U.S. Department of Agriculture. Record Group 16. National Archives and Records Administration, Washington, D.C.

U.S. Department of Justice. Records of the Federal Bureau of Investigation. Record Group 65. National Archives and Records Administration, Washington, D.C.

U.S. Department of State. Records of the U.S. Department of State Relating to Political Relations Between the United States and Mexico, 1930–1944. Record Group 59. National Archives and Records Administration, Washington, D.C.

U.S. Employment Service Records. War Manpower Commission. Record Group 211. National Archives and Records Administration, Washington, D.C.

U.S. Employment Service. Texas Labor Market Reports, 1940–1946. American History Center, University of Texas, Austin, Texas.

U.S. Fair Employment Practice Committee. *Final Report, June 28, 1946.* Washington, D.C.: U.S. Government Printing Office, 1947.

U.S. Fair Employment Practice Committee. *First Report, July 1943–December 1944.* Washington, D.C.: U.S. Government Printing Office, 1945.

U.S. Fair Employment Practice Committee. Record Group 228. National Archives and Records Administration, Washington D.C.

U.S. Office of Coordinator of Inter-American Affairs. Department of State. Record Group 229. National Archives and Records Administration, Washington, D.C.

U.S. President's Commission on Migratory Labor. Stenographic Report of Proceedings, July 13–October 18, 1950, Vols. 1–4 U.S. President's Commission on Migratory Labor, Stenographic Report of Proceedings, July 13–October 18, 1950, Vols. 1–4, Microfilm 1 (of 4) (Washington, D.C: Ward and Paul, 1950), p. 150.

U.S. President's Commission on Migratory Labor. Stenographic Report of Proceedings, Brownsville Hearings, July 13–October 18, 1950, Vol. 1–4. Washington, D.C.: Ward & Paul, 1950.

U.S. War Manpower Commission. Record Group 211. National Archives and Records Administration, Washington, D.C.

Wood Warburton, Helen, and Marian M. Crane. *The Work and Welfare of Children of Agricultural Laborers in Hidalgo County, Texas.* U.S. Department of Labor Children's Bureau Publication 298. Washington, D.C.: U.S. Government Printing Office, 1943.

Archival and Other Primary Sources

Alkali Workers' Industrial Union, CIO Local 153. Agreement Governing Wages and Working Rules Between the Alkali Workers' Industrial Union Local 153 and the Southern Alkali Corporation, Corpus Christi, 1944. FEPC Records, Federal Archives and Records Administration, Washinton, D.C.

Alkali Workers' Industrial Union, CIO Local 153, United Gas, Coke and Chemical Workers of America. Constitution and By-Laws, Corpus Christi, 1943. FEPC Records, Federal Archives and Records Administration, Washinton, D.C.

Alkali Workers' Industrial Union, CIO Local 12078, United Gas, Coke and Chemical Workers of America. Contract. Corpus Christi, 1943.

Andrés de Luna Papers. LULAC Collection. Mexican American Library Program, Nettie Lee Benson Latin American Collection, University of Texas at Austin, Texas.

Archives of the U.S. Latinos and Latinas and World War II Oral History Project. University of Texas at Austin, Texas.

Archivo Francisco Castillo Nájera, Archivo Histórico Genaro Estrada, Secretaría de Relaciones Exteriores, México, D.F.

Archivo Manuel Avila Camacho. El Archivo de la Nación. Mexico, D.F.

Archivo Rafael de la Colina, Archivo Histórico Genaro Estrada, Secretaría de Relaciones Exteriores, México, D.F.

Butler, Eugene. "The Effect of the War on Farm Labor." Papers Presented at Annual Meeting of Texas Agricultural Workers' Association, Fort Worth, January 11–12, 1944, Center for American History, University of Texas at Austin, Texas.

Canyes, Manuel S. "The Third Conference of the Inter-American Bar Association." *Bulletin of the Pan American Union* (November 1944): 613–16.

Castillo Nájera, Francisco. "Relaciones Culturales Entre México y Los Estados Unidos de América." Discurso pronunciado en la "Academia Norteamericana de Ciencias y Artes," Boston, April 6, 1943.

Clyde Johnson Collection. The Bancroft Library, University of California, Berkeley, California.

Coke Stevenson Papers. Texas State Library and Archives Commission, Archives Division, Austin, Texas.

Corpus Christi Caller-Times. *Corpus Christi: 100 Years.* Corpus Christi, Tex.: Corpus Christi-Caller Times, 1952.

Dallas Morning News. *1941–42 Texas Almanac and State Industrial Guide.* Dallas: A. H. Belo Corporation, 1942.

Edmundo E. Mireles Papers. Mexican American Library Program, Nettie Lee Benson Latin American Collection, University of Texas at Austin, Texas.

Ernesto Galarza Papers. Department of Special Collections, Stanford University, Stanford, California.

Fair Employment Practice Committee. Investigation of Alleged Complaints Against the Southern Alkali Corporation; Alkali Workers' Industrial Union, Local No. 12078 of District 50, United Mine Workers' of America, 1942. FEPC Records, Federal Archives and Records Administration, Washington, D.C.

Federación Interamericana de Abogados. *Memoria de la Tercera Conferencia de la Federación Interamericana de Abogados.* 3 vols. México: Talleres Tipográfico Modelo, S. A., 1945.

Francisco Castillo Nájera, "Los Estados Unidos y la situación internacional, consecuencias para México," May 3, 1941, Archivo Francisco Castillo Nájera, 1–29, Archivo Histórico Genaro Estrada, Secretaría de Relaciones Exteriores, México, D.F.

Hohn, Caeser. "The Farm Labor Situation in Texas." *Papers Presented at Annual Meeting of Texas Agricultural Workers' Association,* Fort Worth, Texas, January 11–12, 1944, 63–64, Center American History, University of Texas at Austin, Texas.

Jack Rabin Collection on Alabama Civil Rights and Southern Activists. Historical Collections and Labor Archives, Special Collections Department, University Libraries, Pennsylvania State University.

John Herrera Papers. Houston Metropolitan Library, Houston, Texas.

Manuel C. Gonzales Papers. Mexican American Library Program, Nettie Lee Benson Latin American Collection, University of Texas at Austin, Texas.

Southern Alkali Corporation. Southern Alkali Corporation Brochure. Corpus Christi Southern Alkali Corporation, 1944. FEPC Records, Federal Archives and Records Administration, Washington, D.C.

Southern Alkali Corporation. Southern Alkali Corporation Contract. Corpus Christi Souther Alkali Corporation, 1944. FEPC Records, Federal Archives and Records Administration, Washington, D.C.

Vinson, Curtis. "Race Issue Arouses Ire of Mexicans." *Dallas Morning News,* October 24, 1943, Online Clipping Service, Texas Legislative Reference Library, State Capitol, Austin, Texas.

Secondary Sources

Acuña, Rodolfo. *Occupied America: A History of Chicanos,* 3d. ed. New York: Harper Collins, 1988.

Almaraz, Félix D. *Knight without Armor: Carlos Eduardo Castañeda, 1896–1958.* College Station: Texas A&M University Press, 1999.

Alvarez, Luis A. "The Power of the Zoot: Race, Community, and Resistance in American Youth Culture, 1940–1945." PhD dissertation, University of Texas at Austin, 2001.

Arizpe, Lourdes. "El éxodo rural en México y su relación con la migración a Estados Unidos." *Estudios Socológicos* Vol. 1, Num. 1 (1983): 9–33

Arnesen, Eric. "Whiteness and the Historian's Imagination." *International Labor and Working-Class History* 60 (2001): 3–32.

Balderrama, Francisco E. *In Defense of La Raza: The Los Angeles Mexican Consulate and the Mexican Community, 1929 to 1936.* Tucson: University of Arizona Press, 1982.

———. "México de afuera y los consulados Mexicanos, 1900–1940." *Revista Mexicana de Ciencias Políticas y Sociales* 27, num. 10 (1981): 175–86.

Balderrama, Francisco E., and Raymond Rodríguez. *Decade of Betrayal: Mexican Repatriation in the 1930s.* Albuquerque: University of New Mexico Press, 1995.

Barrera, Mario. *Race and Class in the Southwest: A Theory of Racial Inequality.* Notre Dame, Ind.: University of Notre Dame Press, 1979.

Beal, Elithe Hamilton. "Good Fences Make Good Neighbors." *Southwest Review* 30, no. 1 (1944): 42–47.

Blackwelder, Julia. *Women of the Depression: Caste and Culture in San Antonio, 1929–1939.* College Station: Texas A&M University Press, 1984.

Blanton, Carlos K. *The Strange Career of Bilingual Education in Texas, 1836–1981.* College Station: Texas A&M University Press, 2004.

———. "George I. Sanchez, Ideology, and Whiteness in the Making of the Mexican American Civil Rights Movement, 1930–1960." *Journal of Southern History* 72, no. 3 (2006): 569–604.

Botson Jr., Michael R. *Labor, Civil Rights, and the Hughes Tool Company.* College Station: Texas A&M University Press, 2005.

Brinkley, Alan. *The End of Reform: New Deal Liberalism and War.* New York: Alfred A. Knopf, 1995.

Brody, David. *In Labor's Cause: Main Themes on the History of the American Worker.* Oxford: Oxford University Press, 1993.

Bronder, Saul E. *Social Justice and Church Authority: The Public Life of Archbishop Robert E. Lucey.* Philadelphia: Temple University Press, 1982.

Brookshire, Marjorie. "The Industrial Pattern of Mexican American Employment in Nueces County, Texas." PhD dissertation, University of Texas, Austin, 1954.

Buenger, Walter L. *The Path to a Modern South: Northeast Texas between Reconstruction and the Great Depression.* Austin: University of Texas Press, 2001.

Campbell, Randolph B. "The 'Prosperity Decade' and the Great Depression, 1921–1941." In *Gone to Texas: A History of The Lone Star State,* edited by Randolph B. Campbell, 360–95. New York: Oxford University Press, 2003.

———. "World War II and the Rise of Modern Texas, 1941–1971." In *Gone to Texas: A History of The Lone Star State,* edited by Randolph B. Campbell, 397–437. New York: Oxford University Press, 2003.

Cardoso, Lawrence A. *Mexican Emigration to the United States, 1897–1931: Socio-Economic Patterns.* Tucson: University of Arizona Press, 1980.

Carreras de Velasco, Mercedes. *Los Mexicanos que devolvio la crisis, 1929–1932.* México, D.F.: Secretaría de Relaciones Exteriores, 1974.

Castañeda, Carlos E. "Why I Chose History." *Americas* 8 (April 1982): 475–83.

Castañeda, Jorge. *Mexico and the United Nations.* New York: Manhattan Publishing Company, 1958.

Cline, Howard F. *The United States and Mexico.* Cambridge, Mass.: Harvard University Press, 1953.

Cohen, Elizabeth. *Making a New Deal: Industrial Workers in Chicago, 1919–1939.* New York: Cambridge University Press, 1990.

Collins, William J. "Race, Roosevelt, and Wartime Production: Fair Employment in World War II Labor Markets." *The American Economic Review* 91, no. 1 (2001): 272–86.

Craig, Gordon A. "The Historian and the Study of International Relations." *American Historical Review* 88, no. 1 (1983): 1–11.

Craig, Richard B. *The Bracero Program; Interest Groups and Foreign Policy.* Austin: University of Texas Press, 1971.

Crain, Forest Burr. "The Occupational Distribution of Spanish-Name People in Austin, Texas." Master's thesis, University of Texas at Austin, 1948.

Daniel, Clete. *Chicano Workers and the Politics of Fairness: The FEPC in the Southwest, 1941–1945.* Austin: University of Texas Press, 1991.

Daniels, Cletus E. *Bitter Harvest: A History of California Farmworkers, 1870–1941.* Ithaca, N.Y.: Cornell University Press, 1981.

Davis, Harold E. "Practicing the Good-Neighbor Policy." *Journal of Higher Education* 17 (1946): 196–200, 226.

de la Garza, Rodolfo O. "Chicanos and U.S. Foreign Policy: The Future of Chicano-Mexican Relations," 399–416. In *Mexican–U.S. Relations, Conflict and Convergence,* edited by Carlos Vázquez and Manuel García y Griego. Los Angeles: UCLA Chicano Studies Research Center Publications and Latin American Center Publications, 1983.

de León, Arnoldo. *Ethnicity in the Sunbelt: A History of Mexican Americans in Houston.* Houston: Center for Mexican American Studies, University of Houston, 1989.

———. *Mexican Americans in Texas: A Brief History.* Arlington Heights, Ill.: Harlan Davidson, 1993.

Domínguez López, Emelia Violeta. "El Programa Bracero 1942–1947: Un Acercamiento a Través de los Testimonios de Sus Trabajadores." Tésis, Facultad de Filosofía y Letras, Universidad Nacional Autónoma de México, 2001.

Dozer, Marquard. *Are We Good Neighbors? Three Decades of Inter-American Relations, 1930–1960.* Gainesville: University of Florida Press, 1959.

Driscoll, Barbara A. *Me voy pa' Pensilvania por no andar en la vaganzia.* México: D.F.: Consejo Nacional Para la Cultura y Las Artes y Universidad Nacional Autónoma de México, 1996.

Eckhardt, Robert. "Economic Crisis in the Southwest." *The Texas Spectator,* June 9, 1947, 3–4.

Escobedo, Elizabeth R. "Mexican American Home Front, The Politics of Gender, Culture, and Community in World War II Los Angeles." PhD dissertation, University of Washington, 2004.

Faulk, Odie B. *Land of Many Frontiers; A History of the American Southwest.* New York: Oxford University Press, 1968.

Fernandez, Raul A. *The Mexican-American Border Region: Issues and Trends.* Notre Dame, Ind.: University of Notre Dame Press, 1989.

Finch, George A. *The American Journal of International Law* 38, no. 4 (1944): 684–87.

Flowers, John G., ed., *Report of Conferences on Professional Relations and Inter-American Education.* San Marcos: The Southwest Texas State Teachers College, 1944.

Flyvbjerg, Bent. *Making Social Science Matter: Why Social Inquiry Fails and How it Can Succeed Again.* New York: Cambridge University Press, 2001.

Fogel, Walter. *Mexican Americans in Southwest Labor Markets.* Advance Report 10, Mexican-American Study Project. Los Angeles: UCLA Graduate School of Business Administration, 1967.

Foley, Neil. "Becoming Hispanic: Mexican Americans and the Faustian Pact with Whiteness." In *Reflexiones 1997: New Directions in Mexican American Studies,* edited by Neil Foley, 53–70. Austin: University of Texas at Austin, Center for Mexican American Studies, 1998.

———. "Over the Rainbow: Hernandez v. Texas, Brown v. Board of Education, and Black v. Brown." In *"Colored Men" and "Hombres Aqui": Hernandez v. Texas and the Emergence of Mexican-American Lawyering,* edited by Michael A. Olivas, 111–21. Houston: Arte Público Press, 2006.

———. *The White Scourge: Mexicans, Blacks, and Poor Whites in Texas Cotton Culture.* Berkeley: University of California Press, 1997.

Forrest, Suzanne. *The Preservation of the Village: New Mexico's Hispanics and the New Deal.* Albuquerque: University of New Mexico Press, 1989.

Fraser, Steve, and Gary Gerstle. *The Rise and Fall of the New Deal Order, 1930–1980.* Princeton, N.J.: Princeton University Press, 1989.

Gamboa, Erasmo. *Mexican Labor and World War II: Braceros in the Pacific Northwest, 1942–1947.* Austin: University of Texas Press, 1990.

Gamio, Manuel. *Mexican Immigration to the United States: A Study of Human Migration and Adjustment.* Chicago: The University of Chicago Press, 1930.

García, María Rosa. "Las Relaciones Entre México y los Mexicanos en Estados Unidos; Una Historia de Encuentros y Desencuentros." *Viceversa* 80 (January 2000): 22–25.

García, María Rosa, and David R. Maciel. "El México de Afuera: Políticas Mexicanas de Protección en Estados Unidos." In *Al Norte de la Frontera: El Pueblo Chicano,* edited by David R. Maciel and José Guillermo Saavedra, 375–413. México, D.F.: Consejo Nacional de Población, 1988.

García, Mario. *Mexican Americans: Leadership, Ideology and Identity, 1930–1960.* New Haven, Conn.: Yale University Press, 1989.

———. "Americans All: The Mexican-American Generation and the Politics of Wartime Los Angeles, 1941–1945." *Social Science Quarterly* 65 (June 1984): 279–89.

———. "Mexican-Americans and the Politics of Citizenship; The Case of El Paso, 1936." *New Mexico Historical Review* 59, no. 2 (1984): 187–204.

García, Matt. *A World of Its Own: Race, Labor, and Citrus in the Making of Greater Los Angeles, 1900–1970.* Chapel Hill: University of North Carolina Press, 2001.

García, Richard. *Rise of the Mexican American Middle Class: San Antonio, 1929–1941.* College Station: Texas A&M University Press, 1991.

García y Griego, Manuel "El Comienzo y el Final: La Interdependencia Estructural y Dos Negociaciones Sobre Braceros." In *Interdependencia, ¿Un Enfoque Útil Para el Análisis de las Relaciones México-Estados Unidos?,* edited by Blanca Torres. México, D.F.: Colegio de México, Centro de Estudios Internacionales, 1990.

Garfinkel, Herbert. *When Negroes March: The March on Washington Movement in the Organizational Politics for FEPC.* Glencoe, Ill.: The Free Press, 1959.

Gómez Arnau, Remedios. *México y La Protección de Sus Nacionales en Estados Unidos.* México: Centro de Investigaciones Sobre Estados Unidos de América, Universidad Nacional Autónoma de México, 1990.

Gómez-Quiñones, Juan. *Chicano Politics: Reality and Promise, 1940–1990.* Albuquerque: University of New Mexico Press, 1990.

———. *Sembradores, Ricardo Flores Magón y El Partido Liberal Mexicano: A Eulogy and Critique,* Monograph No. 5 (Los Angeles: UCLA Chicano Studies Research Center, 1973).

———. *Mexican American Labor, 1790–1990.* Albuquerque: University of New Mexico Press 1994.

———. "Mexican Immigration to the United States and the Internationalization of Labor, 1848–1980: An Overview." In *Mexican Immigrant Workers in the United States,* edited by Antonio Ríos Bustamante, anthology no. 2, 13–34. Los Angeles: UCLA Chicano Studies Research Center Publications, 1981.

———. "Notes on an Interpretation of the Relations Between the Mexican Community in the United States and Mexico." In *Mexican-U.S. Relations, Conflict and Convergence,* edited by Carlos Vázquez and Manuel García y Griego, 417–39. Los Angeles: UCLA Chicano Studies Research Center Publications and Latin American Center Publications, 1983.

———. "Piedras Contra la Luna, México en Aztlán y Aztlán en México; Chicano-Mexican Relations and the Mexican Consulates, 1900–1920." In *Contemporary Mexico: Papers of the IV International Congress of Mexican History,* edited by James W. Wilkie, Michael C. Meyer, and Edna Monzón de Wilkie, 494–527. Los Angeles: University of California Press, 1976.

———. *Roots of Chicano Politics, 1600–1940.* Albuquerque: University of New Mexico Press, 1994.

———. "Toward a Perspective on Chicano History." *Aztlán* 2 (Fall 1972): 1–49

Gómez-Quiñones, Juan, and Luis Leobardo Arroyo. "On the State of Chicano History; Observation on Its Development, Interpretations, and Theory, 1970–1974." *Western Historical Quarterly* 7 (April 1976): 155–85.

Gonzalez, Gilbert G. *A Century of Chicano History: Empire, Nations, and Migration.* New York: Routledge, 2003.

———. "Culture, Language, and the Americanization of Mexican Children." In *Latinos and Education: A Critical Reader,* edited by Antonia Darder, Rodolfo D. Torres, and Henry Gutiérrez. New York: Routledge, 1997.

———. "Interamerican and Intercultural Education and the Chicano Community." *Journal of Ethnic Studies* 13, no. 3 (1985): 31–53.

———. *Labor and Community: Mexican Citrus Worker Villages in a Southern California County, 1900–1950.* Urbana: University of Illinois Press, 1994.

———. "Labor and Community: The Camps of Mexican Citrus Pickers in Southern California." *Western Historical Quarterly* 22, no. 3 (1991): 289–312.

Gonzalez, Guadalupe. "The Foundations of Mexico's Foreign Policy: Old Attitudes and New Realities." In *Foreign Policy in U.S.-Mexican Relations,* edited by Rosario Green and Peter H. Smith, 31–32. San Diego, Center for U.S.-Mexican Studies, University of California, San Diego, 1989.

Gonzalez-Souza, Luis F. "La política exterior de México ante la protección internacional de los derechos humanos." *Foro Internacional* 18, núm. 1 (1977): 108–38.

Goodrich, Leland M., and Maried J. Carroll. *Documents on American Foreign Relations,* Vol. 5 (July 1942–June 1943). Boston: World Peace Foundation, 1944.

Green, George N. *The Establishment in Texas Politics: The Primitive Years, 1938–1957.* Norman: University of Oklahoma Press, 1979.

———. "The Good Neighbor Commission and Texas Mexicans." In *Ethnic Minorities in Gulf Coast Society,* edited by Jerrell H. Shofner and Linda V. Ellsworth, 111–27. Pensacola, Fla.: Gulf Coast History and Humanities Conference, 1979.

Green, Rosario, and Peter H. Smith. *Foreign Policy in U.S.-Mexican Relations,* Dimensions of U.S.-Mexican Relations, Vol. 5. San Diego: Center for U.S. Mexican Studies, University of California, San Diego, 1989.

Grove, Wayne A. "The Mexican Farm Labor Program, 1942–1964: Government-Administered Labor Market Insurance." *Agricultural History* 70, no. 2 (1996): 302–20.

Guerrant, Edward O. *Roosevelt's Good Neighbor Policy.* Albuquerque: University of New Mexico Press, 1950.

Guerrero, Salvador. *Memorias: A West Texas Life.* Edited by Arnoldo de León. Lubbock: Texas Tech University Press, 1991.

Guglielmo, Thomas A. "Fighting for Caucasian Rights: Mexicans, Mexican Americans, and the Transnational Struggle for Civil Rights in World War II Texas." *Journal of American History* 92, no. 4 (2006): 211–36.

Gutiérrez, David G. "Significant for Whom? Mexican Americans and the History of the American West." *Western Historical Quarterly* 24, no. 4 (November 1993): 519–39.

———. *Walls and Mirrors: Mexican Americans, Mexican Immigrants, and the Politics of Ethnicity.* Berkeley: University of California Press, 1995.

Guzmán, Ralph. "La repatriación forzosa como solución política concluyente al problema de la inmigración illegal, una perspective histórica." *Foro Internacional* 18, núm. 3 (1978): 494–513.

Haney Lopez, Ian F. *White by Law; The Legal Construction of Race.* New York: New York University Press, 1996.

———. "White Latinos." *Harvard Latino Law Review* 6 (Spring 2003): 1–7.

Harris, William H. "Federal Intervention in Union Discrimination: FEPC and West Coast Shipyards During World War II." *Labor History* 22, no. 3 (1981): 325–47.

Hoffman, Abraham. *Unwanted Mexican Americans in the Great Depression: Repatriation Pressures, 1929–1939.* Tucson: University of Arizona Press, 1974.

Hooks, Gregory. *Forging the Military-Industrial Complex: World War II's Battle of the Potomac.* Champaign: University of Illinois Press, 1991.

Iriye, Akira. "The Internationalization of History." *American Historical Review* 94, no. 1 (1989): 1–10.

Jeffries, John W. *Wartime America: The World War II Home Front.* Chicago: Ivan R. Dee, 1996.

Jenkins, Lou Ella. "The Fair Employment Practice Committee and Mexican-Americans in the Southwest." PhD dissertation, Georgia State University, 1974.

Johnson, Clyde. "CIO Oil Workers' Organizing Campaign in Texas, 1942–1943." In *Essays in Southern Labor History: Selected Papers, Southern Labor History Conference, 1976,* edited by Gary M. Fink and Merl E. Reed, 173–87. Westport, Conn.: Greenwood Press, 1977.

———. "The Battle for Baytown," June 1984, Copy of book-length manuscript in author's possession.

Karl, Barry D. *The Uneasy State: The United States From 1915 to 1945.* Chicago: University of Chicago Press, 1983.

Katznelson, Ira. *When Affirmative Action Was White: An Untold History of Racial Inequality in Twentieth-Century America.* New York: Norton, 2005.

Kesselman, Louis C. *The Social Politics of FEPC: A Study in Reform Pressure Movements.* Chapel Hill: University of North Carolina Press, 1948.

Kibbe, Pauline. *Latin Americans in Texas.* Albuquerque: University of New Mexico Press, 1946.

Kirstein, Peter N. *Anglo over Bracero: A History of the Mexican Worker in the United States from Roosevelt to Nixon.* San Francisco: R and E Research Associates, 1977.

Konvitz, Milton R. "The Extent and Character of Legally-Enforced Segregation." *Journal of Negro Education* 20, no. 3 (1951): 425–35.

Koppes, Clayton R. "The Good Neighbor Policy and the Nationalization of Mexican Oil: A Reinterpretation." *Journal of American History* 69, no. 1 (June 1982): 62–81.

Kreneck, Thomas H. *Mexican American Odyssey: Felix Tijerina, Entrepreneur and Civic Leader, 1905–1965.* College Station: Texas A&M University, 2001.

Kryder, Daniel. "The American State and the Management of Race Conflict in the Workplace and in the Army 1941–1945." *Polity* 26, no. 4 (1994): 601–34.

———. *Divided Arsenal: Race and the American State during World War II.* Cambridge: Cambridge University Press, 2000.

Leuchtenburg, William E. *Franklin D. Roosevelt and the New Deal, 1932–1940.* New York: Harper and Row, 1963.

Larson, Henrietta M., and Kenneth Wiggins Porter. *History of Humble Oil and Refining Company, A Study in Industrial Growth.* New York: Harper and Brothers, 1959.

Ledesma, Irene. "The New Deal Public Works Program and the Mexican Americans in McAllen Texas, 1933–36." Master's thesis, Texas A&M University at Pan American, 1977.

———. "Unlikely Strikers: Mexican-American women in Strike Activity in Texas, 1919–1974." PhD dissertation, Ohio State University, 1992.

Lee, James Ward, Carolyn N. Barnes, Kent A. Bowman, and Laura Crow, eds. *1941: Texas Goes to War.* Denton: University of North Texas Press, 1991.

Leininger Pycior, Julie. "Henry B. Gonzalez," in Profiles in Power: Twentieth-Century Texans in Washington, edited by Kenneth E. Hendrickson, Michael L. Collins, and Patrick Cox, 295–308. Austin: University of Texas Press, 1993.

Levine, Rhonda. *Class Struggle and the New Deal: Industrial Labor, Industrial Capital, and the State.* Lawrence: University Press of Kansas, 1988.

Little, Wilson. *Spanish-Speaking Children in Texas.* Austin: University of Texas Press, 1944.

Lotchin, Roger W. "The Historians' War or The Home Front's War?: Some Thoughts for Western Historians." *Western Historical Quarterly* 26, no. 2 (1995): 185–96.

Luján, Roy. "Dennis Chavez and the Roosevelt Era, 1933–1945." PhD dissertation, University of New Mexico, 1987.

Maciel, David R., and José Guillermo Saavedra, eds. *Al Norte de la Frontera: El Pueblo Chicano.* México, D.F.: Consejo Nacional de Población, 1988.

Majka, Linda C., and Theo J. Majka. *Farm Workers, Agribusiness, and the State.* Philadelphia: Temple University Press, 1982.

Manuel, Herschel T., James Knight, J. A. Floyd, and R. C. Jordan. *Word-Number Test of Scholastic Aptitude for Grades 4 to 7.* Austin, Tex.: The Steck Company, 1939.

Marden, Charles F. *Minorities in American Society.* New York: American Book, 1952.

Márquez, Benjamín. *LULAC: The Evolution of a Mexican American Political Organization.* Austin: University of Texas Press, 1993.

Marshall, F. Ray. *Labor in the South.* Cambridge, Mass.: Harvard University Press, 1967.

———. "Some Factors Influencing the Upgrading of Negroes in the Southern Petroleum Refining Industry." *Social Forces* 42 (1963): 186–95.

Martínez-Matsuda, Verónica. "The Making of the Modern Migrant: Labor, Community, and Resistance in the Federal Migratory Labor Camp Program, 1935–1947." PhD dissertation, University of Texas at Austin, 2009.

Mason, Kenneth. *African American and Race Relations in San Antonio, Texas, 1867–1937.* New York: Garland Publishing, 1998.

Mata, Desireé. "A Time When all the Young Men Disappeared." *Narratives* 4, no. 2 (2004): 102.

Mazón, Mauricio. *The Zoot-Suit Riots: The Psychology of Symbolic Annihilation.* Austin: University of Texas Press, 1984.

McCain, Johnny. "Contract Labor as a Factor in United States-Mexican Relations, 1942–47." PhD dissertation, University of Texas at Austin, 1970.

McWilliams, Carey. *Ill Fares the Land: Migrants and Migratory Labor in the United States.* Boston: Little, Brown and Company, 1942.

———. *North from Mexico: The Spanish-Speaking People of the United States.* New York: Greenwood Press, 1948.

Mecham, J. Lloyd. *A Survey of United States–Latin American Relations.* New York: Houghton Mifflin, 1965.

Meeks, Eric V. "Protecting the 'White Citizen Worker': Race, Labor, and Citizenship in South-Central Arizona, 1929–1945." *Journal of the Southwest* 48, no. 1 (2006): 91–113.

Menchaca, Martha. *The Mexican Outsiders: A Community History of Marginalization and Discrimination in California.* Austin: University of Texas Press, 1995.

Meyer, Agnes E. "A Look at Labor Camps." *The Spectator,* June 30, 1947, 6–7, 11.

Milkman, Ruth. *Gender at Work: The Dynamics of Job Segregation by Sex during World War II.* Champaign: University of Illinois Press, 1987.

Miller, Michael Nelson. *Red, White, and Green: The Maturing of Mexicanidad, 1940–1946.* El Paso: Texas Western Press, 1998.

Monroy, Douglas. *Rebirth: Mexican Los Angeles from the Great Migration to the Great Depression.* Berkeley: University of California Press, 1999.

Montejano, David. *Anglos and Mexicans in the Making of Texas, 1836–1986.* Austin: University of Texas Press, 1987.

Morales, José G. *Unión de dos pueblos, la entrevista de Monterrey,* México: Unknown Publisher, 1943.

Morín, Raul. *Among the Valiant: Mexican-Americans in WWII and Korea.* Los Angeles: Borden Publishing Company, 1963.

Morris Broom, Perry. "An Interpretative Analysis of the Economic and Educational Status of Latin-Americans in Texas, With Emphasis upon the Basic Factors Underlying an Approach to an Improved Program of Occupational Guidance, Training, and Adjustment for Secondary Schools." PhD dissertation, University of Texas at Austin, 1942.

Morton Blum, John. *V Was for Victory: Politics and American Culture during World War II.* New York: Harcourt Brace Jovanovich, 1976.

Nash, Gerald D. *The American West Transformed: The Impact of the Second World War.* Bloomington: Indiana University Press, 1985.

———. "Spanish-Speaking Americans in Wartime." In *The American West Transformed: The Impact of the Second World War,* chapter 7, 107–127. Bloomington: Indiana University Press, 1985.

Neale, Ronning C. *Law and Politics in Inter-American Diplomacy.* New York: John Wiley and Sons, 1963.

Nordyke, Lewis T. "Mapping Jobs for Texas Migrants." *Survey Graphic* 29, no. 3 (1940): 152–60.

Obadele-Starks, Ernest. *Black Unionism in the Industrial South.* College Station: Texas A&M University Press, 2000.

O'Conner, Harvey. *History of the Oil Workers' International Union.* Denver: Oil Workers' International Union, 1950.

Ojeda, Mario. *México, El surgimiento de una pólitica exterior activa.* México: Secretaría de Educación Pública, 1986.

Olivas, Michael A., ed. *"Colored Men" and "Hombres Aqui": Hernandez v. Texas and the Emergence of Mexican-American Lawyering.* Houston: Arte Público Press, 2006.

O'Neill, William. *A Democracy at War: America's Fight at Home and Abroad in World War II.* New York: Free Press, 1993.

Orozco, Cynthia E. "The Origins of the League of United Latin American Citizens (LULAC) and the Mexican American Civil Rights Movement in Texas with an Analysis of Women's Political Participation in a Gendered Context, 1910–1929." PhD dissertation, University of California, Los Angeles, 1992.

———. "Regionalism, Politics, and Gender in Southwest History: The League of United Latin American Citizens' Expansion Into New Mexico From Texas, 1929–1945." *The Western Historical Quarterly* 29, no. 4 (1998): 459–83.

Padilla, Ezequiel. *En El Frente de la Democracia: Discursos.* México: Cía. Editora y Librera ARS, 1945.

———. *Free Men of America.* New York: Ziff-Davis Publishing Company, 1943.

———. *Paz Permanente y Democracia Internacional.* México: Secretaría de Relaciones Exteriores, Departamento de Información Para El Extranjero, Serie Cultural, 1944.

———. *Three Speeches at Río de Janiero.* Mexico: Department of State for Foreign Affairs, The International Press Service Bureau, 1942.

Pagán, Eduardo Obregón. *Murder at the Sleepy Lagoon: Zoot Suits, Race, and Riot in Wartime L.A.* Chapel Hill: University of North Carolina Press, 2004.

Palomo Acosta, Teresa. "The Farm Placement Service of Texas." *The Handbook of Texas Online.* http://www.tsha.utexas.edu/handbook/online/.

Paredes, *With His Pistol in His Hand: A Border Ballad and Its Hero.* Austin: University of Texas Press, 1958.

———. *A Texas-Mexican Cancionero: Folksongs of the Lower Border.* Urbana: University of Illinois Press, 1976.

Pastor, Robert A., and Jorge G. Castañeda. *Limits to Friendship: The United States and Mexico.* New York: Vintage Books, 1989.

Perales, Alonso. *Are We Good Neighbors?* San Antonio: Artes Gráficas, 1948.

———. *En Defensa de Mi Raza.* 2 vols. San Antonio: Artes Gráficas, 1936–37.

Perry, George Sessions. *Texas, A World in Itself.* New York: McGraw-Hill Book Company, 1941.

Peyton, Green. *San Antonio: City in the Sun.* New York: McGraw-Hill, 1946.

Pratt, Joseph A. *The Growth of a Refining Region.* Greenwich, Conn.: JAI Press, 1980.

Proctor, Ben. "Texas from Depression through World War II, 1929–1945." In *The Texas Heritage,* edited by Ben Proctor and Archie P. McDonald, 165–86. Arlington Heights, Ill.: Harlan Davidson, 1992.

Pike, Fredrick B. *FDR's Good Neighbor Policy: Sixty Years of Gentle Chaos.* Austin: University of Texas Press, 1995.

Polenberg, Richard. *America at War: The Home Front, 1941–1945.* Englewood Cliffs, N.J.: Prentice-Hall, 1968.

Privett, Stephen A. *The U.S. Catholic Church and Its Hispanic Members: The Pastoral Vision of Archbishop Robert E. Lucey.* San Antonio: Trinity University Press, 1988.

Raat, W. Dirk. *Mexico and the United States: Ambivalent Vistas.* Athens: The University of Georgia Press, 1992.

Reed, Merl E. "Black Workers, Defense Industries, and Federal Agencies in Pennsylvania, 1941–1945." *Labor History* 27, no. 3 (1986): 356–84.

———. "FEPC and the Federal Agencies in the South." *Journal of Negro History* 65, no. 1 (1980): 43–56.

———. *Seedtime for the Modern Civil Rights Movement: The President's Committee of Fair Employment Practice, 1941–1946.* Baton Rouge: Louisiana State University Press, 1991.

Ríos-Bustamante, Antonio, ed. *Mexican Immigrant Workers in the U.S.* Los Angeles: UCLA Chicano Studies Research Center Publications, 1981.

Rister, Carl Coke. *Oil: Titan of the Southwest.* Norman: University of Oklahoma Press, 1949.

Rivas-Rodríguez, Maggie, ed. *Mexican Americans and World War II.* Austin: University of Texas Press, 2005.

Rodríguez, Eugene. *Henry B. Gonzalez: A Political Profile.* New York: Arno Press, 1976.

Rodriguez, Robert. "A Survey of Texas Gulf Coast Area Mexican-American World War II Veterans." PhD dissertation, University of Houston, 1997

Rosales, Francisco Arturo. *!Pobre Raza!: Violence, Justice, and Mobilization Among México Lindo Immigrants, 1900–1936.* Austin: University of Texas Press, 1999.

Rosales, Rodolfo. *The Illusion of Inclusion: The Untold Political Story of San Antonio.* Austin: University of Texas Press, 2000.

Ross, Malcolm. *All Manner of Men.* New York: Reynal and Hitchcock, 1948.

———. "Those Gringos." *Common Ground* 8 (Winter 1948): 3–18.

Ruchames, Louis. *Race, Jobs, and Politics: The Story of FEPC.* Westport, Conn.: Negro Universities Press, 1953.

Ruiz, Vicki. *Cannery Women, Cannery Lives: Mexican Women, Unionization, and the California Food Processing Industry, 1930–1950.* Albuquerque: University of New Mexico Press, 1987.

———. *From Out of the Shadows: Mexican Women in Twentieth-Century America.* New York: Oxford University Press, 1998.

Saenz, José de la Luz. *Los México-Americanos en La Gran Guerra y Su Contingente en Pró de la Democracia, La Humanidad y La Justicia.* San Antonio: Artes Gráficas, 1933.

———. "Racial Discrimination, A Number One Problem of Texas Schools." *The Texas Outlook* 30, no. 12 (1946): 12, 20.

Salinas, Cristina. "A Border in the Making: The INS and Agricultural Relations in South Texas During the Mid-Twentieth Century." Master's thesis, University of Texas at Austin, 2005.

San Miguel Jr., Guadalupe. *"Let All of Them Take Heed": Mexican Americans and the Campaign for Educational Equality in Texas, 1910–1981.* Austin: University of Texas Press, 1987.

———. "The Struggle against Separate and Unequal Schools: Middle Class Mexican Americans and the Desegregation Campaign in Texas, 1929–1957." *History of Education Quarterly* 23, no. 3 (1983): 343–59.

Sanchez, George I., and Henry J. Otto. *A Guide for Teachers of Spanish Speaking Children in the Primary Grades.* Austin, Tex.: State Department of Education, 1946.

Sanchez, George J. *Becoming Mexican American: Ethnicity, Culture, and Identity in Chicano Los Angeles, 1900–1945.* New York: Oxford University Press, 1993.

Sanchez, Joanne Rao. "Latinas of World War II: From Familial Shelter to Expanding Horizons." Paper presented at the Latino Latina World War II Forum, Washington, D.C., September 12, 2004.

Santillán, Richard. "Rosita the Riveter: Midwest Mexican American Women During World War II, 1941–1945." In *Mexicans in the Midwest,* edited by Juan R García, Ignacio M García, and Thomas Gelsinon. Tucson: Mexican American Studies & Research Center, University of Arizona, 1989.

Salisbury, Richard V. "Good Neighbors? The United States and Latin America in the Twentieth Century." In *American Foreign Relations: A Historiographical Review,* edited by Gerald K. Haines and Samuel J. Walker. Westport, Conn.: Greenwood Press, 1981.

Saragoza, Alex M. "Recent Chicano Historiography: An Interpretive Essay." *Aztlán* 19 (1998–1990): 1–77.

Schmidt, Fred H. *Spanish Surnamed American Employment in the Southwest.* Prepared for Equal Employment Opportunity Commission. Washington, D.C.: U.S. Government Printing Office, 1971.

Schorr, Daniel. "'Reconverting' Mexican Americans." *The New Republic,* September 30, 1946.

Scruggs, Otey M. "Texas and the Bracero Program, 1942–1947." *Pacific History Review* 32, no. 3 (1963): 251–64.

Silva Herog, Jesús. *Una vida en la vida de México.* México, D.F.: Secretaría de Educación Pública, 1986.

Sitkoff, Harvard. *A New Deal for Blacks: The Emergence of Civil Rights as a National Issue.* New York: Oxford University Press, 1978.

Smith, Peter. *Talons of the Eagle: Dynamics of U.S.-Latin American Relations.* New York: Oxford University Press, 1996.

Takaki, Ronald. *Double Victory: A Multicultural History of America in World War II.* Boston: Little, Brown and Company, 2000.

Talbert, Robert H. *Spanish-Name People in the Southwest and West.* Prepared for the Texas Good Neighbor Commission. Fort Worth: Leo Potishman Foundation, 1955.

Tanner, Myrtle. "The Study of Spanish in Texas Schools." *The Texas Outlook* 28, no. 5 (1944): 38–39

Taylor, Paul S. *An American-Mexican Frontier, Nueces County, Texas.* Chapel Hill: The University of North Carolina Press, 1934.

———. *Mexican Labor in the United States: Imperial Valley,* University of California Publications in Economics, Vol. 6, No. 1. Berkeley: University of California Press, 1928.

———. *Mexican Labor in the United States: Chicago and the Calumet Region,* University of California Publications in Economics, Vol. 7, No. 2. Berkeley: University of California Press, 1932.

———. "Migratory Farm Labor in the United States." *Monthly Labor Review* 44 (March 1937): 537–49.

Tomasek, Robert D. "The Political and Economic Implications of Mexican Labor in the United States Under the Non Quota System, Contract Labor Program, and Wetback Movement." PhD dissertation, University of Michigan, 1957.

Torres, Blanca. *Historia de la Revolución Mexicana, Periodo 1940–52, México en la Segunda Guerra Mundial.* México, D.F.: El Colegio de México, 1979.

———, ed. *Interdependencia; ¿Un enfoque útil para el análisis de las relaciones México-Estados Unidos?.* México, D.F.: El Colegio de México, 1990.

Valdés, Dennis Nodín. *Al Norte: Agricultural Workers in the Great Lakes Region, 1917–1970.* Mexican American Monograph No. 13, Center for Mexican American Studies. Austin: University of Texas Press, 1991.

Vargas, Zaragosa. "In the Years of Darkness and Torment; The Early Mexican American Struggle for Civil Rights, 1945–1963." *New Mexico Historical Review* 76, no. 4 (2001): 382–413.

———. *Labor Rights Are Civil Rights; Mexican American Workers in Twentieth-Century America.* Princeton N.J.: Princeton University Press, 2005.

Vásquez, Carlos, and Manuel García y Griego, eds. *Relations between the Mexican Community in the United States and Mexico.* Los Angeles: UCLA Chicano Studies Research Center Publications, 1983.

Vázquez, Josefina Zoraida, and Lorenzo Meyer. *México Frente a Estados Unidos (Un Ensayo Histórico, 1776–1988).* 2nd ed. México, D.F.: Fondo de Cultura Económica, 1992.

Velez-Ibañez, Carlos. *Border Visions: Mexican Cultures of the Southwest United States.* Tucson: University of Arizona Press, 1996.

Verge, Arthur C. "World War II and the Metropolis, 1941–1945, The Impact of the Second World War on Los Angeles." In *The American West, The Reader,* edited by Walter Nugent and Martin Ridge, 234–54. Bloomington: Indiana University Press, 1999.

Villarreal, Jesse J. "Short Cuts in Teaching English As a Second Language." *The Texas Outlook* 28, no. 7 (1944): 11.

Waddell, Brian. *The War against the New Deal: World War II and American Democracy.* DeKalb: Northern Illinois University Press, 2001.

Walsh, Jess. "Laboring at the Margins: Welfare and the Regulation of Mexican Workers in Southern California." *Antipode* 31, no. 4 (1999): 395–420.

Warner, Charles A. "The Oil Industry in Texas Since Pearl Harbor." *Southwestern Historical Quarterly* 61, no. 3 (1958): 329–40.

———. "Texas and the Oil Industry." *Southwestern Historical Quarterly* 50 (1946): 7–24.

Weeks, Oliver D. "The League of United Latin American Citizens: A Texas-Mexican Civic Organization." *Southwestern Political and Social Science Quarterly* 10 (1929): 257–78.

Welles, Sumner. *The Time for Decision.* New York: Harper & Brothers, 1944.

Werner, Herbert. "Labor Organizations in the American Petroleum Industry." In *The American Petroleum Industry: The Age of Energy, 1899–1959,* edited by Harold F. Williamson, Ralph L. Andreano, Arnold R. Daum, and Gilbert C. Klose, 827–45. Evanston, Ill.: Northwestern University Press, 1963.

West, Stanley A., and Irene S. Vásquez. "Early Migration from Central Mexico to the Northern United States." In *The Chicano Experience,* edited by Stanley A. West and June Macklin, 17–31. Boulder, Col.: Westview Press, 1979.

Wilkie, James W., Michael C. Meyer, and Edna Monzón de Wilkie, eds. *Contemporary Mexico: Papers of the IV International Congress of Mexican History.* Los Angeles: University of California Press, 1976.

Wilson, Steven H. "Brown over "Other White": Mexican-Americans' Legal Arguments and Litigation Strategy in School Desegregation Lawsuits." *Law and History Review* 21, no. 1 (2003): 145–94.

Winkler, Allan M. *Home Front U.S.A.: America during World War II.* Wheeling, Ill.: Harlan Davidson, 2000.

Wood, Bryce. *The Dismantling of the Good Neighbor Policy.* Austin: University of Texas Press, 1985.

Woodbridge, Hensley C. "Mexico and U.S. Racism: How Mexicans View Our Treatment of Minorities." *The Commonweal,* June 22, 1945, 236–39.

Zamora, Emilio. *El movimiento obrero Mexicano en el Sur de Texas, 1900–1920.* México, D.F.: Secretaría de Educación Pública, 1986.

———. "The Failed Promise of Wartime Opportunity For Mexicans in the Texas Oil Industry." *Southwestern Historical Quarterly* 95 (1992): 23–50.

———."Fighting on Two Fronts: José de la Luz Saenz and the Language of the Mexican American Civil Rights Movement." In *Recovering the U.S. Hispanic Literary Heritage,* edited by José F. Aranda Jr. and Silvio Torres-Saillant, 214–39. Vol. 4. Houston: Árte Público Press, 2002.

———. "Labor Formation, Community, and Politics: The Mexican Working Class in Texas, 1900–1945." In *Border Crossings, Mexican and Mexican-American Workers,* edited by John Mason Hart, 139–62. Wilmington, Del.: Scholarly Resources, 1998.

———. "La guerra en pro de la justicia y la democracia en Francia y Texas: José de la Luz Sáenz y el lenguaje del movimiento mexicano de los derechos civiles," *ISTOR, Revista de Historia Internacional* 4, núm. 13 (2003): 9–35.

———. "Mexican Nationals in the U.S. Military During World War II," Paper presented at the Latino Latina World War II Forum, Washington, D.C., September 12, 2004.

———. "Mexico's Wartime Intervention on Behalf of Mexicans in the United States." In *Mexican Americans and World War II,* edited by Maggie Rivas-Rodríguez, 221–43 Austin: University of Texas Press, 2005.

———. *The World of the Mexican Worker in Texas.* College Station: Texas A&M University Press, 1993.

Zieger, Robert H., and Gilbert J. Gall. "Labor Goes to War, 1939–1945." In *American Workers, American Unions, The Twentieth Century,* chapter 4, 104–143. Baltimore: The Johns Hopkins University Press, 2002.

Zorrilla, Luis G. *Historia de las Relaciones Entre México y Los Estados Unidos de America, 1800–1958,* Tomo II. México, D.F.: Editorial Porrúa, 1966.

Index